HOLDING IT TOGETHER

HOLDING IT TOGETHER

How Women Became America's Safety Net

JESSICA CALARCO

PORTFOLIO | PENGUIN

PORTFOLIO / PENGUIN
An imprint of Penguin Random House LLC
penguinrandomhouse.com

Most Portfolio books are available at a discount when purchased in quantity for sales promotions or corporate use. Special editions, which include personalized covers, excerpts, and corporate imprints, can be created when purchased in large quantities. For more information, please call (212) 572-2232 or e-mail specialmarkets@penguinrandomhouse.com. Your local bookstore can also assist with discounted bulk purchases using the Penguin Random House corporate Business-to-Business program. For assistance in locating a participating retailer, e-mail B2B@penguinrandomhouse.com.

LIBRARY OF CONGRESS CATALOGING-IN-PUBLICATION DATA
Names: Calarco, Jessica McCrory, 1983– author.
Title: Holding it together : how women became America's safety net / Jessica Calarco.
Description: New York : Portfolio/Penguin, [2024] | Includes bibliographical references and index.
Identifiers: LCCN 2024005078 (print) | LCCN 2024005079 (ebook) | ISBN 9780593538128 (hardcover) | ISBN 9780593538135 (ebook)
Subjects: LCSH: Working class women—United States. | Working poor—United States. | Poor women—Employment—United States. | Work and family—United States. | Labor policy—United States.
Classification: LCC HD6095 .C175 2024 (print) | LCC HD6095 (ebook) | DDC 305.48/230973—dc23/eng/20240202
LC record available at https://lccn.loc.gov/2024005078
LC ebook record available at https://lccn.loc.gov/2024005079

Printed in the United States of America
1st Printing

Book design by Alissa Rose Theodor

For all who care

Contents

Preface

American women today might be shocked to learn that Congress once voted to fund an affordable national childcare system—a system that turned out to be highly effective but was dismantled almost as soon as it began.

In 1942, as US troops were being shipped off for battle, the men of the War Manpower Commission found themselves fretting about how to keep the economy from collapsing at home. They had to keep the factories open. And they had to meet wartime production needs without falling short on domestic demand.[1]

The situation was particularly dire in Mobile, Alabama, where the shipyards were struggling to find enough men to meet the Navy's needs. So, Burton R. Morley, the regional director of emergency management, wrote a letter to the War Manpower Commission asking for permission to recruit women to build the ships instead. Morley noted that "there are a very considerable number of women in Mobile who, according to Social Security Board standards, should be available for employment," and that if they were to recruit "available surpluses of women," they could just about cover the gap. Morley, however, was skeptical that women—particularly middle-class white women—would be willing to take "masculine" jobs.[2]

Thus, Morley proposed an ad campaign targeting women and touting their importance to the war effort, arguing that "pressure should be applied to force their utilization." The Commission agreed. Soon after, it published a flyer that read: "If Hitler came to Mobile, every woman would defend her home with a gun, a knife or her bare fingers. But Hitler and his hordes will not come if women help to build ships, more ships to transport our men, tanks, planes and munitions to the battle lines on other Continents—or if women take other jobs directly aiding the war."[3]

Evocative as it was, the flyer failed. Women didn't come streaming to the Mobile shipyards. The problem wasn't, as Morley assumed, that women were staying home because they were offended by the idea of doing "men's" jobs. The problem was that women, especially mothers, had no substitutes for the jobs they were already doing as the generals of the home front: caring for the children and the sick and the elderly while also running scrap drives, planting victory gardens to keep food on the table, and scrimping and saving wherever they could to preserve supplies for the troops.[4]

At the time, childcare options were extremely limited.* And even if mothers were able to find childcare, it wasn't easy to find paid work. State laws and employer policies often barred married women from employment or relegated them (and especially the Black, Latina, and immigrant women among them) to the most menial and low-paying jobs.† In the run-up to World War II, such policies and practices had become even more common, the product of Depression-era rhetoric scapegoating married women, who were perceived to be working for "pin money" rather than out of "economic necessity," and who were thereby criticized—including by the first woman to serve as secretary of labor—for hoarding American jobs.[5]

It shouldn't surprise us, then, that ad campaigns weren't enough to fill the gaps in the labor force left when men shipped off to war. By December 1942, nearly 100 percent of unmarried women without children were working. But most of them were already working for pay before the war, and economists estimated that the US would need at least four million married women and mothers of young children on board. At the time, only one out of every thirty of those women was working for pay.[6]

In the end, getting married women and mothers of young children to join the wartime workforce took changes in policy—and a particularly cre-

---

* Before World War II, the government had merely dabbled in childcare, setting up a few hundred nursery schools during the Great Depression to provide care for low-income families and jobs for the unemployed. During World War II, the government used funding allocated through the Lanham Act to expand those existing centers and offer federal funding for communities across the US to build even more.

† At the time, many labor unions also barred women from joining to protect the "family wage" they had fought to secure for men.

ative advocate. Katharine Lenroot, chief of the US Children's Bureau, saw an opportunity to convince Congress that funds from the Lanham Act, which were meant to go toward housing and other infrastructure projects in key defense-production centers, could also be used for childcare. In 1941, she wrote to heads of the Office of Education and the Works Progress Administration, figuring that the more agencies she had on board, the better. "It would appear," she wrote, "that the practical way of implementing the resolution and developing a sound nationwide program for the care of children of working mothers would be to have a national project . . . [that] would include various types of care; such as, public child-care centers for care on perhaps a twelve or fifteen hour basis if necessary, day nurseries, nursery schools, recreation centers for school children, nurseries for infants, and such other facilities as might be necessary in industrial defense and military centers. Such facilities are urgently needed in these defense areas if children are to be given proper care while their mothers contribute to our national defense effort."[7]

While the other two agencies were eager to team up with Lenroot and the Children's Bureau, Congress (and Texas representative Fritz Lanham himself, the originator of the bill) refused to play ball until after it was clear that other efforts to recruit women had failed. It took a full year—until August 1942—for Congress to agree that the Lanham Act funds could be used for childcare. It took even longer to work out the details, and Congress didn't begin allocating funding for childcare efforts until 1943.* Local communities got to choose how they used the funding, but in most places, mothers working in any paid job could get up to six days a week of full-time childcare with free meals and snacks and educational programming offered in small-class-size settings—all for $10 or less per day in today's dollars. Most centers were open at least twelve hours a day, and some ran round-the-clock to accommodate factory production hours. Many communities also used the federal government money to offer affordable before-school, after-school, and

---

* As Paul McNutt of the Manpower Commission stated in 1943, "The first responsibility of women with young children, in war as in peace, is to give suitable care in their homes to their children. . . . If any such women are unable to arrange for the satisfactory care of their children at home during their working hours, adequate facilities should be provided for the day care of their children during working hours."

summer care for older children. As one flyer for the program advertised, participants would enjoy "Expert guidance, Active life with youth of own age, Experience in arts, crafts, drama, nature study, music, Supervised games and play."[8]

In the wake of those changes, and by the end of the war, labor force participation among US mothers with young children had risen from one in thirty to one in six. Those numbers are certainly impressive. But they could have been higher still. In the end, only a fraction of US families received childcare through the Lanham Act because only some communities qualified for funding, and because the federal government left it up to those communities to apply, match the funding they got from the federal government, navigate complex bureaucratic rules, and figure out how to build and run a childcare system from scratch.*[9]

The solution was also temporary. Congress never intended to build a permanent national childcare program. At the time, most government officials believed that women should only be employed out of necessity—either because they didn't have a husband who could support them, or because they were needed to do jobs that men couldn't or wouldn't fill. And so, when the men were done with fighting, Congress cut off the funds for childcare. Without that childcare, millions of women were forced back home or into underpaid feminized jobs as teachers, nurses, social workers, hairdressers, and secretaries in the postwar corporate boom.[10]

Women, of course, weren't happy about these developments. A Roper poll conducted in 1945 showed that two-thirds of women who had joined the labor force wanted to keep the "men's" jobs they'd had during the war.[11] As one woman told *Independent Woman* magazine in 1945:

---

* That's what happened in Mobile, where local officials applied for federal funding to set up childcare centers but then failed to allocate any matching funds. By the end of 1943, there wasn't enough money left to keep the centers open, and almost all of the mothers working in the shipyards were forced to head back home. A 1943 report from the Alabama Office for Emergency Management noted that "critical shortages [of workers in Mobile] have increased by 75 percent since the last period," adding that those losses were driven primarily by the loss of mothers with young children. The report explained the workforce shortages by noting that "day care facilities were recently suspended because of the city's failure to match the Lanham Act funds"—a decision that stemmed from "community attitude toward women in industry," which could be seen in the fact that "women who used the day care facilities were bluntly told they should be home caring for their families."

I hear on all sides that I should go back to the kitchen. That sounds to me like the stuff they were saying in Germany when Hitler went into power. Do they think I'm working just for fun or pin money? They should know that it's no easy task for a woman to take care of her husband and her young children and at the same time keep a job.

Or, as another married woman acknowledged in that same story:

Now I am worried, too. Unlike most of my associates, I am not entirely dependent on my salary, but I contend that I have a right to a job and a right to work. Will there be enough jobs to go around . . . and if not, will there be discrimination against women workers who are today one-third of the working force in our entire nation? Will I be deprived of the opportunity to continue to put my skill and education to use?

The discrimination she anticipated was ultimately what came to pass. After the war, not only were childcare centers shuttered, but states and private employers reinstated the kinds of pre-war policies that made it difficult for married women and mothers to work for pay.[12]

Adding insult to injury, other institutions—from the media to the medical establishment—also colluded to create the perception that women would have to be "crazy" (or maybe not even "real" women) to want a job when they could stay home. By the late 1940s, as historian Stephanie Coontz explains, formerly employed women who "had trouble adjusting to 'creative homemaking' were labeled neurotic, perverted or schizophrenic," and "institutionalization and sometimes electric shock treatments were used to force women to accept their domestic roles and their husbands' dictates."*[13]

The thing is, it didn't have to be this way. After the war, many of our European allies needed women in the workforce to help rebuild bombed-out cities and replace men who died in battle. And so they invested in building more equitable economies. In France, for example, World War II prompted

---

* Those same shock treatments were also recommended for women seeking abortion on the assumption that a woman who didn't want a baby must be severely emotionally disturbed.

a move toward policies for paid family leave, universal childcare, child tax credits and subsidies, and free universal healthcare.[14]

We in the US could have followed their example. The postwar boom left us with plenty of money to build a national childcare system and a national healthcare system and offer more support to families in need. But we chose short-term profits over long-term prosperity—which meant not building a stronger social safety net and forcing women to stand in for that net instead.[15]

American women are still paying the price of that choice today. Nearly eighty years and multiple feminist movements after the closure of the Lanham Act childcare centers, caregiving responsibilities remain a huge stumbling block on the path to equality between women and men. Even though women now represent almost half of the US workforce, they're still paid substantially less than men are. And they're still doing more of the unpaid work—on average, almost two hours more per day.[16]

Meanwhile, women in countries with strong social safety nets have fared better overall. The average Frenchwoman, for example, spends almost an hour less per day on unpaid work than her American counterpart. And the gap between women's and men's time on unpaid work is smaller in France as well. This doesn't mean, however, that Frenchmen do more unpaid work than their American counterparts. In fact, Frenchmen spend about thirty minutes less per day on housework and childcare than American men do, and almost two hours less per day on paid work. Put differently: the worker protections that helped Frenchwomen had spillover benefits for Frenchmen. In the US, by contrast, men and women are all worse off than they could be, and there are more inequalities between them as well.

This sad state of affairs is the product of policy choices we've made over and over again. Choices to rely on women to hold it together for their families, their communities, and the whole economy, and choices to deny women the support they deserve for their toils. As I'll explain, these policy choices drag all Americans down, albeit to varying depths. These choices have also rippled out from childcare and served as justification for underinvestment in other aspects of our social safety net, like healthcare and eldercare—because if women are the ones we expect to care for the children, then we might as well ask them to take care of the sick and the elderly while they're at it. And that's how the systems in place have come to affect far more than just women—undermining the security and stability of everyone else in American society, too.

This book is an ode to the women who do the work of holding it together and an effort to show how their underpaid but essential labor keeps our society—and our economy—from falling apart. I want them to see that they serve as the safety net in a society that has forced them to make do without the support they need. I want to show them how America's self-help culture deludes women into thinking that if they're struggling to manage it all, it must be because they didn't wash their face, get out of their own head, or let that shit go. In reality, if women are twisting in the wind, it's because we're the ones working overtime and being underpaid on a project that someone else gets to claim as their own. If we demand better, they'll call us ungrateful. If we resist, they'll threaten us until we comply. And so, unless and until we band together, we're stuck supporting a system designed for someone else's gain.[17]

I make this case to and for the women who live this reality and who, up to this point, have felt powerless to change it. To reach these women—to anger and embolden them—they must feel seen. And my hope is that through up-close, unflinching accounts of the women I've studied, readers will locate themselves both as individuals and as part of a collective of women and allies who can build a path out of self-blame.

HOLDING IT TOGETHER

Introduction

Around the world, women carry more of the load than men do, shouldering a disproportionate share of the unpaid caregiving labor, often while working in underpaid jobs. What sets American women apart is that they're expected to hold it together without the kind of institutionalized support systems on which women in other countries rely.[*][1]

Consider a young woman I'll call Akari—all the names of the people whose stories I'll tell in this book have been changed for privacy reasons; it's the least I can do in exchange for their generosity with their stories and their time.

One chilly morning in November 2021, I talked to Akari by phone during the brief window she had between dropping off her kids and starting her shift at one of her three part-time jobs. Between those three jobs—two weekday jobs in retail and a weekend shift at a high-tech manufacturing facility—Akari, who is biracial white and Japanese, was spending roughly fifty hours a week working, plus another ten hours a week commuting. Even so, her earnings were typically between $2,800 and $3,000 a month—varying depending on how many hours she could get. That's far less than the $7,300 a month living wage for a household with an adult and two children in the Indiana town where Akari and her children live.[†] And it has left

---

[*] Consistent with this possibility, research shows that overall inequality explains the relative size of the gender wage gap in different countries, such that if the US had less income inequality overall, the gender gap would be smaller as well.

[†] Living wage is a measure of the amount of money that a worker working full-time (2,080 hours a year) would need to earn to cover the cost of living for a household of their size in the community where they reside.

Akari with nearly $20,000 in debts and forced her to work so many hours for pay that she rarely gets to spend time with her kids.

This wasn't always the case. When I first met Akari in 2019, she was pregnant with her son, Ren, staying home full-time with her two-year-old daughter, Mei, and engaged to her long-term partner, Theo, who is white, and who was running his own home maintenance business, which brought in about $30,000 a year. Akari had left the workforce when Mei was born in 2017. At the time, Akari was making less than $10 an hour working in retail, and she calculated that she and Theo would end up with more money at the end of each month if she quit than if she kept her job and paid for full-time childcare.[2]

Things were stable for Akari and Theo up until the summer of 2020, when Theo died unexpectedly—the victim of a seemingly random act of gun violence that, years later, has yet to be explained.*

The first few months after Theo's death were a blur of grief and government forms. Like roughly half of all US adults, Theo didn't have any life insurance, and the little they had in savings wasn't enough to keep paying rent. Amid pandemic layoffs, and with local childcare centers closed, Akari had little hope of finding a job, let alone one that would pay all their bills. Relying on family also wasn't an option—Akari's mother had moved back to Japan to live with her own parents after getting divorced when Akari was a teen. So, with guidance from a local nonprofit organization, Akari applied for welfare and food stamps.† She also got on the waitlist for an apartment in a public housing community, and she and the kids moved into a shelter to improve their spot on the list.‡[3]

Relying on public assistance was challenging for Akari emotionally.

---

* The police investigated, but no one was ever charged for Theo's murder.

† By welfare, I'm referring to a program called Temporary Assistance to Needy Families (TANF). Food stamps, meanwhile, is the colloquial term for the Supplemental Nutrition Assistance Program (SNAP).

‡ Despite a nationwide shortage of affordable housing, Akari was eventually able to secure an apartment in a public housing community operated by her local Public Housing Authority and funded through the U.S. Department of Housing and Urban Development's RAD (Rental Assistance Demonstration) program. To qualify for a project-based voucher, Akari had to complete a drug test and provide income-related documentation. She was then assigned a spot on the waitlist based on her circumstances; living in the shelter improved her spot on the list.

Growing up in a middle-class suburban family, Akari never knew anyone on welfare, likely because the program's strict eligibility requirements are designed to ensure that only a tiny fraction of Americans receive cash support.* Akari had also learned from conservative family members to be skeptical of government dependency. "I believe welfare is temporary," she explained resolutely. "It's not supposed to be a lifestyle. It's other people's tax money. So, when you need it, you use it, you appreciate it. But it's not a lifestyle."[4]

The lifestyle that Akari could afford on welfare was far from an extravagant one.† As a single mother of two in Indiana, the most that Akari could receive in cash welfare benefits was $288 a month. Even with extra support in the form of housing assistance, Medicaid, food stamps, and subsidized preschool and childcare, those benefits were rarely enough to make ends meet, and they came wrapped in a lot of red tape. Public housing, for example, came with strict rules about visitors and not leaving the lights on overnight, and food stamps couldn't be used for diapers or wipes, let alone gas or car insurance. "Having a vehicle is really difficult if you're on welfare," Akari told me with a sigh. And yet, to keep her meager welfare benefits, Akari was also required to try to find paid work, which—living in a county where a patchwork bus system was her only other option for transportation—meant that she had to find a way to keep paying for her car.[5]

In another cruel twist, Akari learned that as soon as she started getting a paycheck of her own, her welfare benefits would be docked each month dollar for dollar based on her earnings, and she would get less support through food stamps each month as well. Earning money would mean qualifying for federal and state earned income tax credits (EITC), along with child tax credits. But she would have to use that extra money to pay the higher costs she would be hit with for other services—like rent and childcare—that are priced on a sliding scale.[6]

Having to reckon with all those extra costs is how Akari went from being a stay-at-home mom, to being on welfare, to having not one, not two, but three part-time jobs in a span of a little over a year. The first part-time

---

* Less than 1 percent of the US population is receiving TANF benefits at any given point in time.
† Akari was surprised to learn how little her welfare benefits covered and how punitive the program could be. "Everybody deserves better than welfare," she told me, recalling what she thought when she got her first check.

retail job Akari found, in the fall of 2020, paid less than $10 an hour, didn't offer employment benefits like health insurance or paid sick leave, and typically only scheduled Akari for a few hours a week.* Yet Akari had little choice about which job to take because her children's Head Start preschool program only ran from 8 a.m. to 3 p.m., and even if she paid for extended-day childcare, the kids still had to be picked up by 6 p.m.

Akari added a second part-time low-wage retail job in early 2021, but it didn't help all that much. Akari's bosses rarely scheduled her for more than twenty-five hours a week across both jobs, which meant she was usually bringing home less than $2,000 a month between wages, welfare, and tax credits combined.† That money barely covered rent, utilities, childcare, prescriptions, food, gas, and car insurance. When she fell short—which was often—she had to rely on local food pantries and pregnancy resource centers just to keep diapers on Ren and make sure they all had enough to eat.[7]

The precarity of that arrangement led Akari to add a weekend job at a manufacturing facility in the fall of 2021. On Saturdays and Sundays, Akari would get up at 5 a.m., drive to the plant, and work the line and the heavy machinery from 6 a.m. to 6:30 p.m. both days.

The kids, meanwhile, spent weekends at Theo's sister's house. On Friday evenings, Akari would drop off Mei and Ren, and they would stay with their aunt and cousins through Monday morning, when Akari would pick them up to take them to school. Akari hated that she didn't get to spend the weekends with her kids, but she figured it was better to let them—and Theo's sister and her family—get a good night's sleep rather than disrupt everyone's schedules by dropping the kids off before dawn on the weekends or picking them up after they would otherwise be in bed. Theo's sister wouldn't take money from Akari to watch the kids on the weekends, but Akari would give her a bag of beauty products she could buy at a discount from one of her retail jobs whenever she had some extra money to spend.

---

* US employers are only required to provide health benefits and other benefits like unpaid family leave for full-time employees—those who work thirty hours a week or more. Some employers skirt the rules by capping workers' hours or hiring them as independent contractors.

† In March 2021, Congress increased the annual Child Tax Credit from $2,000 to up to $3,600 per eligible child. This expanded Child Tax Credit expired in December 2021, returning to $2,000 per child per year.

As Akari waved goodbye each weekend, she would think of the stability she was trying to build for her children, but she could see on Mei's and Ren's faces the toll her absence was taking on them. "My daughter," Akari told me in November 2021, "has PTSD because of her father's death. She went from having a dad who works and being a daddy's girl and having a stay-at-home mom who always cared for her. And now there's no dad, and mom's always working. So in her mind she lost both parents."

That sacrifice, however, didn't leave Akari much better off financially because it pushed her at least partially over the benefits cliff. With income from three part-time jobs, Akari suddenly found herself making just a bit too much money to qualify for welfare, food stamps, Head Start, and public housing, and having to pay more for other programs where she was still on the sliding scale. "There's not really a nice transition," Akari lamented, adding that, in the short term, and from a short-term cost-benefit perspective, she would be better off going back on welfare and quitting her new weekend manufacturing job.[8]

Yet Akari was aware that the clock was ticking. Even the states with the most generous welfare benefits have a five-year lifetime limit on eligibility—Indiana's cap is two years for adults and five years for children—though soft diversion tactics ensure that almost no one stays in the program that long.* "Welfare's not gonna last forever," Akari told me resignedly, "and I'm just gonna get older. Right now, I can work, but what am I gonna do when I'm sixty, you know? I can't have anything saved up if I'm on welfare. You can't move up. You have to stay within that line. Right now, where I'm at, I lost all my welfare services. But if I continue to work, eventually I can maybe get a raise."[9]

———

Akari's story is gutting. Gutting because of the depths of the personal tragedy it contains. And gutting because of how common stories like Akari's are and what those stories portend: that the US not only makes it difficult and

---

* These soft diversion tactics include offering families onetime lump sum cash payments. Taking those payments will typically push families out of the welfare program, because TANF eligibility rules include asset limits. In Indiana, for example, families may not receive welfare benefits if they have assets in excess of $1,000, not including their primary vehicle or home.

demeaning to access what little protection it offers but also forces women to be the ones who protect their families from precarity and protect the economy from crumbling, too.

───

As the protectors, women are tasked with being the primary childcare providers for their families and also the kin-keepers, the family health managers, the family budget managers, and the head volunteers. They're the ones who take care of elderly family members and other relatives who've found themselves down and out financially, struggling emotionally, or in need of support with their own responsibilities for care. They're the ones bearing primary responsibility not only for taking care of family members who are sick but for all the work it takes to keep them safe and well, including researching and avoiding potential health threats, taking them to the doctor for checkups, managing medications, and ensuring that their family members are eating nutritiously and getting plenty of exercise. And they're often the ones who do the inventory and the planning and the shopping, the ones who know how much is left in the checking account or the cash jar, and the ones who figure out how to make ends meet when money is short.*[10]

Women also keep this country running by filling the underpaid jobs in our economy—accepting low wages to keep the costs of goods and services more affordable for everyone else. As of 2023, women represented 47 percent of the total US workforce, but they earned only 73 cents for every dollar earned by men. The picture is a little better if we only consider full-time employed women. Those women are earning 83 cents for every dollar that men do (albeit with bigger gaps for Black and Latina women and for mothers†). But focusing on full-time employed women ignores women like Akari

───

* Data from the American Time Use Survey show that moms spend more than twice as much time caring for kids every day as dads do, and women without children spend twice as much time caring for extended family as do men. Women also spend three times as much time every day on housework as men do, regardless of whether they have kids at home. And despite all they're doing for their families, women also spend roughly the same amount of time as men do volunteering in their communities.

† The motherhood wage penalty accounts for 80 percent of the overall gender gap in pay between full-time employed men and women.

who've been pushed into part-time, part-year, and often low-wage labor because those are the only jobs they can get.*[11]

Women shouldn't have to be doing so much for so little. And they wouldn't have to if we had a real social safety net. With the right investments and policies, countries can protect people from exploitation† and grant them dignity throughout their lives.‡[12]

Rather than build that kind of sturdy social safety net, the US has slashed holes in the meager net we do have and left the remainder to wither and rot. Policymakers have kept the federal minimum wage stalled at $7.25 an hour for decades, allowed states to chip away at the value of welfare benefits and institute work requirements and time limits for government assistance,§ and attacked the unions that could fight for higher pay or essential protections like guaranteed paid sick leave, paid family leave, or paid vacation time, safe working conditions, reasonable work hours, retirement pensions, and overtime pay. In the process, they've left forty million Americans struggling to

---

* The reality is that women hold nearly 70 percent of the lowest-wage jobs in the US economy and are systematically underrepresented in higher-paying jobs, too.

† Freedom from exploitation means not being forced to take whatever job you're offered, not being paid less than you deserve for your labor, and not being compelled to work so many hours or so many years to make ends meet that you have no energy left to care for your family or your community or even yourself. In practice, this freedom would likely require strong pro-union policies, higher minimum wages and unemployment benefits aligned with cost-of-living standards, and guaranteed paid sick leave, paid family leave, and paid vacation time, along with strict limits on paid work hours.

‡ Living with dignity means having unpolluted air to breathe, clean water to drink, nourishing food to eat, comfortable clothes to wear, and safe shelter to live in, with access to safe and reliable means of sanitation, transportation, and communication, with access to the care we need for our minds and bodies and those of our loved ones, and with opportunities for rest and solitude when we need it, opportunities to shape society's decisions, and opportunities to experience joy. To ensure dignity, we would likely need to invest in affordable housing programs for middle- and low-income families, robust cash benefit programs and food assistance for those in poverty, and old-age pensions that provide sufficient guaranteed income when people retire, along with free (or nearly free) high-quality, universally accessible systems for childcare, eldercare, healthcare, and public education, from preschool up through college, with funding for those systems set to the level where care work is sustainable and dignified.

§ Even the most "generous" states only give families enough to get them halfway to the federal poverty line. Meanwhile, stingier states, including Indiana, offer a maximum benefit of less than $300 a month, and haven't increased benefits to account for rising costs.

keep a roof over their heads, thirty-four million without sufficient food to eat, and thirty million without health insurance. And they've left more than thirty-five million American kids attending under-resourced schools and nine million without access to affordable childcare.[13]

Without a net, societies crumble. That's why people in the US are more depressed, more sick, and more likely to die young than people in other high-income countries.* It's why we work longer hours but produce less. Why we have a higher poverty rate.† Why our economy isn't growing as fast. And why we have more political unrest.[14]

The situation would likely be even worse if women weren't filling in the gaps in our economy and our threadbare safety net. What would have happened, for example, if Theo's sister hadn't been willing to take care of the kids on the weekends so Akari could add a third part-time job to her schedule? What would have happened if the women running the food pantries didn't collect the donations that Akari relied on when the food stamps ran out each month? What would have happened if Akari hadn't been willing to work three jobs to make ends meet? And what would have happened to Akari's employers—and to the US stock market—if they had to pay Akari what she deserved for her labor and cover her health insurance and other benefits to boot? In the absence of a robust social safety net, the US avoids catastrophe and keeps our society and our economy from crumbling by relying on women as the invisible glue.

---

* The average life expectancy in the US was 76 years in 2021, which is far below the average life expectancy for high-income countries (80 years). Most Western European countries, for example, have life expectances in the range of 80 to 84 years, with Canada and Australia in this category as well. Many countries in Asia also have life expectancies higher than the US, including China (78), Thailand (79), Japan (83), and Singapore (84).

† Economic inequality is typically measured using the Gini coefficient, on a scale from 0 (perfect equality) to 1 (perfect inequality). Among OECD countries, only Turkey, Bulgaria, Mexico, Chile, Costa Rica, and South Africa have higher Gini coefficients (i.e., are more unequal) than the US, which has a Gini coefficient of .40.

THE DIY SOCIETY

It's easy to assume that the situation was always this dire. And yet, there have been moments throughout our history as a country where things could have gone another way.

Consider Franklin Roosevelt's New Deal. During the decades following the Great Depression, US civic and corporate leaders adopted a shared sense of obligation to preserving collective well-being. They created Social Security and Medicare. They passed minimum wage laws and established the forty-hour workweek. They offered health insurance and pensions for workers when they retired. Following World War II, however, and as we saw with the closure of the Lanham Act childcare centers, the US put the brakes on efforts to expand the social safety net and then began to dismantle the net we already had.[15]

As historians Naomi Oreskes and Erik Conway explain in their 2023 book, *The Big Myth: How American Business Taught Us to Loathe Government and Love the Free Market*, that shift was first engineered by a group of ultra-wealthy businessmen in the 1930s in the US. These men, many of whom were associated with the National Association of Manufacturers (NAM), didn't want to pay for Roosevelt's social safety net. So they set off in search of a way to make people believe that our country would be just as safe—or even better off—without a net.[16]

What they found was neoliberalism—the idea that people and corporations should be free to pursue and keep whatever profit they can generate without support or interference from the state.* Put differently, neoliberalism is a belief in social and economic survival of the fittest. It's the insistence that people and corporations should try to get ahead by whatever means necessary (even cheating—since rules go against the whole spirit of freedom anyway), that those who fall behind aren't deserving of sympathy, and that those who get ahead should be celebrated, regardless of the means they used to reach those ends.

In the 1930s and '40s, NAM members paid to import the Austrian

---

* According to the Supreme Court's 2010 Citizens United decision, corporations are people, too.

economists who developed neoliberalism and install them in elite US universities, where they would train the next generation of American economists.* Those trainees included Milton Friedman, who is famous for arguing that a corporation's only job is "to make as much money as possible" for its shareholders, and that taxes and regulations should be cut "under any circumstances and for any excuse, for any reason, whenever it's possible."[17]

NAM then leaned on Friedman for guidance in launching a massive pro-business propaganda campaign. They co-opted popular radio and television programs and set up neoliberal think tanks to convince the American public that society wouldn't fall apart—and might even be better off—without a net. Their message included two core arguments that still permeate popular thinking and policymaking, despite the lack of evidence to support these claims.† First, that if we lower taxes on billionaires and big corporations, the money they save will "trickle down" to the rest of us. And second, that if we don't have a social safety net, we won't need one because people will make better choices and keep themselves safe.‡[18]

These claims had a certain truthiness to them. With the backing of venerated economists and pop culture figures, they were easy for the public to accept. That acceptance then paved the way for the election of neoliberal politicians, most of them Republicans but also Independents and even some Democrats, including pro-union-Democrat-turned-anti-union-Republican Ronald Reagan, who hosted the NAM-funded *General Electric Theater* as part of their propaganda campaign. In the spirit of you-scratch-my-back-I'll-scratch-yours, politicians like Reagan then installed neoliberal economists like Friedman in powerful policymaking positions, where they still predominate today.[19]

---

* One of these economists was Friedrich von Hayek, who went on to win a Nobel Prize for his later-debunked theory that political freedom requires economic freedom—or, put differently, that the more the government intervenes in the market, the more intervention will be required, until eventually totalitarianism ensues.

† "By the 1970s," Oreskes and Conway note, "what had begun as a self-interested defense of business prerogatives—one that was factually dubious and characteristically supported by gross distortions and misrepresentations of history—had been transmogrified into a seemingly intellectually robust body of thought."

‡ Friedman sums up this take in one of his more famous quotes: "When you start paying people to be poor, you wind up with an awful lot of poor people."

From that position of influence, these neoliberal economists and their cronies engineered what political scientist Jacob Hacker calls "the great risk shift" in his book by the same name. By cutting taxes and regulations and slashing social welfare spending,* they shifted responsibility for Americans' well-being away from the government and from employers and onto individuals and families. We now spend a smaller percentage of our GDP on social programs than we have at any point in US history, with that percentage projected to fall even further in the years ahead.[20]

Through its budget cuts and rhetoric of "good choices," the great risk shift made us into what I call a "DIY society": one where people are expected to solve their own problems, rather than count on the government or even their employers to support them. And one where people who fail to solve their own problems are shamed and denied support.

In exchange for our DIY efforts, the engineers of the great risk shift promised widespread prosperity—prosperity that would support workers and families in facing the added risk they were handed. But that promise never panned out. Rates of economic growth in the US were actually lower in the thirty years following the great risk shift than they were during the thirty years before, and the growth that did occur never trickled down. Instead, billionaires and big corporations took all the extra money they saved by lowering taxes and loosening regulations and held on to it as tightly as they could.† As a result, and after accounting for inflation, low-income and

---

* The maximum US corporate tax rate fell from over 50 percent in the 1960s to just above 20 percent in 2023, and the maximum rate for personal income tax followed in lockstep, falling from over 90 percent in the 1960s to only 37 percent today. Regulation changes also made it easier for companies to avoid taxes, pollute, and downsize workers, and harder for workers to unionize and fight back. Those changes left more money in the hands of billionaires and big corporations and less for policymakers to fund the social safety net, prompting cuts to education, transportation, healthcare, childcare, and other social services. Social Security and Medicare were among the few programs that remained mostly untouched, as they support elderly people who disproportionately vote for the GOP.

† Since the 1980s, only the highest US earners have experienced substantial growth in income; adjusting for inflation, incomes in the middle and the bottom of the ladder have barely budged. Growing income inequality also widened wealth gaps. According to a 2022 report from the Congressional Budget Office, in 1989, the top 10 percent of families, by income, held 63 percent of all the net worth in the US; by 2019, that number had risen to 72 percent, with much of the increase coming from earners in the top 1 percent. That increase came at the expense of middle-income families whose share of the net worth fell during that same time span, and at the expense of lower-income families, who rarely have any net assets and who, in many cases, went further into debt.

middle-income households in the US actually have less wealth today than they had twenty years ago. Only the highest-income households are better off wealth-wise, and they've continued to accumulate larger and larger shares of the total US wealth.[21]

MAINTAINING THE ILLUSION

That DIY society is merely an illusion. An illusion that seems real because of the magic that women perform. As we saw with Akari, and as I'll show in this book, families in the US accepted the responsibilities—and the risks—that came with a DIY society because they could dump them onto women. And because they could trust that women would either find a way to carry that weight or find someone else to dump it on—usually another woman more vulnerable than them. In essence, the US has decided that we can get by without a social safety net because women will protect us instead.[22]

That choice is drowning women and leaving our whole society sicker, sadder, and more stressed. Yet the engineers and profiteers of our DIY society refuse to see women struggling, because acknowledging those struggles would shatter the illusion. Ignoring women leaves us exactly where they want us—keeping society afloat without any buoy to hold us, and so out of breath that no one can hear us if we cry.

The magic of women makes the idea of a DIY society seem plausible and makes it seem—despite all the hard evidence to the contrary—like Friedman and his cronies were right. When women can make something out of nothing, then it's easy to assume that the free-market proponents were right all along—that we really can get by without a net.

The reality, of course, is that women aren't actually holding it together, or at least not as well as it might seem. As I'll show in this book, being the stand-in for the social safety net has taken a serious toll on women and left their families and communities less secure. I'll also examine how we've managed to persuade women (or force them, in some cases) to be the glue that holds it all together. And I'll consider why no one seems to care (or even believe) that women are being torn apart.

As a sociologist, I have spent more than a decade examining how people with power and privilege get ahead in our society, who gets hurt in the process, and how we justify leaving them behind. For this book, my research team and I conducted more than four hundred hours of interviews with families, most of them in Indiana, that we followed from 2018 to 2022. I also conducted two national surveys, each with more than two thousand parents across the entire US.

My initial goal was to write a book on the best-laid plans of parenting. I wanted to know how families plan to raise their children, what prevents families from following through on those intentions, and how they feel about any discrepancies in the end. So I started with pregnancy. My research team and I found prenatal clinics that would let us sit in the waiting room with our clipboards and our tablets, and we'd invite the pregnant people who were there for their six-month checkups—the one where they have to drink the syrupy-sweet glucola and try not to gag as they wait the two hours for their glucose test for gestational diabetes—to take a survey about the kind of parents they hoped to be. Two hundred and fifty pregnant patients—all of whom are cisgender women*—completed that initial survey. We then followed up with those same women at six months, twelve months, and eighteen months postpartum, inviting them to participate in surveys and in-depth interviews about their experiences parenting young kids. Most of the initial participants—the women we'd recruited during pregnancy—stuck with the project over time, though not all of them participated in surveys or interviews at every wave.

The interviews that we conducted typically lasted at least an hour and, in some cases, three or more. We let the participants choose where they wanted to be interviewed, which meant that my research team and I spent hours sitting with moms at kitchen tables or on back porches or on the floor in living rooms as kids played nearby. In other cases, moms preferred not to be interviewed at home, so we met at local coffee shops, or in their office at work, or in the children's area of the local public library, or we talked by video call or over the phone. Those video and phone options also came in handy because some of the initial participants left Indiana, moving to New

---

* It is important to note that just as not all women can experience pregnancy, not all people who experience pregnancy identify as women. Rather, gender nonbinary people and transgender men may also become pregnant and may also give birth to a child.

York, California, Oregon, Wisconsin, Texas, Georgia, and many other places in between.

This hybrid format for interviews also meant that we were well prepared for a shift to a virtual-only arrangement when the Covid-19 pandemic hit in March of 2020. And the response, during those early pandemic waves of data collection, was huge—many of the participants in our pandemic surveys and interviews noted that they were grateful for a chance to be heard. As the pandemic continued, I also expanded the study, including surveys and interviews with the original pre-pandemic participants, with their spouses or partners, and with other parents in their social networks as well. In total, and across all the pre-pandemic and pandemic waves of data collection, my team and I conducted 1,110 surveys with 374 participants and 312 in-depth interviews with 142 of those same participants.

The interviews we conducted both before and during the pandemic were often long and emotionally raw. We went into the interviews with some set questions, but we also probed their responses with unscripted follow-up questions and let the conversations meander, following our participants' leads. In that meandering, participants often reflected not only on the decisions they were making as parents but also on the hardship, loss, and uncertainty they were facing at the time of the interview and on how those experiences re-opened scabbed-over wounds. They talked about rape, child abuse, intimate partner violence, abortion, pregnancy loss, child death, infertility, divorce, unemployment, economic hardship, postpartum depression, and so much more. To that end, it's important to note that some of the stories that I share here will include these traumas.

The families in my study vary in their social class status—the level of formal education they've completed, the types of jobs they've held, their amount of money they bring in from paid work, the division of labor in their households, and the wealth and debts they've accrued.[23] Not surprisingly, given these variations, the families in this study also have a wide range of experience with the social safety net. Some, like Akari's, are just barely scraping by financially and have relied heavily on programs like welfare, food stamps, Medicaid, rental assistance, EITC, and subsidized childcare. For others, the social safety net is like a city in a country they have no intention of ever visiting. They may be vaguely aware of its existence, but they've never been there, and they'd probably need help finding it on a map.

The families in my study also come from a range of different racial and ethnic groups—Asian American, Black, Latina, and white. That said, and in part because the initial recruitment for the study took place in Indiana—a disproportionately white but also (politically) red state with blue pockets* — the group isn't as racially and ethnically diverse as the US population but does include women with far-ranging political views. Some participants identify as Republicans or conservatives—including, maybe surprisingly, Akari. Others identify as Democrats or liberals, and still others identify as moderate or Independents or want nothing to do with politics at all. At the same time, and possibly because Indiana's religious and political landscape has created a particularly hostile climate for LGBTQ people† and others who don't fit "traditional" family forms, this study also includes only a small number of queer families‡ and disproportionately includes married-couple families, with fewer moms who are cohabiting, unpartnered, separated, widowed, or divorced.[24]

A focus on Indiana families, including many rural and small-town families, is illuminating, given that books about American motherhood tend to focus on liberal, highly educated women living in cities or suburbs on the coasts. At the same time, as a sociologist, I'm aware of how factors like place

---

* According to the US Census Bureau, as of 2020, Indiana's population was 78 percent non-Hispanic white, 10 percent Black, 3 percent Asian or Pacific Islander, and 8 percent Latino. By contrast, the US population as a whole was 59 percent non-Hispanic white, 14 percent Black, 6 percent Asian or Pacific Islander, and 19 percent Latino. In the 2020 election, 57 percent of Indiana voters chose Donald Trump, and 41 percent chose Joe Biden. That said, there were also five counties in Indiana—disproportionately urban counties and those with large universities—where Biden received a majority of the vote.

† Mike Pence, for example, was the governor of Indiana before becoming vice president under Donald Trump. In both those roles, and in his bids for Congress, Pence made numerous anti-LGBTQ statements and took actions to limit the rights and freedoms of LGBTQ people.

‡ Compared to different-sex couples, same-sex couples often have more egalitarian divisions of paid work and household labor. This is not to say, however, that gendered forces do not affect same-sex couples. Rather, in same-sex couples, birthing partners and partners in lower-status positions (e.g., those with less formal education and lower incomes) may still take on more of the housework and caregiving labor, and women in these couples are still subject to gender and motherhood-related wage penalties.

and race and income intersect to shape women's life chances, so I wanted to understand how the lives of the families I was following compared to those of other families across the US. Thus, I also conducted two separate national surveys, each with more than two thousand parents or guardians of children under eighteen—the Institutions, Trust, and Decision-Making (ITD) study, which was fielded in November and December 2020, and the Parenting in Tumultuous Times (PITT) study, which was fielded between December 2021 and January 2022. For those interested in the wonkier details of running this kind of study, I'd recommend checking out the appendix.[25]

Mothers aren't the only ones who stand in for the US social safety net. Some men, nonbinary people, and women without children are also stuck in this same boat. Yet a focus on mothers is useful because they're often the ones at the bottom of the DIY society pyramid scheme. The engineers and profiteers of our DIY society exist at the top of the pyramid, and they promise riches to anyone who can climb up to join them. But they've taken away the social safety net—the net that would make it possible to climb without all-consuming risk. Without that net, the safest path upward involves climbing on the backs of others. And mothers, especially the most vulnerable mothers, are often the ones providing stability at the base of the pyramid. The ones who make it seem like those higher up have achieved their success DIY.

These patterns raise questions about how the US gets women to stand in for its social net—how we keep them from revolting en masse. So that's where we'll turn in part 1 of our story, considering how the US renders women ready to exploit. We'll see how that process begins with treating women—and anyone else who could give birth—as mothers-in-waiting, because equating womanhood and motherhood creates the perception that women are "naturally" suited to caregiving, and because framing caregiving as women's "natural" purpose makes it easy to justify underpaying them for caregiving labor, since the assumption is that they should just be grateful to get to do what they love.

Of course, not every woman gets caught in the mommy trap, but the engineers and profiteers of our DIY society go to great lengths to catch as many as they can. That involves leaving women in lower- and middle-income families with nowhere to turn for support and nowhere to hide from the caregiving expectations foisted on them and leaving even women in high-income families with choices that are morally fraught. To that end, and as we'll see in part 2 of our story, good choices won't save us, even if the engineers and profiteers of our DIY society try to tell us myths that persuade us they will. Finally, we'll consider what a real social safety net would mean for most of us, why the engineers and profiteers want us all stuck in precarity, and how we could force them to build the net we need despite their protestations by forming a union of care.

Part I

HOW WE GET WOMEN TO HOLD IT TOGETHER

Chapter 1

MAKING THEM
MOTHERS-IN-WAITING

In the US, we groom girls to stand in for the social safety net from the time they're old enough to hold a baby doll. We teach them to be meek while boys are loud and to obey where boys rebel. We give them toy vacuum cleaners to play with, task them with caring for younger siblings and cousins and neighbors, and keep close tabs on their movements, while boys are allowed to run wild. In essence, we train girls to be what sociologist Miranda Waggoner calls "mothers-in-waiting," because equating womanhood and motherhood makes it seem as though girls and women are "naturally" better suited to care.[1]

This kind of grooming goes a long way in pushing girls and women toward model motherhood, but it isn't a guarantee that they all will fall in line. And so, rather than take the risk that too many women will refuse the work of the social safety net, the engineers of our DIY society have turned motherhood into a trap. As we'll see in this chapter, the laws and the culture of American society are designed to force women—and anyone who can be pregnant—into motherhood, into caring for children, and into bearing the risks that come with filling those roles.

FORCED INTO MOTHERHOOD

Growing up, Brooke never wanted to be a mother. This ran counter to her upbringing as a white woman in a conservative evangelical Christian family. And yet, for Brooke, home wasn't a happy place. Her parents had a volatile on-again, off-again relationship. As a result, she had been sent to live with her grandparents for long stretches as a child. She told me, "Until I knew for sure that I had, like, a solid life, I never wanted to bring a child into the world." With a dry laugh and a glance at the six-month-old baby in her lap—her second child—Brooke added, "So I just opted to never have children—until I accidentally got pregnant."

Brooke and Brendan met in college and started dating. "We were typical college kids," Brooke recalled a little wistfully, as if describing someone else's life. "We liked to go out on weekends, we slept in, we skipped class sometimes. But then we ended up pregnant, or I ended up pregnant, and [Brendan] decided that he would rather finish school."

Brooke and Brendan initially planned to get an abortion, and Brendan's parents even offered to pay. Brooke, however, decided to talk things over with her own parents first. Brooke's mom, who had left college herself when she got pregnant with Brooke's older sister, took Brooke to get an ultrasound and promised that she would help Brooke raise the baby on her own, without Brendan or his family involved. "It's funny," Brooke explained, "how seeing a heartbeat on an ultrasound machine can change your perspective on life."

The possibility of that kind of change of heart is why legislators in Republican states like Indiana, where Brooke lives, tried to make it as difficult as possible to get an abortion, even under *Roe v. Wade*. If her mother hadn't taken her for an ultrasound, Brooke likely would have gotten one anyway as part of a state-mandated abortion consultation. That consultation would have had to be at least eighteen hours before the actual abortion procedure, adding further time to mull things over, and it would have included counseling designed to discourage her from going ahead with her plans.[2]

Brooke initially thought she and the baby would be able to live with her parents and that they would help her financially so she could finish college. Once her son, Carter, was born, however, Brooke realized that things wouldn't work out the way she thought they would. Brooke's parents both worked low-wage jobs and couldn't afford to pay for childcare for Carter. Without childcare, it was difficult for Brooke to stay enrolled in school. She couldn't take night classes because she worried about leaving Carter alone with her parents; they struggled to manage their anger, and unlike Brooke, who described herself as "not big on spanking," they were quick to use physical punishment with her when she was a child.

Brooke decided to set out on her own. She applied for welfare, WIC (a version of food stamps for low-income families with infants), rental assistance, and subsidized childcare. Brooke also got a paying job in retail, working for the same store as her mom. Brooke was grateful to have money coming in, and grateful that having an income made her eligible for EITC. Yet that money wasn't enough to offer a sense of security, and retail wasn't the job she wanted long-term. "I absolutely hated it," Brooke recalled.

The director of Carter's childcare center saw Brooke's unhappiness at work as an opportunity. At the time, the center was struggling with staff turnover. So the director begged Brooke to quit her retail job and come on board. Despite paying only minimum wage, the position came with free childcare, which was costing Brooke nearly as much as rent. She warily accepted the job. "I thought I was gonna hate it," she said, but she "absolutely fell in love with it. Children have taught me so much. Children have taught me patience, they've taught me to think outside the box."

Despite the job's emotional payoff, the financial rewards left a lot to be desired. Even when she got promoted to assistant director of the center a few years later, Brooke's salary was only $25,000 a year. Brooke appreciated the raise. Yet the extra money didn't go as far as it could have, because, like Akari when she took on her third part-time job, Brooke found herself suddenly ineligible for some forms of government support and having to pay a great deal more for others that operated on a sliding scale.

Rather than wallow, Brooke tried to stay hopeful, imagining a future where she finished college and became a nurse. While taking a state-mandated parenting class for WIC recipients, Brooke had met another single mom who had pulled herself and her three kids out of poverty by getting a nursing degree. Talking about her friend, Brooke's voice glowed with admiration, saying, "I just think about everything she went through, and now she has a house, she's got a car, her kids go to private school—like, she's got it!" Brooke figured that if she followed a similar path, she could earn $75,000 a year or more— enough that, in her mind, she wouldn't have to worry about the future for herself or her child.*3

With no one to care for Carter in the evening, however—Brooke still

---

* Given the salaries earned by registered nurses, 90 percent of whom earn at least $59,000 a year, many women turn to degrees and certificates in nursing as a pathway to upward social mobility.

didn't trust her parents to watch him—taking night classes wasn't an option. And quitting her job, even with how little it paid, seemed too risky. So Brooke just kept working at the childcare center, even after she met and married her husband, an auto mechanic, and after she gave birth to her second child.[4]

Whether from their families, their schools, or their churches, the message to young girls and unmarried women in the United States is often "Don't have sex!" or even "Sex is a sin!" That kind of abstinence-based messaging is far from effective, especially for young adults and teens.[5]

What can be prevented is unintended pregnancy and parenthood, and that's where the US falls short. Other countries reduce unintended pregnancy by teaching kids how sex works, by making birth control free and easy to access, and by making healthcare universal and easy to afford. Going a step further, other countries also reduce unintended parenthood by reducing the stigma around abortion and making these services free and readily available to use.[6]

In the US, we fail on all these fronts. And we have the high rates of unintended pregnancy and parenthood to show for what we have (or haven't) done.* Roughly half of all US pregnancies are unintended, and roughly half of the American women who become pregnant unexpectedly end up having and raising the child.† By contrast, in other high-income countries in Europe and East Asia, only about a third of pregnancies are unintended, and less than a third of those are carried to term. Becoming a parent unexpect-

---

* In the US, unplanned pregnancies are particularly common among teenagers, people without college degrees, people with limited financial resources, and people with limited access to healthcare—a group that is disproportionately composed of Black, Latina, and Indigenous young women and girls but also includes young white women, including many like Brooke who grew up in conservative religious families.

† Firm statistics on unintended pregnancy are somewhat difficult to come by, in part because some people who experience unintended pregnancy were intending to get pregnant *eventually*, just not right now, and in part because of cultural stigma that may discourage parents from implying, even in an anonymous survey, that their child wasn't wanted. Before the 2022 *Dobbs* decision, however, estimates suggested that, in the US, slightly more than one-third of unintended pregnancies ended in abortion, and roughly one-sixth ended in spontaneous miscarriage.

edly is particularly disruptive for teen girls and young women. And yet, US rates of teen pregnancy and parenthood are alarmingly high. In the US, 57 out of every 1,000 girls ages 15–19 become pregnant, and 60 percent of those go on to give birth. That's more than double the rate in Denmark,* but not because Danish teens are having less sex. During a mini-exchange trip to Denmark when I was in high school, I was shocked to learn that my host—a fellow 16-year-old girl—was allowed to have her boyfriend sleep over in her room and shocked to see her birth control pills just sitting nonchalantly on the bathroom sink.[7]

It would be so easy for the US to reduce unintended pregnancy, but instead, we've chosen the other way. On June 24, 2022, I was editing this very chapter when my phone buzzed with a text from my husband, saying simply, "overturned." I cried on my keyboard that morning, backspacing over the sentence I had previously written here: "At least for now, abortion is still legal in the United States, though a Supreme Court decision on *Dobbs* is due any day." June 24 was the day the Supreme Court issued its decision in the *Dobbs* case, which ended the legal protections for abortion services that were established under *Roe v. Wade* in 1973 and secured under *Planned Parenthood v. Casey* in 1992.[8]

FORCED TO HAVE MORE KIDS

Laws alone, however, aren't the only force trapping women in motherhood. Even before *Dobbs*, a toxic mix of pro-natal messaging and barriers to abortion access was already pushing women into poorly timed pregnancies or having more children than they planned. In late 2019, Audrey and her husband, Colby, decided they were ready to try for a second baby. They had both grown up in white evangelical Christian families with lots of siblings, and they wanted to give their daughter, Harmony, who was a toddler at the time, that same experience as a child.

Audrey and Colby were still trying to get pregnant in March 2020 when Audrey lost her job in retail, leaving her to care for Harmony, whose

---

* In Denmark, only 22 out of every 1,000 girls ages 15–19 get pregnant, and only 30 percent of those pregnancies result in the birth of a child.

childcare center closed. Colby, a healthcare provider, started working over-time to meet the increased Covid demand.

Unemployment was hard for Audrey. Going back to work full-time had been the thing that helped most in overcoming the postpartum depression she experienced when Harmony was born, and returning to a full-time care-giving role left Audrey slipping back into the gloom. The loss of Audrey's job also led to conflict with Colby, who was feeling pressured to take on more overtime at work to maintain their roughly $80,000-a-year household in-come. As Audrey told me a few months into the pandemic, "I think some of it was that he didn't really know how to deal with the stress of his job and took it out on me and took it out on us." He wasn't abusive, she hastened to add, but he was touchy and grumpy. "We just pretty much ignore each other because we know we're going to get into a fight."

Given the stress and conflict at home, Audrey decided that they should stop trying for a second baby. She told Colby multiple times that she wanted to wait. Audrey and Colby were relying on the withdrawal method to avoid pregnancy, which is far-from-guaranteed birth control. Yet, like many men, Colby preferred not to wear condoms, and, like many women, Audrey has health conditions that make it too risky for her to take hormonal birth con-trol pills.[9]

Audrey was aware of the risks of relying on withdrawal—she has a col-lege degree and was a social worker before having kids.* So she asked Colby to be careful and to always pull out during sex unless she said otherwise. Usually, he would ask if he was unsure. But once, Colby didn't ask and didn't pull out, and Audrey happened to be ovulating.

Colby's actions, and the resulting pregnancy, weighed heavily on Au-drey. "It's very clear that it wasn't something I was okay with," Audrey told me, referring to the fact that Colby didn't pull out. "It wasn't something that I consented to." When she saw the two lines on the pregnancy test, she was "REALLY pissed off."

Audrey wanted to talk about what she'd experienced with Colby, but her

---

* Audrey decided not to go back to work as a social worker after having Harmony because the $30,000-a-year salary didn't seem worth it for a job that Audrey described as "not good for my mental health."

friends and family members dismissed her concerns. "I think that the term 'sexual assault' is appropriate," Audrey explained, but "other people I've spoken to have mixed opinions." In the end, one of Audrey's sisters-in-law—the wife of Colby's brother—was the only person who made her feel validated in viewing what happened as assault. Recalling that conversation, Audrey said, "I was like, 'Yes! Thank you!' That was really helpful—it made me feel like I wasn't just overexaggerating or anything like that."

Audrey's only close friends at the time were other mothers who were part of what she called her "church family"—the members of her evangelical Christian church. As a new mom living hours away from the town where she grew up, Audrey relied heavily on the women in her new church family. When Harmony was born, it was the leader of Audrey's church moms' group who volunteered to go to the hospital with Audrey if Colby was stuck at work. And after Audrey lost her job during the pandemic, weekly church services and Bible study groups and moms' group meet-ups were the only regular adult interactions she had with anyone other than Colby. At that point, she and Colby weren't talking very much, either, which led Audrey to lean even more heavily on the women at church. When I asked Audrey what she would do without support from her church family, she told me, "I genuinely don't know how we would do it. Especially living so far from home. I do not know what we would do without our church. Like, they've just been—they've been everything to us. They've helped us out with meals and helped us out by giving me stuff to help with nursing, they've given us baby clothes, they've just been there to talk to us when we need advice."

The members of Audrey's church family were supportive, but not of abortion and divorce. Both were, according to Audrey, "against our faith and our belief system." Those beliefs left Audrey feeling very alone in navigating the decisions she had to make in the wake of the sexual assault and the unintended pregnancy that followed. She considered both getting an abortion and leaving Colby, but she worried about how her family and friends might judge her for those choices. So, instead, Audrey stayed with Colby and tried to feel excited about having a second child.

A difficult pregnancy made that enthusiasm hard to muster. Audrey and Colby continued to fight frequently, and Audrey was struggling with both depression and hyperemesis gravidarum—severe nausea and vomiting that extends beyond the first trimester. Audrey also had to revisit the baby's traumatic conception any time anyone congratulated her on the pregnancy. "When people ask," Audrey explained, "and I say that I didn't want to get pregnant, I think people think I mean it was an accident. And it wasn't an accident. It was a choice; it just wasn't my choice."

After the assault, Colby had promised that he would go with Audrey to therapy to talk through their past and try to find a way forward. And yet, by 2022, Colby still hadn't seen his promise through, despite the difficulties in their relationship remaining unresolved. Audrey feared what would happen if Colby didn't seek help, as his father had been abusive to his family—including what she described as "emotionally, physically, and sexually abusive" to Colby's mother. Even so, Audrey didn't have plans to leave.

Audrey worried that if she and Colby were to divorce, "it would be financially much more difficult." Audrey would likely have qualified for about $1,200 a month in child support from Colby,* and she could have gone back to paid work herself. Yet given her work history, Audrey wasn't sure she would be able to find a job that paid enough to cover her share of the cost of childcare, let alone keep up with payments on her credit card debt, medical debt, and car loans, which totaled more than $40,000. Audrey also worried that divorcing Colby would push her off his employer-sponsored health insurance. As someone with multiple chronic medical conditions, Audrey didn't want to jump through the hoops of finding new doctors. And she wasn't sure whether Medicaid or other low-cost coverage would give her access to the kind of mental healthcare she was able to get on Colby's plan.

And so, rather than ask for a divorce, Audrey tried to maintain a precarious peace with Colby by basically living separate lives. Colby put all his energies into paid work, while Audrey focused on the kids. Despite the peace it offered, that division of labor was challenging for Audrey. Lingering depression made bonding with new baby Melody difficult. Audrey initially thought Melody might have a speech delay but discovered, after visiting a specialist, that "it's just that she doesn't get one-on-one attention that Harmony did when she was this age." That realization led to deep guilt for

---

* Childcare support payments estimated with this calculator: https://www.alllaw.com/calculators /childsupport/indiana.

Audrey—guilt compounded by the fact that Audrey felt she had also failed Harmony since getting pregnant with Melody. "Even though I was there," she explained, "I wasn't present. So that feels really hard."

It's easy to think of abortion as a young woman's issue. But the reality is that before the 2022 *Dobbs* decision, 60 percent of people who received abortions were already raising a child of their own, and half of those already had two or more kids. *Dobbs*, then, tightens the motherhood trap not only by making it harder for women to avoid having children but also by making it harder for women to control the number and the timing of the children they do have.

Of course, and as Audrey's story illustrates, it doesn't take laws to keep women with children from having abortions. Pre-*Dobbs*, women in communities with high rates of unintended pregnancies already faced considerable social pressure to choose parenthood, even if they didn't plan to have children, or to have so many children, or to have a child at that particular time. That pressure comes from women's families, friends, and faith communities. And it leads women to worry that if they choose abortion they will be labeled, judged, or ostracized.[10]

Now, maybe you're thinking, "Why care what other people say? Isn't it worse to have a child you're not ready to raise than to risk being shamed for making a choice your community doesn't support?"

But the thing is, stigma comes with consequences. In tight-knit communities like Audrey's, where everyone knows and depends on each other, breaking a social norm can mean being cut off from your entire support network in a single sudden swoop. Recall that all Audrey's mom friends were members of the same conservative church that taught Audrey to see abortion and divorce as sinful. And recall that the only person in Audrey's network who was willing to acknowledge the truth about what happened with Colby was Audrey's sister-in-law, who was married to Colby's brother and thus likely wouldn't have been able to help Audrey financially or even logistically. In that context, it's easy to see why Audrey chose to continue the pregnancy and stay with Colby, when choosing otherwise would have meant setting fire to the makeshift safety net she'd sewn for herself. And without a sturdy public safety net to fall back on, that seemed like too big a risk to take.[11]

Choosing motherhood, however, can still come with risks for women, even those who have strong support networks and are in a relatively privileged position financially. Recall how Audrey struggled to bond with Melody and how the depression she experienced in the aftermath of the assault and the pregnancy made it difficult for her to give Harmony the kind of attention Audrey thought she should be able to give her after becoming a stay-at-home mom.

Meanwhile, and as we'll see in our next story, the risks of motherhood are even greater for women in more precarious positions. And they're compounded by the feebleness of our social safety net and by our willingness to punish women who fail at holding together its broken threads.[12]

FORCED OUT OF MOTHERHOOD

When Sylvia, who is white, was about fifteen and living with her mother in rural Indiana, her older brother, Dustin, moved back in with his girlfriend, Destiny (who is also white), and their infant daughter, Maizie. Dustin would disappear for days on end because of his opioid addiction. Destiny, meanwhile, was struggling with severe postpartum mental illness but couldn't afford treatment, making it difficult for her to care for Maizie, let alone try to hold down a job. Sylvia and Dustin's mother was supporting the whole household financially, with multiple part-time, low-wage, no-benefit jobs as a home health aide.* That left Sylvia to do most of the work of caring for Maizie after school and most nights as well.[13]

Things gradually began to improve for Destiny, but then she got pregnant again. Destiny, whose relationship with Dustin was fraying by that point, took Maizie and the new baby, Onyx, and moved out on her own. Raising an infant and a toddler alone turned out to be more than Destiny could handle, especially because she experienced even more severe postpar-

---

* To avoid offering benefits like healthcare, home healthcare agencies often cap workers' hours or hire them as contractors, forcing them to work multiple jobs to make ends meet.

tum mental illness the second time around, leading Destiny to also begin abusing drugs.

The Department of Children's Services got involved when, according to Sylvia, Destiny threatened to kill her kids.* Rather than offer support for Destiny's struggles with addiction and mental health, DCS simply took Destiny's children away.† DCS gave custody to Dustin, who officially lived with Sylvia and their mother but was rarely at home. Sylvia, who was about eighteen at that point, wasn't convinced that her brother would be a better parent than Destiny, and she worried that the way DCS treated the situation would make things worse for Maizie, Onyx, and Destiny. "DCS is very stressful," Sylvia recounted, years later, adding hesitantly at first and then more forcefully, "Their decisions—their decisions suck."[14]

Sylvia's mom was working as many hours as she could to support the household, and Dustin just wasn't around much, so childcare again fell to Sylvia. "It was stressful in the beginning," she recalled, "but I coped and learned how to be a parent."

Bedtimes with the kids were particularly rough. During those early years with her niece and nephew, she rarely got the rest she needed because she often ended up sleeping with Maizie instead of sleeping alone in her bed. "I would put her in the Pack and Play and all she would do was cry," Sylvia recalled, adding, "It's a high-pitched squeal, bust-your-eardrums cry." Sylvia was occasionally successful in getting Maizie to sleep separately, but that took a lot of practice and skill. "Like, you can put her in her own bed," Sylvia explained, "but you still have to lay with her and be very quiet and like ninja-move out of there."

---

* Sylvia described Destiny's experience as "postpartum depression," though she may also have been experiencing another related condition called "postpartum psychosis," which is much less common but also far more serious. In a meta-analysis of research on postpartum psychosis, psychologist Rachel VanderKruik and her colleagues find that about one in a thousand pregnant people experience psychosis after giving birth. They note that "clinical features of postpartum psychosis include elated, dysphoric or labile mood, agitation, bizarre or disorganized behavior and thought processes, and insomnia, while psychotic symptoms can often include mood-incongruent delusions, hallucinations, or delusions of control, with content often related to the infant or self (e.g., harm to the infant or self)."

† Research shows that fear of child removal plays a key role in discouraging low-income families from applying for the kinds of government assistance for which they might otherwise qualify, because contact with government agencies can prompt reports that trigger the investigations that may ultimately lead to children being taken away.

After a two-year battle with both DCS and addiction, Destiny eventually regained custody of Onyx and Maizie. Through those years, Dustin remained absent most of the time—like his father before him, whom Sylvia called "an ass and an alcoholic," Dustin never told anyone where to find him and would only show up occasionally. That left Destiny struggling to make ends meet while also taking care of both kids.

Hoping to avoid further run-ins with DCS, Destiny asked if Sylvia could (informally) take partial custody of Maizie and Onyx—keeping them with her at her mother's house every other week. Sylvia loved Maizie and Onyx as if they were her own children. So she agreed. Sylvia abandoned her plans of going to college, and she and Destiny both got jobs as home health aides like Sylvia's mother—a job Sylvia hated—and began splitting both parenting duties and the $200-a-week cost of childcare. "I only had to pay half," Sylvia recalled, "but I mean, a hundred dollars is a hundred dollars. We struggled some weeks."

Despite that support from Sylvia, Destiny never got the help she really needed—drifting in and out of sobriety—and she became less and less involved in her kids' lives. When I last talked to Sylvia in 2022, Destiny was dating a long-haul truck driver and spending weeks at a time with him on the road. Dustin, meanwhile, has never been a reliable presence for Maizie and Onyx—Sylvia isn't even sure where he lives. As a result, Sylvia is still her niece and nephew's primary caregiver. They live with her full-time, even though she's married now and has a daughter of her own.

Sylvia is far from alone in her role as surrogate parent. In the wake of the opioid crisis, the US is seeing unprecedented rates of drug-related illness and death. As opioid addictions and deaths have ramped up, so has the number of children removed from their homes for parental neglect. Between 2000 and 2017, the percentage of US children who were removed from their homes because of parental drug use more than doubled. At this point, 40 percent of child removals in the US are related to a parent's alcohol or drug use, and in states like Indiana that have been hit particularly hard by the opioid crisis, that number is over 60 percent.[15]

When these children are taken from their parents, most are placed with kin. Today, 2.5 million US children are being raised by someone other than their parents, and in the vast majority of those cases, children are placed with grandparents, other relatives, or close family friends. In Indiana, because of the prevalence of opioids, the percentage of children living with grandparents or other extended family is more than double the percentage for the US as a whole.[16]

Dustin, of course, was the one whom the state officially tasked with caring for Maizie and Onyx when Destiny was deemed "unfit." And yet, like Dustin himself growing up, and like roughly a third of all kids in the US today, Maizie and Onyx didn't end up having a regularly present dad.[17]

Instead, and as in most cases where children are removed from their homes, the work of caring for Maizie and Onyx fell primarily on women—first Destiny, then Sylvia and Sylvia's mom. All that responsibility takes a heavy toll on caregivers like Sylvia, affecting their physical and mental health and often trapping them below or just above the poverty line. In Sylvia's case, for example, caring for Maizie and Onyx kept her from going to college, pushed her into a low-income, no-benefits job she hated, and likely even pushed her into getting married and having kids of her own at a young age.[18]

It didn't have to be this way. With a stronger and less punitive social safety net, Destiny and even Dustin might've gotten the help they needed to maintain custody of their children and to raise them in a stable and supportive home—and Sylvia's life might have taken a very different course. In reality, the US social safety net, with its often-draconian child welfare laws, provides only limited support for those nonparental caregivers and also makes only halfhearted efforts to help parents like Destiny and Dustin to successfully and permanently reunite with their kids.[19]

These patterns aren't unique to white families like Sylvia's, and, in fact, they have historically and disproportionately affected Black families in the US. Consider the crack cocaine epidemic of the eighties and nineties. As waves of addiction and death crashed over low-income Black communities, and as sociologist Dorothy Roberts details in her book *Shattered Bonds*, US government officials ripped millions of Black children away from their mothers, promising to save them from the rising tide. Rather than save the children, however, those government officials merely rearranged their lives, foisting most of them onto grandmothers or aunts or other female relatives, causing the number of children being raised by nonparental family members to increase by 40 percent in just ten years. That shift didn't come with any real support for the relatives who were raising these children, leaving many of them to suffer financially, logistically, emotionally, and even physically under the weight of their new caregiving roles.[20]

Meanwhile, the mothers of those torn-away children arguably fared even worse. Demonized by anti-drug crusaders, and abandoned by the state, many of them, like Destiny, found themselves not only struggling to get their children back but spiraling into despair. And that spiral shouldn't surprise us. As we'll see in our next story, mothers are the first to catch the blame for anything that goes wrong in their children's lives.

FORCED TO TAKE THE BLAME

Ayanna didn't plan to get pregnant in high school, but she had her first child just before graduation and her second a little over a year after that. Despite the stress of new parenthood, Ayanna, who is Black, managed to enroll in college—a small historically Black college that specializes in supporting low-income and nontraditional students who need more support than others might to make their way through school. After finishing her degree, Ayanna got a full-time job as a social service case manager. In 2016, when Ayanna was twenty-five and her kids were in elementary school, Ayanna then met and married her husband, Marquis, who is Black, has a bachelor's degree, and works full-time in a warehouse shipping job. In 2017, when Ayanna and Marquis had their first baby together, they were earning about $60,000 a year.

By the time I met Ayanna in 2019, her life had taken a turn down a rocky path. Less than a year earlier, Ayanna had lost her eight-year-old son, Jayce, to kidney disease. Ayanna was also having a hard time relying on family for support in managing her son's death. Her own mother believed that Jayce's kidney disease was caused by vaccines and blamed Ayanna for having him immunized, creating enormous guilt for Ayanna, even though Ayanna wasn't convinced that Jayce's death had anything to do with vaccines. Faced with Jayce's death and her mother's accusations, Ayanna found herself struggling both mentally and physically, including gaining a substantial amount of weight.

Her relationship with Marquis was also suffering—she rated it a 7 on a scale of 1 to 10.

Given that stress, getting pregnant again wasn't on Ayanna's radar. And yet, when it happened, Ayanna saw the pregnancy as a bright spot amid all the gloom. Six months into her pregnancy, she was excited about the new baby and hopeful that the next few months would go well.

Yet there were already signs of trouble. High blood pressure, gestational diabetes, and a urinary tract infection were all red flags to the doctors, and they warned Ayanna that she would likely have to be induced early rather than wait to give birth until her daughter Anissa had reached full-term. Even still, Ayanna held out hope that she could give birth without medical intervention, the way she had done before. "I'd love for my baby to come on her own," Ayanna explained, adding, "I am scheduled to be induced but I prefer a natural, unassisted vaginal birth with my best friend and husband by my side."

In the end, Ayanna's doctors decided to induce her two weeks before her due date, and things quickly went downhill from there. After the induction, Anissa's heart rate dropped, and Ayanna's labor wasn't progressing. The doctors made the decision to switch to an emergency C-section, during which the placenta started separating from Ayanna's uterine wall, leading to sudden, severe bleeding. "Anissa inhaled blood and had to be resuscitated," Ayanna explained. Anissa was in the NICU for ten days.

During those ten days, Ayanna was terrified for her daughter and for herself as well. She knew that Black women are disproportionately likely to die from pregnancy-related complications. Given how awful she felt after giving birth, Ayanna was afraid that she might become one of those statistics herself. "Recovery was hard, as I had never had surgery before and was obese," she recalled. "I was terrified seeing that many women, especially Black women, were experiencing death and other complications after giving birth via C-sections. I made sure I took the blood thinners and blood pressure meds and walked as much as possible. There was a nurse who explained EVERYTHING to me and that helped me so much."[21]

Even with that help, Ayanna continued to struggle physically and mentally after she got home. It took Ayanna almost six months to feel as though she had recovered from childbirth—the result of a series of ongoing health issues, including urinary problems, bowel problems, difficulty concentrating, physical exhaustion, and frequent stress. By the time Anissa was six months old, Ayanna had also been clinically diagnosed with anxiety and depression. Even with treatment, she was still feeling down, depressed, and hopeless at least several days a week, and she also described regular bouts of panic and anxiety.

Faced with those struggles, and with her own grief from Jayce's death still so fresh, Ayanna didn't want to go back to her job and to the work of helping others manage their own trauma. Yet she didn't think Marquis and the rest of her family would support her desire to leave the workforce because Marquis wasn't earning enough to support the family on his own. That pressure to keep working was also compounded when the Covid-19 pandemic hit and Marquis's employer cut his hours on the job. The stress of all that upheaval, on top of the pain of grief and the exhaustion of parenting three young children, led Ayanna and Marquis to separate in 2021. As of 2022, they were still living apart.

When we treat women as mothers-in-waiting, we condition them not only to sacrifice themselves for their children but also to step up if anything goes wrong with their children and to accept responsibility and blame. This kind of mother-blaming isn't unique to the US. What sets us apart, however, is that our underinvestment in the social safety net stacks both motherhood and childhood with so much risk that we're almost destined to fail.[22]

Consider, for example, the risks that come with pregnancy and childbirth in the US today. Despite all the medical advancements the US has made in the past hundred years, we still have the third-highest rate of maternal mortality of all the countries in the OECD (only Mexico and Costa Rica lose more people to complications related to pregnancy and childbirth). And those rates are continuing to increase. Maternal mortality in the US has nearly doubled since 2016, particularly in the wake of Covid-19.[23]

These overall numbers are troubling, but the situation is actually worse than it seems when we examine the data more closely because rates of maternal and infant mortality divide sharply along race and class lines. Black women like Ayanna, for example, are roughly two and a half times as likely as white women to die from pregnancy-related complications. And those gaps are even larger for highly educated women than they are for women without college degrees.*[24]

Given these risks, it shouldn't surprise us that many women today are afraid to become pregnant and that those fears are particularly common among women from vulnerable groups. Take Sierra, another Black mom we'll meet in chapter 8. "I was scared for my life," she recalled of labor with her first child. Her fear led her to wait as long as possible to be hooked up to monitors or stuck on a birthing bed. Instead, she says, "I walked around the hospital until I couldn't take the pain anymore."[25]

And yet, even if women make it through childbirth, the risks don't stop there. Sleep deprivation, memory problems, and even teeth falling out are all common postpartum problems, and one in seven mothers also experiences postpartum depression or anxiety. The mental and physical toll of motherhood also persists as children get older and is compounded the more time that moms spend with their kids.[†] American men, by contrast, are actually happier when they spend more time with their kids, which is ironic given that the majority of Americans believe that women are the ones more "naturally" suited for childcare.[26]

That pattern could be taken to mean that men are better suited than women for caregiving, but the more likely reality is that our treatment of mothers makes motherhood more stressful than fatherhood, including how

---

* I teach these statistics in my Introduction to Sociology class, and I once had a student—a pre-med student—raise his hand and ask, "But isn't that just biology?" And what he meant was: Aren't Black people just more likely to have the kinds of preexisting conditions that make them more likely to die? "Well," I told him, "it's not that simple." Black people in the US are more likely to have certain chronic conditions like heart disease and high blood pressure. But that doesn't mean that Black people are biologically predisposed to have worse health outcomes. Instead, what research shows us is that racism gets inside people's bodies—weathering their cells, putting stress on their hearts, promoting inflammation, and limiting their choices—in ways that can affect their chances in life. Compounding those challenges, Black people in the US are also subjected to medical racism—treated with skepticism about whether their pain is as bad as they say it is, denied access to necessary treatments, and even misdiagnosed by tools designed for white people's use.

† Compared to non-mothers, moms in the US are more exhausted, more stressed, and in worse health. And compared to moms who work for pay full-time, stay-at-home moms are worse off with regard to their mental health. These struggles are particularly common among low-income stay-at-home moms, but the patterns hold across the income spectrum—regardless of how much money their families have, moms who stay home full-time with their kids are more likely to be sad, angry, and depressed than paid working moms.

we blame mothers when anything with their kids goes wrong. Recall how Ayanna's mother blamed Ayanna for Jayce's death because Ayanna was the one who took Jayce to get his childhood vaccines. It's exceedingly rare for vaccines to cause serious illness or death. And yet, rampant misinformation leads many families—and particularly families that have other reasons to distrust the US medical system—to look to vaccines when otherwise healthy kids suddenly get sick. Like Ayanna, mothers are the ones who typically make health decisions for their families, and so they also end up catching the blame.[27]

That blame, meanwhile, leads to feelings of guilt for mothers—even if they're pretty sure they didn't do anything wrong. Recall Ayanna's guilt around Jayce's death and Anissa's birth, as well as Audrey's guilt when depression kept her from giving enough attention to her kids. That kind of guilt is common among mothers. And as sociologist Caitlyn Collins finds in her research, it's particularly common in countries like the US where there are giant holes in the social safety net.[28]

The holes in our safety net are big enough for children to fall through, and falling comes with huge risks of harm. Since the 1970s, infant and child death rates have been higher in the US than in other wealthy nations. Over that time span, the risk of death was 76 percent higher for American infants than for the average infant in an OECD country, and 57 percent higher for American kids ages one to nineteen. Most of these deaths are also preventable—in 2020, guns surpassed car accidents as the leading cause of child death in the US, followed by overdose, cancer, and other diseases, including Covid-19. We're the only wealthy country in the world where guns are the leading cause of child death. That preventability makes child deaths especially egregious, because we can't say there's nothing we could have done. And yet, rather than treat child well-being as a collective responsibility, the US gifts that responsibility to women and wraps it in guilt to keep them from regifting it to someone else.[29]

The engineers of our DIY society need women to fill in and be the protectors because they've left us all teetering on the edge of precarity, and they want to maintain the illusion that we can get by without a sturdy net to catch us if we fall.

Of course, not every girl or woman wants to do that work or is able to, at least not right away. Like Brooke, some girls have no plans to be mothers. Others, like Sylvia and Ayanna, want to wait until they're older—until they've finished college and found a steady partner and a steady job. And still others, like Audrey, Ayanna, and Destiny are already doing the work of mothering and can't take on more right now.

Resistance to motherhood—or mothering responsibilities—poses a problem for the engineers because trapping girls and women in motherhood is the quickest way to conscript them into doing the work of the social safety net. The engineers could let the reluctant among us off with a free pass. But that might give other women too many ideas.

So the engineers construct girls and women as mothers-in-waiting. They create the perception that every girl should grow up to be a woman, that every woman should be (or at least should want to be) a mother, and that every mother or would-be mother should happily sacrifice herself to care effectively and responsibly for any child who happens to come her way. The engineers can then sit back and wait for girls and women to either be lured into the trap by the power of norms or be pushed in by the power of laws.*[30]

---

* Of course, traps like these don't catch everyone. As we've seen with Brooke, Audrey, Sylvia, Destiny, and Ayanna, some women are more vulnerable than others by virtue of the traumas they've experienced or their positions in hierarchies of privilege and power.

Chapter 2

LEAVING SOME WOMEN WITH NO CHOICE

Once they're caught in the motherhood trap, it doesn't take much to get women to stand in for the social safety net. All it takes is denying them access to paid family leave and affordable, reliable childcare. Without that support, mothers and mothers-in-waiting can be easily rejected from male-dominated jobs or relegated to lower-paying positions, since employers can raise questions about whether they'll be able to commit to the work.* And once women are locked out of high-paying jobs, they then have little choice but to fill in the gaps where systems like childcare, healthcare, education, transportation, and eldercare have faltered or failed. Little choice, that is, because the best-paid jobs they can get are underpaid jobs, often in the care-giving sector, and because it seems "logical" for women to take on more of the unpaid caregiving than men.[1]

As I'll show in this chapter, this one-two punch is particularly debilitating for women in lower- and middle-income families—women who often don't have the resources to avoid or delay falling into the motherhood trap or to buy their way out by outsourcing care.[2]

NOWHERE TO TURN

Erin is a typical white, married, stay-at-home mother. She's typical in the sense that, like the majority of stay-at-home mothers in the US, her family is

---

* In the US, employers often assume all women are eventually going to become mothers and that motherhood—unlike fatherhood—is an all-consuming role. Employers then use these presumptions to justify passing on qualified women candidates, especially for jobs in male-dominated fields, and paying the women they do hire less than similarly qualified men.

just barely scraping by—very different from the kind of Real Housewife we might see enjoying a boozy Tuesday brunch on TV. In the PITT study data I collected in 2022, only 7 percent of stay-at-home moms had household incomes of $100,000 or more. Instead, almost 75 percent had household incomes under $50,000, and half had household incomes under $25,000 a year. As a result, roughly half of the stay-at-home moms were receiving food stamps and Medicaid, and more than two-thirds reported at least some difficulty paying all their bills.

With these numbers, it's easy to think, "These women should just get a job!" And the thing is, most of them wish they could, and many of them are already cobbling together side gigs to bring in whatever little money they can. As we'll see with Erin, if mothers in the US aren't part of the formal economy, it's usually because we've left them with no other choice.[3]

Erin met Mark in college, though like about a third of all college students, neither of them finished their degree.* Mark, who is also white, thought he'd be better off trying to work his way up at the mine in the small town in Indiana where he grew up, and he asked Erin to marry him and follow him there. Erin agreed and got a job in the same small town, working at a grocery store. Together, they were earning about $30,000 a year. That was barely enough to cover the basics: $1,500 a month for rent and utilities for a small apartment, $500 a month for the premiums on a bare bones health plan with a $5,000-a-year deductible, a few hundred a month for food, and a couple hundred more a month for car payments and auto insurance, since living in a small town meant they couldn't rely on public transportation to get to the grocery store or even to work on time. Erin, who managed the family budget, could usually make it work each month. But any unexpected expenses got put on the credit card and were usually left to accumulate debt.[4]

Erin's monthly calculus got even more complicated when she gave birth in 2016. Neither Erin nor Mark was offered paid family leave through their employers, and they couldn't afford for both of them to take more than a week off unpaid. Going back to work meant they needed someone to care for

---

* Roughly one-third of college students leave their program without a degree. Among first-time undergraduate students, nearly a quarter leave within their first year. These rates are higher among students at two-year colleges than among those at four-year schools.

their son, Carson, but they were earning too much to qualify for Indiana's public childcare program and too little to pay full cost for childcare.* Relying on family for help also wasn't an option because Erin's family lived hours away in another state, and Mark's mom and dad and stepmom were still working full-time and had their own bills to pay.[5]

At first, Erin thought she could make it work by switching to a part-time night shift at the store. Erin stayed home all day with Carson, while Mark worked at the mine. Then, after Mark came home in the evening, Erin would head to her job. That arrangement made sense financially, but the stress of it wore on Erin, just as it did for my mom when she and my dad tried something similar when I was born. Erin only got to sleep when Carson was napping during the day and between breastfeeding sessions after she got home late at night. By the time Carson was a few months old, she was exhausted and on edge all the time. "It was terrible," Erin recalled. "It was really hard. I was ALWAYS tired."[6]

Erin thought about switching to a day shift, but she couldn't get the numbers to work. Most of the high-quality, licensed childcare centers in her community had year-long waitlists, and even if a spot somehow opened up, it would take her whole paycheck to cover the cost of care. Meanwhile, the other jobs Erin could get as a mom without a college degree living in small-town Indiana—jobs in childcare, retail, food service, cleaning, or as a home health aide—probably wouldn't pay any better and might even end up being worse. In the end, Erin quit. "I was like, I don't wanna pay somebody to raise my child so I can go work at a job that I'm so-so about! So, we're gonna have to make this work," Erin recalled. "And my husband was full on board."[7]

Switching to one income, paradoxically, made things easier for Erin's family financially because it made them eligible for more government support. As a family of three with a $15,000 annual household income, they could qualify for EITC, food stamps, WIC, and Medicaid, though Erin was reluctant to apply. Like Akari, she had internalized the stigma around government dependency. "I know it's for people like us, but at the same time

---

* To be eligible for vouchers for subsidized childcare, families in Indiana must have incomes within 127 percent of the federal poverty line for their family/household size, which in 2016 for a family of three was $20,160 per year.

I was like, I don't quite feel like we're to that point yet where we need Medicaid. I don't wanna use it, I don't wanna abuse the system or anything."[8]

Erin never signed up for food stamps, but she eventually gave in and enrolled in WIC and Medicaid because that was the only way she could afford a surgical procedure that Carson needed, which would have cost $1,000 out of pocket otherwise. Erin recalled balking at the costs of the procedure, saying, "I'm like, I don't even have *ten* dollars!" Even after deciding to enroll, however, Erin found herself facing the work of trying to cut through all the red tape. "So many forms," Erin recalled, "and you have to get so much information that you normally don't have on hand, like copies of everyone's birth certificates. And they give you ten days to get it all in, and I've got a kid! I can't just run around and get this all done." It took Erin multiple tries over months to get the final approval done.[9]

Medicaid, EITC, and WIC didn't solve all of Erin's money problems, forcing her to find creative ways to make their budget work. Diapers, for example, were a challenge for Erin, as they are for many low-income moms.* "They're so expensive," Erin recalled. "Like twenty-five bucks for a decent pack of diapers that'll last me a week. I'm going to die!" In the end, Mark's stepmother, Debby, came through. She was able to purchase diapers more than 50 percent off with her employee discount at the hospital where she worked. There were purchase limits on the discounts, though, so Erin would try to make every diaper last as long as possible, even when it led to rashes for Carson, so she wouldn't have to buy more at full price.[10]

In 2019, Mark got promoted to a new $35,000-a-year job with health insurance. Erin hoped that would be the end of their money stress, but it didn't work out that way. Mark's health plan, for example, which included medical, vision, and dental coverage, cost the family $400 a month in premiums and came with a deductible of $7,000 a year. With a sigh, Erin noted,

---

* Sociologist Jennifer Randles finds that because WIC and food stamps do not cover diapers or wipes, many low-income mothers rely on food pantries for these supplies and often try to stretch them beyond recommended use. Although some critics argue that these women should be using cloth rather than disposable diapers, research suggests that the costs (including laundering) are similar, particularly if families do not have the time and/or resources (i.e., a washing machine and dryer) to launder cloth diapers themselves. Research also shows that disposable diapers reduce the risk of diaper rash and other diaper-related illnesses, which can be a concern for families who are trying to cut down on other healthcare-related costs.

"It's so expensive. So much money for a decent plan—not a great plan, a *decent* plan! Unless it's like a crazy emergency, I'm not gonna cross seven thousand dollars! So, what's the point in paying four hundred dollars a month? I could just set that money aside for medical emergencies!" Even when the plan did cover the cost of care, Erin had to wait months to get reimbursed, fronting money she didn't have. Erin and Mark decided to keep the plan anyway but use healthcare as sparingly as possible—that way they wouldn't add to the $10,000 in medical debt they had already accrued. Erin reflected, "I've tried so many different things to make it all work, to get to the point where we weren't going broke for insurance."

In his new job, Mark also felt pressured to prove he deserved the promotion, which meant that he spent even less time at home. When their second baby, Julian, was born in 2019, Mark took less than a week off before going back to the office, though he had a few weeks of paid time off banked that he could have used. That left Erin alone for twelve hours a day with an infant and a super-active toddler, even while she was still recovering from childbirth. The isolation and exhaustion of that period stretched Erin to where she thought she might break. "It's difficult," she said, sighing, "and you don't necessarily notice it right away. It kinda builds up slowly over time. And then you get to the point where, like, two weeks have gone by, and you haven't really talked to another adult, and you're emotional and you feel kinda crazy. And it's like, I gotta get out! I need a break!"

In those moments, Erin often thought about the freedom that a job might offer, but the math still didn't add up. On top of the childcare problem, Erin worried that no one would hire her, or that she'd get a job and end up losing it, given that her responsibilities as the default parent would come ahead of her paid work.* Erin told me, "My [whole] salary would go towards daycare anyway and you know, when the kids are sick or something, then it wouldn't really be worth it for me to go to work. So, after the initial honeymoon period of 'Oh, I wish I could have a job,' I'm kind of like, 'Yeah, no, I'm good.'"[11]

---

* Research shows that mothers are significantly more likely than fathers to lose their jobs involuntarily.

The US social safety net isn't big enough or strong enough to guarantee safety for any of us, let alone safety for all. Sure, there are government programs that aim to prevent families from going hungry or getting stuck without a roof over their heads. But, as we saw with Akari, those programs aren't designed to lift families out of poverty. They just make poverty a little easier to bear. Moreover, and as we saw with Erin, those programs only protect the poorest among us. The DIY message to the rest of us is figure it out on your own.

That figuring out part falls disproportionately to women, who often have little choice but to fill the gaps in the social safety net. As we'll see in our next chapter, some women can afford to pay other women to fill those gaps for them. But most women—women in low-income and middle-income families like Erin's—have to MacGyver a net with whatever bits of tape and string they can find.[12]

That work falls to women like Erin, in part, because once we catch them in the motherhood trap, we leave them with nowhere to turn. In the absence of guaranteed paid family leave and universal childcare, mothers quickly become the default parents. The ones who are expected to drop everything to meet kids' needs. Recall how Erin was the one who changed her work schedule and sacrificed sleep so she and Mark could go without childcare when Carson was born. Recall also how Erin was hesitant to try to go back to the workforce, despite being unhappy as a stay-at-home mom, because she knew she'd be the one who'd have to take a day off work any time the kids got sick and had to stay home.[13]

Generations ago, mothers like Erin might have turned to their communities for support, but we've stripped their communities to the bone. In 2020, I asked ITD participants where they could turn for help in the next month.* Among parents in households with incomes under $50,000 a year, only 26 percent said they had someone they could rely on to loan them $200,

---

* Participants were asked, "During the next month, if you needed help, could you count on someone to provide any of the following forms of support? Please mark all that apply." Options included: "Loan you $200"; "Co-sign a bank loan for $5,000"; "Provide regular support with remote learning, hybrid learning, or homeschooling"; and "Help with emergency babysitting or childcare."

and only 4 percent had someone who could cosign a loan of $5,000 or more. Only 17 percent had someone they could ask for regular assistance with childcare, and only 20 percent said they had someone they could count on for occasional emergency childcare. Like these parents, Erin was mostly on her own. She got help with discount diapers, but that was basically it for financial and logistical support.

Married mothers could ask their spouses for more help in holding it all together. But, as we saw with Erin and Mark, the fastest way to make a tight budget work is often with dad at the office and mom at home. Why? Because employers reward fathers with daddy bonuses while subjecting moms to motherhood penalties limiting their wages and opportunities to advance. Before they had kids, Erin and Mark were making similar amounts of money. But like most male-dominated jobs, Mark's job at the mine had more avenues for promotion than Erin's job at the grocery store. And once Erin took time off to raise her kids, she wasn't sure they would let her back in the door, let alone offer her the kind of raise that Mark was able to earn.[14]

Of course, to earn their daddy bonuses, men like Mark must prove their worth. They prove it, in turn, by being the ideal worker—committing themselves to their employers as if they have no family or other obligations at home. Consider the ITD data. Among employed parents I surveyed, dads were more than twice as likely as moms to say they would face consequences in their jobs for adjusting their work schedules to meet their families' needs (56 percent vs. 26 percent). And for dads, that risk got bigger the more they earned, while the same wasn't true for moms.* Being the ideal worker thereby gives dads like Mark a shot at climbing the corporate ladder or at least climbing off the bottom rung. And yet, the more time that married dads like Mark devote to their paid work, the more unpaid work they leave to their wives, and the more likely that those women are to decide it isn't worth it to have a paid job of their own.[15]

This brings us back to where we started Erin's story, with the realities of stay-at-home moms. Like Erin, most of the stay-at-home mothers my team

---

* ITD participants were asked, "Please state whether you agree or disagree with the following statements. I would face consequences in my job for adjusting my work schedule to meet my family's needs." Options ranged from (1) strongly disagree to (7) strongly agree. The percentages reported here reflect those participants who said either "somewhat agree," "agree," or "strongly agree."

and I interviewed weren't home because that's where they would be happiest. They were home because they got stuck in childcare's missing middle. They ran the numbers and figured out that their families would be better off financially and logistically if they left the workforce and stayed at home.[16]

Of course, those numbers don't come out the same for everyone. Plenty of mothers in middle- and low-income families don't have partners or don't have partners whose incomes are high enough to support the family on their own. In those cases, and as we saw with Akari, Brooke, Sylvia, and Destiny, women are typically forced to be the social safety net for their families while also working low-wage jobs.[17]

And that's exactly where the engineers of our DIY society want women, or at least most of them: forced to choose between staying home with their children or filling low-wage jobs. Whichever choice they make in that scenario, women are maintaining the myth of our DIY society by doing the necessary work that isn't profitable so that more of the profitable work can be done by others more privileged than them.*

Yet staying home doesn't protect women like Erin from precarity because of how difficult the great risk shift has made it for families to get by on just one job. In the absence of universal, affordable healthcare, for example, families like Erin's are "going broke for insurance." And in the absence of affordable housing, those same families are stuck unable to buy a house and paying exorbitant rates for rent.[18]

Because of this precarity, there's a good chance that Erin will go back to the workforce eventually—likely when her youngest is old enough for public school. In the US, the public education system is the closest we have to a high-quality universal, affordable childcare system. As a result, mothers who leave the workforce when their children are little often return when their

---

* Now, when I say that the work forced on women isn't profitable, I don't mean it isn't valuable. As we'll talk more about in our next chapter, I mean that some jobs can't be easily automated or outsourced to other countries with even weaker worker protections, and they're so labor-intensive that they leave little profit to be made. Childcare, eldercare, healthcare, and education are prime examples. So are personal care services like hairstyling and housecleaning, as well as food production, grocery sales, fast food, and lots of other jobs in retail and customer service, too. Under these conditions, it's difficult for employers to turn a profit; just to keep the doors open, they may have to set costs sky-high.

children start elementary school. That's the path my own mom eventually took—a path that started very similar to Erin's.[19]

My mom originally wanted to be a child psychologist, but she ended up having me before she could finish her college degree. We didn't have family nearby or money for childcare, so my mom stayed home with me during the day; when my dad got home from work, she went to work the night shift in a temp-work clerical job. The stress of that split shift eventually got to be too much for my parents, just as it did for Erin and Mark. So, my mom switched to a part-time day-shift clerical job at an insurance agency and found a home childcare provider who could watch me while she worked. Her job, however, came with so little in wages that it barely covered the cost of childcare, and it also came with so much sexual harassment—this was the eighties, after all—that she hated going to the office every day. And so, when my younger sister was born, my mom quit her job, started selling Mary Kay makeup, and got licensed as a home childcare provider, watching other people's kids at our house to help pay the bills while she was at home.*[20]

It took until I was in middle school for my mom to go back to college, taking night classes to get an elementary education degree. And it wasn't until I was in high school and my youngest brother started elementary school that she got a permanent teaching job. A career in teaching felt like both a natural and a logical choice for my mother. Her life as a mom already re-volved around school, and teaching meant she could—at least in theory—be home after school and during summers and other school breaks—times that my dad couldn't take off, and times that the US education and childcare systems make it difficult for families to cover.[21]

Working full-time, however, quickly created its own problems. My mom, like many employed women, was essentially working a double or triple shift—one shift in the classroom, a second shift of housework and parenting, and a third shift caring for elderly family and neighbors.† As a teacher, she found

---

* One recent survey found that parents of kids under eighteen are twice as likely as other US adults to have side gigs. Research has also shown that mothers of young children use entrepreneurial endeavors to try to manage financial precarity, and these efforts often make them ready targets for multi-level marketing schemes.

† Being home gave my mom more flexibility to help when my grandmother was diagnosed with brain cancer and to assist with errands and day-to-day companionship for another elderly neighbor and the disabled adult nephew who had come to live with her after his own mother had died.

there was rarely time during the school day for lesson plans and grading, and no time during the school year for learning new curriculum or working toward the master's degrees and other certifications she'd need to move up in terms of salary. As a mom and caregiver, however, she found that it was difficult to manage all that unanticipated extra work while also being present at home. As the oldest, I tried to help as a sort of substitute parent— getting my siblings off the school bus in the afternoon, helping them with homework, feeding them snacks, making dinner, and, once I got my driver's license, doing various drop-offs and pick-ups before going to my own part-time job.[22]

And that's how it all comes full circle. Given how little support we've offered them, women in lower- and middle-income families often have to take whatever they can get. What they can get, in turn, is often piecemeal and relies on the labor and availability of other women and girls. For girls, and as we saw with Sylvia, those early caregiving responsibilities give them the kind of experience that makes it seem as though anyone assigned female at birth is "naturally" suited for care and that leads us to expect women to hold it together, even as they're collapsing inside.

NOWHERE TO HIDE

The problem, of course, is that when women prove they can hold it together, we thank them by giving them more to hold. As we'll see in our next chapter, women in high-income families may have the resources to dodge that handoff and the risk that comes with it. But once women in lower- and middle-income families become the default parent, they often become the default caregiver for the rest of their family and their community because we've left them nowhere to hide.

That includes women like Patricia—a Black single mom living below the poverty line. Stereotypes often vilify poor Black single mothers as greedy or lazy for their dependence on government programs. In the 1980s, Ronald Reagan built his campaign for president on wildly exaggerated stories about a type of woman he called the "welfare queen." The reality is that although Black mothers are more likely than white mothers to be living in or near poverty, it's not because they're unwilling to work. In fact, Black mothers' workforce participation rates are similar to those of white mothers, and when Black mothers are in the workforce, they work more hours than white mothers, despite being paid, on average, $2.50 an hour less.[23]

Patricia, for example, makes less than $10 an hour as a customer service representative, and before the Covid-19 pandemic, she used to work full-time. At that point, in early 2020, Patricia was still married to her children's father, Rodney, who is also Black, and they were living together with their three kids. Their two oldest were in elementary school, and their youngest was just shy of two years old. Rodney was working full-time as a construction laborer, and together they were making $28,000 a year.

That income was low enough that Patricia and Rodey qualified for support through EITC, food stamps, WIC, childcare subsidies, and Medicaid, but it still didn't make life easy day to day. When asked about her family's financial situation, Patricia laughed and said, "If money could grow on trees!" Continuing more somberly, Patricia added, poetically, "I'm managing. We may not have the things we want, but we have the things we need." As an example, Patricia pointed to the subsidized childcare she got for her youngest, noting that she wouldn't otherwise be able to afford to keep her job, but she worries that the center is understaffed. In a similar way, Patricia described being both grateful for and frustrated with WIC and food stamp restrictions. Patricia had to rely on tuna fish or other canned meats for protein, and the small amount of fresh fruit and vegetables she was allotted each month could easily be gone in a few days. With a sigh, she noted, "Milk goes fast, bread goes fast. All that stuff goes fast when you have more people in the house." As a result, Patricia often found herself leaning on local food pantries and other charity organizations, especially at the end of the month.

Patricia, however, wasn't just managing the family budget—she was also the default parent at home. Patricia had taken her customer service job—a job she found repetitive and demoralizing—specifically because it was the best work-from-home job she could find. At the time, remote work jobs were rare in the US, and concentrated in high-income professional occupations—not the kinds of jobs open to someone like Patricia, who started but never finished a college degree. Working remotely made it possible to be there for her children while also working for pay full-time. If one of the kids got sick or if the schools had a snow day, Patricia didn't have to figure out backup care or skip work, which, because she didn't have access to paid leave, would also mean skipping income and possibly losing her job. Patricia could also be home before school and after school with her older children, so she wouldn't have to pay for extra care.[24]

Patricia's day-to-day grind was exhausting, but she was managing to hold it together. And so, when the Covid-19 pandemic hit, her family assumed she could manage what they thought would be just a little more. Like many of the couples I interviewed, Patricia and Rodney never even talked about who would care for the kids when the virus and the lockdowns hit. That work just fell to Patricia, and Rodney kept leaving the house every day for work.

Pandemic parenting, of course, ended up being markedly different from dealing with a handful of snow days, and different even from dealing with the annual onslaught of winter sniffles and stomach bugs. Every day was chaotic. The kids were constantly interrupting Patricia during her work time, leaving her frustrated and completely overwhelmed. "You start getting a headache," Patricia said with a heavy sigh, "and they want you to sit and listen to them talk and everything. And it's like, 'Just go! Please! Everybody just leave me alone!'"

Patricia didn't like being so short with her kids. She wanted to enjoy the time she got to spend with them, and she felt guilty about experiencing it as a chore. "I have to work on that more," she chided herself during those early lockdowns. "When it's time to clock out, I need to not clock out mentally as a mother, too."

She also felt like she was letting her kids down. When her son came to her and told her his teacher had yelled at him, Patricia assumed that her son had misbehaved. Eventually, however, Patricia figured out that the teacher yelled at her son merely for asking for help with a math problem, and that "the teacher's not helping him the way she should." Patricia felt as though she had failed her son, and talking to her own dad about the situation made her feel even worse because his advice left Patricia feeling guilty for not helping her son learn to communicate more effectively at school. "My dad," she recalled, "was like, 'Start talking to him more! That'll build his confidence up!'"

With that sense of failure weighing heavily on her conscience, Patricia decided in the fall of 2020 to switch to working four days a week instead five. She figured that arrangement would give her more energy to focus on the kids' needs.

Patricia also kept that same schedule once the kids were back in in-person school and childcare in January 2021 because, by that point, Patricia was unexpectedly pregnant with twins. Between the early pregnancy exhaustion and the sleep debt she'd accrued during the pandemic, Patricia hoped that the extra day would give her time to rest and catch up on chores like laundry, groceries, and cleaning.

But her extended family saw an opening. Patricia is one of the only people in her family with a reliable vehicle. She and most of her relatives also live in Indianapolis, which in 2019 was ranked as the worst major city for public transportation in the US. While Patricia's family could take public buses to get to the grocery store or doctor visits, trips that would take fifteen minutes by car would easily take over an hour on the bus. The pandemic also made relying on public transit not only logistically difficult but medically risky. So Patricia rarely griped when her family asked for help with rides, even when, as Patricia explained, "your whole day that you had to yourself is dedicated to running errands for someone else."[25]

In addition to being her family's chauffeur, Patricia was also their emotional rock. Her mom and older sister would call her whenever they got lonely and pressure her to come around on her days off. "They comment, too," she explained, "about how they miss you so much and all that other stuff. So I can tell they rely on me for a level of support."

Patricia wanted to carve out more time for herself, but she found it difficult to say no to extended family and to close family-like friends. "I'm learning boundaries," she told me in early 2021, adding, "I'm trying to work on saying, 'Hey, listen, this is my day. I need my day to myself.'" When push came to shove, however, Patricia rarely followed through in saying no, because of the support she'd previously gotten from the people around her and the support she might need again someday.

That someday came when Patricia and Rodney divorced just before the twins were born late that summer. Patricia and Rodney had previously separated and gotten back together a few times. Their fights usually centered on the fact that Rodney wasn't helping enough with the chores or the kids, even when he was between jobs. The pandemic, including Rodney's refusal to wear a mask or take other precautions to keep the family safe, was Patricia's final straw.

After Rodney left, however, Patricia was hit by the heaviness of holding it together on her own. "It's pretty depressing," Patricia said mournfully, "to have two brand-new babies and you're doing this by yourself because you and your partner couldn't get along." She continued, "It's just—you created all these kids with this one person, and they're not there to join in. It's not like they're in jail. And it's not actually like they're trying to be part of the kids' lives anyway—they're not getting their own life together enough to be able to be a balance for the kids. But it's just all on you. It's all on you."

The divorce also affected the family financially. Patricia and the kids had to move into a smaller place with only two bedrooms. And Patricia also had to help Rodney out with money because he wasn't keeping up with the payments on the car that he needed to keep driving the twenty minutes to visit the kids. "I was just paying that for him," Patricia explained with resignation, adding that the payments "made it where my finances kind of got backed up a little bit." As a result, Patricia had to spend a few months doing double duty—working from home while caring for twin infants—because she could only afford to take a few weeks of maternity leave, because she had to wait for a spot to open up at the childcare center that would accept her vouchers, and because she couldn't afford to pay for alternate care. "I was depressed," Patricia said matter-of-factly. "I was depressed on how I was going to keep my job and still trying to manage the needs of my twins. It was a struggle trying to answer calls and type and try to burp a baby and feed a baby and change a baby. And oh, two babies have had a blowout at the same time—that just about had my hair out."

Rodney wasn't around to help much. So Patricia found herself relying on close friends and family and grateful that she hadn't pushed them away before. Her friend drove her around while she was still recovering from her C-section. Her mom or her dad would occasionally come over to watch the older kids so she could take the twins to their doctor visits. And they all listened when Patricia just needed a supportive ear.

That support was valuable to Patricia, but it wasn't enough to keep her darker feelings fully at bay. When my team and I last talked to Patricia in late 2021, she talked about how she has to remind herself to stay positive. And she talked about how she tries to use what little downtime she can find to keep her house picked up because "when the clutter comes, so does the depression."

—

One of my graduate school advisors once warned me that the reward for service is more service—that I shouldn't be too quick to volunteer, or say yes to requests, or go above and beyond in those efforts, because I'd get pegged as someone who gets stuff done and thereby be given even more work to do. She was talking about service in academia—things like committee work and article reviews and mentoring—but the same idea applies with caregiving, too.

Once women show that they can successfully juggle all the responsibilities that come with being the default parent, it's easy for the people around them to assume that they would be capable of keeping a few more balls in the air. Cover a colleague's shift at work? She'll do it. Bring cupcakes for the bake sale? She's on it. Give grandma a ride to the doctor? She's got that, too.

Women, especially mothers, are the go-to because they've proven, time and again, that they can get shit done, even with limited resources and limited time. And yet, just because women can work minor miracles doesn't mean that work comes without a cost. As we saw with Patricia, being the backstop is exhausting, not to mention expensive and sometimes infuriating, too.

In these moments, the advice for women is often "Just say no!" That's what my advisor was trying to tell me to do. But that advice ignores the fact that many women—especially women in lower- and middle-income families—often have nowhere to hide.

Put differently, women like Patricia can't just say no when other people ask them for help, because they know they'll need help themselves someday, and because they know that the people asking them have nowhere else to turn. Recall, for example, how Patricia was reluctant to turn down her mother's ride requests, in part because she never knew when she might need to call on her mom for emergency babysitting and because she didn't have the resources to hire someone instead.* This lack of options is particularly common for women like Patricia because the great risk shift has left their families and communities teetering close to collapse.† In 2022, there were almost 38 million Americans living in poverty and more than 63 million living within 150 percent of the poverty line. That's nearly 20 percent of everyone in the US. Meanwhile, nearly a quarter of Americans have no emergency savings, and another third have savings, but not enough to last for three months. Few communities are untouched by this kind of precarity, but Black, Latino, and Indigenous communities are affected more than most, with rates of poverty double or nearly double those for white and Asian communities in the US.[26]

That kind of precarity destabilizes families and communities, leaving people more desperate while making it more difficult to rely on each other for support. Take Patricia in her relationship with Rodney. As a Black man without a high school diploma, Rodney has limited prospects for stable employment, let alone the kind of job that would give him the flexibility to work from home and care for the kids. That leaves Patricia to be both the primary breadwinner and the primary caregiver, a role in which Patricia is far from alone. In the US today, 69 percent of mothers in the lowest-income families and 68 percent of Black mothers are the primary breadwinner for their household. That's compared to only 30 percent in the highest-income households and 37 percent among white moms. As sociologist Dawn Dow explains in her book, *Mothering While Black*, those differences are a product of our country's history of discrimination and a function of the precarity that

---

* Patricia was also hesitant to send her mother on long bus rides where she might contract Covid-19.

† This precarity can be seen in the fact that Black babies are 50 percent more likely than white babies to be born prematurely, and that even high-income Black people have a higher risk of heart disease than their white counterparts, regardless of their weight and how much they smoke or exercise. These effects can also be seen in the fact that schools with more Black students have fewer resources to spend on learning—to the tune of $2,200 less per year per student enrolled. They can be seen in the fact that white students are 50 percent more likely than Black students to finish a college degree after they start one, and in the fact that Black students take on more debt to pay for their degrees than white students do, while having a harder time paying off their student loans. These inequalities are the product of strategic segregation, targeting, and underinvestment in Black communities. Such efforts have not only subjected Black communities disproportionately to threats like environmental toxins, police violence, and traumatic microaggressions, but also prevented them from accumulating the wealth they would need to escape those threats.

history perpetuates. Black women, for example, often can't rely on their partners to be the primary breadwinners, because Black men are pushed out of school and locked out of jobs that would pay enough to support their families, and because even if they stay in school, Black men are often overlooked by employers and denied the same kind of "daddy bonus" that white men get income-wise when they have kids.[27]

As we saw with Patricia and Rodney, and with Ayanna and Marquis, the stress of those arrangements can destabilize families and relationships. Financial precarity is the primary reason why low-income couples and especially low-income Black couples are particularly likely to break up and why they're less likely than other couples to ever get married at all. Even breaking up, however, didn't keep Rodney from depending on Patricia in a way that she could never depend on him. And yet, Patricia couldn't simply turn him away when he asked for help with things like car payments, because she knew he had nowhere else to turn for support, and because she was grateful that Rodney wasn't in jail and at least had the opportunity to see their kids and help her out from time to time.[28]

Precarity forces families and communities to look for the mothers—the ones who have shown they can hold it together—and ask them to hold even more. When it's clear that employers and policymakers aren't willing to invest in your community, the only option for survival is to mine the resources and talents of your own. And yet, the same precarity that forces communities to rely on women like Patricia and Erin also prevents those women from saying no. Even when they're stretched to the breaking point, saying no feels too risky because precarity means they never know when the tables will turn.[29]

Chapter 3

LEAVING OTHERS
MORALLY TRAPPED

The more gaps in our social safety net that are filled by women like Akari, Brooke, Sylvia, and Patricia, the easier it is for more privileged women to climb out of the motherhood trap. In our DIY society, women in higher-income families have the resources to outsource the work of cleaning their homes, feeding their families, and caring for their children and their aging parents, particularly if the exploitation of women in more vulnerable positions makes those services available at lower costs. And the more labor that women outsource, the easier it is for them to compete with men in the workforce and secure the kinds of high salaries that give them leverage in demanding more support from their partners and their families at home. Put differently, more money buys women more choices, but those choices are morally fraught.[1]

That's because, in our DIY society, the only way to avoid the risk of precarity is to dump that risk downstream. Which means that we're all complicit in the exploitation of women, and none of us can fully extract ourselves from that system, since, despite what the engineers and profiteers might tell us, none of us are fully capable of caring for ourselves. As a result, and as I'll show in this chapter, even women in high-income families are drowning—drowning in the guilt of dumping the risk they've been handed, and drowning in the flood of risk they still face, especially if they try to hold it all themselves.[2]

DUMPING THE RISK

Before they had kids, Holly, who is white, was finishing up a PhD and working part-time from home as a data analyst; her wife, Kathleen, who is also white, was working full-time in law enforcement while taking classes toward a master's degree. Financially, things were comfortable for Kathleen and Holly. Together, they were earning about $75,000 a year—more than the $53,000-a-year living wage for a couple without kids in their small city. Like many same-sex couples, Holly and Kathleen also had a fairly egalitarian division of paid work and housework, and they planned to split parenting responsibilities equally when they had kids.

The problem, however, was childcare. Holly and Kathleen didn't have family nearby who could help them care for an infant. If family wasn't an option, they wanted a state-licensed center with highly trained and experienced staff. What they found, however, were high prices and years-long waitlists. Even though they started their childcare search not long after Holly got pregnant, their best option was a part-time spot that wouldn't be available until Willa was almost nine months old.

To make it work in the meantime, Holly and Kathleen decided that Holly would step into the default parent and caregiver role. Holly was earning less money and could work remotely while caring for Willa. And as Holly explained with a wry laugh, "My wife and I complement each other well. I hate how heterosexist this is, but it's very mom-dad." Like many two-mom couples, they decided that it was "logical" and "natural" for Holly, the birthing parent, to take on more of the load.[3]

At the beginning, Holly was able to work at her normal pace while Willa slept. But as Willa grew and spent less of the day napping, that arrangement got increasingly difficult for Holly to manage. When Willa was six months old, Holly decided to cut back to less than fifteen hours a week of paid work and to only work during the times when Kathleen was able to be home to help.

Holly was hopeful that things would get better once Willa started childcare in the fall of 2019, but when Covid hit, the center closed, and they ended up right back where they were before, with Holly doing most of the childcare while also trying to fit in a few hours of paid work around diaper changes, mealtimes, story times, and endless rounds of peek-a-boo. When asked in April 2020 what the hardest part of the pandemic had been for her so far, Holly said without hesitation that it was childcare.

In the fall of 2020, Holly got word that the childcare center would be reopening and that there would be a full-time spot available for Willa. It seemed like Holly's chance to finally go back to full-time paid work. But then, when Holly asked her boss about transitioning to a full-time position, he dragged his feet in submitting the paperwork. Like many managers in high-tech industries, he seemed skeptical that a mother could commit to full-time work, and Holly had to appeal to his boss to get the paperwork through.[4]

Just before Holly was scheduled to go back to a full-time position, child-care left her in the lurch again. Because of staffing shortages, the center could only offer care 9 a.m. to 4 p.m.* "I usually stop working around, like, three thirty now," Holly explained in February 2021, adding, "It's a little bit in flux because I'm working full-time now and so I feel guilty and obligated to work later." At 3:30 p.m., Holly would leave to pick up Willa from child-care, then let Willa "watch TV or play with the iPad or something" for a bit while Holly tried to do a little more work. After that, Holly and Willa would work together on chores until Kathleen got home around 5:30 p.m.

Holly was desperate for reliable full-time childcare and frustrated that she was still paying more than $1,200 a month for part-time hours and what she perceived as worse quality of care. During the pandemic, many of the more experienced staff left the center and, according to Holly, were replaced with staff who had little training or experience in childcare. Holly was un-moored by scant communication from teachers to parents, and she worried children were being rushed to potty train to make life easier day-to-day for the staff.

When Holly approached the center director with her concerns, however, she learned that the challenges they were facing with retaining and recruit-ing experienced teachers were a function of the center's financial constraints. To keep costs low enough for families like Holly's to afford, and as we saw with Brooke in chapter 1, the center could only hire staff who were willing to

---

* Even if the childcare providers were working an eight-hour shift, they couldn't provide eight hours of care, because they would need to use part of their shift to set up in the morning and part of their shift to clean up after the children left in the afternoon. And even eight hours of care wouldn't have been enough to allow for full-time work for parents, given the additional time that parents would have to spend commuting to their workplaces after dropping their children off and then after work before picking their children up in the afternoon.

work for low wages and without benefits like health insurance or paid leave. Those conditions were taking a toll on workers long before the pandemic. Willa's lead teacher, for example, had surgery two years before the pandemic and in 2021 was still paying off the medical debt. To pay down those debts and keep food on the table, she also took a second job on top of her full-time work at the childcare center. And when the childcare center reopened after months of being closed during the pandemic, she quit, deciding it wasn't worth it to go back to childcare, since she could earn more in other roles.

Through conversations with the teacher before she left, Holly and Kathleen came to understand that their own sanity and financial security depended on their childcare center overworking and underpaying its workers, and they became much more acutely aware of both the economic and racial dynamics that arrangement entailed. Holly said, "Kathleen and I just felt really guilty about being complicit in this thing where it's like, 'Oh, we have all these women of color watching our kids and we're not really taking good care of them.'"

The guilt of that complicity weighed heavily on Holly, even as she recognized that she needed reliable, affordable childcare if she was going to be working for pay full-time. "We have more money than we ever had," Holly explained after she went back to working full-time, "and there's so many people who are homeless or who aren't getting enough food or they've been out of work for so long. So it's a little bit odd to have more than we need right now. But also, it could change at any moment in a way, when there's not that social safety net. So, you're like, do I just hoard it in a giant pile and sleep on top?"

▬▬▬

For women in a DIY society, outsourcing risk and responsibility is the best way to keep motherhood from becoming a trap. It's the best way to avoid the burden of being the default parent, and the best way to keep those default caregiving responsibilities from ballooning to include not just your kids but everyone else.*[5]

———

* In the US, access to affordable, reliable full-time childcare is the best predictor of women's labor

At the same time, and as Holly outlines so astutely, outsourcing care is ethically complicated, because, in the absence of a robust social safety net, that outsourcing often requires women to exploit the labor of others more vulnerable than them.* Take childcare workers. In the US, more than 90 percent of those workers are women.† They are among the lowest-paid workers in the US economy, and they rarely have access to benefits like health insurance or paid sick leave. And yet, like Brooke, they're often pushed into childcare because they have no better options they can take.[6]

That low pay may seem tough to square with the high cost that US families pay for childcare—on average, $1,200 per kid per month. But it's a function of the fact that high-quality childcare is extremely labor-intensive to provide.‡ That labor intensiveness makes it difficult for childcare centers to keep their doors open, let alone turn a profit every month. Unlike businesses in other industries, childcare providers can't bolster profits by automating production or shifting it to workers in countries with lower costs of living or laxer labor laws. Growing also isn't usually a viable option, because increasing sales doesn't guarantee profits when margins are razor-thin.§ Neither is opting for less experienced workers—as we saw with Holly, that risks driving families away. And childcare providers can't just keep raising prices—eventually they'll run out of families who can pay.[7]

These problems aren't unique to childcare. Eldercare, healthcare, and education all fit this same framework, as do personal care services like hairstyling

---

force participation. And outsourcing other types of care—like cooking and housecleaning—also makes it easier for women to work for pay full-time.

* Exploit, that is, in the sense that the people—usually women—who fill these gaps in the social safety net are paid far less than the value that their labor generates for society and for the economy as a whole.

† Nannies and au pairs are typically women without children or older women whose children are grown. They are also disproportionately Black, Latina, and immigrant women. These types of workers, however, represent a small fraction of the US childcare workforce overall. Instead, most childcare workers work in centers, and most center-based workers (which include care workers who provide care in their own homes) are white women, many of whom have young children themselves.

‡ To keep kids safe, for example, most states require that childcare centers maintain low student-to-provider ratios—usually 4:1 for infants and 8:1 for older kids. That means that the cost of those provider salaries—plus all the costs of running a center—are divided over a small number of families.

§ If there is only a small difference between the revenue generated from each sale and the costs of producing the item sold, then the costs of acquiring more customers (e.g., through advertising) may eliminate any potential profit gains.

and housecleaning, as well as food production, grocery sales, fast food, and lots of other jobs in retail and customer service, too. And so, US employers in these industries often end up cutting compensation to the bare minimum, and even using workarounds—like capping worker hours—to avoid having to offer benefits like health insurance and paid family leave. That approach saves money in the short term. And yet, as we saw with Brooke's childcare center, it leaves businesses chronically understaffed and dealing with high churn.[8]

Other countries have figured out how to solve these problems. First, they lift many low-profit services like childcare, healthcare, and eldercare out of the free-market system, thereby removing the profit pressures their US counterparts continue to face. They also help workers and employers in other industries with low profit margins, both by setting stricter minimum wage laws and by covering the cost of benefits that the US expects employers to pay or push onto workers instead. In Norway, for example, where the childcare system is funded primarily through government support, the average salary for a childcare worker is equivalent to more than $40,000—nearly double the average salary for childcare workers in the US. Unlike most US childcare workers, Norwegian childcare providers also have access to free healthcare, free college education, and free childcare for their own kids, as well as guaranteed retirement pensions, paid sick leave, paid family leave, and a minimum of twenty-one paid vacation days every year.[9]

In the US, low-profit industries solve these problems by exploiting the women who get caught in the mommy trap.* That includes women like Brooke, who have little choice but to take low-paying jobs in childcare; women like Sylvia, who end up as home health aides; women like Patricia, who work in customer service; and women like Akari and Audrey, whose best options, at least in the short-term, are low-wage jobs in retail stores. Rather than fight that kind of exploitation, the US government helps it along by making our safety net's meager protections contingent on participation in paid work. Under those punitive work requirements, mothers who

---

* Similar patterns of exploitation can be seen among incarcerated workers, immigrant workers, Black and Latina workers, and workers without college degrees. In each case, employers exploit the vulnerability of systematically marginalized groups to force them into taking hard-to-fill jobs with limited benefits and low pay.

need social services but can't find paid work can be forced into unpaid work experience placements with government agencies, community organizations, or even private companies.* The stated purpose of these work requirements is to help women become self-sufficient. And yet, research shows that work experience placements rarely turn into or train participants for full-time, long-term jobs. Which suggests that the real purpose of government work requirements may be to help low-wage employers fill hard-to-fill jobs.[10]

The rest of us have an interest in ignoring the exploitation of women, because it makes our lives more affordable and helps us get ahead in our own careers. If, for example, childcare wages suddenly increased, then—in the absence of government subsidies—childcare centers would have to raise their prices. Those higher prices would then push even more families out of the market for childcare. Priced out of paid childcare, most families would shift that responsibility onto mothers, just as Erin's family did. And the same thing would happen if we simply raised wages in other sectors dominated by women. Rising prices for goods and services like home health care, restaurant meals, and even haircuts would price more families out of the market for those services and create more unpaid work for women in families to do.[11]

Exploitation effectively drives a wedge between women. It disincentivizes those higher up on the social ladder from caring about those on the rungs below. Holly and Kathleen, for example, needed full-time childcare to do their jobs effectively. Yet they could only afford it if the women who provided that care were underpaid. And so, even when confronted with the harsh realities their daughter's teachers were facing, there wasn't much they could do but sit with their guilt.[12]

Given that guilt, we might expect more high-income families to stop paying to outsource care. And yet, the precarity of our DIY society makes it easy for the privileged among us to set aside their sense of complicity. Recall how Holly resigned herself to sitting on the pile of resources she and Kathleen had managed to accumulate, saying that even though her family was

---

* Participants perform this labor in exchange for welfare benefits, which in many states works out to $4 or less per hour.

better off than they ever had been, "it could change at any moment . . . when there's not that social safety net."*[13]

Faced with our own insecurity, it's easy to stifle the guilt we might feel when we drop off a sniffly kid at preschool without first testing them for Covid, even if their teachers don't get paid sick days. It's easy to ignore the twinge we might feel using grocery pickup to save time, even if the workers who picked our groceries are paid so little they have to rely on food stamps or food pantries so their kids can be fed. And it's easy to rationalize hiring someone to clean our house or pick up our laundry or take our elderly parents to doctors' appointments so that we can work longer hours at the office to help our own families get ahead. Even higher-income families are swimming in so much risk that it often seems like the only way to keep from drowning is to hoard whatever lifelines are available and to dump as much of our own risk as possible downstream.[14]

Dumping that risk, however, doesn't always save women from being the default parent or the default caregiver at home. Rather, except in rare circumstances, even high-income women often end up disproportionately responsible for filling the gaps in the childcare system and in the rest of our broken safety net.[15]

STILL DROWNING DESPITE DUMPING THE RISK

Virginia is part of the growing cohort of women who flip the gender script. She has more education than her husband, Charles—she has a PhD to his master's—and she has a higher-paying job. As a tenure-track professor at a leading research university, Virginia was making $75,000 a year in 2020, while Charles, a middle school math teacher, was making $45,000 a year.[16]

Virginia earns more than Charles (both are white), but her gender, coupled with the perceived flexibility of her job, still led her to become the default caregiver for her aging parents and the default parent for her two kids. In January 2022, for example, her two-year-old son, Wally, had to quarantine

---

* In essence, the precarity of our DIY society helps to explain what sociologists call opportunity hoarding—the tendency of privileged families to leverage their resources to secure more resources, rather than spreading the wealth.

for two weeks after a Covid exposure and then for another ten days after he went back to childcare, where he was almost immediately exposed again. Charles, who was back to teaching in person by that point, could have used sick days to stay home with Wally, but it seemed like too big a risk to use them in case he ended up getting sick himself. Meanwhile, Virginia had the flexibility to tell her students and her colleagues that she would meet them on Zoom, so she stayed home with Wally instead. "I've paid two thousand dollars to have twelve days of care in the last six weeks. And that's even with a partial refund," Virginia lamented when she talked with my team in February. "I've paid two thousand dollars to watch my own child."

Having flexibility didn't just mean watching Wally. Instead, the flexibility to work from home meant that almost all of the domestic responsibilities fell to Virginia. That included the chores like grocery shopping, cooking, laundry, lunch-packing, bill-paying, and scheduling, as well as noticing what needed to be done. "I'm the one who does a lot of the invisible labor," she explained, adding, as an example, "I'm the one who makes sure that there are diapers and if something is getting low it's restocked." Virginia acknowledged that Charles is responsible for some things, like the cars, but she saw an overall imbalance in their relationship, saying, "There's a real weight to being a woman in a family."

During the pandemic, Virginia's mother, who has Alzheimer's, got to the point where she could no longer handle things like cooking and cleaning and scheduling. Virginia's dad could have taken on those responsibilities, and her brother could have helped, too, but they fell to Virginia instead. Virginia recalled a conversation with her brother that initially seemed sweet but left her frustrated when she thought about it looking back. Sitting on the porch together during a visit with their parents, he had given her a big hug and told her, "I'm sorry this had to happen, but you're the matriarch now. It's all on you, and I see you holding the world up."

Having to hold up the world created tension not only in Virginia's relationship with her extended family but also in her relationship with Charles. In 2021, Charles's back went out and he stopped doing the dishes—the one daily chore he had reliably done before. Virginia explained that he stopped "because he couldn't lean to put stuff in the dishwasher." Virginia was skeptical that loading the dishwasher would cause Charles's back to flare up again as he insisted, but she accepted (albeit grudgingly) that after-dinner cleanup had been permanently moved from his to her plate.

All those extra chores made it difficult for Virginia to feel as though she could ever concentrate well enough to make progress on her research. "I do actually have a brain," she said with a sardonic laugh. "I love thinking. And I would love to be able to do that again sometimes."

At the same time, Virginia also balked at the suggestion—a suggestion she had seen echoed in various announcements and emails from her employer—that she would be more productive at work if she invested in a little "self-care." "A shower is not self-care," she said, scoffing. "A shower is fucking bodily maintenance for a human care. Self-care is not making a nice meal. That's just a requirement for a mammal. Self-care is just a way that institutions have offloaded the responsibility of enacting humane work practices."

Virginia insisted that what she really needed was institutional support. "What do I need?" she asked rhetorically, during an interview in early 2022. "I need childcare. I need the child tax credit to come back. I need a financial cushion. I need time and reliable care for my children. I need consistency. I need institutions to step up and do what they are supposed to do to be humane. But they're not humane. Institutions don't take care of you. Institutions take care of themselves."

⎯⎯⎯

As I'm writing this, I'm home with my conjunctivitis-infected six-year-old, and all I can say is "Amen." On the one hand, I'm grateful that I can still get paid when I'm working from home. That my colleagues and students are willing to wait a little longer for emails, assignments, and drafts. That they're willing to chat over Zoom instead of in person, or push a meeting back a few days. On the other hand, the flexibility of my job makes it difficult to prioritize work when illness or weather or another minor catastrophe disrupts the precarious arrangements my family and I have made. Especially when my goopy-eyed six-year-old pulls on my arm and asks, "Will you come play Legos with me? It feels like no one loves me anymore." And even when saying yes means having to stay up late on my laptop catching up on the work that I missed during the day.

Like me and like Virginia, women in dual-income families often are (or at least are perceived to be) the parent with more job flexibility. That gendered flexibility has benefits, but it also comes with gendered costs.* As we saw with Virginia and Holly and even Patricia in our last chapter, it's hard to avoid becoming the default parent when you have the more flexible job. Even having the resources to outsource care doesn't protect women from being the backstop when the makeshift net they've stitched gives way.[17]

Of course, workplace flexibility isn't actually the problem here, and neither are the emotional manipulation skills of six-year-olds. Instead, the real problem is that we've dismantled the social safety net in ways that demand more flexibility from workers and families while making that flexibility unequally open to all.

Consider, for example, what plays out when kids get sick and have to stay home. In the US, childcare centers can't afford to lose any revenue, and they can't afford to lose any staff. At the same time, childcare centers can't typically afford to pay for health insurance for their employees or give refunds when kids have to stay home. That's why childcare centers often have rules saying kids can't come in with symptoms of illness—or even within twenty-four or forty-eight hours of having been sick. Those rules help protect the institution by limiting the spread of disease. And yet, in the absence of policies guaranteeing paid leave and protections for parents and guardians whose kids get sick, those same rules also leave families scrambling to care for sick kids. In the ITD study, I asked employed parents how easy it is to manage when their kids get sick. Only 40 percent said it would be easy for them to take time off if their kids had to stay home because of illness, and less than a quarter said they have reliable access to emergency childcare. Faced with

---

* That includes costs in terms of the division of responsibility in families and financial costs in the sense that workers who request flexibility, especially women and those who request flexibility for caregiving reasons, are often passed over for promotions and paid less than their peers. These costs stem from employers' assumption that women will use that flexibility for caregiving responsibilities and that women who devote more time and energy to caregiving won't be as committed or as productive on the job.

those shortfalls, some families end up sending sick kids to school or child-care anyway, even if they know that their kid might end up getting their classmates or teachers sick. Meanwhile, others might have one parent take time off or ask to work remotely and keep their kids home, even if they know they'll be judged or penalized by their employers for devoting less than their full attention to their work.[18]

Those impossible choices typically fall to moms, even when dads have access to flexible policies like paid time off or the option of working from home from time to time. In the PITT study, 84 percent of moms in mom-dad families said they would be the ones primarily responsible for caring for a child who got sick or had to quarantine. And even when moms in mom-dad families were the primary breadwinner for their household, 77 percent said they'd still be the primary caregiver if their kids had to stay home.[19]

Of course, there are some dads and nonbinary parents who end up as the default parent and caregiver. And yet these cases aren't a model of what we should be striving for. Instead, and as we'll see in our next story, they're further evidence of how our underinvestment in the social safety net forces whoever is most vulnerable to do more of the invisible work of care.[20]

FLIPPING THE SCRIPT . . . AND THE RISK

Ivan is one of the only 7 percent of American dads who stays home with his kids full-time.* Ivan is also unlike many other stay-at-home fathers, in that he's home specifically for caregiving reasons, not because he's retired, ill, disabled, still in school, or unemployed.[21]

To Ivan, however, it seemed logical to be the primary caregiver. Before they had kids, Ivan and his wife, Nancy, both of whom are white, were both working for pay full-time, but their jobs were very different in terms of flex-ibility as well as pay. Nancy, as a nurse practitioner, worked four ten-hour shifts a week in a prenatal clinic, making $125,000 a year. Ivan, by contrast, was working as an art appraiser, earning less than half of what Nancy was

---

* By contrast, 27 percent of American mothers are stay-at-home moms. Stay-at-home mothers are also more likely than stay-at-home fathers to say that they're home specifically for caregiving reasons (more than three-quarters of stay-at-home moms, compared to only a quarter of stay-at-home dads).

making, and able to do almost all of his work from home. When their daughter, Cecilia, was born in 2019, Ivan volunteered to stay home full-time with her, and Nancy was thrilled with that choice. They agreed that Ivan would still do about ten hours of appraisal work a week and that Nancy would increase her work hours, going to five ten-hour shifts a week instead of four in order to help pay down the more than $200,000 in debt they still had on their college and graduate school student loans.

Their arrangement had benefits for the family and especially for Nancy, who had struggled with severe postpartum depression while home on maternity leave. Ivan was glad to be in a position where he could take that stress off her plate; as he explained, "She functions at her best not being the primary childcare person. So I'm happy for her to be the breadwinner and go out and be validated by that. Likewise, it's validating to have her express that she's pleased to be the one going out to the world and having me home with Cecilia."

At the same time, being a full-time caregiver was hard on Ivan. Nancy could see how desperate he was for a break from the constant demands at home. And unlike many of the breadwinner dads in families I interviewed, Nancy not only noticed when Ivan was struggling but also tried to help as much as she could, including by taking Cecilia for an hour every night when she got home so Ivan could have time alone. When things were more financially stable, Nancy also went back to working four days instead of five so Ivan could sleep in one day a week and focus more on his appraisal business, and so that she could help with errands like buying groceries. When Ivan was diagnosed with cancer, Nancy paid for babysitters to help when Ivan went to doctors' appointments and when he was recovering from surgery. And when Nancy became pregnant with their second baby, she arranged for Cecilia to go to childcare three days a week so that on those days, Ivan, who was at this point in remission, would only have to manage the new baby at home.

When men are in Nancy's position, they very rarely go to those lengths. Compare Nancy to Colby, Audrey's husband, whom we met in chapter 1. When Audrey was struggling, Colby didn't cut back his work hours or find a babysitter to help Audrey part-time. Instead, he just took on more and more overtime, and even when he was home, he left Audrey to handle the house and the kids. Breadwinner dads like Colby rarely spend their own incomes to outsource care. Instead, spending on childcare and housework and other domestic responsibilities is determined almost entirely by women's income.[22]

Breadwinner moms like Nancy, by contrast, often go above and beyond with housework and childcare to compensate for their nontraditional paid work roles. In fact, research shows that in different-gender couples, moms who outearn their partners do more of the housework and childcare than moms whose partners' earnings closely match their own. Put differently, couples are best able to achieve an even split with domestic responsibilities when moms earn exactly as much as dads do—not less and not more.[23]

These patterns, however, don't just apply to different-gender couples. They can also be seen in couples that don't fit the version of gender as a two-sided coin. Mandy and Alex, for example, have three kids together. Mandy, who identifies as a woman, is currently the primary breadwinner, working two jobs—as a university administrator and an adjunct college professor—and earning about $65,000 a year. Alex, who is gender nonbinary, is currently staying home with the kids full-time, though that wasn't always the case. When Mandy gave birth to their first baby in 2014, she was working on a PhD and teaching college classes online part-time, making about $15,000 a year, while Alex, who has a bachelor's degree, was working full-time as a bicycle mechanic, making about $30,000 a year. They agreed that Mandy would care for their first child while teaching online and writing her thesis, and then, once Mandy finished her PhD and got a full-time job, Mandy would have more babies, but Alex would step in as the primary parent, at least until all the kids were old enough to be in school full-time.[24]

Having Alex at home made it possible for Mandy to get ahead career-wise, but it also led to guilt. Mandy, for example, worried that for Alex, shouldering the bulk of the caregiving would breed resentment. And she worried that she wasn't spending enough alone time with Alex because she couldn't afford to pay for a babysitter for nights out and still cover all their bills, including $2,500 a month for rent, $500 a month for health insurance, $1,200 a month for food, plus payments toward their $5,000 in credit card debt and the more than $120,000 she and Alex still owed on their student loans. Considering those worries, Mandy tried to work from home as often as she could so that she could see Alex during the day. Mandy also tried to avoid getting sucked into work during her off hours, so she could focus on things like cooking and grocery shopping and take some of the burden off Alex. "I've been doing a much better job of setting boundaries with my job," Mandy explained in 2022. "So, for example, there would be days when Alex was just in meltdown mode because they were so stressed out with parenting. Being able to say to my job I'm taking today off or I'm not taking on any more projects because I need to be here physically and emotionally for my family has been good."

Having a stay-at-home partner is good for women in some ways, but it doesn't solve the larger precarity problem our DIY society creates. Sure, women with stay-at-home partners might make more money than they would otherwise, and they might get more sleep or have more time for exercise. But because of gender wage gaps, families where mom is the primary breadwinner tend to have fewer financial resources, on average, than families where most or all of the earnings come from dad. Moreover, and because of how our society judges families who don't follow traditional gender scripts, breadwinner moms may still end up doing the extra labor required to be the kind of involved parent and supportive partner that breadwinner dads rarely are and ought to be.[25]

Compare, for example, Nancy to Tom, who is also the primary breadwinner in his family and who also works in a high-paying healthcare job, earning roughly $90,000 a year as an athletic trainer. When their children's school and childcare center closed at the start of the Covid-19 pandemic, Tom's wife, Stephanie, stopped taking the part-time shifts she used to work as a physical therapist. Tom, meanwhile, kept working as though nothing had changed. "She does it all," he told me in March 2021. "She does all the laundry. She does all the housecleaning. I try and do most of the outside stuff but she'll obviously, especially during football season, she'll help with a lot of that." As justification for that decision, Tom pointed to the gender wage gap in their family, noting nonchalantly, "We never really relied on her money." Tom, like many breadwinner fathers in families my team and I talked to, treated Stephanie's income as nice but superfluous.

Like many other breadwinner fathers, and unlike Nancy, Tom also assumed that Stephanie was doing just fine in managing all her responsibilities, saying, "How she does it, I don't know. Days I'm home with the boys by myself it's like it's all I can do is focus on keeping them alive and she's doing it all." Stephanie might have looked like she was holding it together, but there were cracks showing at the seams. In 2021, Stephanie recalled the early months of the pandemic and how hard it was to help her older son with virtual kindergarten while also taking care of her younger son, who had just turned two. Stephanie also noted, with a great deal of guilt, how she often gave her two-year-old an iPad to keep him busy, how she let the house become an "absolute disaster" rather than try to keep it as clean as she needed it to be for her own sanity, and how she would hide from the kids in her bedroom to escape the stress of it all.

When women are the primary or even the co-breadwinners, they rarely have the luxury of being so oblivious to their partners' stresses and needs. During the Covid-19 pandemic, for example, Janet, who is white and makes $70,000 a year as a financial administrator, was able to work remotely full-time. Her husband, Russell, who is also white and who makes $120,000 a year as a behavioral clinician, could only work remotely part of the time. This left Janet to handle most of the care for their three kids—two in elementary school, plus a toddler—while their school and childcare center were closed. Janet wanted Russell to do more. And yet, when he did occasionally stay home, the result was what Janet described as "chaos." Russell quickly got angry that the kids "didn't just behave and do their work." In the end, Janet concluded that it wasn't worth asking Russell to do more at home if he was just going to get angry with her and the kids. Instead, until their children were able to go back to in-person school and childcare, Janet tried to manage on her own—a choice that led to "significant depression issues," frequent drinking, and substantial weight gain, "like forty pounds in three months."[26]

Russell, meanwhile, isn't the only man who gets angry when pushed to do more at home. In the ITD survey, which I fielded in December 2020—at the height of the Covid-19 pandemic, when many schools and childcare centers across the US were still closed—I asked parents how often they had yelled at their kids over the past two weeks. Among dads who were doing some of their work remotely, nearly half said they had yelled at their kids at least once a day.* That's compared to only a quarter of the dads who weren't doing any of their paid work from home.†[27]

Men like Tom and Russell could take a page out of Nancy's playbook. They don't have to go all the way to being stay-at-home parents like Ivan or Alex, but they need to check in with their partners and look for signs that their partners are struggling, even if it seems like everything is okay. And they need to step in to do more of the housework and childcare and other domestic responsibilities and strive to do that work calmly and patiently without having to be reminded or even asked.

At the same time, telling men to do more isn't a viable structural solution to the burden our DIY society places on women or to the precarity that system creates. Telling men "Do more!" doesn't change the incentives that men have to dump the risk they face onto the women in their families—the same set of incentives that leads privileged women to dump the risk they've been handed onto others more vulnerable than them. Telling men "Do more!" also doesn't change the gendered structure of our economy, the gendered pressures that men face to prioritize paid work over caregiving, or the gendered differences in socialization that leave men less prepared to do the work of care.[28]

Unless we change the incentives and eliminate the constraints, telling men "Do more!" also risks forcing women into the role of gender police and cleanup crew. Put differently, unless men like Tom and Russell *want* to change their behavior, the women around them will have to constantly remind them what to do, and they'll have to pick up the slack when men let things slip. Take Candace and Garrett, a white married couple who both

---

* In the ITD survey, participants were asked, "Over the past few weeks, how often did you yell at your children?" Responses included: "not at all," "less than once a week," "about once a week," "a few times a week," "about once a day," "a few times a day," "about once an hour," and "a few times an hour." The percentages reported here include parents who said they have yelled at their children once a day or more often.

† Dads who were doing all their work from home fared only somewhat better, with more than a third of them (36 percent) saying they were yelling at their kids once a day or more. Like Russell, angry dads were also disproportionately white, highly educated, high-earning professionals, likely because those were the dads who were most likely to have the kinds of jobs that offered remote work options during the pandemic, and because they reported larger pandemic-related increases in their childcare and housework time compared to other dads.

work for pay full-time. They each earn roughly half of their $75,000-a-year household income, Candace as a public school teacher and Garrett as a supervisor at a distribution center. Two weeks after their son Hayden was born in 2018, Garrett went back to the warehouse, while Candace stayed home (at partial pay) for three months. Garrett told Candace that he was going to start working more overtime to make up for her lost income while she was on family leave, but Garrett started getting home later and later, leaving Candace alone with Hayden for thirteen- or fourteen-hour stretches. Candace got suspicious about whether Garrett was really spending all that time working, and she eventually found out he was taking extra time for himself, like meeting up with friends, before coming home. When Candace confronted Garrett, he promised to come straight home in the evening but continued working overtime, even after Candace went back to work and even in 2020, after their second son was born and the pandemic closed their childcare center. Garrett's absence left Candace to care for a newborn and a toddler full-time while also teaching online and managing all the housework and other responsibilities at home.

That overlapping triple shift exhausted Candace to the point where her therapist even encouraged her to ask Garrett for more help. Despite her therapist's urgings, Candace was reluctant to broach the topic with Garrett because she worried he would get defensive, noting that when she does ask for help, "To him, it feels like I'm saying he doesn't do anything ever. I've got to do baby steps, that way I don't upset him."

Candace worried that Garrett would leave her if she pushed too hard, especially after she caught him messaging other women on Snapchat and asking them for "dirty" photos. When Candace approached Garrett about what she had found on his phone, he gaslit her, insisting that the online conversations were innocent and accusing Candace of being too jealous and too controlling and not wanting him to have any friends. That pushback left Candace too afraid to ask for the help she needed because she didn't want to lose Garrett, and she wasn't sure she could give the kids the kind of life she wanted for them if she had to raise them on her own.[29]

Despite those fears, Candace might be happier if she left Garrett. Sociologist Joanna Pepin and her colleagues find that unmarried moms actually spend less time on housework, get more sleep, and have more free time than married moms do—in large part because they're not picking up after their husbands in addition to picking up after their kids.[30]

Candace is right, however, to worry about financial precarity. She earns too much on her own to qualify for government assistance like welfare, food stamps, Medicaid, or subsidized housing or childcare. Yet even with child support from Garrett, it might be difficult for Candace to maintain her current standard of living, especially without a sturdy social safety net, and with more than $50,000 in student loan debt, medical debt, credit card debt, and vehicle debt, plus $250,000 still outstanding on the mortgage for the home they own. In essence, and as we also saw with Audrey, the lack of a social safety net can persuade American women to stay for the sense of security with partners they might otherwise leave.[31]

The women we've met in this chapter are certainly facing less precarity than the ones we met in our last. As we've seen here, however, it would be a mistake to assume that privilege offers full protection against the gendered risks and responsibilities of our DIY society. Rather, our lack of a real social safety net leaves even higher-income families swimming in so much risk that the only way to keep from drowning in the short-term is to dump that risk downstream—from men to women and then onto other women more vulnerable than them. At the same time, and as we'll see in part 2 of our story, it would also be a mistake to assume that the women from our last chapter would be able to climb out of precarity by making all the same choices that their more privileged counterparts have made.[32]

Part II

WHY WE HAVEN'T FIXED THIS AND HOW WE COULD

Chapter 4

GOOD CHOICES WON'T SAVE US

Rather than acknowledge the burden that women are carrying, the engineers of our DIY society have taken a page out of Garrett's playbook and gaslit the women who complain. They tell us that if we're struggling, it's probably our own fault for being lazy or making bad choices. And they tell us that if we just keep swimming, we'll keep our families afloat, even as the risk creates dangerous riptides.[1]

To support their gaslighting, the engineers have funded neoliberal think tanks like the American Enterprise Institute (AEI) and its Institute for Family Studies (IFS) to pump out research "proving" that if we all just make the right choices, we can get by without a social safety net. Take, for example, a report on the so-called success sequence published by the AEI/IFS in 2022. The authors of the report argue that if young people want to achieve success in America today, all they have to do is follow a three-step sequence: finish at least a high school education, work full-time (or have a partner who does), and get married before having kids. This idea of the success sequence has been around since the mid-2000s, and it has attracted substantial public attention. *Washington Post* columnist George F. Will went so far as to call the success sequence "insurance against poverty." And *New York Times* columnist David Leonhardt cited success sequence research in claiming that when it comes to poverty, "family structure is part of the problem," and the "new norm" of out-of-wedlock childbirth "doesn't seem to be a healthy one." As evidence, proponents of the success sequence often point to surveys showing that among millennials who followed all three steps by their mid-thirties, only 3 percent were living below the poverty line.[2]

These numbers might seem convincing, but the promise of good choices ultimately rings hollow, both because correlation doesn't imply causation, and because the federal poverty line is a paltry measure of success.* As we'll see in this chapter, women often find themselves crumbling under the weight of the responsibility we've heaped on them, even if they try their best.[3]

MARRIAGE WON'T SAVE WOMEN

Jocelyn, like many young women in low-income rural communities, believed that marriage was the key to success. Finishing high school, getting married, and adopting breadwinner-homemaker roles had mostly worked out for her parents, so Jocelyn figured that she and husband Kyler could do the same. Jocelyn and Kyler are both white and have high school diplomas, and they got married in their early twenties. Jocelyn hoped they would have at least five children—one more than her mother's four. "My mom stayed home other than once when my dad was laid off from work," Jocelyn explained, "and so that was always kind of my goal. And I wanted to homeschool my kids."[4]

Jocelyn had her first baby, Declan, in 2013, but she wasn't able to stay home with him the way she would have preferred. With only a high school education, Kyler was struggling to find full-time work, so he took a part-time minimum wage job at a pet store while also trying to start his own pet care business on the side. Like many small businesses in the US, Kyler's wasn't profitable and couldn't cover their bills.† Jocelyn, however, wanted to be a good wife. She didn't want to ask Kyler to give up on his dreams. And so, to help with finances, she got a low-wage, no-benefits job as a grocery

---

* The federal poverty line closely aligns with the federal minimum wage, which makes it very difficult for Americans to qualify as officially poor. Working at $7.25 an hour for forty hours a week and fifty weeks a year would yield a total income of $15,080; that's above the $14,580 federal poverty threshold for a person living alone. Thus, the only way that someone can be officially poor in America is by having dependents or by working for pay at less than minimum wage or less than full-time. For these reasons, the living wage is arguably a better indicator of poverty than the federal poverty line. By that measure, which also accounts for regional variations in cost of living, a person living alone in Indiana would need to be making $32,000 a year to comfortably make ends meet.

† Data from the US Bureau of Labor Statistics (BLS) show that roughly 20 percent of small businesses close in their first year of opening, and only 25 percent survive fifteen years or more. BLS data also show that the median income for self-employed workers in the US is only $32,020 per year.

store cashier, working as many hours as they would schedule her for. Jocelyn was able to take that cashier job only because her mother was able to provide Jocelyn with free childcare, though Jocelyn and Kyler gave her a little money when they could.[5]

That arrangement worked well enough until Jocelyn gave birth to her second son, Silas, in 2015. Without access to paid family leave, she had to go back to work after just a few days—a choice that left her in serious pain. "I had a lot of hip problems," she recalled, "so I ended up having to quit that job. And I started working for myself cleaning houses. That way I was moving around instead of staying stationary in one spot." Like Kyler, however, Jocelyn struggled to build up a solid client base, leaving her income volatile month to month.

That volatility left Jocelyn and Kyler relying on credit cards—and paying only the minimum—especially after Kyler lost his pet store job. Kyler saw losing his job as a sign that he should focus on his pet care business. But Jocelyn knew the bills needed to be paid, so she took on a second job in food service. "There were days when I was there until two o'clock in the morning and had to be back to open at six a.m., and that was horrible," Jocelyn recalled. "And it was just easier to not sleep. Because by the time I got home and showered and ate I was gonna get an hour and a half. And there's no point. Better to be tired at work than accidentally oversleep and lose my job."

The stress of those arrangements took a toll on Jocelyn's relationship with Kyler, and losing childcare made things even worse. Not long after Jocelyn started working her second job, Jocelyn's mother had to move out of state to take care of Jocelyn's ailing grandmother. Kyler and Jocelyn decided that the best of all the terrible options would be a split shift, with Kyler working a part-time day-shift job during the week and Jocelyn working for pay nights and weekends instead. That split shift, however, didn't work out well, just as we saw with Erin and Mark.

Frustration turned to violence, which ultimately prompted Jocelyn to leave. "The only reason that relationship ended," Jocelyn explained, "was that he actually hurt me. I've always grown up with, like, 'You don't just leave because you want to; you make it work as much as you can.'" Jocelyn, who had grown up very religious in an evangelical Christian family, wasn't keen on the idea of leaving a marriage, but she had limits.

Leaving, however, left Jocelyn relying on a threadbare system of government support, including welfare, food stamps, housing subsidies, EITC, and Medicaid. Adding insult to injury, the Indiana government also collected child support from Kyler and kept the money as reimbursement for Jocelyn's welfare benefits, rather than pass it through to Jocelyn and the kids.[*6]

At the advice of a friend, Jocelyn turned to a local crisis pregnancy center that was affiliated with an evangelical Christian church. Like many other crisis pregnancy centers, its primary mission was to discourage pregnant women from seeking abortion services, but it also offered pregnant women and parents a host of free or low-cost supplies and services, including diapers, maternity and baby clothes, and even donated high chairs and cribs.[†] Even with that support, it was a struggle for Jocelyn to afford basics like food and childcare and rent.[7]

Those financial pressures led Jocelyn to quickly move in with another man she started dating not long after she and Kyler broke up. Wesley, who is white and has only a high school diploma, was still living with his own parents at the time. Having four adults in one house created tension; Jocelyn says, "we were fighting constantly." Despite the stress of that arrangement, Jocelyn stuck things out with Wesley because living with him and his parents meant she didn't have to pay for rent or for childcare, and she could go back to working night and weekend shifts in paid roles and caring for the kids during the day.

Cohabitation quickly turned to marriage, after Jocelyn unexpectedly be-

---

* Unlike some states, Indiana does not have a "pass-through" child support program. Instead, Indiana law stipulates, "The amount of child support assigned to the state each month will be the lesser of the following: 1) The amount of TANF benefits received that month; or 2) The amount of child support due to the recipient during that month. Any child support payments collected while the recipient receives TANF benefits will be kept by the state. When the recipient no longer receives TANF benefits, the assignment terminates, with respect to current child support; however, any assigned child support that was unpaid during the TANF benefit period will remain assigned to the state."

† Pregnant people who visit crisis pregnancy centers will likely be given information about alternatives to abortion and warned of potential abortion risks. As one such organization states on its website, "You will receive accurate information about pregnancy, fetal development, life-style issues, and related concerns. The pregnancy center does not provide abortion or referrals for abortion, but we are committed to offering accurate information about abortion procedures and risks. You may refuse any information you do not wish to receive." In some communities, like Jocelyn's, these centers are even located right next to health clinics offering abortion services, creating added confusion for people seeking abortions and other reproductive healthcare.

came pregnant again. With a new baby on the way, Wesley, who is also an evangelical Christian, proposed that they get married and that Jocelyn stop working for pay. Given what she'd been through with Kyler, Jocelyn was initially wary of getting married again and leaving herself financially dependent on a man. "Wesley made that decision for me," she explained, "because I was in this mindset of 'I have to keep working; I have to, I have to, I have to.'" Wesley countered that because he had a full-time job, they could afford to have Jocelyn stay home, and Jocelyn eventually relented despite her fears. "I don't wanna say [he] made me quit but he kind of did," Jocelyn told me.

Jocelyn's fears were warranted. In 2020, after Jocelyn had not only a third but also a fourth child, Wesley lost the new $40,000-a-year waste management job he had just started before the pandemic. Because he was a new hire, he didn't qualify for unemployment benefits, missing the cutoff for eligibility by just twenty days.* Wesley eventually found a part-time job in truck repair that required more than an hour's commute each way. He used the family's only vehicle to get to work, which left Jocelyn quite literally trapped at home with the kids. Her only option to help financially was to care for neighbors' kids in her own home, but even that didn't help much. Jocelyn knew that the clients she could find in her low-income rural community were also struggling, so she took whatever money she could get— usually less than $100 per week per child.[8]

Once he was able to go back to working full-time, Wesley persuaded Jocelyn to once again stop doing paid work and focus on caring for their little ones and homeschooling their older kids. By that point, in 2022, Jocelyn, who wasn't even thirty years old, had given birth to her fifth child and was pregnant unexpectedly with her sixth. Because of her church's teaching on birth control, Jocelyn relied on cycle tracking and other "natural family planning" methods. Based on those teachings, Jocelyn assumed that she wouldn't get pregnant before her period came back after her fifth pregnancy, which led to what she called an "oops" with her sixth child.[9]

---

* States set eligibility requirements for unemployment insurance, including minimum income requirements and minimum duration of employment requirements. In Indiana, for example, a worker must be a resident of the state and must have been working for pay in the state for the last twelve months. Wesley had changed jobs a number of times before the pandemic and, as a result, had not met these minimum duration requirements.

Supporting and homeschooling six kids on a $40,000-a-year income wasn't easy, and it left Wesley and Jocelyn with a mountain of bills and more than $20,000 in medical debt, credit card debt, and car loans. Given that financial precarity, Jocelyn occasionally broached the idea of going back to paid work, but Wesley repeatedly persuaded her that they'd be better off with her staying home. "I don't have a college degree or anything like that," Jocelyn acknowledged. "Whatever amount I would be making probably would only cover the cost of childcare. So there's not a whole lot of a point in me going back. The only thing we've discussed was going and working an opposite shift from my husband so we can kind of play off of each other's schedules, but then we would never see each other." Jocelyn had already tried that kind of split shift both with Kyler and Wesley, and she wasn't eager to go there again.

As rates of both single motherhood and child poverty rose rapidly in the 1980s and '90s, Republicans and Democrats began blaming the latter on the former. They argued that the US welfare system was incentivizing single motherhood and thereby incentivizing families to stay poor. In the end, those arguments proved so politically persuasive that Congress voted to dump our old welfare system—Aid to Families with Dependent Children, or AFDC, which was built by FDR in the 1930s—and replace it with the hollowed-out version—Temporary Assistance to Needy Families, or TANF—we still have today.[10]

TANF's proponents, which included both Ronald Reagan and Bill Clinton, argued that the key to fighting poverty was not stronger social safety nets but stronger families, and that the key to stronger families was marriage and engagement in paid work. Based on these beliefs, TANF's architects included strict work requirements, as we talked about with Akari, and they also created incentives for states to reduce the amount of cash they give to poor families and redirect the savings in other ways. In light of those incentives, states now spend only 22 percent of the TANF funds they get from the federal government on direct cash payments to families, compared to 71 percent in 1997, the first year TANF was in place.* Since the early 2000s, the federal government has also encouraged states to spend those savings on marriage promotion campaigns, including by setting aside over $100 million every year to match the money that states spend funding pro-marriage ads and organizations that teach relationship skills.[11]

The US government justifies its emphasis on "healthy relationships" by pointing to what they consider evidence of the benefits of marriage. The Department of Health and Human Services website, for example, states that "[m]ore than 30 years of research show that when children are living with their married, biological parents, they have better physical, emotional, and academic well-being" and that "[s]tudies have shown that people live longer, have less stress, and are more financially stable in a healthy family environment where both parents are present, share the responsibility of the household, and raise the children."[12]

Now, these arguments might seem reasonable, but they should be sounding our correlation-is-not-causation alarm. They assume that unmarried parenthood causes the kind of poverty and precarity that hurts kids' futures, when it's usually the other way around. As we saw with Patricia and Rodney, poverty and precarity are the primary reasons couples break up or avoid getting married in the first place. And it's poverty and precarity—not family structure—that really matter for kids' chances for success in their lives.[13]

Marriage advocates tend to ignore this more nuanced interpretation of the evidence or even misuse the data outright. Take *Hillbilly Elegy* author J. D. Vance. In his successful 2022 bid for a Republican Senate seat, Vance blamed poverty on the "sexual revolution" and on the abandonment of marriage†—vilifying unmarried mothers like Akari, Brooke, and Patricia,

---

* The federal government has effectively capped welfare spending, which has been stuck at $16.5 billion a year since 1996, with no adjustments for inflation. As a result, the real value of federal funding for welfare has fallen by 40 percent since 1996. Going a step further, welfare rules also incentivize states to reduce welfare eligibility and cut the real value of benefits and then redirect the money they save toward other initiatives, including marriage promotion campaigns. Notably, the beneficiaries of these marriage promotion classes and programs need not be welfare recipients themselves.

† *Hillbilly Elegy* has been roundly criticized for the way it blames poverty on people's "bad" choices and perpetuates stereotypes linking single motherhood with laziness, immorality, and greed.

even without calling them out by name. Vance went so far as to suggest that married couples should stay together for the good of the children, even if the relationship becomes violent, as Jocelyn and Kyler's did, contradicting the evidence outright.[14]

Marriage advocates also ignore the fact that marriage promotion rarely works. These programs do little or nothing to help couples stay together, despite what their proponents claim. Moreover, by reducing the amount of money that states are giving directly to low-income families, marriage promotion campaigns may actually increase the risk of violence because they take up resources that could otherwise help families financially through difficult times.[15]

Without those resources, stress is more likely to lead to violence. In the US, surveys show that one in three women has experienced physical, sexual, or emotional abuse from a partner, and that one in four has experienced severe violence or abuse. That's higher than the risk faced by women in many other high-income countries that give families more support.[16]

Without an adequate social safety net, American women who experience violence in their relationships are also less able to escape. As we saw with Jocelyn, American women who leave abusive relationships often have to figure out how to navigate the limited programs the US does offer for low-income families and also how to fill in the gaps. Maybe not surprisingly, then, it often takes multiple attempts for women to leave abusive relationships, if they do so at all. Moreover, as we saw with Jocelyn and Wesley, women who do leave may end up moving quickly into new and often less-than-ideal relationships because our tattered social safety net makes it so difficult for them to get by on their own.[17]

▬

Now, you may be thinking, "But Jocelyn still could've made better choices; if she'd gone to college, she would've had better job options, more choices partner-wise, and more bargaining power in negotiating for support." Like marriage promotions programs, however, that just-stay-in-school logic also has a correlation-is-not-causation flaw.

COLLEGE WON'T SAVE WOMEN

Take Lillian, who ended up on WIC despite being married, working a full-time job, and having finished both college and a master's degree.

Lillian's goal was to become a marriage and family therapist. Given growing demand for mental health services, Lillian, who is white and Jewish, figured there would always be plenty of jobs for her and that it would be easy to jump back into working if she took a few years off to have kids. Growing up, Lillian's mother had left the workforce for a few years while her children were little, then gone back to working full-time once all the kids were in school. Lillian wanted to be there for her own future kids in a similar way.[18]

After graduate school, Lillian found a job right away, but things didn't work out as she planned. By that point, in 2016, Lillian had met and married Desmond, a Black South African immigrant who was attending college in the same city where Lillian was living in graduate school. Although Desmond hadn't yet finished his degree, they decided to move to Indiana to be close to Lillian's family so they could start having kids right away.

Even with a master's degree, the best job Lillian could find in Indiana was with the Department of Children's Services (DCS), working with families like Destiny's that had lost custody of their children or that were going through other types of difficult times. The job felt meaningful to Lillian, but it paid only $30,000 a year and didn't come with benefits like paid family or medical leave.

Given how little Lillian was making, she and Desmond figured that they couldn't afford to pay for Desmond to finish his college degree full-time. So, instead, he enrolled in part-time college classes and found a part-time job as a leasing agent at an apartment complex, bringing in less than $10,000 a year. With so little money coming in, Lillian and Desmond had to be careful about what they spent each month, even with some support from Lillian's family to help make ends meet.

Things got more complicated financially when Lillian had their first baby in 2017 and when, six months after giving birth, she got pregnant again. Each time, Lillian experienced pregnancy complications that made it difficult to go back to work right away. As a result, Lillian took three months of unpaid leave after each pregnancy. In the meantime, they got by on Desmond's meager earnings, monetary gifts from Lillian's family, free childcare from Lillian's mother, and, after their second baby was born, assistance through WIC. "I had no idea we were eligible," Lillian recalled, telling me how a nurse at the hospital told her she would qualify during the months while she was on unpaid leave.

Lillian was grateful for WIC's support, but it wasn't much, and she hated the hoops she had to jump through, like complicated application forms and regular weigh-ins to ensure that her son was getting the nutrition for which the government had paid. "It wasn't easy," Lillian explained, "in terms of, like, getting all of the documents they needed and all of that. And it's embarrassing." When she ran into acquaintances at the WIC office, she worried that they judged her—or that they would think she was judging them. "There's stigma attached no matter what."

That was early 2019. In late 2021, when I last talked to Lillian, things were a little more stable financially, but it had been a rocky few years in between. In 2020, Lillian's mother was diagnosed with advanced-stage cancer, which made it too risky for her to continue providing childcare. Lillian and Desmond, however, couldn't afford full-time childcare for one kid, let alone two. So Lillian quit her job at DCS—a job she had come to despise because of its lack of support for working parents—and became an independent contractor with a service that offers therapy online.

Lillian hoped that switching to remote work would solve their childcare and money problems, but the plan fell through on both fronts. It was almost impossible to focus on her patients while caring for the kids full-time. Even when Desmond was home to help, Lillian could rarely find a quiet space where she could work uninterrupted. As a result, Lillian was typically only able to see two or three patients a day. And as an independent therapist, she only got paid for the patients she saw. Lillian also lost the employer-sponsored health insurance she had with DCS. But given her income and Desmond's, they were still making too much to qualify for Medicaid. So she ended up buying a plan through the Affordable Care Act's Health Insurance Marketplace. Between premiums, copays, and other out-of-pocket expenses, it was costing her $1,200 a month. Ironically, because of how much she was paying herself for insurance, Lillian could only take patients who could afford to pay out of pocket—not those who wanted to use Medicaid or even private insurance to pay. Because our insurance system is so complicated, Lillian would have either needed to hire someone to do her billing or cut back on the number of patients she saw to have time to do that work herself.

Given that she was earning more per hour than he was, Lillian could have asked Desmond to quit his own job and care for the kids. Yet she was reluctant to do so because of the pressure that Desmond felt to earn more money. Lillian explained, "I think he's embarrassed about how little he's bringing in financially." As far as she knew, Desmond hadn't been fully open with his family about the fact that Lillian was earning more than he was.

So when Desmond decided to take the real estate licensing exam and try to start his own business as a Realtor, Lillian supported him. With home prices soaring during the pandemic, Desmond thought it would be a good time to get in the game. He also convinced Lillian they should spend $250 a month so he could rent a small office space to look more professional to potential clients. Despite those efforts, Desmond found it difficult to stake his claim. In the last three months of 2021, Desmond only closed on one house—for a commission of $800. Like many first-time homebuyers, his clients kept getting overbid, which meant that Desmond didn't get paid.[19]

When I asked Lillian in late 2021 about the biggest challenges she was facing, she told me without hesitation: "Finances, for sure." Continuing, Lillian told me, "We don't make savings. We make our bills, but some bills I let sit and wait. Like, we'll sit on this credit card bill. We'll let this psychiatrist visit wait. We'll pay that later. You know? There's a lot of financial awareness of what's coming and what's going out." Lillian and Desmond were able to balance it all, for the moment. But Lillian knew that could change any time. "If I were to be out of work, it would completely change our lives," she said. "I mean . . . we'd be back to making almost nothing."

The weight of that risk was heavy on Lillian. Sighing, she told me, "I just wish that as parents you could have the space to take care of your mental health, to take care of your children, and the basic needs that they have. And to not constantly worry that you were going to go bankrupt because of making decisions between those things. As privileged as we are financially right now, it changes in a second. And that just shows that, like, if we're worried about that right now, then people who are not as financially well-off or don't have the same privileges or opportunities in life—I mean, they're set up to be destitute at a certain point."

———

For more than a half century, the US has pushed the message "Stay in school." In the 1970s, that meant "Finish high school."* By the early 2000s, it meant "Go to college." In a 2009 speech before Congress, President Barack Obama argued that, going forward, "every American will need to get more than a high school diploma." In that same speech, Obama equated dropping out of high school with "quitting on yourself" and "quitting on your country."[20]

On some level, that message makes sense. College graduates earn 50 percent more than workers with only high school diplomas, and they're only half as likely to be unemployed. College degrees are also associated with higher rates of marriage and lower divorce rates. And college-educated adults are disproportionately likely to make "good choices" health-wise like avoiding cigarettes, getting regular exercise, and eating nutritious food, have better overall health, and even live longer.[21]

Once again, however, claims about education as a guaranteed ticket to prosperity should be sounding our correlation-is-not-causation alarm. Even if the statistics seem promising, we can't assume that increasing rates of college enrollment will automatically reduce precarity or that getting a college degree will automatically protect women from bearing the brunt of the risks that their families face. Lillian, for example, had not only a four-year college degree but also a master's degree. And yet the best jobs she could find in her hometown—where she wanted to live because it would make raising a fam-

---

* One 1973 public service announcement depicts a young man walking past unhoused people on a city street, taking a flyer out of a trash can, and then following the directions on the flyer to a local employment office. The ad tells the listeners that people without high school educations have double the risk of unemployment as those who have finished their degrees and offers a stern warning to stay in school.

ily easier and more affordable—didn't pay enough or offer the kinds of benefits that would keep her and her family consistently above the poverty line.

Like with marriage, economic precarity makes it more difficult to stay in school. In dozens of other countries around the world, from Argentina and Brazil, to Greece and Germany, to Kenya and the Philippines, higher education is treated as a public good. Students who are admitted to college can go for free, just as they would to public K-12 schools, or by paying nominal fees. In the US, the public higher education system used to operate similarly. In 1960, a student at a public university in Indiana would have paid about $200 a year in tuition, or the equivalent of about $2,000 today. Those low costs were the product of public investment in higher education, including federal government money and money from the state of Indiana. At the time, Indiana's public universities, like the one Lillian attended, only had to rely on student tuition and fees to cover about a quarter of their budget because tax funding covered the rest. Over time, however, Indiana—like most states and the federal government—decreased its funding for higher education, shifting more and more of the cost of higher education onto students and their families instead. Today, public universities in Indiana rely on tuition and fees to cover more than 60 percent of their budgets. That shift has led to a massive increase in public university tuition, which today costs more than $11,000 a year for in-state students, and almost $40,000 a year for students attending from out of state. Meanwhile, the federal government has also reduced the public money available to help students pay those rising college costs. Federal Pell Grants, for example, which used to provide enough funding for low-income students to cover 75 percent of the cost of tuition, now cover only 30 percent.[22]

Pushing those costs makes it more difficult for students—and particularly students from low- and middle-income families—to get college and graduate degrees. To keep up with tuition payments and afford room and board, students from low- and middle-income families often have to work part-time or even full-time jobs during college. Working long hours for pay makes it more difficult for those students to finish their degrees, particularly if, like Desmond, they're also raising children or helping care for other family members while they're going to school. College classes also don't typically count toward the kind of work requirements associated with programs like welfare and food stamps.* That's how Brooke ended up getting pushed out of college, and that's part of why a third of college students never finish their degrees. Even if they don't finish, however, students still have to pay back the debt they have taken on to go to college†—debt that further compounds the precarity of their situations by making it more difficult for them to buy houses, get married, have children, and care for aging family members. Patricia, whom we met in chapter 2, for example, still has more than $30,000 to pay off on loans toward a degree she started more than a decade ago but never completed. And her experience is common in the US, particularly among Black students, whose families have been systematically denied access to the kind of wealth that might otherwise buoy them in finishing college and paying what they owe.[23]

Even though college is more expensive and harder to finish, the payoff for higher education isn't as high or as consistent as it used to be. Before the great risk shift, college graduates in the US enjoyed a substantial "college wage premium"—the difference in income between the average college graduate and the average person with only a high school diploma. Those wage premiums allowed families—disproportionately white families like Lillian's parents'—to buy homes and build lasting wealth. That apparent promise of prosperity led to a rapid increase in college enrollments. All those graduates, however, flooded the market, creating more competition, stifling wage growth, and causing the college wage premium to fall. As a result, college students today can't expect the same payoff job-wise or income-wise that their parents or grandparents got before them. Among US college graduates, more than a third are underemployed, in the sense that their jobs don't require college degrees, a quarter have annual incomes of less than $38,000, and only a quarter are earning more than $70,000 a year.[24]

The situation for women college graduates is even more precarious because their college wage premium is even lower than men's. In the US, the

---

* Food stamp recipients can be exempted from work requirements if they are caring for a child under six years old, but this is not the case for TANF recipients, who are required to work, regardless of whether they are also the primary caregiver for a child.
† The average student at a public university takes on more than $30,000 in loans to get a four-year college degree.

difference between the median income for a woman with a four-year college degree and the median income for a woman with only a high school diploma is about $25,000 a year. For men, that difference is more than $33,000 a year. That's because women college graduates have lower median incomes than men with the same level of education—$63,000 versus $80,000 per year—with even bigger gaps between men and women who complete graduate or professional degrees.[25]

These differences in income reflect, in part, the gendered sorting and valuing of jobs that we talked about in chapter 2. Consider, for example, Lillian's job as a mental health counselor. In 1970, 43 percent of workers in these jobs were women, compared to 75 percent today. In the wake of that shift, and like other jobs that have gone from majority male to majority female—including book editors, Realtors, and even biologists—the real wages for mental health counselors have also declined over time.* In 1980, for example, the median income for mental health counselors like Lillian was more than $24,000 a year—or the equivalent of almost $87,000 in today's dollars. By contrast, the current median salary for mental health counselors in the US is less than $49,000 a year. Put differently, the real wages for workers in Lillian's field have fallen by almost half in the last fifty years, despite growing demand for the services Lillian provides.[26]

Given those falling wages, it's easy to think that Lillian picked the wrong career path and she would've been better off going to school for business or a computer science degree. And yet, that assumption about the payoff of jobs in male-dominated fields like science, technology, engineering, and mathematics (STEM) is also subject to the correlation-is-not-causation flaw.

---

* Notably, the same thing doesn't happen when men move into careers that have historically been done by women. Rather, even within feminine-typed occupations, and even after controlling for other factors that may affect salaries, women earn less than men. This is also despite the fact that when men do enter into feminine-typed occupations, it is often because they have been laid off from a non-feminine-typed job.

STEM WON'T SAVE WOMEN

By the time she was in her early thirties, Teresa was already making $125,000 a year as a manager at a major biotech company I'll call Chescom, working ten-hour days plus weekends. She had earned an engineering degree from an elite private college and was enrolled in a part-time MBA program at another elite private university. The end result of all of this education and effort would hopefully be a senior director role and, further down the line, eventually a C-suite job.

To get to that point, however, Teresa had to take on about $150,000 in student loans, and all that debt left her feeling ambivalent when her husband, Cole (both are white), broached the idea of having kids. "He wanted kids *so* badly," Teresa told me. "His whole life, he's always wanted kids." Teresa was less certain, as she was the one covering most of their bills. At the time, Cole, who was also working for Chescom, was making only $60,000 a year, despite working fifty or sixty hours a week, and he still had more than $150,000 left to pay on his own student loans. After trying a year of law school, he had switched to a master's program in nonprofit management, then taken a job at Chescom when he couldn't find work for a nonprofit organization that would pay enough to pay off his loans.

Despite her hesitations, Teresa agreed to go off the pill (which, like many women, she hated because of its side effects), and she ended up getting pregnant right away. Teresa was excited to be pregnant, but she found it was like being constantly spotlit. "I was planning to work up until I went into labor," Teresa recalled, "but I was getting frustrated because I could not walk down the hall without somebody asking, 'Oh, how are you feeling? Oh, you must be so ready! Oh, you must be so anxious!'" Eager to escape those comments, Teresa decided to work from home during her last month of pregnancy instead.[27]

Childcare also turned out to be more complicated than Teresa anticipated it would be. Almost as soon as she knew she was pregnant, Teresa began touring childcare centers and putting her name on waitlists. In the process, she learned that a spot wasn't likely to open up until her daughter, Aurora, was six months old. Chescom, meanwhile, didn't give Teresa or Cole enough paid family leave to fill that gap—Teresa was able to take three months off, while Cole only got three weeks. They agreed that Cole would take one week off when Aurora was born, then take the other two weeks when Teresa had to go back to work, but that still left a gap of over a month to fill. So Teresa paid her younger sister to nanny for Aurora in the interim, and she adjusted her work schedule—going in at 7:30 every morning—so she could be home in the early afternoon.

Teresa hoped that things would be easier once Aurora was in full-time childcare, but the supportive work community she'd built before getting pregnant was suddenly more hostile when she went back to work. After maternity leave, for example, Teresa blocked off three forty-five-minute slots a day on her public calendar, labeling them as "Teresa's pumping time." As one of the few women leaders in a male-dominated organization, Teresa thought it was important to normalize breastfeeding and new motherhood rather than do what she called "coding the language," such as by marking the times as private appointments instead. Her colleagues were less than receptive, including older female colleagues who had children but had relied on formula. When Teresa told one woman that she needed to end a meeting early to pump, the woman responded derisively, "Yeah, but you're choosing that."

Comments like those frustrated Teresa. "I can't just skip it," Teresa insisted, "because: A) the baby will run out of milk, and B) I will physically have discomfort and potentially can get like clogged ducts and infections from that decision. So, it's not as easy as just saying like, 'Oh, I'll just skip it today.' Which is I think what people think."*[28] Teresa gave up pumping at work when Aurora was six months old. At that point, Teresa got the sense that even the colleagues who had initially defended her pumping time would no longer be on board.

Management also made things difficult. Before she had Aurora, Teresa had started a women's group, in part to persuade the company to provide designated parking spaces for pregnant workers and rooms—other than the bathrooms—to use for lactation at work. After many months of meetings

---

* Mastitis, an infection of the milk ducts that can result from disruptions in a lactating parent's feeding schedule, affects approximately one in four postpartum parents. In our interviews with postpartum mothers, my team and I found that physical problems like mastitis and painful engorgement were among the most common reasons why mothers stopped breastfeeding sooner than they planned.

and emails, Chescom still hadn't budged on the parking spaces but did provide space for lactation rooms. Those rooms, however, didn't have sinks that lactating workers could use for washing pump parts when they were done, meaning that Teresa had to keep negotiating with Chescom's higher-ups.[*][29]

Around the same time, Teresa got word that her boss was being promoted, creating a chance for Teresa to move up into his job, but she decided not to apply. "A year ago," she noted, "hands down, absolutely I would have applied. Like, if you would have asked me 'What's your goal?' I would say my goal is to get his job. But then it's like—at what cost? Life is short and I don't want to be one of those absentee parents." Another woman at her office—a mother of four who is ten years Teresa's senior—warned her against taking the job, recommending that she focus on her family in her thirties and her career in her forties and fifties, once her children wouldn't need her so much. Teresa acknowledged that her boss was also a parent. Yet she recognized that, for very gendered reasons, the demands of parenthood were different for him. "He also has three kids," Teresa explained, "but his wife is a stay-at-home mom, so he has a slightly different support situation."

Teresa, by contrast, not only has a full-time employed husband but also, like Virginia and many other primary breadwinner wives, tries to do at least half of the housework and childcare, and sometimes more. Teresa, for example, does all the cooking and most of the cleaning, while Cole does the dishes and mows the lawn, unless he has to work or doesn't get around to it, leaving Teresa to do his chores instead. Childcare also falls more heavily on Teresa, despite her efforts to negotiate for equal roles. Take bedtime: Cole will change Aurora into her pajamas, but Teresa is the one who reads Aurora books until she falls asleep. So even though Teresa and Cole have a similar number of bedtime responsibilities, Teresa typically spends more time with Aurora every night than Cole does.[30]

Like Jocelyn and Lillian and many of the other employed women my team and I interviewed, Teresa also sacrificed her own opportunities for advancement so her husband could try to get ahead in his career. Cole was

---

* In Indiana, where Teresa works, the law requires that employers with more than twenty-five employees "provide a private location, other than a toilet stall, where an employee can express the employee's breast milk in private and, if possible, to provide a refrigerator for storing breast milk that has been expressed." The law does not stipulate that the lactation space must have a sink.

miserable working at Chescom—he took the job only because it paid better than his other options—and Teresa explained that it didn't feel right for her to apply for a promotion "with Cole being unhappy and working long hours." Teresa also acknowledged the judgment Cole got, including from his own parents, for not being the primary breadwinner, noting, "I think it's hard for him as the man." So when Cole floated the idea of running for a local government position, Teresa not only encouraged him to go for it but also volunteered to run his campaign. "Multiple days a week," Teresa explained, "he needs to go knocking on doors and talking to voters, and the baby and I come with him as much as we can."[31]

In the end, Cole lost the election, which contributed to a bout of depression and anxiety that further limited Cole's contributions at home. At first, Cole tried to cope with the loss with exercise—spending hours after work and on the weekends going for long bicycle rides and leaving Aurora with Teresa at home. Eventually, however, all that physical exertion caught up with Cole. "I overtrained," he explained, "and my body shut down, and then I had nowhere for all of this stress and anxiety to go, and I just broke down." Unable to exercise, Cole sank into a deep depression and had to turn to therapy and medication to gradually find a way through.

Cole's mental health struggles and the onset of the Covid-19 pandemic led Teresa to pass up another opportunity for promotion at work, even though it was heavily hinted to her that she would get the role. Teresa explained, "I feel like I give enough to the company, and I don't want to give more because that means I'll be sacrificing how much I can give to my family." Yet it was hard to say no. With a dry laugh, Teresa added that she probably would have applied if she were a man.

———

The tech revolution coincided with the great risk shift and offered the engineers of our DIY society the perfect illustration of their up-by-your-own-bootstraps promise of prosperity. By 1980, tech companies were growing so fast that they were desperate for workers, willing to hire anyone who had programming skills regardless of whether they had a college education, and willing to train anyone who was willing to learn. That year, *The New York*

Times published an article telling the story of two IBM employees who had worked their way up the ranks to steady high-paying jobs as engineers. Neither had obtained a bachelor's degree. Instead, they both went to community college for two-year degrees, got entry-level jobs as trainees, and got regular on-the-job instruction that helped them move up from there. The article notes that one of the employees, Patricia Eyrich, "thought of becoming a school-teacher, but the job opportunities appeared slim." With computing, by contrast, the article points to "a serious shortage of computer-trained personnel" and a need for employees with a wide range of technical capabilities, "from those with basic mathematical training to heads of departments holding master of science or master of business administration degrees." "Because of the manpower shortage," the author promises, "salaries should continue to be good." As if to prove that point, the article ran alongside a half page of ads for jobs in engineering, business, and financial risk management, offering salaries of up to $300,000 a year.[32]

All those zeroes made tech seem like a sure bet for future success. Around that time, for example, my dad was in high school in West Baltimore, and a guidance counselor encouraged him to sign up for community college classes in computer programming because his public high school had run out of math classes for him to take. In 1989, economist Estelle James and her colleagues offered similar advice to parents, saying, "[W]hile sending your child to Harvard appears to be a good investment, sending him to your local state university to major in Engineering, to take lots of math, and preferably to attain a high GPA, is an even better private investment." Two decades later, President Barack Obama established the $4.35 billion Race to the Top competition, following the same logic to give more money to states that outlined the strongest plans for improving education in STEM.[33]

Today, salaries in high-tech fields remain higher than in many other parts of the US economy. Software engineers, for example, have a median salary of $109,000 a year—more than double the $48,000 median wage for mental health counselors like Lillian, despite the fact that only the latter requires a college degree.* Meanwhile, even the lower-level workers in high-tech

---

* According to the US Bureau of Labor Statistics, the typical entry-level education for computer hardware engineers, software developers, and mental health counselors is a four-year-college

sectors—the janitors and the factory machine operators, for example—earn more than their counterparts in other fields.[34]

Given these gaps, the message to young people is often "If you want to make real money, pursue a career in STEM." But STEM isn't the guarantee it might seem to be. Women in STEM jobs, for example, not only make less than men in similar roles but also find themselves subject to frequent hostility and abuse. Recall how Holly had to fight to get a full-time position in tech after giving birth. And recall how Teresa had to fight to get her biotech company employer to put basic pregnancy and breastfeeding protections in place. Those fights reflect the fact that STEM fields remain heavily male-dominated, despite efforts by organizations like Stemettes, Girls Inc., and Girls Who Code, which have sprung up since the 1990s to increase representation of women in business, engineering, and tech.[35]

That male dominance makes things difficult for women in part because it reinforces the invisibility of care. Given how high incomes tend to excuse men from domestic responsibilities, employers in male-dominated industries can get away with treating their workers (or at least most of their workers) as if their only obligation is to the job that pays their bills. That presumed lack of obligations increases the stigma that workers face when they take time off for parental leave or if they work from home or cut back their hours to care for an aging parent or a sick child. That's why men are less likely than women to take the parental leave to which they're entitled, and why most dads who do take time off take less than ten days. This choice also sets a precedent. It reinforces the idea that mothers are the default parents and sets them up to do more of the parenting long term.*[36]

Now, women could also shirk caregiving obligations the way men do to devote more to their jobs. Yet research shows that women face judgment for not putting family first, including from other women, as Teresa did with her colleagues at work. Surveys show that Americans perceive mothers—but

---

(bachelor's) degree, though employers in all these industries typically prefer to hire employees with advanced (master's) degrees.

* We know that the more involved dads are in the first six weeks, the more involved they tend to be over the rest of a child's life. Although these patterns may be correlational, qualitative research suggests that fathers' early involvement (or lack thereof) may shape parenting dynamics in lasting ways.

not fathers—as worse parents simply for working for pay if they could afford to stay home full-time. And mothers are viewed even more unfavorably if they're working full-time in male-dominated industries and if they're described as "successful" in their jobs.*[37]

Considering these judgments, women like Teresa—those employed in high-status male-dominated fields—often decide to either abandon any plans of having children or pump the brakes career-wise to catch up with caregiving obligations at home. Teresa, for example, said she might consider leaving her job for a part-time position as a yoga instructor if she and Cole didn't have all those loans to pay. And Teresa is far from alone in that kind of dreaming. Among college STEM majors, for example, women are twice as likely as men to say they're considering leaving STEM for another career. Meanwhile, the women who do persist in science tend to make sacrifices either at work or at home. In a study of midcareer science professors, only 50 percent of the women had children at home, compared to 70 percent of the men. And among science professors who had children within five years of completing their PhDs, only 53 percent of the women got tenure, compared to 77 percent of the men.[38]

These patterns then become self-reinforcing because higher-ups in tech industries use them to justify underinvesting in women in STEM. Sociologist Natasha Quadlin conducted an audit study of US employers using a set of fake résumés for recent college grads. These résumés were designed to be extremely similar, apart from three key factors—the gender of the student, their major, and their college grades. Quadlin then submitted these résumés as part of applications for more than two thousand entry-level jobs. What

---

* To arrive at these findings, Professors Tyler Okimoto and Madeline Heilman conducted surveys of hundreds of people across the US. They presented participants with one of a set of short stories describing either a mother or father of two young kids. The researchers varied certain parts of the story—like whether the parent was working for pay full-time, whether they were working in a male-typed (e.g., financial advisor) or female-typed (e.g., employee assistance counselor) occupation, whether they were "successful" in their job, and whether their partner earned enough that they could afford to stay home. The researchers then asked participants to rate whether they thought the parent in the story they read was a good parent or not. Comparing participants' responses across these different stories, they found that mothers are perceived as less effective parents when they're working for pay full-time, particularly in male-dominated fields, when they're "successful" in their jobs, and when they're working for pay by choice rather than out of economic necessity.

she found was disheartening. High-achieving men were nearly twice as likely as high-achieving women to get invited for an interview, and for STEM majors, the differences were even larger than that. In those cases, high-achieving men were three times as likely as women to get invited to interview for the job. Quadlin then surveyed the hiring managers for those positions, and what she found was that hiring managers dismissed the résumés of high-achieving women because they perceived those women as "less likeable" than high-achieving men. If, in turn, a woman with a STEM degree does manage to find a position, research shows that because of persistent sexism, the gap between her income and that of her male counterparts will likely get larger the higher up the career ladder she climbs.*[39]

Now, my point here is not to say that women shouldn't get married or go to college or pursue degrees and careers in male-dominated fields. Rather, my point is that these "good choices" won't necessarily save women from precarity or from being forced to stand in for the social safety net. The engineers and profiteers have designed our DIY society to force women to be the ones who hold it together, regardless of the choices they make. And the "good choices" rhetoric is merely a diversion—a way to justify not building a real social safety net by creating the perception that women don't need or deserve support.

To that end, and as we'll see in our next three chapters, the engineers and profiteers have constructed a whole set of myths to lure us into believing that we can get by without a net. These myths pit us against each other. And they guilt and gaslight women into either accepting the risk that's been dumped on them or dumping it further downstream.

---

* Research by Hadas Mandel and Assaf Rotman shows that "women receive lower rewards to their higher education across the entire wage distribution, and this gender gap increases at the very top education premiums—the top quarter, and even more so, the top decile."

Chapter 5

THE MERITOCRACY MYTH

mericans love a good rags-to-riches story, but we've never really liked the poor. In 1766, ten years before signing the Declaration of Independence, Benjamin Franklin wrote, "The best way of doing good to the poor is not making them easy in poverty, but leading or driving them out of it." This model might seem benevolent, but it isn't. Instead, Franklin, who grew up the son of a poor candlemaker but retired wealthy at age forty-two, is implying that people are poor either because they don't know how to do any better or because they're too lazy to try. And so, Franklin's model "solves" poverty not with government handouts but with punishment, compulsory moral education, and forced work.[1]

How do you go from humble beginnings to that kind of callousness toward poor people? By believing the meritocracy myth—a myth that treats success as the product of the kinds of "good choices" that we talked about in chapter 4. Franklin himself helped write this myth in his *Poor Richard's Almanac* and his 1758 essay *The Way to Wealth*. Under the guise of Poor Richard, Franklin presented himself as a kind Pied Piper for people in poverty, offering them—in exchange for the price of his publications—maxims to follow, like "God helps them that help themselves," "A penny saved is a penny earned," and "Early to bed, and early to rise, makes a man healthy, wealthy and wise."[2]

These proverbs and the thinking behind them have plagued us for generations. They have wormed their way into the minds of the American people and, as we'll see in this chapter, undermined support for the social safety net, even among people who, without the meager net we have, would likely be poor themselves.

PRECARITY IS THE COST FOR MORAL SUPERIORITY

Take April, who opposes all efforts to expand or strengthen the social safety net and insists that faith, hard work, and good discipline are the surefire route to prosperity, despite relying on programs like Medicaid and EITC herself.

April grew up in an upper-middle-class white family. Both her parents went to college and worked full-time in healthcare. They earned enough to send April to childcare full-time when she was little, and enough that they were able to help her get a four-year degree at a public university without having to take on any debt. Church wasn't a big part of April's early life, but in college, she joined a student group for evangelical Christians, which is where she met her now-husband, Mateo, who is Latino.

After finishing his degree, Mateo went on to seminary and became an assistant pastor at their church. While Mateo was still in seminary, April supported them both by working full-time for a religious charity organization that paid her $30,000 a year. The organization's mission was to "strengthen" families, which included helping families who were at risk of having their children removed or whose children had already been placed in foster care. One of April's responsibilities was to provide temporary childcare for children in low-income families, many of them low-income Black or Latino families, while their mothers were dealing with court cases or social service agencies or in the hospital giving birth.

That role shaped April's beliefs about the link between parenting, behavior problems, and children's chances in life. Reflecting on her work years later, April explained, "There's some [parents] who don't believe in any discipline at all, who think their child should just make all of the decisions. Then there's some [parents] who will just do whatever works. And oftentimes it's laziness." April postulated that kids raised without "discipline" would suffer in life because they would never learn "to do what's right."

By "discipline," April means physical discipline. April told me, "The Bible says, 'Spare the rod and hate your child.'" From that message, April took that spanking is good for children, telling me, "The happiest kids I know have been disciplined well."

That belief in the importance of physical discipline led April to quit her job and stay home full-time after giving birth to her son, Diego. As Diego's mother, April saw it as her responsibility to raise him as a "young Christian man" and "teach him how to obey with a happy heart, right away, no excuses." April also stressed that her disciplinary responsibility as a mother would be incompatible with full-time employment, cautioning, "The discipline route is hard and long." When Diego was six months old, for example, April decided that rather than babyproof the house, she would "houseproof our baby." If Diego tried to play with an electrical outlet, April would flick his hand to teach him not to touch the outlet. "And then," she explained, "I tell him I love him, it's okay; now, let's try again. And he learns—'Okay, if I don't obey there are consequences. If I obey, there are blessings.'"

April would repeat this flick-explain-reassure sequence as many times as it took for Diego to absorb the message. April said, "That can be like days of me teaching him, 'Don't touch the outlet. Don't touch the outlet.' But that means every time we go somewhere, he won't be touching the outlets after spending the hard work of the three days, or however long it takes to teach him you don't play with outlets." She acknowledged that this approach was time-consuming and emotionally taxing. But April didn't have sympathy for parents who did otherwise, saying, "I think it's more of a lazy parenting move to say, 'Oh, I'm not gonna put the hard work in to teach my child.'"

Putting in that work meant that April and Diego had to make ends meet on his salary as an assistant pastor—which was only $30,000 a year. Based on that income, April was able to enroll the family in Medicaid and claim the EITC and child tax credits. April's family also could have qualified for food stamps, but April didn't apply. Money was tight, though it helped that neither April nor Mateo had student loans, since their families paid for college. And it helped that they only had to make about $600 in mortgage payments each month, rather than paying rent, because their families had given them the down payment on a house.

Things did get more challenging financially in 2020. Pandemic restrictions on large gatherings led their church—which was also Mateo's employer—to see a dip in donations. So Mateo didn't get the raise he'd been promised, and he wasn't sure whether he would continue being paid in full and on time. Given that uncertainty, April tried to scrimp and save as much as possible. Sometimes that meant she would eat only Diego's leftovers for her own breakfast or lunch, particularly in 2021 when food prices rose sharply.

Despite that hardship, April was quick to assert a moral boundary between her family and other families whom she saw as truly poor, insisting that her family's faith and good choices would see them through. "I know a lot of things are going up right now in price and there's inflation," April explained in 2021, adding, "but thankfully thus far we've been able to be pretty frugal and to feel like there's not really anything that we want that we don't have." Drawing on stereotypes of so-called welfare queens, April also took aim at other low-income mothers—implying that if they were struggling financially, it was probably because they were making poor financial choices, like spending money on manicures or hiring babysitters so they could have time for themselves. "I'd never do those things," April insisted. "I'm not often spending a lot of time by myself, but I feel like I have everything I could ever need. I feel lacking in no area of my life. I mean, I shower every day and I have plenty of food."[3]

Confident in her family's good choices, April also insisted that her family could have gotten by without the Covid pandemic relief checks that the government sent in 2020 and 2021. "We can still pay all of our bills," she maintained. "I really felt we didn't need the stimulus package. We weren't eagerly awaiting that. We're used to living off of one relatively meager salary."

April applied those same expectations to other people, believing that if they just had as much faith and made the same good choices she did, they would also be able to make ends meet in challenging times. Consider April's responses to a series of survey questions that I posed to her and to other parents I interviewed as part of an online survey fielded in November 2021. Each question asked participants to choose which of two statements better matches their views. April's choice in each pair is italicized below.

Question 1:
- *Most people who want to get ahead can make it if they're willing to work hard*
- Hard work and determination are no guarantee of success for most people

Question 2:

- *People who are rich have worked harder than most other people*
- People who are rich have had more advantages in life than most people

Question 3:

- *People who are poor have not worked as hard as most other people*
- People who are poor have faced more obstacles in life than most people

Question 4:

- *Poor people today have it easy because they can get government benefits without doing anything in return*
- Poor people have hard lives because government benefits don't go far enough to help them live decently

Each time, April selected the statement consistent with the meritocracy myth—the one suggesting that "good choices" are the key to success and that those who don't make "good choices" don't deserve sympathy or support.

In that same survey, April also expressed opposition to every effort I suggested for strengthening the social safety net—from universal, affordable childcare, to free universal healthcare, to free public college tuition, to guaranteed paid sick leave and family leave, to raising the minimum wage.*

April's views may seem surprising, given that without our current, though meager, social safety net, her family could easily fall below the pov-

---

* These views can be seen in April's responses to a series of survey questions I posed in that same survey in November 2021. In these questions, I described a set of policy changes the US could make and asked whether participants would support those policy changes or oppose them. April, in turn, opposed all of the following: 1) a single national childcare program, run by the government, that uses tax dollars to provide free or very low-cost public childcare (less than $40 per month per child) for all families with children in the US; 2) a single national health insurance system, run by the government, that uses tax dollars to provide free healthcare to all people in the US; 3) a national paid family leave program guaranteeing mothers six months of full-salary paid leave following the birth or adoption of a child; 4) a national paid family leave program guaranteeing fathers and gender nonbinary parents six months of full-salary paid leave following the birth or adoption of a child; 5) a national paid leave program guaranteeing all workers six weeks of full-salary paid time off each year; 6) raising the federal minimum wage to $15 an hour; and 7) using tax dollars to make public college and university tuition free for all US students.

erty line. Without Medicaid, April and Mateo would likely be spending $500 a month or more for health insurance bought through the Affordable Care Act's health insurance marketplace, like Mark and Erin did. Without federally subsidized home mortgages (or the down payment money they got from their parents), April and Mateo could easily be spending $2,000 a month for rent on a two-bedroom apartment in their neighborhood. Without EITC and child tax credits, they might struggle to even make their mortgage payments every month. And without taxpayer-subsidized public education, April's and Mateo's parents might not have been able to cover the full cost of their college tuition, which likely would have left them stuck with monthly payments to make on student loan debt.

April's views, however, are shared by many and in some cases most Americans. And they're a reflection of the myths we've been sold.

SELLING THE MERITOCRACY MYTH

To see what I mean here, let's go back to Benjamin Franklin's *The Way to Wealth*. Franklin's writings inspired the mid-nineteenth-century New Thought Movement, which preached that people can think their way to health and prosperity. Take New Thought founder Phineas Quimby, who wrote in 1861 that "man's happiness or misery depends on himself" and who argued, channeling Franklin, that what the poor and the sick need is wisdom, not charity, to escape their plight in life. Or take Quimby's student Mary Baker Eddy, who went on to found Christian Science, and who wrote in 1875 that "health is not a condition of matter, but of Mind." As Kate Bowler explains in her book *Blessed*, proponents of New Thought believed if you think positive thoughts, your life will get better; if you think negative thoughts, your life will get worse; and if you think positive thoughts but bad things happen anyway, you probably weren't thinking positively enough.[4]

That New Thought Movement laid the groundwork for the "prosperity gospel," a set of beliefs that emerged in the early twentieth century but are still held today by most Christians, particularly evangelical Christians like April and Mateo, and even some non-Christians in the US. The prosperity gospel teaches that God rewards those who are faithful and hardworking not only with salvation after death but also with salvation on earth in the form of wealth and good health.[5]

Consider, for example, how evangelical megachurch pastor and bestselling author Joel Osteen reassures his readers:

> Quit telling yourself, "This is all I'll ever have. Granddaddy was broke. Momma and Daddy didn't have anything. My dog is on welfare. My cat is homeless." Let all of that go and have an abundant mentality. "This is not where I'm staying. I am blessed. I am prosperous. I am headed to overflow, to the land of More Than Enough."[6]

Osteen is promising here that if people just keep having faith and "doing the right thing," God will lift them from hardship to prosperity. Taking these ideas a step further, evangelical churches often teach that Christians are obligated both to pursue prosperity and to evangelize—to help other people do the same.[7]

Franklin and New Thought also laid the groundwork for generations of secular self-help writers, including Norman Vincent Peale, whose 1952 self-help book *The Power of Positive Thinking* spent 98 weeks as number one on the *New York Times* bestseller list, remained on the list for 186 weeks, and has sold more than five million copies through multiple rereleases over time. Although Peale himself was a Christian minister like Osteen, his book had a strong secular appeal, including in the high-powered corporate world and with moderate and right-wing politicians. Peale had close relationships with Presidents Richard Nixon, Ronald Reagan, and Donald Trump. Trump has even cited *The Power of Positive Thinking* as his primary spiritual guide.[8]

The book's central message is "Change your thoughts and change your world." Peale goes on to write that although people may experience hardships or tragedies, "By methods I shall outline, obstacles are simply not permitted to destroy your happiness and well-being. You need be defeated only if you are willing to be. This book teaches you how to 'will' not to be."[9]

Echoes of Peale's philosophy can be seen today in any self-help book that treats the right mindset as the first step to success. That includes Rhonda Byrne's bestselling book *The Secret*, which was originally published in 2006. The book admonishes readers to "remember that your thoughts are the primary cause of everything" and promises, based on the so-called laws of attraction, that if readers just think hard enough about wealth, health, and happiness, they can attract everything they desire.[10]

Whether they come in a more religious or secular flavor, self-help books and motivational speakers are often selling versions of the myth of meritocracy. They offer messages like "Expect great things and great things will come" and "Shoot for the moon. Even if you miss, you'll land among the stars" (both quotes from Peale). And they create the perception that good people will be rewarded and that people who are "blessed" with health, wealth, or happiness must have done something to be deserving of their rewards.[11]

The truth is much more complicated. As we saw in chapter 4, neither the right mindset nor the right choices will guarantee rewards in a DIY society. Certainly, successful people may—and often do—work hard, but hard work doesn't automatically result in success.* Consider, for example, the data on paid work. As of 2022, the highest-paid workers in the US economy worked only four more hours a week, on average, than the lowest-paid workers, and both groups averaged more than a full 44 week (46.6 and 42.2 hours per week). That's despite the fact that the lowest-wage jobs in our economy are often part-time jobs that cap workers' hours—caps that allow employers to get around government rules requiring employers to offer full-time workers benefits like health insurance and family leave. As we saw with Akari, those caps often force workers to work multiple jobs to make ends meet. Which is why, as of 2023, 10 percent of the US workforce had multiple jobs; why women, especially unmarried moms of young children, are the group most likely to supplement their primary job with a second part-time position or gig work; and why it's disheartening to see research results like those from sociologists Christin Munsch and her colleagues, who found that employers don't reward women for working long hours in the same way they do for men.[12]

Just as hard work doesn't guarantee rewards, people can also be punished

---

* In the US, the average full-time worker now works at least forty-seven hours a week, and 26 percent of US workers work fifty hours a week or more. These trends are driven, in part, by the decline in real wages, which has forced lower-income workers like Akari to take on multiple jobs. They are also driven, in part, by pressures toward overwork in elite professional jobs, and by new technologies like email, cell phones, and widespread internet access that allow workers to be constantly on call.

just for being who they are. Consider an audit study conducted by sociologist Devah Pager in which she hired actors—young Black and white men—gave them nearly identical résumés, and sent them out to submit those résumés with applications for a range of entry-level jobs. She found that young Black men had only a 14 percent chance of getting called back for an interview, compared to a 34 percent chance for young white men. The disparity continues the further into the process applicants get, such that young Black men who do get interviews are still far less likely than white candidates with similar résumés to ultimately get selected for entry-level jobs.[13]

BUYING THE MERITOCRACY MYTH

Despite the evidence disproving the meritocracy myth, Americans continue to believe. More than 70 percent of US adults believe that hard work alone—not luck or help from other people—determines who gets ahead in our society, and more than 90 percent believe that hard work plays at least some role.* That's far higher than in many other countries, like France, where only about 50 percent of people believe that hard work plays any role in who gets ahead.[14]

These beliefs also span political, religious, generational, and racial divides. The Pew Research Center, for example, found that belief in the meritocracy myth is particularly common among two seemingly disparate groups of Americans. The first is Republicans, including both fiscal conservatives and evangelical Christians.† The second is a group Pew calls the "faith and family left." This group, which tends to vote Democrat, is much younger and more racially diverse than the Republicans, but is also more religious than others on the left.‡ Despite their differences, these groups share a belief

---

* Since the 1970s, the General Social Survey has included the question: "Some people say that people get ahead by their own hard work; others say that lucky breaks or help from other people are more important. Which do you think is most important?" Response options include "hard work," "luck and help," or "both equally."

† Among fiscal conservatives, 88 percent believe in the meritocracy myth, and the same is true of 81 percent of evangelical Christians.

‡ Not surprisingly, research using these same survey questions shows that belief in the meritocracy myth doesn't break down neatly along political or demographic lines. Although these beliefs are disproportionately common among Republicans like April (85 percent), more than half of Demo-

that—whether through prayer or simply positive thinking—people can will their way to success.[15]

What makes the meritocracy myth appealing to so many Americans? One reason is that precarity and inequality make it psychologically soothing to believe in a definite and self-determined path to success.[16]

We like to think of ourselves as the land of opportunity, but the US makes upward mobility far more difficult than most people realize and makes downward mobility a serious risk. Given those constraints, it would be easy for Americans to feel hopeless, and many already do. Like an emergency valve, the myth of meritocracy releases that hopelessness. It offers reassurance to the downtrodden that if they just keep working hard and maintaining the right mindset, they can overcome whatever obstacles they encounter. And it offers the convenience of not having to wait around for whatever support that others might be willing (or unwilling) to provide. In a study of college students, for example, psychologists Jacob Shane and Jutta Heckhausen found that, regardless of their own backgrounds, students who expressed stronger beliefs in the meritocracy myth tended to have higher aspirations for themselves and took more short-term steps to try to achieve their goals than did students who attributed success to luck. Put simply, attributing success to hard work prompts us to stay more focused in pursuing future goals.[17]

The meritocracy myth, however, is like cigarettes. It offers comfort in the short term, but its residue builds up in the body, leaving scars that are difficult if not impossible to undo. Consider the research on African Americans from low-income backgrounds, which shows that those among them who believe the myth of meritocracy have worse health outcomes (like hypertension) over time. That's because meritocratic beliefs promote "John Henryism"—a term inspired by the story of a man who collapsed after trying (and ultimately failing) to win a race against a machine. As public health scholars Naa Oyo A. Kwate and Ilan H. Meyer explain, meritocratic thinking encourages "single-minded determination" even in the face of insurmountable obstacles

---

crats (53 percent) also hold them. Similarly, and while white people like April are the most likely to share these attitudes (67 percent), the majority of Black (54 percent) and Latino (63 percent) adults in the US adopt a similar stance.

and leads people to respond to their resulting failures with demoralization and self-blame.[18]

At the other end of the social and economic spectrum, meritocracy messages operate less like cigarettes and more like gold stars, reassuring people who aren't struggling (or are struggling less than others) that they are good and worthy—and that they shouldn't feel ashamed of the advantages they enjoy.* In a highly unequal society like the US, almost everyone is better off than someone else. As we saw with Holly, those gaps can easily lead people higher up on the ladder to feel guilt for their privilege and thus to feel a sense of obligation to reach back and help others to climb. But the meritocracy myth erases that sense of guilt and obligation by making inequality seem justified. Psychologists Shannon McCoy and Brenda Major found, for example, that exposing people to subtle meritocratic messages—like *The Little Engine That Could*—made them more inclined to accept social inequalities, even when those inequalities negatively impact people like them.[19]

In a similar way, the meritocracy myth also boosts people's self-confidence by giving almost all of us other people we can feel superior to. While looking down the ladder could lead to feelings of guilt, the meritocracy myth tells us instead to be proud of how high up we are, regardless of how much of that height we have actually climbed. Those feelings of superiority are a powerful drug. Take research by sociologists Arthur Alderson and Tally Katz-Gerro, who find that in countries where belief in meritocracy is widespread, people who perceive themselves as better off than others around them are happier and more satisfied, regardless of the absolute level of resources or opportunities they have in their lives. The benefits of looking down also get bigger as gaps between the ladder's rungs get wider, meaning that the more unequal the society we live in, the more substantial the psychological payoff of comparing ourselves to those further down.[20]

Messages like Osteen's, Byrne's, and Peale's encourage these kinds of down-the-ladder comparisons by teaching believers not to dwell on the challenges they're facing and rather to focus on the blessings they have. Re-

---

* Research shows that even when the rich are willing to blame "bad luck" for other people's lack of success, they are rarely willing to concede that luck played a role in the success that they personally have experienced, seeing their own success as the product of merit instead.

call that even as April's family didn't have enough to eat, April didn't want to dwell on the hardship her family was facing. Instead, she insisted that they had what they needed and that their faith and frugality would see them through.

WHAT THE MERITOCRACY MYTH COSTS THE SOCIAL SAFETY NET

Counting your blessings and staying positive might not seem problematic. However, if you believe that *you* can achieve health and wealth and happiness through prayer and positivity, then it's easy to assume that others should be able to do the same. In essence, the meritocracy myth encourages its believers to assume that people who are struggling simply haven't tried hard enough.* It suggests that if people like Patricia just worked harder and changed their attitude, they wouldn't need government support.

As we saw with April, those beliefs make it easy to judge those who are struggling. Recall how April equated poverty with laziness and morality, assuming that the bad behavior she saw in the low-income kids she worked with was the product of their parents' laziness in not disciplining them at home.† Those assumptions are common among many groups of Americans, and they undermine the empathy we might feel toward those whose plights are just a little bit worse than our own. Studies have shown, for example, that roughly half of Americans think that most people in poverty aren't doing enough to improve their lives. These beliefs are common across the income spectrum, including among people who are living just below or just above the poverty line.‡ In fact, people like April who are living just above

---

* Surveys show that two-thirds of US adults (65 percent) believe that most people can get ahead if they're willing to work hard.

† Consider, for example, the advice Joel Osteen gives to parents. He writes in his book *You Are Stronger Than You Think*, "Your child may be off course, making bad choices. It looks permanent, but that is not his destiny. . . . You can stand in the gap for your children. Yes, they make their own decisions, but as parents, you have a God-given authority. . . . God hears your prayers. He sees your faithfulness. He sees you believing when you don't see things changing, thanking Him when you could be complaining. Your time is coming."

‡ Among people living below the poverty line, 39 percent agree that people in poverty aren't working hard enough, as do 44 percent of those living just above the poverty line. As of 2023, the

the poverty line—and thus just beyond the eligibility threshold for many government programs—are particularly likely to be critical of people on welfare, buying into the stereotype that they just don't want to work.[21]

These beliefs also undermine efforts to strengthen the social safety net and make its protections universal—by raising questions about the deservingness of people who are struggling, and by channeling that skepticism into support for punitive policies that force people to prove they're worthy of government support. Universal programs are built on the notion that *everyone* is deserving of things like high-quality healthcare, childcare, eldercare, and education, as well as adequate income, reasonable work hours, paid time off, and a comfortable retirement. If you believe that some people are simply lazy—that they will mooch off others without giving back what they can— then it's easy to oppose a more universal safety net.

The alternative, then, becomes the kind of restrictive net we currently have: a net that uses complex and costly barriers to test whether applicants can "prove" they're worthy of support. In the US today, safety net programs are gated by eligibility criteria so opaque that many people—as we saw with Lillian—don't even realize they qualify. These eligibility criteria include work requirements that force people like Akari and Brooke to take whatever job they can get; endless forms and appointments that suck up hours of time and come with the risk of embarrassment; and even personally invasive procedures like weigh-ins, which are required for babies receiving WIC benefits, and drug tests, which some states require for recipients of programs like welfare.[22]

An absence of empathy also pushes us toward a more punitive social safety net—one that disciplines people for needing government support. Take, for example, the paternalism of the US food stamp program. We could give people a reasonable amount of money and let them use it as they see fit. Instead, we set the benefit amount so low that mothers on food stamps often end up skipping meals or cutting their own portions so their kids can eat. And we set such strict limits on what can be purchased with food stamps that families not only have to go without the supplies they need—like diapers for Ren or gas for Akari's car—but also without food

federal poverty line, which determines eligibility for many government programs, was $24,860 in annual income for a family of three and $30,000 for a family of four.

they actually enjoy—like Patricia's family being forced to eat canned meat instead of fresh.[23]

Anyone with empathy would balk at the horrors of this system. But the meritocracy myth lures us to shrug and look the other way. Consider some data from the Pew Research Center's American Trends Panel, which includes more than twelve thousand English- and Spanish-speaking adults in the US.* Analyzing these data, I found that belief in the meritocracy myth is closely correlated with derision toward people in poverty and with opposition to efforts to expand and strengthen the social safety net.†

In an analogous way, the meritocracy myth also justifies our use of the prison-industrial complex to punish those who fall through the holes in the net. Before the 1800s, incarceration was rare in the US. Inspired by the Second Great Awakening in American Protestantism, and its distinction between the "deserving poor" (who should be loved in Christ-like fashion) and the "undeserving poor" (who should be punished and then rehabilitated), Protestant Christian activists and secular social reformers—including Benjamin Franklin—argued for a new carceral system. They pushed for the state construction of penitentiaries that would reform the "undeserving" through forced labor, penitence, and prayer.[24]

The earliest of these new penitentiaries were built in the US following the Panic of 1819—the first great depression in the US. As historian Andrew Browning explains, widespread unemployment was the catalyst that governors needed to embrace a new model of imprisonment that forced people convicted of crimes—including crimes of debt or poverty—to work for little or nothing in pay. In the aftermath of the Civil War, Southern policymakers

---

* Wave 59 of the Pew Research Center's American Trends Panel, which I use in the analyses described here, was fielded in January 2020 with a sample of 12,638 English- and Spanish-speaking US adults ages eighteen and up. The data presented are weighted descriptive statistics and are weighted with the variable WEIGHT_59. For the data and documentation, see "American Trends Panel Wave 59," Pew Research Center, 2020, https://www.pewresearch.org/politics/dataset /american-trends-panel-wave-59/.

† Compared to those who don't believe the meritocracy myth, Americans who do believe the myth are nearly three times as likely to agree that "poor people today have it easy because they can get government benefits without doing anything in return." Those who do believe the myth are also roughly twice as likely to oppose policies that would establish a national healthcare program, with similar patterns of opposition toward increasing the value of government welfare benefits and making college tuition free for all.

followed a similar logic in creating the Black Codes—a set of laws used to convict Black people of ridiculous "infractions" like selling produce on the side of the road or quitting a job without permission from their employer. Once they were convicted, and because of loopholes in the Thirteenth Amendment that allowed incarcerated people to be required to perform unpaid labor, Black people could be effectively reenslaved. By creating a literally captive workforce, this early incarceration system generated huge profits for prison owners, for states, and for the companies and plantation owners that contracted with prisons for labor to produce goods like candles and furniture, as well as to build infrastructure like railroad lines.[25]

Our modern system of mass incarceration is similarly racist and exploitative. In 2023, there were nearly two million people incarcerated in US jails and prisons, and they were disproportionately poor and Black.* In addition to doing the work of running prisons, they also do the jobs that no one else wants to do, for pay far below the minimum wage and without any protections against exploitation and abuse. A report from the American Civil Liberties Union describes how incarcerated people

> work as cooks, dishwashers, janitors, groundskeepers, barbers, painters, or plumbers; in laundries, kitchens, factories, and hospitals. They provide vital public services such as repairing roads, fighting wildfires, or clearing debris after hurricanes. They washed hospital laundry and worked in mortuary services at the height of the pandemic. They manufacture products like office furniture, mattresses, license plates, dentures, glasses, traffic signs, athletic equipment, and uniforms. They cultivate and harvest crops, work as welders and carpenters, and work in meat and poultry processing plants.[26]

Meanwhile, even if they eventually get out of prison, the stigma of incarceration follows people in ways that make it difficult to find even minimum

---

* In 2022 and 2023, Black people accounted for 39 percent of the US prison population and 35 percent of those incarcerated in local jails, compared to only about 14 percent of the US population overall. Research also shows that incarcerated people are disproportionately from low-income households, with pre-incarceration incomes more than 40 percent lower than incomes of non-incarcerated people of similar ages.

wage jobs, which increases the chance that they'll end up in prison again. American consumers could protest and refuse to support businesses engaged in this kind of exploitation. Yet we don't, because the meritocracy myth tells us that incarcerated and formerly incarcerated people aren't deserving of sympathy, and because even if we tried, these practices are so ubiquitous they're almost impossible to fully boycott.[27]

HOW MERITOCRACY DELUDES AND DIVIDES US

By offering justification for these types of inequities, the meritocracy myth keeps us divided along lines of class and race. Race as a concept and a system of hierarchical categories was developed by European colonizers to justify exploiting others' lands, lives, and labors for their own financial gain. As sociologists Celeste Watkins-Hayes and Elise Kovalsky explain, one of the most effective ways to justify exploitation is to deny the humanity of the group being exploited, and one of the most effective ways to deny a group's humanity is by constructing them as a separate and inherently lesser race.[28]

In a similar way, the meritocracy myth also deludes us into believing that race and class divisions are deserved. Take, for example, racial differences in incarceration and poverty rates. The evidence is clear that these inequities are the product of generations of racist policies—from slavery and the Black Codes to redlining and Jim Crow and the war on drugs. Yet as political scientist Martin Gilens finds in his research, most Americans overestimate the percentage of US welfare recipients and incarcerated people who are Black.* The Americans who overestimate those numbers are more likely to perceive racial differences in poverty and incarceration as the product of Black people's choices, rather than the disproportionate challenges they face. And the Americans who overestimate those numbers are also more likely to reject the need for penal reform and the need for a stronger social safety net.†[29]

---

* Today, for example, Black people represent about 33 percent of incarcerated people, 30 percent of welfare (TANF) recipients, 26 percent of food stamp recipients, 19 percent of Medicaid recipients, and 15 percent of recipients of free or reduced-price school lunches.

† These patterns don't just hold for attitudes about welfare or incarceration. Rather, research shows that whenever white people believe that a problem—like Covid-19—primarily impacts Black people, they're less likely to say that the government should spend money to help.

Ironically, because policies often have spillover effects, underinvestment in the social safety net hasn't just hurt Black Americans. Rather, as writer Heather McGhee explains in her book *The Sum of Us*, underinvesting in the social safety net also increases the gaps in our economic ladder in ways that make life more difficult for anyone who isn't at the very top. Research shows, for example, that since the 1970s, earnings inequalities between Black and white workers have narrowed at the bottom of the educational distribution— not because the situation for Black workers has improved, but rather because the situation for white workers without college degrees has gotten worse. That deterioration has led to despair and disaffection in poor and working-class white communities and contributed to rising rates of drug overdose, gun violence, intimate partner violence, and suicide. Because of these patterns, death rates among white people ages forty-five to fifty-four have risen faster in the past twenty-five years than among people the same age in other racial groups.[30]

THE BENEFIT OF THE MYTH . . .
FOR BIG BUSINESSES AND BILLIONAIRES

The meritocracy myth justifies these tragedies not only by vilifying the people at the bottom of the economic ladder but by glorifying the people at the top. As a result, most Americans have no problem with billionaires. A 2021 Pew Research Center poll, for example, found that only 29 percent of people think billionaires are bad for the country, and among Republicans, that number was only 14 percent.[31]

That same benevolence also extends to specific billionaires, including Elon Musk. Or at least it did before Musk spent forty-four of his billions flushing Twitter down the drain. A 2022 *New York Times* article described how Elon Musk's "brilliance has spawned the world's most valuable automaker." And a 2022 *Wall Street Journal* article described Musk as "the person Silicon Valley would create if venture-funded engineers figured out how to build humans in a lab: the bold innovator fearlessly disrupting one industry after another with a nerdy verve."[32]

Billionaires like Musk use the myth of meritocracy to paint themselves as worthy of their wealth and the power that wealth provides. Take the ulti-matum Musk gave to Twitter employees when he took over the company—either quit or commit to an "extremely hardcore" work schedule involving "long hours at high intensity." "Going forward," Musk wrote to his employ-ees in an email, "[o]nly exceptional performance will constitute a passing grade."

Billionaires like Musk like to make themselves out to be "hardcore," but they can only put up that front because they can pay someone else to do the soft stuff behind the scenes: Cooking for them. Cleaning for them. Manag-ing their schedule. Caring for their kids. Billionaires like Musk have the money to buy that help a million times over. Yet they use the meritocracy myth to sell the lie that anyone who works as hard as they do can be as rich or even as healthy as they are.* And in that sense, they're not all that differ-ent from Ben Franklin, who shamed poor people for not saving pennies while amassing the equivalent of tens of millions of dollars in today's wealth.[33]

By peddling the meritocracy myth, billionaires also fuel the perception that they shouldn't have to pay for everyone else's social safety net. Consider, for example, the rhetoric that killed President Joe Biden's proposal for a billionaire tax. That bill, which would have increased taxes on roughly 700 of the wealthiest Americans, would have generated up to $250 billion in annual revenue, enough to cover almost all of what the US federal govern-ment currently spends on education every year.† At the time, the Democrats controlled both the executive and legislative branches of the government, so it seemed like the bill would pass. And yet, Senator Joe Manchin, a Demo-crat from West Virginia, refused to vote for it, declaring that he didn't like the idea of "targeting" people who had "contributed to society" and people who "create a lot of jobs and invest a lot of money and give a lot to philan-thropic pursuits." Manchin suggested that "we all pull together and row together" instead.[34]

---

* Take tech billionaire Bryan Johnson, whose anti-aging regimen includes a strict vegan diet, an hour a day of exercise, a regular sleep schedule, blue-light blocking glasses, and injections with the blood of his teenage son, all of which he claims are reducing his biological age.

† The bill would tax people with assets of over $1 billion or incomes more than $100 million a year for three consecutive years.

The thing is, today's billionaires exist because we've permitted them to pull ahead of the rest of us, by slashing the taxes the ultra-wealthy used to pay to fund the social safety net. In the 1960s, the highest earners had to pay a tax rate of 90 percent on every dollar they made over $300,000. Today, the highest earners pay only between 32 and 37 percent on every dollar they make over $329,850 a year. That falling tax rate not only left the government with less money to fund the social safety net but also allowed the number of ultra-wealthy people to rise. Since the 1980s, for example, the number of American billionaires has increased from only 13 to more than 700, with some estimates putting the number as high as 927.[35]

The engineers promised that we'd all benefit from that extra wealth at the top of the ladder, but despite that promise, it never trickled down. Instead, and as we talked about in the introduction, the share of the wealth held by everyone but the richest among us has fallen over time. It has fallen so much that after accounting for inflation, low- and middle-income households in the US today actually have less wealth than they had twenty years ago.[36]

That growing divide reflects, in part, the fact that the wealthiest Americans don't even pay the tax rates they're supposed to. We've given them all kinds of loopholes, to the point where most US billionaires pay a far lower tax rate than the average Joe. Elon Musk, for example, paid $0 in federal income tax in 2018. And in the four years prior, Musk paid only $455 million in total taxes, despite reporting an income of $1.52 billion and despite growing his wealth by $13.9 billion on top of what he already had in the bank. That works out to a true tax rate of only 3.27 percent. That's a higher tax rate than some billionaires pay—like Warren Buffett, who paid only 0.10 percent, or Jeff Bezos, who paid 0.98 percent. But it's far lower than the 14 percent federal income tax rate paid by the median American.[37]

Passing a billionaire tax would make it a whole lot easier for the US to build the kind of universal social safety net that would leave the vast majority better off. Unfortunately, the meritocracy myth undermines our will to try. Instead, many of us look favorably on the rich and powerful, because the myth tells us that if, like April, we just stay positive and keep working as hard as we can (and maybe even harder), we too might be rich someday. And because, even if we're not rich yet, believing the myth allows us to feel superior to anyone who's worse off than we are or who doesn't seem to be trying as hard to get ahead.[38]

The meritocracy myth is not the only tool the engineers and profiteers use to divide and delude us into accepting the DIY society and women's role as a substitute safety net. Rather, as we'll see in the next two chapters, myths about gender and motherhood also serve to justify inequality and exploitation and to prevent us from coming together to demand the kind of social safety net that would better protect us all.

Chapter 6

THE MARS/VENUS MYTH

en Are from Mars, Women Are from Venus. I was about ten years old
when I first saw those words, printed in their stark blue and pink, on
the cover of John Gray's "classic guide to understanding the opposite sex."
The book, originally published in 1992, went on to top the *New York Times*
bestseller list, sold more than ten million copies in its first five years, and
recently experienced a massive resurgence in popularity thanks to a viral
TikTok video sharing advice from the book. That advice boils down to the
idea that we'd be happier (and have fewer divorces—Gray is a couple's therapist) if we went back to a time when women knew their place.[1]

To make this argument, Gray asserts that men and women are fun-
damentally opposite and that relationships between them will only work
when both parties embrace their separate roles. Women, he suggests, "value
love, communication, beauty, and relationships," and are thereby best ful-
filled by nurturing. Men, by contrast, value "success, achievement, and efficiency," which makes them best suited for roles requiring competence and
power.[2]

Gray's arguments may sound scientific, but it's merely a pseudoscience
sheen. Instead, Gray is promoting the Mars/Venus myth, which equates
gender (and sexuality) with biological sex, treats both as a set of binary op-
posites, and asserts—without solid evidence—that biology dictates gendered
skills, temperaments, preferences, and needs. As I'll explain, this myth also
helps to undermine support for expanding and strengthening the social
safety net by justifying men's exploitation of women and by muzzling women
who try to complain.[3]

ACCEPTING THE PERKS OF PATRIARCHY

Consider Dennis and Bethany, a college-educated white married couple with two young kids and a "traditional" breadwinner-homemaker division of roles. Dennis identifies as a moderate political independent, reads *The New York Times* every day, and has progressive views on some things, like being open to the possibility of free college for all. As we'll see, however, there's also an ambivalence to Dennis's attitudes about gender, marriage, and family—an ambivalence that undermines his commitment to egalitarianism and to enacting policies that might make things more equal for him and Bethany at home.

On the one hand, Dennis supports the idea of gender equality. In a survey, for example, I asked Dennis, "Do you think it's generally better for a marriage if the husband earns more money than his wife?" to which he responded that "it's just as good for a marriage if the wife earns as much or more." In that same survey, Dennis also said that he would strongly support "a national paid family leave program guaranteeing mothers six months of full salary paid leave following the birth or adoption of a child" and also that he would strongly support a similar policy guaranteeing six months of paid family leave for men.

On the other hand, Dennis is wary of the possibility of gender equality going too far. When asked "Do you think children are better off if their mother is home and doesn't hold a job, or are the children just as well off if the mother works for pay?," Dennis chose the option saying children are better off if their mother is home. Dennis also indicated on his survey that he wouldn't support a national program to provide all US families with free or low-cost childcare.* "As a concept," he emphasized in an interview, "I think it's probably a great idea." Yet he was skeptical of whether, in practice, the quality of care would match what his kids were getting from Bethany at home, and he worried that paying for high-quality care for every child would

---

* Dennis was asked the same survey questions as April. In his responses, Dennis indicated that he opposed a national childcare program, a national health insurance system, and raising the federal minimum wage.

load the country with too much debt and put too much of a tax burden on high-income earners like him.

Dennis was also willing to accept very unequal gender arrangements in his own family, so long as he got the upper hand. Early in their marriage, Bethany was working full-time as a social worker, making about $30,000 a year, while Dennis was working full-time in information technology, making about $90,000 a year. When their daughter, Willow, was born in 2015, Bethany continued working for pay full-time in a flex work arrangement. Two or three days a week, Bethany's mom or her female cousin would come over to watch Willow so Bethany could go to work. On the other days, Bethany cared for Willow while working from home. As Willow got older, it got more difficult for Bethany to continue working full-time while also caring for Willow, just as we saw with Holly in chapter 3.

When Willow was about a year old, Bethany got offered an opportunity to move up into a manager role that would have required her to be in the office full-time. Bethany could have taken the promotion and found full-time paid childcare for Willow. Instead, as Wesley did for Jocelyn, Dennis encouraged her to quit her job and stay home, where she took on not only all the childcare but almost all the housework as well. Explaining that decision, Dennis told me, "She was going to make more money . . . but it was going to be more red tape and more work, and she wanted to hang out and take care of our kids and not spend half of her paycheck finding care."

Dennis recognized that a breadwinner-homemaker arrangement might be perceived as regressive, but he had no qualms about their arrangement, saying, "It's funny, because we're not your typical fifties family where we have to fit these roles and whatever. But it's fine because we don't feel that way. It just kind of worked out that way for us." Dennis repeatedly emphasized that Bethany quitting her job was logical, that "it just made sense."

For Dennis, that separate-and-unequal arrangement "made sense" both financially and in terms of the perks it offered him. When I asked if he ever helped with things like taking the kids to the doctor or staying home when they were sick, he told me, "It's just easier if she takes care of all that. Why use time off when I don't have to? I can use that for more fun things. That's part of the perk of her getting to stay home." Dennis acknowledges the "perks" he gets from their arrangement, like getting to save the time he's not at work for "fun things" like going to the gym, watching sports, or taking vacations rather than using it for housework or parenting tasks.

Dennis, meanwhile, also believes that their arrangement has perks for Bethany and even implied that Bethany ought to be grateful that she "gets" to stay home. He told me that Bethany should be grateful that he doesn't help more with household chores because he wouldn't perform them as well or meet what he sees as her too-high standards. And he recalled that when he has tried to do chores like laundry and dishes in the past, Bethany ended up having to redo them, and so now, "I just let her do that." Of course, Dennis could have learned to do laundry and dishes more effectively. Instead, however, and like the men interviewed by sociologist Allison Daminger for her research on gender inequalities in family life, Dennis treated these differences in his and Bethany's skill sets as flukes of personality, saying, "It's just naturally divvied itself out."[4]

In Dennis's opinion, Bethany is unlikely to go back to work full-time, because, in his view, it's good for the whole family to have her at home. "We're lucky enough she doesn't have to. And it allows her to do stuff at home. She's much happier. Everyone is much happier." According to Dennis, Bethany's hair was falling out from the stress of her job as a social worker. And so, Dennis assumed that it would only make sense for Bethany to go back to paid work if she would be making more money than they would have to spend on childcare. He put it bluntly, saying, "She was making dirt," and concluding that if Bethany went back to her old job, it would be "almost a wash by the time you would talk about paying for childcare or whatever."

Bethany's stance on stay-at-home motherhood is more ambivalent than Dennis's. Dennis said children are better off if their mother is home and doesn't hold a job. Bethany, by contrast, said children are just as well-off if their mother is working for pay. Bethany, who identifies as a liberal Democrat, also strongly supported not only guaranteed paid family leave (like Dennis), but also (unlike Dennis) a national program to provide all US families with free or low-cost childcare, free national healthcare, and raising the federal minimum wage—all policies that would give women a more realistic choice between paid work and staying home.

Bethany's reasons for staying home were also different from what Dennis implied. Dennis said that Bethany was unhappy in her job as a social worker and didn't want to have to deal with the increased workload that would come with a promotion, and that she decided to stay home because she wanted to "hang out and take care of our kids and not spend half of her paycheck finding care." Bethany had a different recollection of her decision to leave the workforce. "Both of our moms stayed home with each of us," Bethany explained, "so it was what we knew. And we knew we could make it work [financially]. So we decided to go for it just because, I mean—it's a lot. Parenting and working and then also managing the childcare. To me, it just was harder as Willow got older and could do more. And I wanted to be there with her and see that." Now, Bethany does acknowledge that she wanted to get to see Willow learn and grow, but it was the last of a long set of reasons she listed for staying home. Before that, she talked about how difficult it was to work full-time while caring for an infant and about the pressure she felt to recreate for Willow the kind of stereotypically idyllic childhood that she and Dennis both had had. Note, in turn, that Bethany never mentioned being unhappy with her job as a social worker—only unhappy with how difficult it was to do that job while also being the primary caregiver for Willow at home.

Bethany and Dennis had both grown up with multiple siblings and being at home also made it easier for Bethany to feel as though she could manage adding another child. By the time Bethany gave birth to their son, Oliver, in late 2018, however, the isolation of stay-at-home motherhood was starting to weigh on her, and she found herself craving more adult interaction than she was getting with just Dennis at home. And so, in 2019, she started a very part-time job teaching group fitness classes—a job she was able to take since the kids could attend the free on-site childcare while Bethany was teaching classes at the gym.

Bethany had to fit working for pay around her family life, while for Dennis, it was the other way around. That distinction became even more apparent when Covid-19 hit and sent everyone home. The gym was closed, so Bethany stopped teaching classes, but she also didn't go back to teaching even when the gym reopened in the fall of 2020, because of new restrictions on childcare eligibility, and because Willow was starting kindergarten online. Dennis, meanwhile, could have continued working from home that fall. But he went back to the office in June 2020—as soon as his employer gave him the go-ahead—because it was easier for him to focus on work without the distraction that came from having the kids underfoot at home. Dennis's decision to go back to the office left Bethany in charge of virtual learning, a responsibility that she hated and left her feeling as though she wasn't patient enough. "I want to take that mouse and just point to whatever she wants," Bethany explained, exasperated, "but I know I need to let her learn."

Bethany was grateful when Willow was able to switch to in-person learning, but even that change didn't ease the pressure as much as she hoped. When my team and I talked to Bethany in 2021, when Willow and Oliver were six and three, her schedule involved getting up at least an hour before the kids every morning to do chores or lead workout sessions for friends over Zoom, then get the kids up, get them breakfast, drive Willow to school by 8:45 a.m., then run errands with Oliver, try to get some housework done, get lunch for Oliver, get him to nap for a bit, drive to pick up Willow from school at 3:45 p.m., then make dinner, feed the kids, bathe them, and get them ready for bed. "At that point," Bethany explained, "I'm exhausted, or worn out, and so I sit down until I fall asleep basically, and then start all over again."

Bethany also expressed frustration with how much of the housework and parenting fell to her. She noted with a wry laugh that "it only took a pandemic" for Dennis to "finally figure out how to clean up Oliver's tray after dinner." Once Dennis went back to the office, however, they quickly slipped back into pre-pandemic roles.

Although Dennis is more involved with the kids than Bethany's father and his father ever were, his style of involvement also tends to create more problems for Bethany than it solves. "Like when they're taking a bath," Bethany explained, "they don't need to play around. Get them bathed, get them out. If Dennis is doing bath [time], like, they'll play for forty-five minutes and then they're all wound up." The longer that bath time took, meanwhile, the longer it took to get the kids to bed, and the longer that Bethany had to wait for a break.

At the same time, Bethany found ways of excusing Dennis for not being more (helpfully) involved. Talking about bath time, for example, Bethany noted, "In his defense, I'm with them all day and he's at work. And so, when he does get home, we have dinner, they might get to play a little bit, but during the week, that's when he wants to see them, or, that's when he gets to see them. So I get that." Note here how Bethany walks back her frustrations with Dennis, stifling her own sense of injustice and coming to his defense. This kind of self-correction was common among mothers my team and I interviewed, who often backtracked when they caught themselves speaking ill of their children's fathers—as though they felt bad for complaining, even if their complaints were valid.

In Bethany's case, other evidence suggested that there was truth to her initial take—that Dennis wasn't happy being home with the kids. Like Russell, whom we met in chapter 3, Dennis acknowledged that he often felt frustrated with the kids and that, during the pandemic, his frustrations often turned to yells. In her own interview, Bethany also noted Dennis's quicker temper but then promptly backtracked, excusing his yelling on the basis of the fact that he wasn't used to spending so much time with them at home. "I think it's harder for him," she decided, "because he's with them at the end of the day, when they're already tired. And so I feel bad for him, because he gets frustrated with them and they get frustrated."

Those same justifications led Bethany to step in when she saw Dennis getting angry, even when it meant taking on more of the parenting responsibility herself. Of course, Dennis could try to keep his frustrations in check—the way Bethany does with the kids all day. And Bethany could demand that he do better, rather than giving him the benefit of the doubt. But the Mars/Venus myth lures them into accepting the status quo. As I'll explain, that myth not only helps men like Dennis justify exploiting women's unpaid labor, but it also teaches women not to complain.

THE ORIGINS OF THE MARS/VENUS MYTH

The Mars/Venus myth puts people in boxes—one pink; the other blue. That myth also goes further in establishing a hierarchy. It gives people a higher social value if they're more pink or more blue than their box-mates. And it puts the whole pink box below the blue.[5]

We police this box-based system with homophobia, transphobia, sexism, and misogyny, all of which operate as ranking systems that justify demonizing or even destroying those who don't fit neatly in their box. Homophobia ranks people based on whether their sexuality "matches" their sex, and it stigmatizes those who aren't straight or who don't seem straight enough. Transphobia determines people's value based on whether their sex "matches" how they express their gender, and then devalues anyone—cisgender, transgender, or nonbinary—who doesn't think, look, or act the way their sex is "supposed" to. Sexism establishes a hierarchy of gender expressions, treating masculinity as superior to femininity, and misogyny then comes in to institutionalize this hierarchy and to punish women who try to challenge men. Together, these systems reinforce the idea that biology distinguishes "real" men and "real" women, that the former are better than the latter, that the "real" ones are better than the "fake" ones, and that anyone who questions the system deserves to be beaten back into their box.[6]

These ranking systems—and the pseudoscientific myth of Mars and Venus they're based on—have deep historical roots. In the early days of anthropology and evolutionary biology, Charles Darwin set off to look for biological evidence to prove that men were the superior sex. Looking at Victorian-era high society, Darwin saw a world divided by gender, with men in positions of power and women confined to the home. Drawing on the racist and classist meritocracy myth we saw in the last chapter, Darwin assumed that his society was the pinnacle of human evolution, and he studied so-called primitive hunter-gatherer societies as a window into our evolutionary past. Rather than consider all the evidence, however, Darwin started with his conclusion—that our contemporary sex and gender hierarchy is the product of natural selection.* Next, Darwin looked for evidence that fit his conclusion, narrowing down to hunter-gatherer roles. Darwin argued in *The Descent of Man, and Selection in Relation to Sex,* published in 1871, that men, as the hunters, had to be "more courageous, pugnacious, and energetic" and to have more "inventive genius" than women. Meanwhile, as the gatherers,

---

* Darwin's idea here is that biology pushed men and women into different roles based on their distinct physical and mental characteristics. Survival (and sexual attraction) then favored those men and women who best filled their assigned roles. As a result, subsequent generations of men and women became increasingly distinct in their traits.

women had to be more nurturing, more cooperative, and more docile in their dependence on men.[7]

Darwin's "evidence" was taken as gospel; and yet recent actual scientific studies have revealed that Darwin was wrong all along. Reviewing all the studies of hunter-gatherer societies conducted between the 1800s and the 2020s, biologist Cara Wall-Scheffler and her team found that in 79 percent of those societies, scholars had documented evidence of women hunting alongside men—and not just hunting occasionally or opportunistically. Instead, as Wall-Scheffler explained in a 2023 NPR interview, women's hunting "was purposeful." Girls and women were being trained from an early age to make their own tools and go hunting. "Women had their own toolkit," said Wall-Scheffler. "They had their favorite weapons. Grandmas were the best hunters of the village." This evidence of women's hunting—and thus of the falsity of the myth of the gender binary—is, as Wall-Scheffler notes, "right there in the literature." Rather than use this evidence to challenge early theories of gender essentialism, generations of anthropologists and biologists accepted the myth and concluded that their own evidence must be the outlier. It wasn't until Wall-Scheffler and her team went back and tallied the evidence that the regularity of these presumed outliers became clear.[8]

In the meantime, centuries of bad science—coupled with a heavy dose of Adam and Eve—have permeated popular culture and reified the myth of men's "innate" intellectual and physical superiority. As historian Kimberly Hamlin explained to NPR, "next to the myth that God made a woman from man's rib to be his helper, the myth that man is the hunter and woman is the gatherer is probably the second most enduring myth that naturalizes the inferiority of women."[9]

BUYING THE MARS/VENUS MYTH

The recent research around sex, gender, and sexuality is clear, and it erodes the idea of a stark binary of pink and blue. But even as the science becomes more definitive about the fluidity of masculinity and femininity, cultural acceptance of the Mars/Venus myth appears to be on the upswing. A 2022

Ipsos poll found that nearly half of American men believe that "traditional" masculinity is under threat, and many of those men blame feminism for the change, saying that it has done more harm than good.* Globally, that puts American men second behind only Russian men in holding such views. That same poll also showed that more than 30 percent of American men believe that women overreact to online harassment, nearly 20 percent believe that women who report abuse are usually making up or exaggerating their claims, and more than 10 percent believe that women who experience violence have it coming to them. Troublingly, these misogynistic views are also more common among men ages eighteen to forty-five than among men their fathers' and grandfathers' age. Gen Zers and millennials, for example, are twice as likely as older men to believe that women are obligated to have sex with their partners, and they're five times as likely to say that it's acceptable to send someone unrequested sexually explicit images online.[10]

Of course, not all men embrace misogyny so openly. Yet studies show that most Americans continue to believe some version of the Mars/Venus myth and that the prevalence of those beliefs empowers people who hold more extremist views.[11]

Take the fuzziness around male/female sex categories—a complexity that a growing share of Americans refuses to accept.[12] A 2022 poll from the Pew Research Center found that 60 percent of US adults believe that whether a person is a man or a woman is fixed and determined by sex at birth. That's compared to 56 percent in 2021 and 54 percent in 2017. These beliefs also aren't limited to older Americans. Even among eighteen-to-thirty-four-year-olds, more than half equate gender with biological sex. Almost three-quarters of Americans also believe that we shouldn't teach elementary-age kids about people who don't fit neatly into sex and gender binaries, and a smaller but still substantial proportion of American adults say that society has gone too far in accepting transgender people and supporting transgender rights.[13]

Despite these perceptions, the evidence reveals that sex is more of a spec-

---

* More than a quarter of American men say that feminism does more harm than good, and only a slightly smaller number blame feminism for the loss of men's social, economic, and political power.

trum than a set of boxes to tick. Nearly 2 percent of babies are born with intersex traits. That's roughly the same percentage of the global population that has green eyes. People with intersex traits can't be easily identified as male or female based on things like their genitalia or their chromosomes, and some intersex traits can't be detected until puberty or later, which means that sex can't be perfectly determined at birth. Meanwhile, even among those who fit within the male/female binary on easily observable measures, there are still wide variations in things like hormones, hormone response, and internal anatomy, all of which can vary across different stages and circumstances of a person's life. Research shows, for example, that spending time caring for young children—or even holding baby dolls—causes a drop in testosterone levels, and it does so for both women and men. Those drops in testosterone also make caregivers, regardless of gender, more sensitive to the needs of their charges. And those patterns become more pronounced the more experience someone has with caregiving. What that means, in turn, is that if more men and boys were given more early opportunities to practice, they might also seem "naturally" suited for caregiving roles. And men like Dennis and Russell might not get as angry when they are called to do the work of care.[14]

Americans are also becoming less expansive in their views of sexuality, despite unmistakable evidence that, like sex, sexuality doesn't operate exclusively on binary terms. Belief in the moral acceptability of gay and lesbian relationships fell between 2022 and 2023 from 71 percent to 64 percent of Americans, and that same poll found that belief in the moral acceptability of changing one's gender fell over that same time period, from 46 to 43 percent. Those declines were driven by changing views among Republicans and weekly churchgoers. In 2022, 56 percent of Republicans saw same-sex relations as morally acceptable, but by 2023, that number had fallen to 41 percent.[15]

Americans' insistence on a strict and biologically based pink/blue binary also extends to issues of gender roles. There's a perception that men and women think, talk, look, and act differently, and that those differences are the product of inherently gendered traits. And yet, research shows that, in reality, men and women aren't as different as we might expect. There aren't, for example, distinctly masculine or feminine communication styles or systematically different masculine and feminine psychological traits. Instead, there's a tremendous amount of overlap physically, psychologically, and temperamentally between men and women, and that's true even when we only consider cisgender heterosexual women and men.[16]

Meanwhile, and to the extent that there are differences in the scripts that men and women follow, those differences are more a product of socialization than biology. In lab studies psychologists find that when adults are asked to interact with a boy baby or even a girl baby they are lead to believe is a boy (i.e., because she is dressed in masculine-typed clothes and called by a masculine-sounding same), they assume that the baby is stronger, more playful, and less sensitive, offer more masculine-typed toys, engage in more physical or aggressive play, and worry less about potential safety risks. Longitudinal studies also show that the more that parents push gender stereotypes on their infants, the more strongly those children will gravitate toward gender stereotypical toys months and even years later when offered a choice of different toys in a lab.[17]

Observational studies also regularly document gendered socialization in real-world interactions between adults and kids. Sociologist Heidi Gansen, for example, finds that most preschool teachers discipline boys and girls differently, demanding higher levels of self-control from girls than from boys, expecting girls to help more with cleanup, and encouraging rather than punishing physical aggression in boys. Similarly, based on observations in middle school classrooms, sociologist Michela Musto finds that teachers give boys, particularly white boys in advanced classes, more leeway to break the rules, and allow them to monopolize class time and talk over girls, unchecked. In light of that treatment, the students themselves come to perceive the white boys in advanced classes as more "exceptionally intelligent" than girls are, even when that doesn't bear out in their grades or test scores.[18]

Despite such evidence, most American men and women continue to believe in a strict and biologically rooted pink/blue binary. A 2017 survey from the Pew Research Center asked men and women about their perceptions of gender differences, and strong majorities of both groups reported that there are gender differences in how men and women express their feelings, in their physical abilities, in their hobbies and interests, and in their approaches to parenting.* A large minority of both groups also believes that men and women have different skills when it comes to paid work.† Men were more likely than women to see these differences as the product of biology, but nearly half of women also saw these differences as biological, rather than as the product of societal expectations and socialization, as research consistently shows.[19]

Such survey results are deeply troubling, especially because, thanks to social desirability bias, they're likely to underestimate how many Americans accept the Mars/Venus myth. Men in particular are likely to pay lip service to progressive gender ideals but abandon them in practice, especially when they become personally inconvenient, such as when they and their partners are deciding where to move for their careers, when they are deciding who should stay home with the kids when they're sick or don't have childcare, or when one partner loses their job. Dennis, for example, encouraged Bethany to quit her job rather than take the promotion at work and put Willow in full-time childcare, and he chose to go back to working in the office in June 2020, even though he could have continued working remotely to be more available to help Bethany with the kids.‡[20]

More bluntly, many American men claim egalitarian beliefs as a convenient shield. That's what sociologist Ellen Lamont finds in her research with young college-educated heterosexual men in the US. By claiming egalitarian attitudes, Lamont argues, these men can "dismiss inequalities that emerge in their romantic relationships as the result of individual preferences so that gendered outcomes are allowed to go unquestioned, thereby leaving gender inequalities intact."[21]

My own interviews display a similar dynamic, showing that men use praise for women's gendered talents to justify not being more involved in

---

* With respect to the expression of emotion, 89 percent of women and 84 percent of men believe that there are important gender differences. With respect to physical abilities, those numbers are 75 and 76 percent. With respect to hobbies and personal interests, the numbers are 67 and 69 percent. And with respect to parenting, those numbers are 68 and 60 percent.

† With respect to paid work competencies, 35 percent of women and 38 percent of men perceive important gender differences.

‡ Such findings are also consistent with survey research showing that support for gender equality in the workplace has increased faster than support for gender equality at home.

the work of care. Recall how Dennis weaponized his own incompetence. He could have learned to do the dishes and the laundry as effectively as Bethany. Instead, he "just let her do that." Or consider how Tom from chapter 3 spoke with awe about his wife, Stephanie, saying "She's doing it all" and "How she does it, I don't know." Tom might have known how she was doing it all—and might have seen how she was crumbling under all of that responsibility—if he had bothered to watch or to ask. Instead, he stuck with the bare minimum of just keeping the kids alive.

To that end, while husbandly reverence might seem endearing, research shows that learned helplessness manifests inequality. It gives men like Dennis and Tom a convenient cover for the fact they're getting off easy. And it operates to gaslight women like Bethany and Stephanie because it makes their complaints seem petty, since their husbands seem so loving in lavishing them with praise.[22]

SELLING THE MARS/VENUS MYTH

The media—both traditional and social media—is playing a key role in reviving the Mars/Venus myth. In 2023, for example, Fox News fired host Tucker Carlson in the wake of accusations of blatant misogyny. A suit against Carlson, filed by former staff member Abby Grossberg, alleges that he "subjugates women based on vile sexist stereotypes." In an interview with NPR, Grossberg recalled how "I ultimately went and complained to one of my supervisors about the abuse and the bullying and the gaslighting I was putting up with at *Tucker*," and how his response was "We're just following Tucker's tone." Fox might seem noble for firing Carlson. Yet given the prevalence of sexist rhetoric across the network's programs and platforms, it's not clear that cutting Carlson cut out all of the rot.[23]

That rot, meanwhile, is even harder to root out on social media, where it can go instantly viral and proliferate in infinite, indelible copies online. Examining one week of Twitter data from June 2017—a week chosen because it was mundane news-wise—sociologist Diane Felmlee and her colleagues found over 2.9 million tweets containing gendered insults like "cunt," "slut," and "whore," averaging 419,000 sexist tweets per day. Using algorithms that evaluate the sentiment of language, they found that most of these tweets were negative in tone and often reinforced vicious gender stereotypes—deriding women for being ugly, stupid, promiscuous, crazy, or old. Going a step further, Felmlee and her colleagues also looked at how other users reacted to these tweets, and they found that replies, retweets, and likes tended to reinforce (rather than resist) the hate and harassment that women face online.[24]

If you've ever tried to confront a sexist troll on Twitter, you've likely discovered that there's a good chance they'll lash back with some version of "Can't you take a joke?" And that's the thing about the modern purveyors of sexism and misogyny. They craft their hate in ways that make it seem all in good fun. Think of the male comedians who tell rape jokes or attack women in the name of humor, like *Saturday Night Live* star Michael Che did to gymnast Simone Biles when she withdrew from the 2020 Olympics. Che posted a string of so-called jokes on Instagram, including one equating Biles's exit to that of convicted sex offender and former gymnastics coach Larry Nassar and suggesting that both had to quit "because of mounting pressure," and another quipping of Biles's exit, "Who said black don't crack?" Beyond comedians, there are also congressmen who refer to their women colleagues with sexist slurs, like in 2020 when Republican Representative Ted Yoho, in front of reporters, used the phrase "a fucking bitch" to refer to Democratic representative Alexandria Ocasio-Cortez.* And those are just the high-profile cases. This kind of casual misogyny happens every day across the US. In 2019, for example, ProPublica uncovered a secret Facebook group for US Border Patrol agents where they jokingly referred to migrant women as "hoes." And in 2023, the LAPD's Sgt. Darcy French filed a lawsuit against the city, alleging that she had been targeted for years with harassment and discrimination—including being passed over multiple times for promotion, forced to transfer divisions, and threatened with demotion—after reporting her colleagues for sharing sexist memes and for making her the subject of degrading messages they posted online.[25]

---

* When asked about the incident, then House Speaker Nancy Pelosi said she wasn't surprised by the incident, noting, in reference to her Republican colleagues, that "I can tell you that firsthand, they've called me names for at least twenty years." Echoing similar sentiments, California representative Barbara Lee said on the House floor that "I personally have experienced a lifetime of insults, racism, and sexism. And believe me, this did not stop after being elected into public office."

Humor makes the nastier parts of the Mars/Venus myth more palatable—like a candy coating on a bitter-tasting pill. Psychologist Thomas Ford and his colleagues find that jokes are more effective than serious messaging when it comes to normalizing sexism and misogyny. In their experiments, they exposed audiences to different types of sexist messages and found that those who heard the humorous versions became significantly more skeptical of women's rights efforts, more tolerant of sexist interactions they were asked to observe in the lab, and more inclined to believe that others around them would tolerate that sexism as well.[26]

Couching sexism in humor doesn't just affect the men who hear those messages; it also makes women less likely to speak up in protest, particularly if a man is the one telling it for laughs. Psychologist Robyn Mallett and her co-authors find that when men express sexism through humor rather than in serious comments, women who hear those messages are more reluctant to push back.[27]

To understand why humor makes sexism go down easy, it's helpful to consider the science. There's still a lot we don't know about how humor works. But we do know that humans tend to laugh in moments of benign incongruity—when we expect one thing and find another, but where the unmet expectation doesn't cause any harm. In those moments, laughter serves a social purpose. It signals to other people that we recognize that a norm or expectation was broken. And it also serves to repair the breach by signaling that we're not offended or upset by the gaffe.[28]

Sexist humor is thereby effective because it gives men cover. When men treat sexism as humor, they're implying that they are not actually sexist. Because if they were actually sexist, then it wouldn't be funny for them to think or do or say something sexist. Or at least it wouldn't be funny in the way of benign incongruity, because it wouldn't be incongruous (since anyone would expect a sexist to think or do or say something sexist) and it wouldn't be benign (since the point of thinking or doing or saying something sexist would be to hurt others, rather than causing people to laugh).

In other words, men may find sexist humor appealing when it gives them a way to manage the incongruity between their sexist thoughts, words, and actions and the more gallant way they want to perceive themselves. Recall how Dennis described his and Bethany's division of household labor as "funny" because, on the one hand, they look like "your typical fifties family where we have to fit these roles and whatever," while, on the other hand, "we don't feel that way." For Dennis, his "typical fifties family" arrangement seems funny because, in his view, he's not a typical fifties man. He wants to think of himself as egalitarian and progressive, despite the way he benefits from patriarchy's perks. And humor allows him to repair that gap. Meanwhile, if I had laughed when Dennis talked about his family being "funny," I would have signaled to Dennis that I see him the way he wants to be seen. But I didn't feel much like laughing that day.

HOW MARS AND VENUS DELUDE AND DIVIDE US

Why do men and boys secretly find sexist messages so appealing? Arguably, it's because those messages allow men to feel justified in dumping the risk of our DIY society onto women, in much the same way that meritocratic messages allow women to justify outsourcing risk onto others in more vulnerable positions than them. As we talked about with Mark in chapter 2, men have an interest in passing the buck risk-wise if they want to be (and be rewarded for being) the kind of ideal worker their employers expect them to be.[29]

To be that ideal worker—to put in long hours and prioritize their work commitments—men need someone managing all of life's other responsibilities. The more hours that a man works for pay, the more likely his wife is to quit her job and become a full-time homemaker.* And the less time that a woman spends working for pay, the more her husband is likely to earn. That's particularly true for men who are higher up on the ladder—men like Dennis, who have high incomes and professional careers. Gender specialization yields bigger financial advantages for these men than for other men, and the premium they get for having a stay-at-home wife has also increased substantially over time.[30]

Unfortunately, men can't simply reject ideal-worker pressures or the incentives of having a stay-at-home wife.† Employers are willing to reward

---

* The reverse pattern doesn't hold for husbands whose wives work long hours.
† Evidence of these gendered breadwinner pressures can be seen in surveys, which show that 76 percent of Americans think men face a lot of pressure to support their families financially (compared to 40 percent who think the same for women), and 68 percent think men face a lot of pres-

men for being ideal workers even more than they're willing to reward women for doing the same. And so, in the absence of a broad and sturdy social safety net, security depends on what you can afford.[31]

The Mars/Venus myth emboldens men to get their wives or girlfriends or even their mothers to be the woman behind the man, by treating women as both the lesser and more nurturing of the two—as the helpmate who exists only to prop men up behind the scenes. Consider how Andrew Tate, kickboxing champion turned webcam sex business millionaire turned Tik-Tok star and frequent talk show guest, talks about women and their roles in relation to men. Tate tells his millions of followers that "real" men make big money (ideally without being dependent on a boss) and have big muscles (ideally big enough to attract a doting girlfriend or wife). Tate's model of manhood depends on having women in the kitchen (and in the bedroom), and he reassures men that it's better for everyone if women just stay home. "We live in a world now," Tate complains, "where if I come along and say women are better with children and men are better at fighting, that I'm somehow fucking sexist when it's clearly true." Going a step further, Tate calls women "intrinsically lazy," saying, "[T]hey have no interest in world conquest. They want to be comfortable. If you show a woman how to make a thousand dollars an hour, she'll think, 'I can work two hours a week.' If you show a man how to make a thousand dollars an hour, he'll think, 'I can make eighteen thousand a day.'" Instead, Tate suggests, women should "prioritize their roles as wives and mothers over pursuing careers." Tate has also said that women should be men's property in marriage, though he later walked that one back as a joke.[32]

These ideas might seem extreme, and yet Tate has millions of followers on social media, and a 2023 YouGov poll found that half of all American adults had heard of Tate, and roughly 40 percent of those like what he says. Among young people, including men and women, those numbers are even higher. Seventy percent of millennials have heard of Tate, and 50 percent

---

sure to be successful career-wise (compared to 44 percent who think women are expected to be successful in their jobs). By contrast, 77 percent of Americans say that women face a lot of pressure to be involved as a parent, compared to 49 percent who say the same for men. And 71 percent of Americans say that women face a lot of pressure to be physically attractive, while only 27 percent say that men face pressure to look a certain way.

like his views. Tate's supporters aren't confined to red states, either. Rather, as journalist Lisa Miller found in her reporting for *New York Magazine*, his influence extends even to boys and men in liberal enclaves like New York City, where many of the left-leaning Brooklyn moms she interviewed were shocked to discover that their teenage sons were watching his videos and listening to his podcast interviews regularly online. Interviewing those teenage boys, Miller found that they're drawn to Tate for the powerful model of masculinity he offers and for the hope he gives them for achieving that model themselves. These boys don't want to see themselves as sexist. Yet Tate's cartoonishly outsized persona, coupled with the high esteem they hold him in, makes it easy for Tate's young followers to dismiss his crasser comments as jokes and to see themselves as less extreme than he is, even as they internalize his ideas.[33]

Tate is effectively selling a version of the Mars/Venus myth, and that myth is appealing because it absolves boys and men of the guilt they might otherwise feel for accepting patriarchy's perks. Given how women are struggling under the weight of the risk we've dumped on their shoulders, it would be easy for men, especially relatively privileged men like Dennis, to feel guilty about not doing more to ease the load that women are carrying. The myth, however, is a sort of inoculation against that kind of guilt. It reassures men that women are happier at home, that they're better at domestic responsibilities than men are, and that men are even doing women a favor by not helping more with housework or childcare, because that way women won't have to be the ones who clean up the mess when men get angry at the kids or leave a pen in their pocket in the wash.[34]

To that end, the Mars/Venus myth also makes it difficult for women to complain about their boyfriends or their husbands so long as those men exceed the bar the myth sets. Dennis, for example, almost seems like a feminist compared to men like Tate. And so when Bethany catches herself complaining about Dennis—like when he's getting the kids riled up at bath time—she's quick to stop herself, because he could be so much worse. Bethany also isn't alone in that kind of self-censorship. Many of the women I interviewed were reluctant to criticize their children's fathers for not doing more at home and were quick to defend those men as "good husbands" and "great dads" for doing the barest minimum at home. Candace, who we met in chapter 3, even defended her husband, Garrett, after she caught him messaging other women online, saying, "I try and limit how much I complain about my husband . . . because I also don't want [other people] being like, 'Oh, Garrett's a piece of crap,' which Garrett's not. He is a good dad. He is a good husband."

The Mars/Venus myth is not, of course, a new myth. It didn't start with Andrew Tate or even John Gray. Instead, versions of this myth have long served to goad women like Candace and Bethany into accepting their "proper" roles and into believing that they would have to be "crazy" to complain. Take, for example, the pseudoscience of hysteria, which has been used for generations to goad women into believing "It's not the patriarchy; it's you."

"Hysteria" comes from the Greek word for uterus, and it was first used by Hippocrates, the founder of Western medicine, to describe female "madness," a broad condition that incorporated symptoms ranging from pain and anxiety to fainting and seizures to emotional outbursts and other erratic or seemingly unfeminine behaviors. Hippocrates attributed such madness to the uterus, which, in his view, would wander through the body if it wasn't full. The proposed solution to hysteria was regular marital sex, which would fill the uterus both with semen (which was believed to have healing properties) and with pregnancies, which would keep the wandering uterus firmly rooted in place. The gendered concept of hysteria persisted over millennia, even though belief in the idea of an actual wandering uterus waned over time.* In the 1800s, hysteria was blamed for falling birth rates among middle- and upper-middle-class white women, who were accused of "race suicide" if they didn't have at least four kids. In the 1900s, hysteria was included in early editions of the American Psychiatric Association's *Diagnostic and Statistical Manual*, where it remained an official diagnosis for mental illness until 1980. And even in 2017, women who participated in the #DayWithoutAWoman protests following the election of President Donald Trump were labeled by

---

* Greek physician Galen, for example, believed that hysteria resulted when a woman's unfertilized "seeds" were allowed to "rot" inside her. And Sigmund Freud blamed "penis envy"—the sense of inferiority that women felt when they were old enough to realize that they didn't have a penis, which could only be cured by giving birth to a male child.

the right-wing media as "rabid feminists" and "crazies" and accused of "hysterics and tantrums."[35]

Through its specter of the "crazy" woman, the Mars/Venus myth emboldens men to punish women who try to challenge the pink/blue binary or call out the injustice they face. A 2022 Ipsos poll, for example, found that nearly half of all American women have experienced online abuse or seen sexist content online in the past two years, and women are more than twice as likely as men to face harassment and other personal attacks online. That same poll also found that a third of women have stopped saying what they think online because of the risks of doing so, and more than a quarter have experienced lower self-esteem because of the online mistreatment that they've been subjected to. Gendered violence, of course, isn't limited to online spaces, and research shows that emotional abuse and physical violence against women is extremely prevalent in the US, too. As we saw with Audrey, Jocelyn, and Candace, there are risks for women who try to call out inequities or ask for more support than their partners are willing to give.[36]

WHAT MARS AND VENUS COST
THE SOCIAL SAFETY NET

A stronger social safety net would reduce those risks for women. And most men would also benefit, at least in an absolute sense. Dennis, for example, acknowledged that they'd have more money if Bethany were able to go back to working full-time and if they didn't have to pay for childcare.[37]

What men would lose would be the perks of patriarchy—the relative advantages that men have over women and in some cases over other men. At home, a stronger social safety net—with policies like universal childcare, universal healthcare, universal college, and more funding for welfare programs so they can adequately compensate social workers like Bethany—would put Dennis and Bethany on more equal footing, giving Bethany more leverage to demand support from Dennis and Dennis less room to wiggle out of domestic responsibility on the grounds that his paid work has a higher monetary value and that her time is better spent on childcare and chores at home. At the office, those policies would give more workers—both men and women—more of a chance to compete with Dennis for high-paying jobs, because they wouldn't be stretched so thin.[38]

If men want to keep the perks they get from patriarchy, then they have an interest in keeping the social safety net small and meager. And that's where the Mars/Venus myth comes in. That myth allows men like Dennis to feel like one of the good men, even if they oppose efforts to strengthen the social safety net. And it does so by creating the (mis)perception that everyone is better off if women do the work of the social safety net instead. Consider some data from the PITT study. In it, I found that opposition to safety net programs like guaranteed paid family leave and free universal childcare was significantly more common among dads who believe the Mars/Vens myth than among dads who reject those ideas.* And which dads were most likely to believe the myth? Maybe not surprisingly, it was affluent, white dads, 69 percent of whom said that kids are better off with their mother at home than if their mother is working for pay.†

Believing the Mars/Venus myth allows affluent white men like Dennis to feel like one of the good men, even if they oppose efforts to strengthen the social safety net. That's because, according to the myth, we all benefit when women stand in for the social safety net. Recall, for example, how Dennis used the myth to dismiss the need for universal, affordable childcare while still trying to portray himself as a good husband and a good dad. In theory, he suggested, free childcare for all is "a great idea." At the same time, drawing on the myth and its gender essentialism, Dennis suggested that such a program wouldn't be worth the taxes on his income or the debt for the national economy—particularly since Bethany was already providing high-quality care for his children and since, in his view, Bethany would be happier

---

* I gauged parents' belief in the Mars/Venus myth by asking, "Do you think children are better off if their mother is home and doesn't hold a job, or are children just as well off if their mother works?" I also asked parents about their support for or opposition to a series of social safety net policies, including a policy raising the federal minimum wage to $15 an hour, a policy guaranteeing six months of paid family leave for parents of new babies, a policy providing free public childcare and preschool for all US children, and a policy creating a new national health insurance program.

† In this case, I define affluent men as those with household incomes of $75,000 a year or more. By contrast, only 47 percent of all parents reported that it is best for children if their mothers do not work for pay.

at home than working for pay full-time. By activating the myth, Dennis was able to perceive a lack of universal, affordable childcare as a benefit for his wife and his kids, even when he has more to gain than they do from maintaining the status quo.

———

Unfortunately, men aren't the only ones who've bought into the idea of the pink/blue binary. And they're not the only ones opposing the kinds of policies that could help dismantle gender inequalities and sexist myths. As we'll see in our next chapter, many women also buy into patriarchal messages, even at the expense of leaving themselves without a net.

Chapter 7

THE SUPERMOM MYTH

In 1983, California mother Judy Johnson made explosive allegations about the owner and staff at her son's childcare center. Johnson accused them of physical and sexual abuse as well as of performing Satanic rituals on children. She claimed that teachers dressed up as witches, sacrificed animals, drilled holes into children, made children fly through the air, forced them to drink the blood of other dead children, and even flushed children down toilets into secret rooms where they were forced to participate in the creation of pornographic films.[1]

Johnson was later revealed to be suffering from paranoid schizophrenia, and all charges were eventually dropped against her son's childcare providers, but it was too late. Helped along by overzealous police, prosecutors, and journalists, her lurid allegations had created a frenzy that swept the nation. Anxious parents began pulling their children out of preschools and childcare centers, and some even lodged their own (often flimsy and flawed) accusations, leading to a spate of similar legal cases against childcare providers across the US.* These new cases led to more news coverage and hand-wringing over the perceived Satanic takeover of the childcare industry, to the point where, in 1984, Senator Arlen Specter of Pennsylvania declared in a Senate Judiciary Committee hearing that the problem had "reached epidemic proportions."[2]

---

* The resulting "daycare panic" was devastating for childcare providers. As historian Richard Beck explains in *We Believe the Children*, "Plummeting enrollment numbers and surging insurance premiums forced many centers to close down, and newspapers reported that some day care directors were advising their employees to avoid physical contact with children if at all, advice intended not to protect children from molestation but rather to protect employees from accusations of sexual assault."

Given the outlandishness of Johnson's accusations, it's easy to wonder why so many families and policymakers bought into the fear. As I'll explain, however, that kind of fear shouldn't surprise us, given the Supermom myth that Americans have been sold.* That myth paints a portrait of children in constant danger and of mothers as the only ones with the power to rescue them from harm.† That myth, in turn, might seem empowering for women. And yet, it weaponizes women's fear to keep them in their "proper" place at home.[3]

SUPERMOM VS. SATAN

Take Kara, who believes that her primary responsibility is protecting her children from sinfulness and from the ultimate damnation that she believes is the punishment for sin. "God puts parents in charge of kids," Kara explained, adding, "We're loving caretakers of their souls." For Kara, an evangelical Christian who is biracial Asian American and white, that caretaking involves teaching children "right from wrong." And like April, whom we met in chapter 5, Kara also believes that proper moral instruction requires "discipline" of the physical kind.‡

In college and graduate school—Kara has a bachelor's degree in psychology and a master's degree in mental health counseling—Kara found that her church's teachings on physical discipline weren't compatible with what she was learning about child development. Kara recalled that her professors taught her that the best way to deal with a child's misbehavior is not to use

---

* I am using this term differently than other commentators, who have used the idea of the "Supermom myth" (or similar terms) to talk about the unrealistic pressures that American mothers face.

† In the case of the daycare panic, and as historian Richard Beck explains, Johnson's accusations captured national attention because of how they resonated with broader concerns about the women's movement in the US. Parents' magazines, for example, drew a straight line between the California case and the supposed dangers of letting mothers of young children work for pay outside the home, publishing articles with titles like "Mommy, Don't Leave Me Here! The Day Care Parents Don't See" and "Can You Work and Have a Happy, Healthy Child?"

‡ Paraphrasing the Bible, Kara explained that "if you discipline your child—if you hit them with the rod which is like spanking in biblical times—then your child will not die. And so it's saying if you do this the right way it's not going to harm them AND it's going to keep them from doing harmful things." Put differently, Kara believed that physical punishment was the only way to keep her children from sinning (i.e., doing harmful things), and thereby the only way to ensure that they would get to live an eternal life in heaven, rather than face eternal death in hell.

physical punishment but rather to ignore it, because if a parent doesn't react to a child's misbehavior, the child will tire of it and stop on their own. Rather than reject her faith, however, Kara concluded that there must be "flaws in the research." "Biblically," she explained, her professors' approach "stops short, because I'm not caring for [my kids'] soul. What I'm teaching them is I don't care enough about you to correct your behavior. And the Bible teaches that we're to raise up our children and correct them and teach them and, like, admonish them, so they know right from wrong."

Kara also faulted researchers for not distinguishing various types of physical punishment. She considered her own approach gentle and loving, noting that spanking, for her, is "a swat," at least for the first offense. Kara noted that her sons will often cry after being disciplined, but she insisted that's okay because it's important that "disobedience brings pain." At the same time, Kara told me that she is always careful to reconcile with her kids after spanking them. She asks them to look her in the eye, and she tells them, "I love you. [Your behavior] was not okay, but I love you. It's over now. Go play."

Kara, like April, believed that the best way to practice this kind of loving discipline was as a stay-at-home mother, and, when her children were old enough, by homeschooling them rather than sending them to public or even private schools. Kara explained that, for her and her husband, the point of homeschooling was not academic. In fact, despite her own educational achievements, when asked how disappointed she would be if her children never graduated from college, Kara said she would not be disappointed at all. Instead, Kara planned to homeschool to ensure that her children were learning "through a Christian worldview."[4] Like many families who homeschool for religious reasons, Kara and her husband, Alec (who is white), were worried about protecting their children from the "worldly" influence of public schools, particularly in the liberal-leaning college town where they live. "I think nowadays," she explained, "especially here, a lot of morals are being pushed on kids from teachers, ill-intended or well-intended, that we might disagree with."

Before kids, Kara had worked full-time for a nonprofit religious organization that provides free or low-cost mental health services, earning about $30,000 a year. Kara liked doing work that helped her community. But when her first son, Sheldon, was born in 2017, she felt compelled to leave the workforce, following in the footsteps of her own mother, who had stayed home. Though leaving the workforce was an easy decision for Kara, home-making itself was hard. She often found herself frustrated with the tedium and monotony of housework. She remembers catching herself thinking, "Why can't my life be the way I want it? I could go change the world and I'm stuck here at home!"

Kara struggled with her role as a mother until she joined the moms' group at her church. Alec works long hours—often fifty hours a week or more—as a software engineer, earning roughly $80,000 a year. As a result, and as we saw with Audrey and her church moms' group in chapter 1, the other moms in Kara's church group became her primary source of adult in-teraction, support, and advice. Kara recalled how they encouraged her to reframe her thinking around stay-at-home motherhood, treating it not as a lost opportunity but rather as essential work. Other moms would tell her in weekly meet-ups and text message chains, "We *are* changing the world! With the kids we're raising. And this is, like, really important work." In the end, Kara concluded that "biblically, it's not about what makes me happy. It's about what we believe is best for our kids. Even if it's hard sometimes, I'm glad to be able to do it. Even if I miss working and I miss being able to have more of a tangible impact on the community."[5]

The members of Kara's church moms' group met at least once a week to discuss Christian parenting books and prayer journal assignments. "I'm learning that I need to be less selfish. Learning to be thankful," Kara ex-plained, talking about what she took from those lessons. "When I feel really burnt out, [I'm learning] to be like, 'Well. This is what God has given me. I can do it cheerfully. And he's given me the strength to get through it, and he'll give me rest when I need it.'" Kara absorbed the message that she should be grateful for the opportunity to be a parent and to parent without complaint, even when it was difficult. "When they're crying in the middle of the night," she said, "I'm so thankful we have kids to cry in the middle of the night."

Alec reinforced that lesson, reminding Kara that it's unacceptable for women to be "lazy" or "grumpy" about their mothering roles. After their second child, Paxton, was born in 2018, Alec only took a week off from work, despite having the option for more paid family leave. He then began spending most of his nights and weekends helping a friend renovate a house he was trying to flip. Kara was less than thrilled. Yet Alec persuaded Kara that she was being "grumpy," "ungrateful," and even "un-Christian" for not wanting him to do the "Godly" thing of helping a friend. Kara conceded to Alec, saying, "[I]t should be a joy for me to take care of our kids while you do that." Kara even came to think of herself as "selfish" for wanting Alec to spend more time at home, noting, "I used to want him to be home as much as possible, but I wasn't trusting that God is working in his heart. Because I was selfish in thinking like, 'Well, I'm watching the kids. Now that you're off work, you should watch them so I can, like, get things done!'"

Alec often reminded Kara of her place in "the hierarchy," which involves putting "God first and then our spouse and then our children." No matter what she was dealing with individually, Kara owed Alec attention, affection, and deference. Alec's job was to have "the final say in things," while her job was to "nurture the people in the house and to be a help to my husband." Accepting those roles, as gratefully as she could manage, made it easier for Kara to justify doing all the housework and almost all the care for their kids. "Now," she said, "I feel like I'm more willing to say, 'I'm taking care of the kids! This is great. I love my role as a wife and mother.' And I think, like, fathers should help, but it's not such a big deal."

Kara found the clear rules and authority structure of the hierarchy reassuring. She noted that in the US today, we tell mothers that it's up to them to make sure that their children are successful, safe, happy, and healthy. And then we bombard them with conflicting advice on nearly every aspect of pregnancy and parenting: whether it's okay to drink alcohol, how long to breastfeed and when to start solid foods, whether to let babies cry it out when they won't sleep, whether to follow the recommended vaccine schedule, what to do with kids who won't follow instructions, and how to help kids who are getting into fights or struggling academically in school. Kara, like nearly every mother my team and I interviewed, talked about how exhausting it is to wade through all this evidence and make all these choices and how demoralizing it is to be judged—often by other women—for choosing "wrong."[6]

Kara's faith offered her a shortcut through the dilemma—one that eliminated both the stress of decision-making and the "mom guilt" that came from comparing herself to other women whose choices differed from her own. Kara explained that following a faith-based approach to parenting has "been, like, the best thing ever, because I don't have to worry about what this parenting magazine says. I don't have to worry about what my friends say or what my family says as long as I'm basing it on the word of God, like in the Bible. Then it'll be okay."

Ironically, Kara's all-consuming fear of sin also made it easier for her to let go of other things she might be afraid of—like the possibility of her kids struggling with school or getting sick. During the Covid-19 pandemic, for example, Kara wasn't worried about herself or her kids catching the virus, and she and her family went back to in-person, unmasked church services and small group meetings as soon as her state lifted its stay-at-home orders in May 2020. "At the beginning," she explained, "we were really tempted to be afraid, but we shouldn't be. Even if it were much more deadly, it would still be our responsibility to trust God and not to be afraid. It would be easy for us to just hole up at home and not talk to anyone and to just let our lives be governed by a fear of the virus and then we wouldn't be following God's commands to love one another, to gather together. We're still going to church and not being afraid."

Kara saw herself as Supermom against Satan. Like April and many of the other evangelical Christian moms my team and I interviewed, Kara viewed sin—and the possibility of not spending eternity in heaven—as the biggest threat to her children, and she believed that it was her role as a mother to protect her kids from moral and spiritual harm.

Given how the media tends to focus on families in coastal cities and suburbs, it's easy to think that Kara's views are fringe. Yet my national surveys reveal that evangelical Christian moms like Kara—and the women in her church group—represent more than a third of all moms with kids under eighteen in the US today. These moms are also disproportionately likely to be stay-at-home moms and nearly twice as likely as other moms to home-school their kids.*

To understand how these women came to see themselves as Supermoms against Satan, we have to go back to the 1970s and evangelical pastor Bill Gothard. Gothard retired from ministry in 2014 at the age of eighty-one, after more than thirty women filed a lawsuit against him, accusing him of sexual harassment and abuse. Before that, Gothard had spent decades teaching a Christian approach to parenting, and his ideas have remained highly influential ever since. That includes the hierarchy of authority that Kara and Alec and their children live by.† It also includes the necessity of physical discipline for children's moral development and the idea that it's best for children if their mothers stay home, homeschool them, and don't work for pay.[7]

To get families to follow these rules, Gothard gave them something to be afraid of, and he wasn't the only one. By the early 1980s, and in the midst of the moral panic that led to witch-hunt-like attacks on childcare providers like the one in California, evangelical Christian leaders across the US were spreading the message that America's moral order was under siege from Satan and that Christians had a responsibility to "take America back for God."[8]

According to evangelical preachers like Gothard, that responsibility falls primarily to mothers, who are tasked with preparing the next generation of Christians to join the fight. Through church moms' groups like the ones Kara and April and Audrey belong to, evangelical moms learn to take up that mantle. They learn from each other, and, now, from books, Instagram

---

* Among mothers of school-age children, evangelical Christian mothers disproportionately reported that they were home full-time with their children (19 percent versus 13 percent of other mothers). In the same survey, 19 percent of evangelical Christian mothers reported that at least one of their children is being homeschooled or attending a fully online/virtual school, compared to 10 percent of mothers who do not identify as evangelical Christians. Having a child attending a traditional public school was also less common among evangelical Christian mothers than among other moms (56 percent versus 65 percent).

† According to Gothard's hierarchy, God is the ultimate authority on all things, but within the context of the family, the order of authority goes husband, then wife, then kids. In practice, this means that wives must never disobey or contradict or question their husbands, that children should show that same deference to their parents, and that husbands have the final say in every decision that gets made.

posts, podcasts, prayer journals, TikTok videos, and blog posts created by other Christian influencer moms. Take, for example, Heidi St. John, a stay-at-home evangelical mother of seven, a fierce advocate of homeschooling and corporal punishment, and a blogger, author, motivational speaker, podcaster, and Republican congressional candidate.* In her books, St. John tells mothers that their role in the fight for moral righteousness is to raise children who will serve as "arrows" in "the Lord of heaven's armies." Their labor will be difficult, she cautions, but "warriors can't afford to be lazy," because "the devil loves a lazy Christian."[9]

Like Kara and April, Christian momfluencers often equate laziness with a lack of discipline. Take Christian relationship expert Karis Kimmel Murray, who is the author of the 2017 book *Grace Based Discipline,* and who also co-hosts a Christian radio segment with an audience of 4.5 million listeners a day. Spanking is central to Murray's approach to discipline. Like April, Murray calls parents who don't spank "lazy," and, like Kara, she argues that not spanking is a form of spiritual "neglect." Murray is also careful to distinguish "corporal punishment" from "grace-based spanking," insisting, as Kara did, that "there is no equivalency between the two."[10]

It's important to note that the evidence is not on Murray's side here. Summarizing decades of scientific research on the physical punishment of children, psychologist Elizabeth Gershoff finds that "spanking is both ineffective and harmful" and concludes that "spanking is a form of violence against children that should no longer be a part of American childrearing." Over time, people who were spanked when they were little show more aggression, more rule-breaking, more depression, more anxiety, more suicide attempts, more problem drinking and drug use, and lower cognitive performance than people who weren't spanked, even after controlling for differ-

---

* On her blog, St. John talks about how she was called by God to homeschool to avoid "hav[ing] our home life hijacked by a worldly philosophy of education" that puts academic success ahead of family and ahead of serving God. St. John also cautions new homeschooling moms that they shouldn't be lured into simply re-creating a traditional public school experience at home, noting, "I don't think God meant for us—or our children—to struggle under the weight of someone else's idea of a 'proper' education. I think—just maybe—He meant for us to be free." In essence, St. John is telling women like Kara that when it comes to their children's education, the only teachers they can trust are themselves and God, which means they have no choice but to be stay-at-home moms. And as we saw with Kara, those messages are appealing, even for mothers who attended public school themselves.

ences when they were young.* Given these findings, mental health experts have argued that spanking should be treated as an adverse childhood experience (or ACE), putting it in the same category as physical and emotional abuse. As we saw with Kara, however, evangelical Christians are often skeptical of scientific authorities and quick to dismiss research-based evidence when it doesn't fit their views. That's the case with practices like spanking. And it's also what we saw with Kara and with other evangelical Christians (particularly white evangelical Christians) disproportionately resisting efforts to reduce the spread of Covid-19.[11]

That lack of trust in authorities increases mothers' responsibility for children's safety by forcing them to be the ones who identify and figure out how to manage potential threats. Yet Christian momfluencers tell women like Kara and April that they just must grin and bear that extra responsibility without complaint. Take Amber Lia and Wendy Speake's 2016 book, *Triggers: Exchanging Parents' Angry Reactions for Gentle Biblical Responses*, which has more than one hundred thousand copies in print. Recalling the early years of motherhood, Lia writes that "I didn't understand why God would choose such a painful method when He could simply make it all better: fix what's broken, heal what's sick, cure our disease, and eradicate our problems." Lia goes on to explain that, as she grew as a mother and a Christian, "it occurred to me that God uses rough sandpaper to make His creations lovely and smooth. And I knew, after a day where I had exploded over my little one's immaturity, that God was using their rough edges to smooth me out and soften my heart. God planned the lion's share of my spiritual growth to be done in the fiery furnace of family life."[12]

Evangelical women are tasked not only with protecting their children from eternal damnation but with doing the same for their husbands, under the hierarchy that Kara follows. Take Debi Pearl's book *Created to Be His Help Meet*, which is now in its tenth edition and has sold more than five hundred thousand copies since it was published in 2004. In it, Pearl tells

---

* Longitudinal studies reveal that at Time 2, children who were spanked at Time 1 demonstrate more externalizing problems (e.g., aggression, rule-breaking, antisocial and oppositional behaviors) and internalizing problems (e.g., depression, anxiety, stress) and also have lower cognitive performance than children who were not spanked at Time 1, even controlling for their behaviors and performance at Time 1.

readers, "God created man with a regular need for a woman, and God commanded the man's wife to see to it that his need is met. Do yourself and everyone else a favor, and devote at least 15 minutes every few days to totally pleasing your man." Pearl also stresses that if women don't meet their husbands' sexual needs, they're "providing an opening" for their husbands to cheat on them with other women, and thereby guilty of pushing their husbands into sin.*[13]

These messages might seem like bitter pills to swallow. Yet, as we saw with Kara, the Supermom versus Satan myth is also powerful because it identifies a clear threat (eternal damnation) and supplies a simple recipe for mothers to follow to keep their families safe: 1) follow the example of biblical wives and mothers (as interpreted by evangelical Christian preachers like Gothard); 2) avoid ungodly influences (like public schools and laziness); 3) do all this work joyfully and without complaining (especially to or about your husband); and 4) when you have doubts, trust your husband and trust in God. This approach appealed to Kara because it cut through the ambiguity of all the conflicting information and advice around parenting, and because it's noncompetitive and reassuring. Any mother who follows this recipe deserves the title of Supermom, and she can keep the title just by asking forgiveness, even if she slips up from time to time.

SUPERMOM VERSUS SUFFERING

Of course, not all mothers are motivated by a fear of Satan—some need a different threat to convince them to don the Supermom cape. That includes Monica, who isn't religious, and whose worries center on ensuring that her children lead "happy" and "successful" lives.[14]

Monica, a white, married, college-educated stay-at-home mom of two, recognizes that, in our deeply unequal society, that kind of success and happiness (and thus the avoidance of suffering) often feels like a zero-sum game. There's "a competitiveness to parenting," explained Monica. "Everybody wants their kid to be the best or the smartest or whatever."

---

* Echoing this same message, TLC's Duggar family offered Valentine's Day advice to couples, leading with number one: "Say yes to sex, even when you're tired."

Monica approached her first pregnancy with the goal of optimizing everything to help her child stay competitive. She enrolled in breastfeeding and parenting classes, joined moms' groups on Facebook, toured childcare centers, spent countless hours Googling, and devoured parenting books, especially biologist John Medina's 2010 book, *Brain Rules for Babies: How to Raise a Smart and Happy Child from Zero to Five*. The book recommended a set of rules for parenting that Monica planned to follow to a tee. No TV or screens for at least the first two years. Nothing but breast milk for at least the first six months, and then only "healthy" food (no meat, no dairy, and no processed foods). No decisions that didn't fully center on her children's physical and emotional well-being.

Monica initially planned to go back to working full-time after her son Ryder was born. And yet, as she prepared for that process, concerns about Ryder's safety and happiness started to creep in. Before she and her husband, Matthew, who is white and has a six-figure job as a software engineer, had even started trying to get pregnant, Monica left her own six-figure corporate job to go back to school to become an elementary school teacher like her own mother had been. She hoped that being home in the afternoons and during the summers would make it easier to meet her children's needs while still having a career. While she was pregnant with Ryder and finishing up her coursework, Monica had toured dozens of childcare centers. And yet something about the idea of childcare kept nagging at Monica. "When you think about it," Monica explained, "having a stranger spend the whole day with your child and kind of raising them—it's really sad." After Ryder was born, Monica still hadn't found a childcare center she trusted, so she looked into hiring a nanny instead. After a few interviews, however, Monica once again found herself dragging her feet. "It's like, you don't know this person who's gonna watch your kid all day," she noted, adding that one of the most stressful decisions you can make as a parent is "leaving your kid in somebody else's hands."[15]

In the end, Monica decided that the best way to ensure Ryder's safety, health, and happiness would be to care for him herself as a stay-at-home mom. By the time Ryder was a year old, Monica had dubbed herself "house manager" and put all her energies into cultivating the optimal home environment for him and for the next baby she and Matthew were planning to have. Explaining that decision, she said, "I think it ultimately came down to the idea that, for at least the first couple of years, it'd be nice for me to be more hands-on raising our kids than going to work and helping raise other kids."

Monica redirected all her career ambitions into raising children who would have the best possible chance at success in life. That included setting high standards for nutrition and beating herself up whenever the kids strayed from her strict dietary rules. "Thankfully he enjoys most of the food we give him, and he eats lots of beans and legumes and vegetables," Monica said proudly when Ryder was six months old, then added, a little cautiously, that "he gets Cheddar Bunny Annie's crackers, too, so he gets snacks and stuff that's probably not the best thing, but I would say it's balanced and healthy." These are organic baked snack crackers. Yet Monica still seemed to beat herself up for allowing Ryder to eat any processed snack food whatsoever. Like many other middle- and upper-middle-class parents, Monica saw eating a "healthier than healthy" diet as a way to give her kids an edge.[16]

The Covid-19 pandemic amplified Monica's concerns about risks to her kids. Unlike Kara, who focused on the spiritual risk of fear and isolation, Monica worried about Ryder's physical safety from the virus and about contracting it herself—she was pregnant with her second son, Zane, when the pandemic hit. And so, while Kara and her family were going back to in-person, unmasked church services in May 2020, Monica and her family were still "trying to take as many precautions as possible," which included wearing masks and gloves to the grocery store and even changing clothes after going out in public. Monica also maintained that level of caution for over a year—keeping her kids home as much as possible until the fall of 2021, when she enrolled Ryder in a half-day, three-day-a-week preschool program.

That decision to send Ryder to preschool was a difficult one for Monica, as it required weighing the risks to Ryder's physical safety against the risk that Ryder wasn't getting enough social interaction and educational instruction at home. "Ryder is clearly a social kid," Monica explained, adding that when they were just at home full-time, she felt "guilty that he doesn't get the socialization. And it's really easy for me to put pressure on myself [and ask]: Should we be doing more educational stuff?" After months of weighing the risks, Monica decided that it would be worse for Ryder to fall behind academically than to contract Covid-19. "Most of my concern and worry is just about him working hard and being happy," she told me. "I want him to be successful. I don't want him to have to struggle."

Note the language Monica uses here. Unlike Kara, who believed that suffering—via discipline—was necessary or even beneficial for children, Monica believed it was her role to protect her children from suffering, including physical pain and illness, as well as from the kind of disappointment that might come from not being "successful" academically or in his professional life. Monica didn't want to go so far as spoiling her children, but she didn't believe that raising unspoiled children required the rod. Although both she and her husband, Matthew, had been spanked as children, they didn't plan on doing the same. Not spoiling Ryder in Monica's view meant teaching him to work hard to get what he wanted. "I don't want to hand everything to him," she stressed.

Given the stress of her intensive approach to parenting and Matthew's limited involvement at home—he often worked fifty or sixty hours a week, leaving the children and the house to her—Monica, like Kara, sometimes felt stifled at home. "Just having the title as mom and being a stay-at-home mom is not enough," she explained. "I want to be doing something in addition to that." Monica also compared herself unfavorably to mothers who worked full-time, noting, "I feel guilty that I, like, don't have to be balancing a full-time job, and I feel like I'm not as strong as these other moms like that are doing all this stuff. I feel like I'm not doing as much." Given those feelings, Kara sometimes caught herself daydreaming about finding childcare for the kids so she could apply for teaching jobs or even go back to the corporate grind. Yet in those moments, Monica stifled her sense of longing by telling herself it was selfish to want to work for pay if she could afford to stay home, and selfish to want someone else to raise her kids.

Monica also reminded herself that trying to "do it all" wasn't likely to alleviate her guilt. She recounted a conversation with a full-time employed friend, who helped her to realize that "no matter what you do, you're gonna have this mom guilt." With a dry laugh, Monica explained, "You just feel like you can't win."

Monica and Kara wound up in similar places, though they got there by heeding two different versions of the same Supermom myth. Like Kara's version, Monica's identifies a clear threat: children's suffering. It also offers basic rules for parents (and usually mothers) to follow to keep their children safe from possible physical, social, and emotional harm.

One difference, however, is that Monica's version is competitive—to prevent their children from suffering, moms not only have to follow the rules but follow them better than everyone else. That's because in a highly unequal society without a sturdy social safety net to fall back on, the best way to avoid suffering is to secure one of the rare spots at or near the very top. Consider, for example, the case of a degree from an Ivy League university— a list that includes eight of the most selective schools in the US. Ivy League graduates earn, on average, $86,000 a year in their first years after finishing school, compared to only about $58,000 a year for students who graduated from other four-year schools. Those gaps in pay also grow over time. At midcareer, Ivy League graduates are making, on average, almost $162,000 a year, while other four-year college graduates are making, on average, only $101,000 a year. All that money buys security, especially in a society as precarious as ours. And so, American mothers—particularly affluent, highly educated, politically liberal-leaning mothers—are often hyper focused on shoring up their kids' futures by making sure they're "good enough" to be one of the nineteen thousand admitted each year to an Ivy League school.[17]

The odds are stacked against them. Less than half a percent of US high school graduates are admitted to Ivy League schools.[18] Yet American mothers are bombarded with messages telling them that if they just work hard enough, if they just feed their kids the right diet, read them the right books, give them the right kinds of screen time, send them to the right schools, and enroll them in the right activities, they will get to post a selfie on their Instagram in a sweatshirt that says "Ivy League Mom."[19]

John Medina's 2014 book, *Brain Rules for Baby*, which Monica treated as her equivalent to a parenting Bible, begins with a list of questions he often gets from parents, including "How do I get my kid into Harvard?" "How can I make sure my little girl is going to be happy?" and "What can my baby learn while she is still in the womb?" In response to these questions, Medina offers a laundry list of things they need to do to ensure their children's health, happiness, and success in life: breastfeed for at least a year, avoid TV and video games, spend lots of time talking to your baby, give them toys that encourage creative self-expression, let them learn by making mistakes and facing "natural" consequences like being cold if they refuse to put their coat on to go outside, and teach them impulse control.[20]

On this last point, Medina goes so far as to suggest that teaching impulse control is "the best way to get your children into a college of their choice." Medina bases this advice on evidence from the marshmallow test experiment that Stanford psychologist Walter Mischel first conducted in 1972. Mischel found that kids who could wait longer for a promised treat did better, years later, on metrics like their SAT scores, and thus concluded that teaching kids to delay gratification would improve their lot in life.[21]

More recent research has poked holes in these conclusions. One study from 2018, for example, found that kids from high-income families delay gratification significantly longer than kids from lower-income families—because kids growing up in the context of scarcity learn by experience that even if they're promised a second marshmallow, it might never come. Medina, however, ignores the correlation-is-not-causation problem and insists that practicing delayed gratification will improve kids' outcomes in the end. Monica implemented that lesson by not just giving her kids whatever they wanted right away.[22]

Mothers like Monica buy books like Medina's because they offer an empowering sense of control. Like the Christian momfluencer books that Kara's moms' group read, Medina's frames mothers as superheroes battling the villains that threaten to harm their kids. Take how *Brain Rules for Baby* is described on online retail sites like Amazon. The ad copy reads, "What you do right now—before pregnancy, during pregnancy, and through the first five years—will affect your children for the rest of their lives." The language here makes it clear not only that mothers (or mothers-in-waiting) are the book's target audience but that mothers have a critical role to play in shoring up their children's success in an uncertain world.

What mom doesn't want to think of herself as a superhero? In a society that devalues caregiving and overvalues men's contributions to the economy, the myth gives moms not only a sense of control in the face of uncertainty but, maybe more important, a way to feel needed and valued for the care they provide. Of course, we could imagine a world where dads are seen as protectors. But because of the Mars/Venus myth, that expectation typically falls to women. And it creates pressure on mothers to be like helicopters—constantly hovering and available to swoop in and protect their children at any time.[23]

To that end, it's important to note that stay-at-home moms like Kara and Monica aren't the only ones who appreciate the ego boost that the Supermom myth provides. Rather, employed moms also want to feel valued for their domestic second shift. And there are versions of the myth that tell them that if they just work hard enough, they can be both Supermom and CEO.*[24]

SUPERMOM CAN HAVE IT ALL

Take Chloe, who is trying to prove that she can be a Pinterest-perfect parent while also holding a demanding full-time job. Since college and graduate school, Chloe has been moving up step-by-step in the public health field and now holds a director role. Even with all her education and professional success, however, Chloe, who is white, is still making only about $50,000 a year—the same amount that her husband, Neil, who is white and has a high school education, earns as a supervisor at a mine.

Despite her role as co-breadwinner and despite all the time she puts in at the office, Chloe is also the one responsible for almost all the "worry work" of parenting, as is the case for most American moms. During the Covid-19 pandemic, for example, it was Chloe's concerns that shaped their decisions about whether and when to send their eighteen-month-old daughter, Georgia, to in-person childcare. In early February 2020—a full month before

---

* When asked about their pre-pandemic employment, 49 percent of mothers in the PITT study sample said they were working for pay at least thirty-five hours a week, 26 percent said they were working for pay less than thirty-five hours a week, and 25 percent said they were not working for pay at all. That's compared to 58 percent of fathers who were working for pay at least thirty-five hours per week, 24 percent who were working for pay less than thirty-five hours per week, and 18 percent who were not working for pay at all. During the pandemic, school closures and layoffs disproportionately affected women's employment. Thus, when asked about their employment at the time of the survey (January 2022), only 38 percent of mothers in the PITT study were working for pay at least thirty-five hours a week, 23 percent were working for pay less than thirty-five hours a week, and 39 percent were not employed.

Georgia's childcare center closed—Chloe asked her boss if she could switch to working remotely while caring for Georgia at home. Chloe, whose mother is an ER nurse in New York City, had a sense that "it's going to get bad." Neil could have put in a request in March to do at least some of his work remotely, but he was worried his boss would get angry, so he kept going to work on-site every day.

Neil's decision to keep going into the office left Chloe to care for Georgia full-time while also working full-time remotely—an arrangement that left her feeling as though she was failing on every front. "The hardest part has been not feeling as productive and as successful in any area," Chloe said in May 2020. "There's just not enough of me to go around. I do deal with a lot of guilt around that."[25]

Given all the stress that Chloe was under, Neil suggested they send Georgia back to childcare when their center reopened in November 2020. Yet, like Monica, Chloe was hesitant: "I think there's a good element of mom guilt in it. I didn't want to make the wrong decision and put her health and safety at risk." At the same time, also like Monica, Chloe was worried that keeping Georgia out of childcare for too long would affect her "emotional health and development." In the end, Chloe decided to split the difference, waiting until February 2021 to send Georgia back to childcare and then, after that, continuing to vigilantly watch the local Covid numbers. Because Chloe was the one who was more worried about the risks of childcare, she felt compelled to be the one to do the work of figuring out how to manage those risks. Neil could have just as easily been the one checking various public health agency websites each morning, but he never volunteered to do so, and Chloe never asked.

That pattern played out across dozens of different parenting worries—from the very big to the very small. Chloe described her parenting fears as like a constant news ticker running in her head, with questions like "Is something going to happen to Georgia? Is she eating the right foods? Is she getting too much screen time? Is she socializing enough? Is she meeting all of her milestones? What if something happens to us and she's alone in the world?" Those fears even led Chloe to say no when Neil suggested that they ask his sister—a mom of three—to watch Georgia for the evening so they could go out together, noting, "I don't want to leave her. Like, that's how every Disney movie starts. The parents leave and something tragic happens. Like, there's no reason I have to worry, but it's there."

Neil, by contrast, rarely worried about the things that Chloe did. In fact, Chloe's more anxious approach to parenting freed him from having to worry, because he could trust that she'd considered it all. Going a step further, Chloe's role as the worry parent also made it seem "natural" for her to be the one who took the steps involved in protecting Georgia from all the threats Chloe was anxious about. For example, and like most of the mothers I interviewed, Chloe was the one who babyproofed the house and kept an eye on Georgia when they were all home together in the evenings to make sure she didn't put something in her mouth that she could choke on or trip into a table when she was learning to walk.

What differentiated Chloe from stay-at-home moms like Kara and Monica was that Chloe's ticker of parenting worries wasn't the only one constantly intruding on her thoughts. It ran alongside another work ticker, with thoughts like "Are you looking professional? Are you looking like you're in charge? Don't blame that on not getting any sleep. That's not an excuse. You chose this. You chose this. You chose this." Becoming a mother made that work ticker tick even louder. "As someone who was coming back from maternity leave as a director," Chloe recalled, "I wanted to show that I was strong and knew what I was doing and having a home life was not going to impact my work." For Chloe, that meant not complaining about the baby or how tired she was. She noted that it's important for professional women to avoid that kind of complaining and that they should not show any weakness. In doing so, Chloe also implied that women should be able to hold it all together, and that, if they struggle to do so, it's because they're not trying hard enough.

That might seem like a lot of pressure for Chloe to put on herself. But keeping that kind of I-can-do-it attitude gave her hope not only for herself but for her daughter and for other women, too. "I'm trying to prove myself," she explained, "but also I don't want to set a bad example for other people. You know, if other women come in, I don't want [my employer] to be like, 'Well, it didn't really work out with Chloe . . .' I don't want to set that up. And I wanna be a strong role model for my child." Chloe also stressed that if she didn't put that kind of pressure on herself, "I don't think I'd be as good at my job."

Chloe appreciated the results she got from her high-pressure approach to work and parenting, but they also came at a cost. "I knew it was gonna be hard," she explained, "but I don't feel like you can really fully wrap your head around wanting to be in two places one hundred percent at the same time."

Chloe sometimes found herself frustrated with Neil for not understanding what she was going through. "Sometimes it's an exhausting week," she explained. "Sometimes I just wanna pick a fight with my husband. You know, just, like, 'You don't get it!'" At the same time, Chloe used Neil's job as an excuse for his more limited role in parenting—a grace she never extends to herself. Talking about why she was the one who handled all the research and doctor visits and follow-up care when Georgia was diagnosed with a minor medical issue, for example, Chloe pointed to the fact that his job is less flexible than hers and that while she gets six weeks of paid time off each year, Neil gets only two.

That's not to say that Neil isn't involved at home. It's just that he plays more of a supporting role. When Chloe is feeling overwhelmed, she'll sometimes tell Neil, "I just need you to handle everything so I can just disassociate with everything for a minute." Neil is quick to step in those moments. Yet like most other fathers, he rarely notices when Chloe is struggling or volunteers to help before Chloe asks.

Chloe, however, doesn't like to ask for help from Neil or anyone else because she feels as though she should be able to do it all. "You feel guilty about complaining," Chloe explained, adding, "It's been hard to say that it's hard." And so, Chloe usually tries to hold it all together on her own and only gets a break when she's about to crack.

———

The myth that Supermom can have it all is more carrot than stick. This version tells moms like Chloe they don't have to give up anything to put on their capes, because they can have it all—and do it all well—if they're willing to work hard. You can be Supermom while also being CEO.

This myth is a corporatized and sanitized retelling of the message promoted by the US women's movement in the 1960s and '70s. The feminists of that era told American women that they deserved to have it all, but that we could only get there with a stronger social safety net, and only if men stepped up at home. As writer and activist Gloria Steinem explained in a *Time* interview, "As long as working women also have to do the work of child and family care at home, they will have two jobs instead of one. Perhaps more important, children will grow up thinking that only women can be loving and nurturing, and men cannot." Or, as she put it more bluntly to Congress, "Most American children suffer too much mother and too little father."[26]

Over time, corporate consultants twisted this message—wringing out the parts about men needing to step up and social safety nets needing to be stronger, leaving only the parts that tell women they deserve to have it all. *Lean In*, by former Facebook COO Sheryl Sandberg, and first published in 2013, is likely the most famous example, though the dilution of feminism began long before that. The book—an expanded version of Sandberg's wildly popular TED Talk—effectively tells women that if they're struggling to get ahead at work, it's because they're letting self-doubt hold them back from really trying. Sandberg tells women to ask themselves questions like "What would I do if I weren't afraid?" and "How can I do better?" Note, in turn, how these questions echo the work news ticker that ran in Chloe's head.[27]

Sandberg also tells women to lean in not only for themselves but for the benefit of other women, promising that "[c]onditions for all women will improve when there are more women in leadership roles giving strong and powerful voice to their needs and concerns." This might seem like an empowering message. But the consequence, as we saw with Chloe, is what we might call "Jane Henryism." Highly educated professional moms, in their quest to prove that they can do it all and be role models for their daughters and for all other women, end up working themselves to the bone.[28]

Sandberg did get pushback for her message. Black feminist writer and activist bell hooks, for example, argued soon after the publication of *Lean In* in 2013 that "Sandberg sees women's lack of perseverance as more the problem than systemic inequality. Sandberg effectively uses her race and class power and privilege to promote a narrow definition of feminism that obscures and undermines visionary feminist concerns." Similarly, feminist philosopher and writer Nancy Fraser saw Sandberg's *Lean In* as the epitome of capitalism's co-optation of feminism, writing in 2013 that "I fear that the movement for women's liberation has become entangled in a dangerous liaison with neoliberal efforts to build a free-market society. That would explain how it came to pass that feminist ideas that once formed part of a radical worldview are increasingly expressed in individualist terms. Where feminists once criticised a society that promoted careerism, they now advise women to 'lean in.' A movement that once prioritised social solidarity now celebrates female entrepreneurs. A perspective that once valorised 'care' and interdependence now encourages individual advancement and meritocracy."[29]

Unfortunately, and like "dangerous" women throughout history, the feminists who questioned Sandberg's *Lean In* message were either deemed crazy or summarily ignored. And so, what we got in the wake of *Lean In* was a gaggle of pseudo-feminist writers who cashed in on Sandberg's message by writing their own books promising that if women just make the right choices, they can have it all without feeling exhausted all the time. Consider, for example, management expert Laura Vanderkam's 2015 book, *I Know How She Does It: How Successful Women Make the Most of Their Time*. Vanderkam markets her book provocatively, asking, "What if balancing work and family is actually not as hard as it's made out to be?" Vanderkam bases this argument on data from hour-by-hour diaries tracking how "successful" women—women who make $100,000 a year or more—spend their time. Vanderkam finds that "these women worked less and slept more than they assumed they did before they started tracking their time. They went jogging or to the gym, played with their children, scheduled date nights with their significant others, and had lunches with friends. They made time for the things that gave them pleasure and meaning, fitting the pieces together like tiles in a mosaic—without adhering to overly rigid schedules that would eliminate flexibility and spontaneity."[30]

Based on these findings, Vanderkam offers advice to her readers. Domestically, she suggests "tak[ing] it easy on housework," ideally by outsourcing it to someone else. Professionally, Vanderkam recommends what she calls "split shifts," putting in seven hours at work, then four hours at home, then another two hours at night after the kids are in bed, which is basically the schedule that Chloe follows. And she recommends carving out an hour a day for leisure, and particularly what she considers productive leisure time, like exercise or crafting instead of watching TV.

Vanderkam's advice may track with how "successful" women spend their time. But in the absence of a sturdy social safety net, the lifestyle requires ample resources—like the money to pay for a housekeeper and full-time childcare and the job flexibility to set your own work hours and work remotely at least part of each day. Put differently, if you're a woman and you're not making $100,000 a year (or more), it will likely be a struggle to meet Vanderkam's standards. And even then, you might only be able to afford those standards by exploiting someone else. That's what we saw with Chloe. Even when she managed to follow some of Vanderkam's advice, she still ended up feeling exhausted, stretched, and riddled with guilt.

That guilt is why mothers like Monica (who used to work in a high-powered corporate job) sometimes end up opting out of the workforce, at least while their children are young. And it's why mothers like Teresa (the high-level executive we met in chapter 4) end up passing on opportunities for promotion, even when they're a shoo-in for the job. These women have been told that they should be able to have and do it all well, and when they struggle to find a way to reach those goals, the Supermom myth leaves them with only themselves to blame.[31]

Like Chloe, highly educated professional mothers often end up assuming, through their own experiences and by talking to other mom friends, that fear and guilt are "normal" parts of mothering. But research shows that isn't the case. Drawing on interviews with over one hundred highly educated professional mothers in the US, Sweden, Germany, and Italy, sociologist Caitlyn Collins finds that maternal guilt varies across countries, with US mothers having the most. Although mothers in all four countries associated guilt with "good mothering," Collins found that the mothers in Sweden—which has the strongest social safety net and the strongest commitment to egalitarian gender norms—expressed by far the least guilt. In the US, by contrast, the lack of a strong social safety net, coupled with weak commitments to gender egalitarianism and expectations of long work hours, creates a situation in which mothers feel like there are no good choices. Strong social safety nets, according to Collins, reduce maternal guilt by increasing the amount of time that professional mothers can spend at home, reducing the incentives for fathers to shirk care responsibilities to focus more on paid work, and creating the expectation that childcare is a cost and a responsibility that everyone should share.[32]

THE COST OF THE MYTH

Our lack of a social safety net, and the resulting financial precarity, allows the Supermom myth to flourish. The threat of precarity gets wrapped up in different villains' costumes—like Satan or Suffering. But those villains are all manifestations of the same core threat. And mothers buy into the myth because it promises they can conquer what they fear.

This is a chicken-and-egg problem. On the one hand, not having a social safety net makes it easier for people to believe the myth. Countries that have introduced paid family leave, for example, subsequently saw bigger increases in egalitarian decision-making at the household level compared to other similar countries that hadn't yet made those changes at the time, and they also saw bigger improvements in children's and mothers' health. A study in Norway compared different-gender couples whose children were born right before and after the government implemented a "daddy quota" in 1993, which (initially) gave fathers an additional four weeks of leave on top of the eighteen weeks of paid leave parents could divide and share. The study found that post-quota families reported 11 percent lower levels of conflict over the household division of labor and were 50 percent more likely to say they were dividing domestic responsibilities equally between women and men. Changing policy is perhaps the best way to get people to change their minds.[33]

Yet, on the other hand, believing the Supermom myth inflates the importance of mothers, making it easy for people—even mothers—to think that the US can get by without a better net. Mothers matter, a lot. But they aren't the only ones who should be protecting children. Nor would children need as much protection if we had a stronger social safety net. Put differently, the Supermom myth leads us to ask the wrong questions—"How can mothers best protect their children?"—rather than: "Why are women the ones tasked with protecting kids?" Or even: "Why do we have so much to fear?"[34]

For individual mothers, this inflated sense of self-importance makes it easy to justify not getting (or even asking for) help with the burden of caregiving, either from fathers or from anyone else. Recall, for example, how Monica couldn't find any childcare providers she trusted; how Kara didn't trust public school teachers with teaching her children moral lessons; how

Chloe was hesitant to send Georgia back to childcare in person or let family members babysit so that she could take a night off.[35]

By making mothers seem like the "natural" and "best" protectors for their children, the Supermom myth also undermines efforts to build a stronger social safety net. Consider the PITT study data, which show that mothers who believe that it's best for kids to have their moms at home are also less supportive than other mothers of policies like free childcare and preschool for all.* Those same mothers—most of whom are themselves stay-at-home parents or working for pay only part-time—are also disproportionately inclined to say that parents' primary responsibility is to give their own children the best chance at being successful, rather than working to ensure that all kids have an equal chance of success.[†36]

These findings harken back to Nancy Fraser's warnings about the dangers of neoliberal feminism. They suggest that believing the Supermom myth may lead mothers to reject the need for a sturdy social safety net, since if kids are safe under moms' watchful eyes, then there's no risk that kids will ever fall. Maybe more troubling, these findings also suggest that mothers—especially mothers who are already able to spend more time at home with their children—may see keeping the social safety net small and weak as a way to maintain their kids' competitive edge over kids who don't have that same support at home. Though, of course, the cost for holding that belief is having to hold it together alone.

---

* I measure these beliefs using mothers' responses to the question: "Do you think children are better off if their mother is home and doesn't hold a job, or are children just as well off if their mother works?" Cross-national comparisons point to similar conclusions, showing that countries with more egalitarian attitudes regarding paid work and family roles tend to have the strongest social safety nets, including longer paid family leave, flexible work arrangements, and universal, affordable childcare.

† PITT participants were asked, "In your opinion, which of the following more accurately captures the responsibility of a parent? Would you say that parents should try to ensure that: 1) their own child has the best possible chance of success, even if that makes it harder for other people's children to be successful, or 2) all children have the same chance of success, even if that makes it harder for their own child to be successful"? Among mothers who believe that it's best for children if their mothers are not working for pay, 51 percent say that parents' primary responsibility is to ensure their individual child's well-being. By contrast, among mothers who believe that it's just as good for children if their mothers work for pay, only 39 percent see it as more important for parents to ensure their individual children's well-being than to ensure that all kids have an equal chance at success in life.

Regardless of which versions of these myths they're telling, the prophets of American self-help culture goad women into competing with each other and gaslight those who struggle into blaming themselves. We could reject those prophets, calling them out one by one for their falsehoods. And yet, as we'll see in our next chapter, the roots and the rot of these myths run deep to maintain the status quo.

Chapter 8

WHAT A BETTER
NET WOULD MEAN

Never let a good crisis go to waste." That saying may or may not have been coined by Winston Churchill, but it certainly captures how European countries responded to the crisis of World War II. As we saw in the preface, much of Europe responded to the war's death and destruction by strengthening their safety nets with programs like universal healthcare, universal childcare, and paid family leave.[1]

In 2020, the US seemed to be at a similar tipping point. As the Covid-19 pandemic and the murder of George Floyd laid bare the deep inequities in American society and the giant holes in our social safety net, it looked like we might finally reject the myths that perpetuate our DIY society, admit that it's only working for a few of us, and build the kind of net that would better protect us all.[2]

In March 2020, Congress passed the CARES Act, which allocated $2.2 trillion in temporary pandemic relief efforts. Despite Republicans' long-standing opposition to increasing government spending, the act was passed by a Republican-controlled Senate and signed by Republican president Donald Trump. It included $300 billion for direct cash payments to taxpayers—up to $1,200 per adult and $500 per child. It also included $260 billion to expand and extend unemployment benefits, $377 billion for small businesses, $100 billion for hospitals, $71 billion for transportation, $31 billion for schools, $25 billion to expand broadband internet access, $17 billion for rent relief, $5 billion for childcare, and $750 million for food banks, plus an eviction moratorium for renters who couldn't make payments and a six-month pause on repayment of student loans.[3]

As the pandemic continued, so did the cascade of relief efforts, flowing out to support the vast majority of families and communities in the US. That included making free lunch available to all school-age children, sending monthly checks to families with kids through an expansion of the child tax credit, boosting support to institutions helped by the CARES Act, extending the eviction moratorium and the pause on student loan payments, and increasing the value of food stamp benefits for low-income families to compensate for rising grocery costs.[4]

These programs were a life raft for millions of Americans who were already drowning before the pandemic, and who surely would've sunk under the flood of risk it wrought. The expanded child tax credit alone lifted more than three million US children out of poverty nearly overnight, reducing the child poverty rate from 15.8 to 11.9 percent. The child tax credit together with increased food assistance and the expanded National School Lunch Program cut the percentage of children experiencing food insecurity by almost a third. Certainly, there were hiccups—like outdated government computer systems causing delays in access to unemployment benefits. Yet research from the Federal Reserve shows that these programs, in total, boosted families' "resilience"—how long they would be able to maintain their standard of living even after the loss of a job—by about fifteen weeks on average. In essence, pandemic relief efforts offered a silver lining of security for millions of Americans in an otherwise desperate time.[5]

A GLIMPSE OF THE GOOD LIFE

Take twenty-year-old Sierra, who in late 2019 was living with her eighteen-month-old son, Kailani, sharing an apartment with a friend in a college town in Indiana. Sierra, who is Black and has only a high school education, was working a minimum wage job in fast food. Though she took as many hours a week as her employer would give her, she typically earned less than $1,000 a month. That was little enough that she qualified for support from poverty programs like welfare, WIC, EITC, and Medicaid, but the benefits weren't enough to make life easy. Money was a constant source of stress.

Kailani's father, Derek, had lived with them for a short time after Kailani was born. But Derek, who is Black and only has a high school diploma, was having trouble finding work in a lily-white town with plenty of college students to fill any open jobs. So he moved back home to Alabama, to a small town with a big poultry-processing facility that employs many of his relatives, and where Derek hoped to get a steady job.

Once Derek moved away, Sierra found herself struggling to raise Kailani on her own. "It's just me," she explained sadly, adding, "It's kind of hard. Like, I can't really do everything by myself." Sierra and Derek weren't together as a couple anymore, but she wanted Kailani to grow up with two parents, and she wanted help with day-to-day parenting demands. So in early 2020 Sierra decided to quit her job at the fast-food restaurant, take Kailani out of the subsidized childcare program he was attending, and move to Alabama as well.

In Alabama, Sierra found an efficiency apartment at a motel, and she started looking for childcare for Kailani and applying for local jobs. Before she got any callbacks, however, the Covid-19 pandemic replaced "Help wanted" ads with "Closed" signs.

Like many other meat and poultry processors, the local poultry plant was hit hard by Covid infections and had to shut down. That left nearly everyone in town looking for work. And it meant that Sierra, as the newcomer, had neither any chance of finding a job in the short term nor anyone to lean on for support. With so many people out of work, local charity organizations were also overrun with demand, which meant that the church that gave out free diapers didn't always have Kailani's size.[6]

Amid supply shortages and panic hoarding, Sierra was struggling not only to get enough diapers for Kailani but also to get enough food to eat. Since every state has its own versions of programs like welfare and WIC and food stamps, Sierra had to reapply in Alabama. Even once she was enrolled, Sierra found herself struggling to use her benefits. With Covid food shortages, and with so many other people out of work and relying on government food aid, qualifying products were almost impossible to find on the shelves. "A lot of people buy all the meat, all [the] milk and cheese and eggs, and it's been hard to get stuff like that lately," Sierra said.[7]

In a stroke of luck or irony, Derek wasn't among the people who had lost their jobs at the poultry plant, because the best job he could find when he moved back to Alabama was a low-wage job at a big box store. Sierra hoped that, working at the store, Derek would be able to pick up the things she needed, like food and diapers and wipes. But with shortages affecting so many products, Derek's employer was saving what little they did have for customers. Employees weren't even allowed to use their breaks to shop—they had to wait until after work. By the time Derek finished his shift each day, all the necessities would be gone.

Just as things began to get dire for Sierra, the US government stepped in with relief, sending out the first stimulus checks in late April 2020.* She could barely believe it. Some of the money went toward car insurance and clothes for Kailani; Sierra was able to save the rest because of another government program that offered rent and utilities relief. "I didn't believe that either," Sierra told me in May 2020. "When that happened, I was just a happy person." Without that support, Sierra would have been unable to stay in her apartment and unable to stay in Alabama near Derek. "That would be hard," she noted. "I wouldn't have no place for me and my son to go. That would have been scary. I'd have to move back with my mom back in Chicago."[8]

Of course, pandemic relief programs didn't alleviate all of Sierra's worries. Car insurance payments, for example, took a sizable chunk out of Sierra's relief check—more than $100 every month. It was frustrating and nonsensical to Sierra that she wasn't driving anywhere but still had to pay.

And yet, more money and fewer expenses meant that Sierra didn't have to stress about finding a job, at least not right away. Sierra hadn't qualified for paid family leave after giving birth to Kailani and had worked as much as she could since he was born. For the first time ever, Sierra got to just spend time at home with her son. "I'm enjoying it," she told me, "because when I used to work a lot, I used to complain how I didn't have enough time to be with my son. We do finger painting, and we color. I just let him scribble and stuff, and we play Connect Four. I taught him how to play that. We do that and watch TV."

For families in poverty like Sierra's, the pandemic safety net was life-changing, even if it didn't fully eliminate the precarity they faced. Families like Sierra's also weren't the only ones who benefited from pandemic relief.

---

* The US federal government passed bills providing three separate stimulus checks. The first checks included up to $2,400 for couples earning less than $150,000, or up to $1,200 for single adults earning less than $7,500, plus $500 per child. The second checks, for up to $600, were sent in December 2020 and January 2021. The third checks, for up to $1,400, were sent in March 2021.

Compared to our pre-pandemic safety net, the response to Covid was more universal with much less red tape. This meant that families who'd previously gotten stuck in our safety net's missing middle—earning too much to qualify for government poverty programs, but too little to be able to easily afford things like food or housing or healthcare or childcare or higher education—were able to access relief they'd never had before.[9]

Take Christine, a stay-at-home mom of three children. She loved the universal free school lunch program put in place during the pandemic,* both because of how it took the stress out of her grocery budget and because of how it gave her "one less thing I have to think about during the day." Or take Mandy, whom we first met in chapter 3. She and Alex were living "check to check" in 2019; she called it a "great relief" to get the pandemic stimulus and child tax credit checks and to not have to make payments on the more than $100,000 that she and Alex still owed on their student loans. And consider also Laura, a married mom of three who lost her job in publishing during the pandemic. With the money from the Covid unemployment benefits and stimulus payments, Laura was able to build the occasional freelance marketing work she'd done pre-pandemic into a small but thriving business. As her own boss, Laura could also work from home full-time and set her own hours, which made it easier to share caregiving responsibilities with her husband, Tony, who had recently left the military and was looking for a full-time job.[10]

———

We could have made our pandemic safety net permanent. And for a moment in early 2021, it seemed like we might go even further, putting in place new policies like affordable childcare, universal preschool, guaranteed paid fam-

---

* Before the pandemic, only students from low-income US families qualified for free or reduced-price school meals, which meant families had to fill out complex applications and prove they "deserved" to qualify. When Covid hit, however, Congress voted to expand the program to offer free breakfasts and lunches for all children. This response wasn't innovative—Sweden, for example, has guaranteed free lunches for all school children since 1997, and for elementary-age children since 1973. And yet, given how supply chain issues limited availability, as Sierra experienced, and how inflation caused grocery prices to soar during the pandemic, many families were very grateful for the extra support.

ily leave, free college, caps on the out-of-pocket cost of prescription drugs, and a higher minimum wage. In January of that year, Joe Biden became president—elected at least in part because voters liked his plan to "Build Back Better" better than Trump's promise to "Keep America Great." Biden's plan didn't go as far as establishing a full European-style social safety net—it didn't include universal healthcare, for example—but it still represented a huge leap in that direction on multiple critical fronts, all paid for by increased taxes on big businesses and billionaires and other Americans with extreme levels of wealth.*[11]

GIVING UP ON HOPE

In the end, however, the crisis didn't save us. We let the money dry up. We brought back the red tape. And we even ripped new holes in our pre-pandemic social safety net.

By early 2022, Congress had not only rejected Biden's Build Back Better plan but also cut off pandemic relief programs on which families like Sierra's had come to rely. The eviction moratorium, the pandemic relief checks, and the monthly child tax credit payments all ended abruptly. The last of those alone pushed millions of families into poverty. A month after the last checks went out, the child poverty rate in the US jumped from 11 to 17 percent, exceeding the pre-pandemic rate.[12]

Sierra and Kailani were among those left out to dry. Without the extra

---

* For kids and families, the plan included twelve weeks of guaranteed parental leave, with subsidies for employers to cover the costs, along with a monthly child allowance of $300 per child, expanded childcare subsidies so that families earning up to 150 percent of their state's median income would pay no more than 7 percent of their earnings for care for infants and toddlers, free public preschool for all three- and four-year-olds, and plans to build new preschool and childcare facilities to meet demand. On the education front, Biden also proposed to modernize public school buildings, guarantee two years of free community college for every student, boost the value of the Pell Grant, and offer debt relief for student loan borrowers. To improve healthcare access, the plan would have reduced prescription drug costs, lowered insurance premiums, expanded eligibility for Medicaid, and improved long-term care coverage for sick and elderly people. Infrastructure-wise, Biden wanted to modernize and expand public transit, build or upgrade more than 1.5 million homes to make them affordable for low- and middle-income families, ensure access to clean drinking water in every community, and reduce the cost of broadband internet. And to improve work conditions, Biden proposed raising the federal minimum wage from $7.25 to $15 an hour, with additional raises and benefits for care workers, plus creating new high-paying jobs and supporting worker unionization to ensure that those jobs remained good jobs long-term.

money from the government, Sierra could no longer keep up with her insurance payments. So she had to give up her car. Not having a car made it more difficult for Sierra to keep the part-time job she had found at a gas station, because she had to walk miles to get to work and often miles back home again if she couldn't get a ride. In the summer of 2022, Sierra gave up on trying to make things work in Alabama and moved with Kailani to Chicago to live with her mom instead.

By early 2023, Congress had gone even further, ending the pause on student loan repayments, cutting off rent relief and universal free school lunches, and rolling back the pandemic expansion of Medicaid, leaving up to twenty-four million more people without healthcare coverage.* Adding insult to injury, Congress also instituted new and broader work requirements for programs like food stamps and Medicaid. And the new Supreme Court, with help from red-state officials, eroded federal and state protections for abortion and eliminated the affirmative action programs that had helped ensure fairness in hiring and admissions to college.[13]

One of the last holdouts was childcare, though even there, Congress let us down, allowing pandemic childcare subsidies to expire at the end of September 2023. That $24 billion could have continued flowing into centers to help raise wages for workers like Brooke, limit the staff turnover that Holly experienced, reduce the long waiting lists like those Teresa faced when her daughter was born, and maybe even make childcare affordable enough for women like Erin to go back to full-time paid work. Now, instead, that money is gone. As a result, according to estimates from the Century Foundation, up to 70,000 childcare centers across the US are likely to close within the next few years, eliminating more than 230,000 jobs and pushing more than three million families over their childcare cliff and into the missing middle, unable to afford or find access to care.[14]

The expiration of the pandemic childcare subsidies came in the middle of a vicious and highly consequential congressional fight. In August 2023, congressional Republicans threatened to shut down the federal government,

---

* The federal government also ended the Covid emergency declaration, making it easier for private employers to force workers back to the office, even if they were happier and more productive at home.

demanding deep cuts to future social safety net spending in exchange for their support in passing a routine funding bill that would allocate the money Congress had already agreed to pay. At first, it looked like Congress might be able to reach an agreement, but Donald Trump, who at the time was the front-runner for the Republican presidential nomination, urged congressional Republicans: "UNLESS YOU GET EVERYTHING, SHUT IT DOWN!" By the time the childcare funding expired in September, Congress still had not reached an agreement. Less than a week later, congressional Republicans, led by a far-right radical contingent, pushed out House Speaker Kevin McCarthy for negotiating with Democrats to pass a temporary stopgap spending bill.[15]

Amid all the turmoil in Washington, the news media had little air to spare for the fact that we'd fallen off a childcare cliff. One notable exception was Fox News. Their take included an op-ed by conservative radio host, author, and relationship coach Suzanne Venker arguing that "the most obvious solution to the ensuing child care crisis is for married parents of non-school-age children to sit down and do the math and decide which one of them will stay home. For most families, that parent will be Mom." Venker also went further in suggesting that childcare "was never meant to be available for every parent who simply wanted to use it" and that women who can afford to stay home shouldn't be putting their children in childcare anyway.*[16]

THE BENEFITS OF UNIVERSAL SUPPORT

It may seem rational to argue that we shouldn't waste government money on supporting people who can find a way to get by without assistance. But making social safety net programs universal amplifies the benefits for the most vulnerable while leaving almost all of us better off.[17]

Consider, for example, the case of universal school lunches. Research shows that those programs are good for families, good for kids, and, from a public health perspective, good for society as a whole. When US school

---

* Venker also drops in some seriously questionable economic logic, arguing that "if far fewer parents use subsidized day care, the industry will become much smaller in scale, thus making it more affordable to those who truly need it."

districts have experimented with making school meals universal, they've seen improvements in kids' nutrition as well as their test scores. Those benefits extend even to kids whose families could afford to pack lunches—possibly because, even in the US, school lunches are more nutritious than the kinds of food most kids would otherwise bring from home.* At the same time, the benefits of universal school meals are most pronounced for kids from low-income families—the kids who would get free lunch or reduced-price lunch either way. That's because when school lunches are free for everyone, low-income kids aren't stigmatized for eating them, and they can get the food they need without shame.[18]

Take also the case of healthcare, which many countries make free or nearly free and easily accessible to all. Since the 1970s, countries with universal health systems have kept healthcare costs contained, with total spending—including government spending, employer spending, and personal spending—on healthcare representing a fairly constant 9 percent of GDP, and with almost all of that money coming from the state. In the US, by contrast, total spending on healthcare costs has increased dramatically over that same time period, from 7 percent in the 1970s to 18 percent of the US GDP in 2022, and the portion of those costs paid by employers and families has increased substantially, too. Consider the average employee and employer contributions to the cost of an employer-subsidized family health plan. Between 1999 and 2022, the employee's share of those costs nearly quadrupled, from $1,543 to $6,106 a year. Over that same period, the employer's share of the costs more than tripled, from $4,247 to $16,357 per employee per year. Given those costs, it's almost no wonder that many US employers try to get around the Affordable Care Act rules—as we saw with women like Akari, Patricia, Sylvia, and Lillian—by capping worker hours or treating workers as independent contractors so they don't have to pay for even part of their healthcare.[19]

School lunch and healthcare aren't exceptions. If the US were to build a Scandinavian-style social safety net with universal benefits like healthcare,

---

* Comparing school lunches and packed lunches, nutrition researcher Alisha Farris and her team found that school lunches contained significantly higher levels of protein, fiber, vitamin A, and calcium and also contained fewer calories, less fat, less saturated fat, and less sugar. The only measures on which packed lunches scored "healthier" were vitamin C, iron, and sodium.

paid family leave and sick leave, affordable childcare, free college tuition, retirement pensions, and free eldercare, then the vast majority of Americans—regardless of their incomes—would end up healthier, happier, and more productive than they currently are. In fact, research shows that universal programs would be so much more cost-effective than our current public/private hybrid system that over the long run, a Scandinavian-style social safety net would pay for itself.*[20]

THE PROFITEERS WHO SANK US FOR THEIR OWN GAIN

In the short run, however, a plan like Build Back Better would have dramatically shifted the balance of power. Regular people would have been substantially better off, while billionaires and big corporations would've had to get by with a little bit less.[21]

That shift provided an incentive to kill the bill. Not because billionaires and big corporations couldn't get by with less money, but because having an outsized share of the wealth is what gives them their power. The more people there are with nothing in the bank, the easier it is for people with millions or billions to monopolize scarce resources—like prime real estate and admission to elite private colleges. And the easier it is for the people with millions or billions to pressure those with nothing into doing their bidding—like working in the factory they run or cleaning their house for a meager wage.†[22]

---

* Sociologist Erik Olin Wright suggests that even big corporations and wealthy elites stand to benefit from a stronger social safety net, though only if we go all the way to the kind of robust social safety net that many Scandinavian countries have—with things like universal healthcare, universal paid sick leave and family leave, free college and university tuition, affordable childcare, affordable housing programs, robust retirement benefits, strong unemployment protections, and generous minimum wage laws. Such a system would reduce some of the costs that employers currently pay (e.g., for employee health insurance) and would also help increase worker productivity (by making workers healthier and happier) and stoke innovation (by positioning workers to fill more "modern" career opportunities).

† The engineers of our DIY society derive their status and power at least in part from the exploitation of others—such as by running or owning shares in companies that underpay their workers or by underpaying for the goods and services they buy. When the social scaffolding is sturdier, and when the safety net is larger, that kind of exploitation is more difficult to accomplish because workers have more power to leave bad jobs or negotiate for the kinds of pay and working conditions that will reduce their precarity. As we saw with Akari, Brooke, Sierra, and so many other people we've met so far in this book, in the absence of a sturdy social safety net, workers can be compelled

And so, killing the bill is exactly what they did, by using their wealth to buy political power. At the time, the House of Representatives was held by Democrats, who are more inclined toward expanding the social safety net. The Senate, meanwhile, had a fifty-fifty split, with Vice President Kamala Harris having the tie-breaking vote. And so, to kill the bill, opponents had to get all the Republicans and at least one Democrat on board.[23]

That key Democrat turned out to be West Virginia senator Joe Manchin, who has a long history of taking big business's side. Manchin, for example, helped pass legislation that allowed the maker of the EpiPen—a lifesaving device for people with allergies—to raise the price from about $100 in 2007 to $600 in 2016, despite the fact that each EpiPen costs only about a dollar to make.* The company in question was West Virginia–based Mylan Pharmaceuticals, which was also Manchin's biggest campaign donor, and which, at the time, was headed by Manchin's daughter, Heather Bresch.†[24]

That history made Manchin an easy target for the opponents of Build Back Better. During the first three months of the bill's negotiations, Manchin took in over $1.5 million in donations from billionaires, big corporations, and super PACs (or political action committees) for his 2022 reelection campaign. With those donations in hand, Manchin's first step was to gut the bill of key provisions like child tax credits, paid family and medical leave, affordable childcare, affordable housing, free community college, and corporate tax increases. In February 2022, even after getting all those

---

to take jobs that pay them less than they need or (arguably) deserve for their labor. That underpayment generates profits for these workers' employers and/or for those who purchase the goods or services that workers are providing by leaving more money in their pockets at the end of the day. Billionaires, big corporations, and their cronies leverage their wealth and the power that comes with that wealth to perpetuate these systems of exploitation and to resist efforts at social change. They do so by disproportionately controlling the tools of wealth generation, by shaping organizational and institutional policies in ways that serve their own interests, and by resisting changes to US tax laws that would make them more progressive and thus eat up a greater share of the wealth they currently keep for themselves.

* By contrast, a similar device still costs $69 in the UK, with the full cost covered by the National Health Service. Given these price differences, Mylan was accused of price gouging in a class action lawsuit.

† After merging with a division of Pfizer, Mylan became known as Viatris. Manchin's daughter, Heather Bresch, began working at Mylan in 1992, became CEO in 2012, and remained CEO through the major price hike that occurred in 2016.

concessions, Manchin, along with Arizona senator Kyrsten Sinema—then a Democrat, now an Independent, and a recipient of similar campaign donations—refused to give the bill the votes it needed to pass in the Senate after passing the House.*[25]

Of course, Manchin and Sinema weren't the only ones who voted to kill Build Back Better. Not a single Republican senator or Republican House representative voted in favor of the bill.† And their votes were also paid for—in many cases, by the same billionaires and big corporations that filled Manchin's and Sinema's coffers with cash. The billionaires included Republican megadonors like Wall Street investor Kenneth G. Langone and real estate developer Harlan Crow, who was later uncovered to be financially backing Supreme Court Justice Clarence Thomas and his family as well. The corporate donors included health insurance companies like Blue Cross Blue Shield and UnitedHealth Group; financial companies like Wells Fargo, Goldman Sachs, and American Express; defense contractors like Lockheed Martin; fossil fuel companies like ExxonMobil; technology companies like Verizon; and even the parent company of Fox News.[26]

These billionaires and big corporations not only killed our chance at a stronger social safety net; they also used the pandemic to get ahead while the rest of us flailed. A *Washington Post* investigation found that of the $4 trillion in federal money spent during the first six months of the pandemic, more than half—$2.3 trillion—went to big companies and their executives and shareholders, while only one-fifth—$884 billion—went to workers and families. Companies took that money—and the lower interest rates they also got from the government—and used them for executives' and shareholders' gain. The Cheesecake Factory, for example, furloughed forty-one thousand workers in 2020, despite claiming a $50 million tax break that was

---

* Not coincidentally, later that spring, Manchin also refused to cast the deciding vote in favor of the John Lewis Voting Rights Act.

† Of course, Democrats also receive campaign donations from big corporations and billionaires, which is part of why support for our DIY society often extends across the aisle. These big donors, however, disproportionately identify as Republicans and give more money to Republican than Democratic campaigns, particularly in the run-up to presidential election years. These big donors also play a disproportionate role in funding Republican candidates for state-level offices. In Wisconsin, for example, an investigation found that GOP candidates received more than four times as much money in campaign donations from big corporations as Democratic candidates did.

supposed to keep employers from pushing workers off their payrolls. The Cheesecake Factory did end up rehiring most of those workers a few months later, but in the interim, the furloughs and tax break saved the company so much money that it posted record profits in 2021.[27]

All those profits left the stock market booming. That might seem like a universally good thing. But the problem is that the stock market is like a casino where only the house and the high rollers win. Technically, anyone with cash to spare can invest in the stock market, but the top 1 percent of US households owns a third of all the money in the stock market, and the top 10 percent of households now control a record 89 percent of all the money in stocks.* What that means, in turn, is that when the stock market is booming, it's also increasing inequalities in US wealth. In 2021, for example, the richest 1 percent of Americans gained $6.5 trillion in wealth, while regular Americans were struggling to pay for rent and childcare and keep food on the table amid rising grocery costs.[28]

These two trends, of course, were closely related. Big corporations and billionaires were pocketing all that extra money the rest of us were spending on higher prices, causing the value of stocks to rise. Some business leaders and economists tried to blame rising prices on greedy workers demanding higher salaries. But the real story is that big corporations used Covid disruptions as a cover to raise their prices and keep them there.† In a *New York Times* investigation, journalists Lydia DePillis and Jeanna Smialek found that despite auto manufacturers' grumblings about pandemic production and supply chain disruptions, they actually continued raising prices long after production and supplies were back on track. Then they went further and cut lower-price models from their car lines, ensuring that prices wouldn't come back down again.‡ By July 2023 there were only three new cars in the

---

* The top 1 percent of US households includes Americans earning $600,000 or more annually and/ or with a net worth of $11.1 million or more.

† Analyses reveal that higher salaries and rising materials and logistics costs can't account for the increase in prices during the pandemic. Rather, companies kept prices high even when their own costs went back down again, and even if they never went up at all.

‡ Instead of making a range of cars for different price points, auto manufacturers cut their lowest-price brands and focused only on making luxury cars—the ones with the highest markup and thus the highest profit margins. With cars in short supply, dealers also jacked up the prices on their existing inventory, including on the used cars that—with fewer lower-price brands on the

US market with a sticker price under $20,000, and the average price of a new vehicle was $48,000. That's more than triple what Sierra would be making every year if she was working forty hours a week at the federal minimum wage of $7.25 an hour, and it doesn't even include car insurance costs.[29]

Now, you may be thinking, "But vehicles are luxuries; you can get by without a car." In the US, however, not having a vehicle makes life difficult if not impossible for people living in rural and suburban communities, as we saw with Sierra and with Jocelyn, and for people living in cities that have invested next to nothing in public transit routes, as we saw with Patricia and her mother. That lack of public transit is a boon for the auto industry because demand stays high, even if high-price premium models are the only option for people to buy.[30]

Of course, auto manufacturers aren't the only ones playing this new "excuse-flation" pricing game. According to the Economic Policy Institute, 54 percent of the inflation that the US economy experienced during the pandemic was the product of "fatter profit margins,"* while labor costs accounted for only 8 percent. And yet, rather than take steps to try to stop the profit-price spiral, federal policymakers focused on curbing wage growth by increasing interest rates and allowing unemployment to rise.[31]

Put differently, billionaires and big corporations exploited the Covid pandemic for their own financial gain. They manipulated policymakers into letting them get away with fleecing American taxpayers and consumers while trying to force their employees to take the blame.

HOW THEY KEEP US FROM FIGHTING BACK

So why haven't Americans revolted against the billionaires and big corporations? After all, there are 330 million of us but only a few thousand of them. If enough of us were willing to vote for politicians who don't support corporate kleptocracy, we could not only build the kind of social safety net

---

market—middle- and lower-income customers were increasingly forced to buy. Even when supply chains improved and plants reopened, prices never went back down again, and many manufacturers permanently discontinued their lower-price lines.

* The report concludes that "this is not normal," noting that between 1979 and 2019, corporate profits accounted for only 11 percent of price growth.

we need but also (through things like increased taxes on billionaires and big corporations) reduce the chances that it gets dismantled again.[32]

But that's where the myths come in. As historians Naomi Oreskes and Erik Conway explain in their 2023 book, *The Big Myth*, billionaires and big corporations have followed the playbook that the National Association of Manufacturers wrote in the 1930s and '40s—the one that imported neoliberalism to the US from Austria, paid to embed those ideas in the American academic and political systems, and underwrote massive pro-business-propaganda-disguised-as-popular-media campaigns.[33]

No part of today's campaign has the nearly universal reach that *General Electric Theater* did, but the engineers and profiteers of our DIY society don't actually need every one of us to believe the myths. In a democracy, they only need more than half of us. And with a little voter suppression thrown in, they need even less than that.[34]

So which of us are the mythmakers targeting? Those more willing to tolerate neoliberalism's inequalities, which, as I'll explain more in a minute, disproportionately means those who lean to the political right.[35]

With that target squarely in their sights, billionaires and big corporations have bought up media companies (and particularly right-leaning media companies) like Fox News, Twitter, and *The Washington Post*. They've endowed business schools and started whole universities (often conservative Christian ones) to train the next generation of political and corporate leaders. And they've funded libertarian and conservative think tanks that pump out seemingly scientific but actually wildly unsubstantiated "research"-based ideas.[36]

The goal here is to lure enough voters into believing the myths that justify our DIY society. And these efforts have been so successful that acceptance of neoliberal ideologies extends well beyond the political right. A 2016 Pew poll of American adults, for example, found that 71 percent of Republicans and 31 percent of Democrats believe that government regulation of business usually does more harm than good, and more recent polls have found similar patterns around specific types of regulation, like regulation of major tech and social media companies, and regulation on how much companies can pollute.[37]

HOW THEY LEVERAGE OUR DELUSIONS FOR POWER

With these ideas firmly entrenched in American psyches, the next step in protecting the status quo is for billionaires and big corporations to give their believers politicians for whom to vote. Sometimes ultra-wealthy people—like billionaire Democrat-turned-Republican Donald Trump, or billionaire Democrat-turned-Republican-turned-Independent-turned-maybe-Democrat Michael Bloomberg—use their wealth to run for office, effectively embodying the myths themselves. More often, they bankroll politicians who are willing to put their face behind these ideas.[38]

Those big money–backed politicians are usually Republicans.* Yet billionaires and big corporations also give some money to Democrats to ensure that they'll have leverage no matter who wins. For similar reasons, big donors spread their donations all over the country and even fund state and local races in places where they don't operate or live. In Wisconsin, for example, a 2021 investigation found that GOP candidates had received more than four times as much money in campaign donations from big corporations—many of them headquartered in other states—as Democratic candidates did.[39]

The point of these donations is to control the outcome of every single election. Take it from Trump-appointed former Secretary of Education Betsy DeVos, a billionaire who has a helpful tendency to say the quiet part out loud. The DeVos family made its money through the multi-level marketing company Amway and has historically been one of the biggest donors to Republican campaigns. A 2020 report found that the family had made more than $82 million in political contributions since 1999. DeVos, in turn, doesn't try to hide her intentions with these donations. In a 1997 op-ed, she wrote, "[M]y family is the largest single contributor of soft money to the national Republican party. . . . I have decided, however, to stop taking offense at the suggestion that we are buying influence. Now, I simply concede the point."[40]

That money doesn't get funneled to just any Republican candidate.

---

* Billionaires and CEOs of big corporations also lean disproportionately to the right in their personal voting behavior and donations.

Rather, research shows that it's increasingly being directed toward candidates with extreme far-right views. Take, for example, the case of senator, writer, and venture capitalist J. D. Vance and his main backer, Peter Thiel. Thiel, who co-founded PayPal, made billions as an early investor in Facebook and donated $10 million to the super PAC that supported Vance's successful 2022 Senate campaign.[41]

Vance, like many contemporary Republican candidates, holds a range of far-right and deeply neoliberal views—views that tip into racism, classism, and sexism and that sometimes even have a fascist or eugenicist bent. He's anti-vaccine, anti-immigration, anti-abortion, anti-welfare, and, as we saw in chapter 4, staunchly anti-divorce.[42]

Some of Vance's positions might seem contradictory. Consider a speech from Vance's 2022 campaign. In it, Vance first complained that "our country doesn't have enough children, meaning that we have too few young workers supporting the broader economy." Now, as we saw with Brooke, Patricia, and Jocelyn, having children (or having more children) can easily trap people into poverty, especially in the absence of a sturdy social safety net. Thus, if Vance is so focused on increasing the US population, we might also expect him to advocate for strengthening the social safety net and making sure that families with children have adequate support. Instead, and later in that same speech, Vance expressed outrage about the "millions of people . . . [on] welfare rolls." In the US, and because of how we determine eligibility for welfare, it's almost impossible for people without kids to qualify for cash assistance. Thus, Vance is effectively complaining that millions of families who've done as he asked by having children are also getting government support.[43]

This apparent hypocrisy makes more sense when we consider that the Vances of the world may think of people as cogs in the economy, not as full human beings. From that perspective, it makes sense not only to force families to have more children than they can manage but to deny those families support. Because, as we've seen with Akari, Brooke, Sylvia, Patricia, Jocelyn, and so many other mothers, financial precarity forces parents and especially mothers to take whatever job they can get, no matter how degrading or underpaid. Put differently, the combination of forced childbearing and a lack of a social safety net makes people easier to exploit for the benefit of big businesses and billionaires.

The people most easily exploited in that kind of system are women like Sierra—low-income single mothers, and especially those who are racialized as Brown or Black. That's why politicians like Vance also vilify women like Sierra, just as Reagan did a generation before. Not because they want these women to have a better life, but because vilifying these women makes them—and their children—easier to exploit. Easier, that is, because blaming people for their "bad choices" (or their parents' "bad choices") makes it seem justified to deny them support.[44]

That need to vilify victims is why neoliberalism goes hand-in-hand with racism, sexism, classism and even fascism and eugenics. And it's why billionaires like Thiel are willing to get in bed with politicians like Vance, despite those politicians' seemingly heinous views. Because building a better social safety net—and thereby eliminating a key mechanism of exploitation—is a bigger threat to billionaires like Thiel than any reputational risk they might face.[45]

Billionaires and big corporations want us divided by race, class, and gender. The more divided we are, the less likely we are to care when people like Sierra are suffering, and the less likely we are to recognize our shared interests— like our shared interest in broadening and strengthening the social safety net. If, in turn, we don't recognize our shared interests, then we're less likely to come together to overthrow our DIY society and challenge the engineers and profiteers who are keeping us from building that net.

Conclusion

LEVERAGING OUR LINKED FATES

On Friday, October 24, 1975, women across Iceland took the day off from paid work, housework, and childcare and took to the streets instead.* Men suddenly felt what it was like to manage the burden women had been carrying, and employers and government officials took notice as well. As BBC News reported, "Banks, factories and some shops had to close, as did schools and nurseries—leaving many fathers with no choice but to take their children to work. There were reports of men arming themselves with sweets and colouring pencils to entertain the crowds of overexcited children in their workplaces. Sausages—easy to cook and popular with children—were in such demand the shops sold out."[1]

The day off, however, was merely the beginning—a collective call to arms. Five years later, Iceland was the first country to elect a woman as president—President Vigdís Finnbogadóttir, who was at the protests with her mother and her three-year-old daughter that day. In the wake of that election and the policy changes that followed, life in Iceland improved dramatically, especially for women and kids. In 1980, the US and Iceland had equal ratings on the Human Development Index—each receiving .57 out of a possible 1.0. By 2015, Iceland's rating had risen to .90, compared to .78 for the US. And today, Iceland's rating is a near-perfect .96, ranking it third in the world behind only Switzerland and Norway and above the US, which comes in at number 21.[2]

Certainly, Iceland still struggles with lingering gender inequalities. But

---

* Notably, and cleverly, protest organizers managed to elicit participation even from women who were skeptical of feminist movements by calling it a "day off" rather than a "strike."

in 2023 it was ranked the best country in the world for women. The US ranked forty-third. We're ranked forty-third because, instead of spending the last fifty years building a sturdy social safety net the way Iceland has, we've left gaping holes in the meager net we do have, and we've left women to hold it together instead.[3]

To get women to do that work, we trap them as mothers-in-waiting and give them nowhere to turn, nowhere to hide, and nothing but morally fraught choices to make. The reward for surviving the game isn't the prosperity we've been promised—it's another round with more responsibility to hold. But if women refuse to play or collapse under all that risk, we shame them for making "bad choices" and for not being the kind of robot-like workers that we've incentivized employers to prefer.

And the thing is, we know how to fix this, and we can afford to do it. The resources are just in the wrong hands. If we wanted to free women from the burden of holding it together, and if all of us, regardless of gender, wanted to be freer from the threat of precarity, we could demand that the profiteers of our DIY society stop hoarding what they've stolen from all of us and use it to build the net we all need and deserve.

The real problem is the lack of will to change things—a lack of will we've been lured into by buying the myths we've been sold. Those myths guilt and gaslight us into accepting the risk that's been dumped on us or goad us into dumping it further downstream. The engineers constructed these myths to delude and divide us. Because to maintain the illusion of a DIY society, the engineers and profiteers of that system need women to hold it together—to fill in the gaps where the DIY model fails.

———

A different version of this book might end with a self-help guide for women. A step-by-step plan for lightening the loads we carry and letting go of our guilt. And certainly, as a woman and a mom myself, I get why messages like that have appeal.

As we should know by this point, however, self-help solutions merely reinforce the misperception that women can avoid precarity by making "good choices." They perpetuate the assumption that women who don't make "good choices"—like choosing the right job, the right partner, or the right timing for their pregnancies—deserve shame instead of support, when, in fact, the women to whom those "good choices" are available are often those with privilege to spare.*[4]

Individuals can't solve structural problems, at least not in an equitable and sustainable way. So with Iceland's Women's Day Off as inspiration, I'll offer a collective solution, which I'll call a "union of care."

THE ESSENTIAL WORK OF CARE

Care is inherently a shared project. Despite what the engineers and profiteers of our DIY society want us to believe, some of our needs can only be met through care, which involves the physical and mental labor of supporting others' well-being. Care is noticing someone else's needs even if they don't ask and being there to listen when they do. It's figuring out a plan to meet those needs and what it will take to execute it. And it's putting our bodies on the line to make sure those needs are met. Supporting others financially is one small part of the care equation, but there's so much more to it than that.[5]

Care flows through networks, and we all exist in networks of care. If I asked you to draw your network, you might put yourself at the center, surrounded by a few family members and close friends. Your real network, however, is likely bigger than you could easily imagine, and certainly bigger than you could easily draw. That's because our networks include not only the people we rely on and the people who rely on us, but also all the people supporting or supported by them. Put differently, while we might imagine our networks of care as small, closed loops, the reality is that each of our connections has other connections, and so on, with links spreading out across space and time.[6]

Of course, just because we exist in these expansive care networks doesn't mean that they're doing what we need them to. Rather, some of us may find

---

* Some women, for example, might have partners who are willing to share the work of caregiving fifty-fifty or even, like Ivan and Alex, take a greater share. And yet, statistics suggest that there aren't enough men—even young men—like that to go around.

that we're giving far more than we get care-wise. And others of us may find ourselves giving equally to those around us, but there's still not enough care to go around.[7]

To that end, the point of a broad and sturdy social safety net isn't to replace these networks. It's to strengthen them and make the work they do more sustainable by bridging gaps and filling in where they tend to fail. That means ensuring that everyone has what they need to contribute as fully as possible to the shared work of care, because it's hard to help others put on their oxygen masks if you don't have your own to put on first. And if there aren't enough masks for everyone to begin with, then there's little incentive to help others who are struggling to put theirs on.

In this analogy, the oxygen masks are the necessities for a life with dignity. That means unpolluted air to breathe, clean water to drink, nourishing food to eat, comfortable clothes to wear, and safe shelter to live in. It also includes safe and reliable means of sanitation, transportation, and communication. Plus access to the care we need for our minds and bodies and those of our loved ones, as well as opportunities for work that is meaningful and not degrading, opportunities for rest and solitude when we need it, opportunities to shape society's decisions, and opportunities to experience joy. The more of us who have these things, the better equipped we will all be to support those who are struggling, and the less incentive we'll have to exploit or oppress others so we can have the sense of dignity we need.

———

There are lots of ways to structure a social safety net that offers this kind of security. But a good first step would be to free the work of meeting people's care needs from the profit pressures that a heavily financialized market economy tends to create. The solutions are clear, and we've discussed them throughout this book: building universal public systems like healthcare, childcare, education, and care for the elderly and disabled, and funding those systems to the level where they can provide the high-quality care that people need to live with dignity from birth until natural death. Achieving that kind of dignity requires treating people as people—in all their messiness and complexity—and not as cogs in a machine, as J. D. Vance might prefer. In practice, that would mean stripping away the checks on "deserv-ingness" built into our current system,* training care providers to build trusting relationships with care recipients, and trusting care providers to act flexibly rather than enforcing unrealistically rigid standards that create more work or punish people in need.[8]

A good second step would be to care for the people who care. That in-volves funding systems of care not only to the level needed to provide affordable high-quality care for recipients but also to the level of sustainability—ensuring that the people who do the work of caregiving, whether formally or informally, are given the resources to do that work effectively and without sacrificing their own needs or personal responsibilities for care. Along those lines, caring for the people who care also means acknowledging that we all have care responsibilities, even if those roles aren't formal or paid. And it means supporting informal caregiving by ensuring that we all have the time and resources to do that work, as well as the energy to do it effectively, which requires time apart from caregiving responsibilities and resources to fully recharge.† That support would come, in part, through programs like guaran-teed monthly stipends for families with dependents, giving them more choice between paid work and care. That system would also involve new policies, including not only guaranteed paid family leave, sick leave, vacation time, and time off to care for dependents, but also stronger minimum wage laws and laws preventing employers from penalizing workers for taking time off or requesting scheduling accommodations related to care.

These policies would go a long way toward providing the security we need to live with dignity, but if we want that social safety net to stay sturdy in the long term, we also have to look out for cracks. That means finding and closing gaps that emerge in the public care system (like the current gaps in after-school and summer break care) and closing loopholes that allow em-ployers to get around care-promoting policies (like the current loopholes

---

* Rejecting the idea that some people are more "deserving" of dignity would not only pave the way for public acceptance of universal public programs like healthcare and childcare, but also for more generosity in funding our existing universal programs—like public education—and for less red tape around the means-tested anti-poverty programs—like unemployment and food stamps and cash welfare—that we already have.

† In that sense, a formal public care system wouldn't supplant informal care networks, but rather would support the work of those networks and step in where they tend to fall short.

that let employers get away with denying health coverage to contractors and part-time workers). It also means designing the formal public care sector to rein in the culture of overwork, which, even when well intentioned, can limit the sustainability of systems of care. If the formal public care sector not only pays its workers extremely well but also puts in place checks on overwork—like ensuring full staffing, setting clear expectations and boundaries, and promoting leaders who walk the walk—then competition for workers might ultimately persuade other private employers to follow the public sector in step.[9]

Of course, some employers may find it difficult to chart this new course without going under. And that's because, as we talked about in chapter 3, care industries aren't the only ones struggling to stay afloat in our highly financialized market economy, and they're not the only ones struggling to ensure that workers get decent benefits or paid a decent wage. Rather, other industries like grocery sales, garment manufacturing, and home construction struggle to turn a profit and often end up exploiting their workers, as we saw with Erin and Desmond, and/or setting prices so high that many customers are priced out of the market or forced to get by with less than they need. To keep these industries sustainable, we might need to expand our traditional definitions of care—and our subsidization of care industries—to include the work of meeting people's other basic needs like shelter, clothing, and food.[10]

These efforts would go a long way in protecting the dignity of paid workers, but paid workers currently represent only 46 percent of the US population. If, therefore, the goal is for everyone to live with dignity, then we also need care systems that aren't tied to paid work—that support people even if they're unable to work for pay for any reason—including because of caregiving responsibilities—or unable to find work that pays enough to meet their needs. In practice, this would mean removing work requirements from programs like welfare and making the cash benefits for programs like welfare, unemployment, disability, and Social Security generous enough to live on with dignity, while also providing real opportunities—including decent jobs in the newly expanded public sector—for those who want to work. Research shows that the best way to protect the dignity of the people at the margins of our economy is to give them money with no strings attached. Enough money, that is, to afford not only the basics but a life with meaning and joy.[11]

Now, you might be thinking, "If we just give people money to stay home, no one will want to work." But the thing is, people are intrinsically motivated to make and do and innovate. They just want to be treated with dignity, and they need to be sustainably rewarded for the work they do. Consider, for example, what sociologists Kathryn Edin and Laura Lein found in interviews with more than three hundred single mothers on welfare. Almost all of those mothers said they would rather support their families with paid work than rely on welfare alone. Yet almost none of them could find a reliable job that would pay them a living wage. And so, caught as they were in such an irrational and inhumane system, these mothers acted as rationally and humanely as they could, which often meant taking what little the government gave them in cash welfare benefits and then relying on (and not reporting) whatever financial support they could get from their children's fathers and whatever under-the-table work they could find to make sure their children got to eat and keep roofs over their heads. Based on these findings, Edin and Lein argue that the women we accuse of laziness or even criminality are often acting out of resignation or even rebellion against systems designed to ensure that they fail.*

And it isn't just single mothers who act that way. "Quiet quitting," for example, is a common tactic used by disgruntled workers—the media may have just coined this term, but labor scholars have long called it "work to rule." The idea is to do only the work that is explicitly required by contract, and it's a highly effective tool. In 2018, for example, the teachers' union in Providence, Rhode Island, was able to negotiate a modest salary increase—raising the starting salary for teachers from $40,547 to $42,712—by refusing noncontractual work like after-hours grading and lesson planning, voluntary extracurricular activities, field trips, after-school meetings, and updates to school newsletters. Teachers are often accused of "laziness" or

---

* Work slowdowns, for example, were a common tactic of resistance among enslaved people in the US, and enslaved people were dubbed "lazy" (rather than strategic) for their unwillingness to work harder.

"selfishness" for these kinds of tactics. And yet, what they're really doing is showing society how we've taken for granted their labor and time.[12]

———

Creating a system that cares for all with dignity would certainly come at a cost. We could reshuffle some of what we are currently spending,* but we'd likely need additional revenue from higher taxes on big corporations and billionaires and others with extreme levels of wealth.† The idea of tax hikes might seem scary. But that fear is the product of neoliberal lore. In reality, a small annual wealth tax on ultra-wealthy families—those with a net worth of more than $50 million—would generate $3.75 trillion in revenue for federal government programs over the course of just ten years.‡ That's more than five times what we'd need to fund an affordable, high-quality universal childcare and preschool program over that time span,§ and it would leave plenty of money for things like universal healthcare as well.[13]

Given the message of thrift that Ben Franklin baked into the American ethos, a multi-trillion dollar price tag net might leave you with sticker shock. Recall from chapter 8, however, that well-funded universal programs are, in

———

* In the case of healthcare, for example, research shows that a shift to a universal public system would ultimately cost the government less than ensuring universal coverage under the current hybrid system, in part because of how current spending (including spending by individuals, employers, and state and federal government agencies) could be reallocated in more efficient ways.

† In the case of early childhood education, for example, management scholar Daniela Viana Acosta and her colleagues estimate that over ten years, it would cost $351 billion to develop a universal public preschool program for all three- and four-year-old children in the US, including $41 billion in new facility construction costs. They also estimate that if the program were made permanent, it would effectively pay for itself by 2053 because "the negative effect of additional debt is offset with improved productivity from additional education and additional caregivers entering the labor market."

‡ This plan was originally proposed by Senator Elizabeth Warren and would include a 2 percent annual tax on households with net worths between $50 million and $1 billion and a 4 percent annual Billionaire Surtax (6 percent tax overall) on households with net worths above $1 billion.

§ These estimates are based on a program designed by Senator Elizabeth Warren, which would be free for the millions of US families making less than 200 percent of the federal poverty line (currently $55,500 for a family of four) and would ensure that, annually, no family pays more than 7 percent of their household income toward the cost of preschool and childcare. Some of the money for that program could come from the $26 billion we currently spend on childcare and preschool programs for low-income families, and from the $55 billion we currently allocate for childcare tax credits every year, with the rest coming from the Ultra-Millionaire Tax.

the end, less costly for society and more effective stability-wise than the kinds of half-assed solutions US politicians typically propose. Instead, the only people who really have something to fear from these changes would be the engineers and the profiteers of our DIY society—the billionaires and big businesses and their cronies who wouldn't have the same grip they currently do on the levers of social and economic power.[14]

These engineers and profiteers won't like it if we dismantle their system and abandon the myths they've carefully constructed to divide and delude us into accepting their authority and the resulting precarity we face. They won't like it, but there are far more of us than there are of them. And we can overthrow them with a union of care.

A UNION OF CARE

For decades, labor unions were the dam that protected us from billionaires and big corporations. That is, until the great risk shift broke the dam. The neoliberal policymakers that came into power under the great risk shift passed a bevy of anti-union legislation. As a result, most Americans now live in places that legally limit union bargaining with policies like right-to-work laws.* The effects of those policies were swift and devastating. Examining US wage data from 1968 to 2019, and treating the uneven rollout of state-level right-to-work laws as a sort of natural experiment, sociologist Tom VanHeuvelen examined how those laws affected incomes. What he found was that passing right-to-work laws made wages more unequal and caused median wages to fall.† Given those outcomes, we might have expected voters to reject anti-union candidates and push to overturn right-to-work laws. But anti-union rhetoric led many Americans to blame the unions instead. That blame then led to declines in union membership, to the point where only about 10 percent of US workers were part of unions in 2022.[15]

Despite their losses, unions are still powerful, as evidenced both by their high-profile recent wins over employers like Amazon, Apple, and Starbucks,

---

* Right-to-work laws prohibit unions from negotiating contracts that require workers to join a union as a condition of employment.

† The income advantage typically enjoyed by unionized workers also fell by half in states with right-to-work laws.

and by Republican legislators' rush to pass even more anti-union laws. Today, union members remain better protected and better compensated than nonunionized workers in those same industries. And unions are also effective in bridging divides between workers—just as their name implies. Research shows, for example, that racial resentments and opposition to affirmative action policies are lower among white union members than among white workers who are not unionized.[16]

So if we already have teachers' unions and nurses' unions and unions of childcare workers and home health aides, why would we also need a union of care?

The problem is that while a labor union model might work for individual care industries, it doesn't solve larger problems like the exploitation of women or the devaluation of care. Right now, unions of care workers exist as separate silos—they're often disconnected from other unions of care workers, and even from other unionized workers in the same industry who work for different employers, and from other caregivers who perform similar labor, either for pay without the protection of a union or as unpaid caregivers at home.* This kind of siloing might make union negotiations easier, but it limits workers' ability to leverage strength in numbers. And it focuses unions on making local and incremental improvements, rather than on fighting for broader changes to policies and structures of power.[17]

Adding another wrinkle, labor unions can easily be pitted against the people they serve. Teachers' unions, for example, are often accused of being "in it for the money" when their unions press for higher pay or better benefits. Politicians and media pundits shame them for being "selfish"—for not caring about the kids, the families, and the communities that depend on the service they provide. Of course, the reality is that strong teachers' unions and decent wages both reduce teacher turnover, which is better for kids in the end.† And yet, because kids and families and communities aren't part of the union, they may struggle to see how they also benefit when teachers win.[18]

---

* That focus on paid work has, at times, led labor unions to operate in ways that disadvantage informal caregivers, such as by using gender essentialist rhetoric—rhetoric that situates men's "proper" place in the workforce and women's "proper" place at home—to defend the idea that workers should be paid a "family wage."

† Research conducted in the wake of Wisconsin's passage of anti-union legislation found that ef-

What we need, then, is something much bigger: a union that bridges the gap between care industries, the gap between paid and unpaid care workers, and the gap between the people who give and receive care. That union, however, will only be as powerful as its membership. And some people might balk at joining such a broad coalition—a group that might seem too disparate to effectively unite.

So how do we get the skeptics to join the union? By reminding them how care links our fates. As political scientist Evelyn M. Simien explains, linked fate is our awareness of the fact that "what happens to the group will also affect the individual member." And when it comes to care, we're all far more connected than it might seem.[19]

Consider the case of a home childcare center. In that center, the caregiver, the children, and their families are part of the same network, whether they want to believe it or not. Just like with a web of string, putting stress on one part of that network creates tension in the rest of the network, and in other networks that network is connected to. Imagine, for example, that a child gets sick, but her parents send her to childcare anyway because they don't have paid time off from work. That child, in turn, might get the caregiver sick, who might then have to close the center temporarily, not only while she's recovering but also to care for her own son, who gets sick and has to stay home from school. With the center closed, meanwhile, all the families would have to scramble to fill the gap in care. Some families might be able to work remotely, but that comes with added stress. Other families might call in Grandma, but that would risk her health. Still other families might end up taking unpaid time off from work, but that would threaten their budgets and possibly even their jobs.* And if some of those parents are also care workers, then taking time off from work could also cause breakdowns for the people for whom they care.[20]

To that end, a union of care would be for anyone who is part of a caregiving

----

forts to limit the power of teachers' unions not only amplified school staffing crises but also led to a significant drop in student test scores—a drop that disproportionately impacted the students who were already struggling academically in school.

* A national poll from the University of Michigan's Mott Children's Hospital found that a third of US parents with children in childcare said they may lose their jobs or lose income if their children are sick and have to stay home.

network. And the point of the union would be to strengthen our sense of linked fate.* That strength can break the engineers' and profiteers' grip on the levers of power because we have the numbers they don't. Acting alone, there's no chance we'll move them. Acting in unison, we might get them to budge.†[21]

This is what the feminists of the 1970s and '80s tried to tell us. They saw where the risk was shifting. They saw our DIY society becoming ever more precarious for families and especially for women. They saw the engineers hatch plans to delude and divide. They tried to warn us and get us to link arms.[22]

Take Silvia Federici, a political scientist and feminist activist who helped create the Wages for Housework movement. In 1975, she wrote, "We want and have to say that we are all housewives . . . Because as long as we think we are something better, something different than a housewife, we accept the logic of the master, which is a logic of division."‡ Federici is talking about housewives, but we could swap in "caregivers" and the message would arguably be the same. That message is a warning that the engineers and profiteers are trying to keep us from recognizing that we are stronger together, tempting us to look with scorn at those who do the essential but often unpaid or underpaid work of caregiving, rather than recognize how care links our fates.[23]

Take also bell hooks, the Black feminist writer whose critiques of *Lean In* we talked about in chapter 7. In 1989, hooks warned her readers that "[i]t

---

* Research shows that women in the US who altered their employment to accommodate Covid-related caregiving responsibilities (e.g., leaving the workforce, reducing and/or changing their hours, changing jobs) report a stronger sense of gender-linked fate than do women whose employment was not affected by the pandemic.

† As political scientist and feminist activist Nancy Fraser has argued, we can only prevent feminism from becoming "capitalism's handmaiden" by "reclaiming the mantle of participatory democracy as a means of strengthening the public powers needed to constrain capital for the sake of justice."

‡ As historian Kevin Sapere explains, the Wages for Housework campaign took inspiration from the Welfare Rights Movement, which sought "compensation for the labor of caring for others" and "emphasized that wages would allow the financial security for women to leave abusive relationships." In the end, however, the Wages for Housework movement remained on the fringes of feminist activism. And rather than offer more robust financial support for women relying on the social safety net while caring for young children, policymakers like Ronald Reagan pledged to "end welfare as we know it" by denying unpartnered women with young children the money they needed to stay home with their children long-term.

is easy for women and any exploited group or oppressed group to become complicit in the structure of domination, using power that reinforces rather than challenge[s] and change[s]."* Here, hooks is critiquing white feminist movements for focusing on empowering white college-educated women to achieve economic equality with white men while ignoring how that empowerment comes at the expense of other women, often Black women, whom they step on as they try to get ahead.[24]

Far too many of us ignored these warnings, lured in by neoliberalism's promise that it's possible for each of us to succeed on our own. We accepted the myths that divide us, denying the deservingness and dignity of others in the pursuit of individual gain. We allowed ourselves to be deluded into believing that care isn't essential labor and that we can get by without a social safety net. And we resigned ourselves to accept the pain and precarity that comes from relying on women to hold it together instead.

A union of care would reject those divisions and treat care as a collective responsibility for ensuring the dignity that everyone deserves. Care would replace achievement as the primary measure of an individual's contributions to society. And the rising value of care would persuade more and more of us to do our fair share.

Imagine, for example, a world where we value care work on par with IT. In that world, Bethany might have earned as much as Dennis, and the dominoes of their resulting choices could have fallen a very different way. Bethany probably would have stayed in the workforce after having children, and if she had, at a salary similar to Dennis's, then there's a good chance that Dennis would have shared much more equally in the parenting and the housework. Meanwhile, if jobs in fields like childcare and social work paid as well as jobs in IT, then Dennis might be more inclined to let his own son play with dolls and pursue a career in caregiving, instead of repeating the cycle again.

Now imagine that the informal work of caring for others is just as valued as commodified care work, and that the needs of caregivers are respected as

---

* Similarly, in her 2000 book, *Feminist Theory: From Margin to Center,* hooks wrote that "[r]uling male groups have been able to co-opt feminist reforms and make them serve the interests of the white supremacist, capitalist patriarchy because feminist activists naively assumed women were opposed to the status quo."

much as those of recipients of care. In that world, Akari wouldn't have to be working her three jobs, or maybe even any of them, because she could be paid for her labor at home. Stay-at-home parents like Erin, Alex, and Jocelyn wouldn't be struggling to make ends meet. And neither would mothers like Patricia or Brooke, who've been forced to accept underpaid labor as the price for meeting their families' care needs. In that world, families would have real choices about how to divide their energies between working for an employer and caring for their families. And those choices wouldn't pit precarity against morality, because families like Holly's could choose to rely on others for support with caregiving while knowing that those caregivers are cared for as well.

This is the world we ought to be imagining. A world where we hold it *together* rather than pretending we can hold it together on our own.

Acknowledgments

I didn't start writing this book until 2021, but its origins stretch back to 2014, and to the sleepless nights I spent scrolling through social media as a new mom on maternity leave. Like many of the moms I later went on to study, I found myself searching for a sense of camaraderie in managing the exhaustion and uncertainty that came with being the default parent, living far from family, and being stuck on a year-long waitlist for full-time childcare. As I scrolled, however, I also saw the tradeoff for that sense of camaraderie—a pressure to compare myself to other moms. I had a sense that there might be a project there. But at the time, I was still struggling to write my first book, *Negotiating Opportunities*, so I filed it away in a folder of future project ideas.

I didn't open that folder until 2017, when my first book was on its way to the printer, when my due date for my second baby was fast-approaching, and when my colleague Brian Powell suggested that I apply to lead the Sociological Research Practicum (SRP) at Indiana University, where I was an assistant professor at the time. Each year, the SRP lead spends nine months developing a study and then six weeks working with the cohort of first-year graduate students to collect or analyze the data involved. I was more than a little hesitant about taking on such a big responsibility pre-tenure, but I figured it might be my best chance to revisit that long-deferred project idea.

I also knew, though, that to do the project justice, I'd need more data than the grad students and I could collect in just six weeks and more funding to collect the data I'd need. So I turned to my colleagues for advice and support. Elaine Hernandez helped me develop a plan for the Social Networks and Parenting (SNAP) Study, a longitudinal study following participants from pregnancy through the postpartum period and examining how the people around us shape our sense of ourselves as parents along with the parenting decisions we make. Elaine also introduced me to prenatal clinics where I could recruit participants and encouraged me to reach out to Brea Perry and Bernice Pescosolido, who connected me with the Indiana Clinical and Translational Sciences Institute and their Networks, Complex Systems & Health Project Development Team, which agreed to fund my initial waves of data collection under the ICTSI NIH/NCRR Grant No. UL1TR001108.

As the SRP lead, I got to work with study director Emily Meanwell, who developed and managed the project infrastructure, including a tracking system to connect participants' data across waves and a file organization and workflow system to keep the project and all the research assistants on track. As an expert on poverty and housing instability and a member of Indiana University's Institutional Review Board, Emily also offered essential advice on ethical and empathetic research, helped me develop guidelines for interviewing about difficult and sensitive topics, and (later) conducted many of the project's highly sensitive interviews.

With a plan, tools, and funding in place, I then hired an amazing team of graduate and undergraduate student research assistants. Amelia Hawbaker became my lead project manager, helping with everything from developing the study protocols, surveys, and interview guides to training the interviewers, coordinating the schedule, and conducting many highly sensitive interviews. Cara Davies programmed the initial wave of surveys and taught me to use Qualtrics so I could program the subsequent waves. Katie Beardall and Melissa Garcia led the in-clinic recruitment, including managing communication with the clinic staff and training the recruitment team; they also helped with many waves of interviews. Hui Chen helped me clean and analyze the initial prenatal wave of survey data, which I used to develop the data collection instruments for follow-up waves. Elizabeth Anderson, Grayson Bodenheimer, Caroline Brooks, Max Coleman, Emily Ekl, Benjamin Hartmann, Monica Heilman, Yingjian Liang, Nora Weber, and Chavonté Wright were part of the first-year cohort who worked with me on the SRP and helped with a wide range of tasks, including developing surveys and interview guides, recruiting participants, conducting and transcribing in-depth interviews, and analyzing the data we collected together. Under-graduate students Leo Banks, Kinsey Bromm, Rachel Desmarais, Natalia Fuentes-Rohwer, Elsie Gasaway, Shanita Hunt, and Katie Orick also helped with recruiting participants, transcribing and verifying in-depth interviews, and analyzing data from surveys and interviews. And sociology department staff members Lisa Aten, Paula Cotner, Julia Mobley, and Susan Risen helped with financial logistics, including sending gift cards to participants after each wave.

Support from Indiana's Social Science Research Funding Program allowed me to extend the project beyond the SRP days, and many of the early team members also stuck with the project for subsequent waves. Amelia, Katie B., Melissa, Elizabeth, Grayson, Monica, Nora, Chavonté, Natalia, Katie O., Lisa, Paula, Julia, and Susan helped with follow-up waves of SNAP and later the Pandemic Parenting Study, and Alisha Kirchoff, Callie Cleckner, Ellis Frieh, Krystina Millar, Megan Bolton, Shelley Rao, and Tabi Wilbur joined the team to help with those follow-up interviews as well. Elizabeth and Max, along with my colleague Andrew Halpern-Manners, also helped me clean, analyze, and develop survey weights for the national survey data I collected for the Institutions, Trust, and Decision-making (ITD) Study and for Parenting in Tumultuous Times (PITT).

The idea for the Pandemic Parenting Study (PPS) came out of the SNAP study interviews that my team and I were conducting in February and March 2020, which offered an early warning of the impact that Covid-19 was already having on families and especially on moms. When I talked to Brea Perry about those findings, she suggested that I reach out to Amelia (Amy) Knopf, a faculty member at the Indiana University School of Nursing, who had experience conducting research on health decision-making in the context of infectious disease. Amy helped me navigate the morass of (mis)information about Covid-19, develop the PPS surveys and in-depth interview guides, and secure funding for three pandemic data collection waves, allowing Cassie Mead, Drew Myers, and Rachel Filippone to join the interview team. And each wave was a Herculean effort. The first PPS wave, for example, involved more than sixty in-depth interviews conducted in a little over four weeks' span.

Of course, neither the SNAP study nor the PPS would have been possible without the support of the clinic staff that welcomed my team and helped with recruiting patients, and without participants' willingness to share their stories, their hopes, and their struggles, and to continue with the project over time. I am eternally grateful to every person who answered my surveys and especially to those who also carved out precious time to talk with me or a member of my research team. The gravity of those conversations pulled me to keep the project going, adding more waves of data collection, even when that meant doing Zoom interviews from my bedroom and while caring for my own kids during the long months when their school and childcare center were closed.

To that end, I am also deeply indebted to the people who've helped me juggle the often competing responsibilities of paid work and family life, including the caregivers who have loved my kids as well as I could. Through their patience and boundless enthusiasm, the educators at BDLC—especially Ronak Albarazinge, Haley Armes, Marianne Bailey, Brittany Blanks, Mady Brown, Kay Dosunmu, Rachel Draughn, Angela Frezza, Jill Hayes, Rachel Hancock, Jenna Johnson, Moriah Kaiser, Jett Mehay, Katy New, Anna Padilla, Mindy Peek, Aubrey Pulley, Sarah Terry-Zagorski, and Raisa Wenz—not only cultivated my children's confidence, curiosity, and creativity but also taught me to be a more empathetic parent, a more effective educator, and a more active contributor to a shared community of care.

Of course, the lessons I got about caregiving started with my own mother, long before I had kids, and this book speaks to her story in so many ways. By age twenty-eight, Anne McCrory had three kids and her own home childcare business, watching up to six kids in addition to her own every day, plus a business selling Mary Kay makeup on the side. In her thirties, she became a preschool teacher while going back to school to get a degree in elementary education and eventually got a full-time public school teaching job. In her forties, while I was living at home for graduate school, she finished a master's degree and a reading specialist certification—we used to do homework together on the couch at night. In her fifties, and during the Covid pandemic, she quit her job—a casualty of the callousness so many Americans directed toward teachers and public schools. Now in her sixties, she's far from retired. She has already written and illustrated two children's books—*When Someday Comes* and *Who's Ready? For the First Day of School!*—

and somehow still finds time to drive around the country, from my sister's house in Virginia, to my brother's in California, to mine in Wisconsin, to visit her eight grandkids and even help me chop back a yard full of hosta plants every fall. My mom is also a sort of reverse Ronald Reagan. She was too young to vote for him in 1976 and 1980, but she was an anti-union, anti-safety-net Republican well into her thirties, then became an Independent, and is now a staunchly pro-union, pro-safety-net Democrat. And in that she gives me hope that views can change.

My dad, meanwhile, has never been the caregiver in our family, but he still deserves a special mention here. He's the one who taught me to love big ideas—he has this story about philosopher Charles Pierce that he loves to tell at parties. He's the one who taught me to set ambitious goals and never settle. And he's the one who taught me to believe in my convictions, even when that meant we disagreed about what was best. I doubt that Duane McCrory will ever read this book cover to cover, but it brings me joy knowing that he's proud of me anyway.

My mother-in-law and father-in-law, by contrast, are eager to read the book and especially excited about the possibility that I might appear as a talking head on one of their favorite cable news shows. Like my mother, Joan Calarco was also a teacher, first at a Catholic school, and then in New York City public schools. Joan retired in her sixties, but she never really stopped teaching. She has volunteered teaching English to immigrants and refugees, tutored the children of family, friends, and neighbors, and, during the pandemic, planned daily "grandma school" lessons to do with my kids over Facetime. Pete Calarco is a former IRS agent, and he taught me a great deal about the corruption of big businesses and billionaires and about the ins and outs of US tax law.

Joan and Pete also deserve credit for raising Dan Calarco to be a stellar son, husband, and dad. Dan is an adventurer, but he respects my need for routine and order, especially in times of stress, and even when it means taking his shoes off when he comes in the house. He's not an academic, but he understands the pressures I face in my job and loves the ambition I bring to my work, even when that means bringing my laptop on vacation or getting up at 5 a.m. to write. And he's willing to have the frequent and often difficult conversations required for a relationship based on an equal division of care.

That isn't to say, of course, that we've managed to find some perfect equilibrium, only that we aim not for a consistent equal but for an ebb and flow that centers (roughly) on equal across many dimensions and adjusts year by year or even hour by hour. There have been times when I was the default parent—especially while the kids were little—but Dan has also stepped up to fill that role, like when he and the kids moved to Wisconsin in 2022, while I stayed behind for five months in Indiana before I could start my new job. Dan is also our kid activity coordinator, our travel planner, our kin-keeper, and our holiday magic-maker, and his willingness to take on that kind of cognitive labor—and hang with the kids while I go for runs and sometimes squeeze in a little extra writing on weekends—makes it possible for me to do the kind of deep thinking that a project like this one requires.

For Layla and Leo Calarco, this project has offered a window into the work that I do while requiring a great deal of patience on their end. They've learned, albeit grudgingly, that if they wake up before their alarms go off in the morning, they either have to go back to bed, make themselves breakfast, or curl up on the rug in my office until my pre-dawn writing time is done. Despite all the time I put into my work, they still seem to admire my efforts, and that admiration sustains me, especially when Layla tells her friends with pride, "My mom is a writer!" At the same time, their quick wit keeps me humble, like when Leo insists, "I think I've written more words than you."

The words for this book began with a quote in an interview I gave in November 2020 with writer Anne Helen Petersen for her *Culture Study* newsletter, which had debuted earlier that year. She is one of the most incisive cultural commentators of our generation, so I was thrilled to have the chance to talk with her about my research, and deeply impressed by the questions she asked. One of the things I said in response—"Other countries have social safety nets. The US has women"—ended up striking a nerve, getting requoted in dozens of news outlets, from *The New York Times* to *Glamour* and *Vogue*, in policy reports from groups like Brookings and the Center for American Progress, and even by Hillary Clinton on the formerly-known-as-Twitter platform X.

That quote also found its way into the hands of Leah Trouwborst, who was an editor with Portfolio/Penguin at the time, and who emailed to ask if I had considered turning my research into a book. At that point, I had just published *A Field Guide to Grad School* and was working on *Qualitative Literacy* with Mario Small, so I wasn't sure about taking on another book project or making the switch to trade book publishing, but conversations with Leah convinced me that I had a valuable message to share. Leah also introduced me to the rest of the Portfolio/Penguin team. That included Niki Papadopoulos and Adrian Zackheim, whose enthusiasm for the project built my confidence, as well as Merry Sun, whose hands-on role as editor has strengthened the book from the details to the core. Merry, along with Leila Sandlin, has stuck with me through many rounds of revisions, adjusting deadlines and acting as a sounding board for possible edits, to prioritize getting it right. Margot Stamas and her marketing team saw the potential in the book and have worked closely with me to get it into readers' hands.

The "other Margo" has been my friend and advocate through this whole process, helping me navigate the ins and outs of trade book publishing, keeping me going with words of encouragement when life made writing complicated, reading countless drafts, and serving as my trusted gut-check for every big decision I had to make. Margo Beth Fleming also understood that I wanted to write a book that not only opened the eyes of those new to sociological thinking but also spoke to those deeply familiar with sociological ideas. To that end, Margo helped me plan a day-long workshop where a set of experts came together to talk about the book and give me feedback on an early draft. Those experts included Allison Daminger, Dan Hirschman, Allison Pugh, and Casey Stockstill, and the day we spent together talking about the book (and sharing some very yummy meals) was among the very best days I've ever had. They helped me connect my work to big ideas across a range of disciplines, reframe my argument to clarify my contribution, and reorganize the chapters for maximum impact. Outside of that workshop, Kathryn Edin also helped me check the manuscript for accuracy, particularly in relation to the wonkier details of poverty policies and programs, and I am extremely grateful for her time and her willingness to share her expertise.

In sum, there have been many hands that went into making this book, and it fills my heart to know that there are so many people who care.

DATA COLLECTION AND METHODS

INTERVIEW DATA

Most of the primary data in this book comes from stories I gathered—with the help of a team including graduate and undergraduate students at Indiana University—from more than 250 families with young children, whom I've been following since 2018. The interviews included in this book were conducted as part of two interrelated studies, the Social Networks and Parenting (SNAP) Study, which was approved by the Indiana University Institutional Review Board under Protocol #1708860416, and the Pandemic Parenting Study (PPS), which was approved under Protocol #2003911048.

For SNAP, my research team recruited pregnant people through three prenatal clinics in Southern Indiana, as well as through online advertisements and flyers posted in the surrounding communities. All pregnant people who attended the clinics for standard screenings for gestational diabetes (approximately 500 people) were invited to participate in an online screening survey, as were potential participants who responded to community-based recruitment notices. Recruitment continued until 250 pregnant people had completed and passed the screening survey and consented to follow-up research. All the pregnant people who completed the screening survey identified as women, and approximately half of these were having their first child, with the other half having older children as well. After completing the brief screening survey, participants were invited by email or by phone to complete a longer online prenatal survey, which, like all surveys used in this study, was programmed in Qualtrics, and which included a range of questions about the decisions mothers intended to make for their children (e.g., regarding vaccines, breastfeeding, co-sleeping, screen time, childcare, behavior/discipline), the kind of parenting-related advice and information they had received from other people in their social networks, their health and their pregnancies, their relationships with their partners, and their home lives and personal backgrounds. Participants who consented to follow-up research were then invited to complete follow-up surveys and interviews at 6 months (N=148 surveys, 61 interviews), 12 months (N=115 surveys, 33 interviews), and 18 months postpartum (N=93 surveys, 27 interviews). Interviews were conducted with support from a research team that included graduate student research assistants. Some interviews were conducted in person in mothers' homes or workplaces or in public places like libraries or cafes, while others were conducted over the phone or through video platforms like Zoom. All interviews were recorded and transcribed. Mothers received $20 gift cards for each survey and interview they completed.

The PPS involved three waves of background/screening surveys and in-depth interviews with SNAP Study participants, as well as with their partners and network contacts. From April to May 2020, all previous SNAP Study participants (excluding those who had specifically opted out of follow-up) were invited to complete the Wave 1 background/screening survey, which was programmed in Qualtrics and included closed-ended and open-ended questions about their experiences during and decisions regarding Covid-19. Participants who completed the Wave 1 survey (N=145) were then invited to write diary entries about their experiences during the pandemic (N=105) and to participate in Wave 1 interviews involving in-depth questions about these same topics (N=66). In-depth interviews were conducted virtually or by phone, with the help of a research team that included graduate student research assistants, and were recorded and transcribed. A few interviews lasted less than sixty minutes (usually because mothers had to cut interviews short due to caregiving responsibilities), but the average length was more than ninety minutes, and some lasted more than two and a half hours.

PPS Waves 2 and 3 followed procedures similar to those in Wave 1, except that partners of the initial participants were invited to participate in both those waves, and at Wave 3, initial participants provided names of other parents in their social networks, who were invited to participate in survey and in-depth interviews as well. Wave 2 was conducted from January to March 2021, including background/screening surveys (N=150) and in-depth interviews (N=57). Wave 3 was conducted from October 2021 through January 2022 and involved background/screenings surveys (N=192) and in-depth interviews (N=68). Participants received $20 gift cards for each background/screening survey and each interview they completed. At each wave, participants were asked a wide range of questions and follow-up questions, including questions about their experiences during the pandemic, the effect the pandemic was having on their lives and their relationships, the decisions they were making during the pandemic, and the sources they relied on for information and support.

SURVEY DATA

In-depth interviews can give us rich stories like Akari's—offering a window into people's day-to-day experiences, their perceptions of those experiences, the meanings they assign to those experiences, and the motivations that guide them as they navigate their lives.[1] Yet interview studies typically focus on depth over breadth. Thus, if the goal is to determine how common some phenomenon is in a population, or whether the prevalence of that phenomenon varies across different social groups, tools like surveys are generally a better bet. Put differently, while interviews and other types of qualitative data are best for answering questions like "How do families get by without an adequate social safety net?" and "Why don't people always use the government benefits for which they are eligible?," quantitative survey data are better suited for answering questions like "What percentage of US families are struggling financially?" and "Are women or men more likely to support expanding the US social safety net?"

Thus, as a supplement to the interview data I collected through the SNAP and PPS studies, I also conducted two national surveys, each with more than two thousand parents and guardians of children under eighteen across the US.

ITD

The Institutions, Trust, and Decision-making Study was approved by the Indiana University IRB under protocol #2010244658. It ran from November to December 2020 and was fielded with support from the survey company Ipsos, which recruited participants through their iSay panels to take an online survey in exchange for points, which can be redeemed for incentives. Eligible participants had at least one child under eighteen living with them and were at least eighteen years of age themselves. Recruitment quotas (based on gender, race/ethnicity, marital status, educational attainment, income, employment status, and region) were also used to recruit a probability sample that roughly corresponds with the demographics of US parents with children under eighteen. Approximately 10,000 panelists were invited to participate in the survey; 3,834 panelists clicked the link to begin the survey. Of these, 1,135 were excluded because they did not meet the selection criteria (agreeing to participate, having a child under age eighteen, and being at least eighteen years of age) or because the quotas had been met. An additional 233 respondents clicked the link but did not complete the survey and were thereby also excluded from the analysis.

The survey questionnaire focused on families' experiences and decisions regarding the Covid-19 pandemic, but it also included a range of more general questions about parenting-related attitudes and beliefs. Some questions were adapted from prior surveys for comparability. Following the completion of the survey, I worked with a statistical expert to develop post-stratification weights, which I apply in all analyses to adjust for extraneous differences between the sample margins and population control totals (for adults living with children under eighteen) obtained from the American Community Survey.

PITT

The Parenting in Tumultuous Times Study was approved by the Indiana University IRB under protocol #13111. It ran from mid-December 2021 through mid-January 2022 and was fielded with support from the survey company Qualtrics, which recruited participants from their Qualtrics Panels to take an online survey in exchange for predetermined rewards, such as points that can be redeemed for prizes or cash. Participants were eligible for the survey if they were living in the US, were at least eighteen years of age, and have at least one child under age eighteen who is living with them. Quota sampling was used to ensure representation of parents from different social groups (e.g., men and women; white, Black, Latino/a, and Asian American parents; parents with and without bachelor's degrees; and parents living in the Northeast, Midwest, South, and West). Mothers, Black parents, and parents who have not completed bachelor's degrees were oversampled to allow for more detailed analyses of variations within these groups; 3,553 respondents clicked the link to begin the survey. Of these respondents, 1,554 were excluded because they did not meet the eligibility criteria, because they exceeded the quotas, because they did not complete the full survey, or because they failed the quality checks. Thus, the final sample includes 2,009 US parents.

Like the first survey, this second survey focused on families' experiences and decisions regarding the Covid-19 pandemic, but it also included a range of other parenting-related questions, including some adapted from other surveys for comparability. When analyzing these data, I apply the post-stratification weights that Qualtrics developed to align the sample (based on gender, race/ethnicity, educational attainment, age, and regional location) with data on parents with children under eighteen from the 2021 American Community Survey.

Notes

PREFACE

1. On the American labor crisis during World War II, see Ruth Milkman, *Gender at Work: The Dynamics of Job Segregation by Sex during World War II* (Champaign: University of Illinois Press, 1987).
2. For Morley's letter, see "Letter from Burton R. Morley, Area Director, to Mr. J. J. Carney, Labor Economist, relating to anticipated in-migration in Mobile within the next six months," November 11, 1942, Office for Emergency Management, War Manpower Commission, Region VII, 1942–1945, National Archives at Atlanta, National Archives Identifier: 281509, NAIL Control Number: NRCA-211-WMC12-WMMIGLET(1), https://catalog.archives.gov/id/281509.
3. For the War Manpower Commission's response to Morley, see "War Manpower job flyer promoting women to register for War Jobs," 1942, Office for Emergency Management, War Manpower Commission, Region VII, 1942–1945, National Archives at Atlanta, National Archives Identifier: 281500, NAIL Control Number: NRCA-211-WMC11-WMJOBFLYER, https://catalog.archives.gov/id/281500.
4. On women's role as the generals of the home front, see Terrence H. Witkowski, "The American Consumer Home Front during World War II," *ACR North American Advances* 25 (1998). On policies limiting women's employment, see Claudia Goldin, "Marriage Bars: Discrimination against Married Women Workers, 1920's to 1950's" (working paper, National Bureau of Economic Research, October 1988), https://doi.org/10.3386/w2747; Megan McDonald Way, *Family Economics and Public Policy, 1800s–Present: How Laws, Incentives, and Social Programs Drive Family Decision-Making and the US Economy* (New York: Springer, 2018).
5. On the limited childcare options prior to World War II, see Susan E. Riley, "Caring for Rosie's Children: Federal Child Care Policies in the World War II Era," *Polity* 26, no. 4 (June 1994): 655–75; Emilie Stoltzfus, *Child Care: The Federal Role during World War II* (Washington, DC: Congressional Research Service, 2000), https://crsreports.congress.gov/product/pdf/RS/RS20615/9. On the relegation of women to low-paying jobs, see Nancy Foner, "Immigrant Women and Work in New York City, Then and Now," *Journal of American Ethnic History* 18, no. 3 (1999): 95–113; Goldin, "Marriage Bars"; Claudia Goldin, *Understanding the Gender Gap: An Economic History of American Women* (Oxford: Oxford University Press, 1992); Susila Gurusami, "Motherwork under the State: The Maternal Labor of Formerly Incarcerated Black Women," *Social Problems* 66, no. 1 (2019): 128–43; Tera W. Hunter, *To 'Joy My Freedom: Southern Black Women's Lives and Labors after the Civil War* (Cambridge, MA: Harvard University Press, 1998); María de la Luz Ibarra, "Mexican Immigrant Women and the New Domestic Labor," *Human Organization* 59, no. 4 (2007): 452–64; Milkman, *Gender at Work*; Stella DeRosa Torgoff, "Immigrant Women, the Family, and Work," *Trends in History*

2, no. 4 (1983): 31–47. On unions' role in restricting work opportunities for women, see Joan Ellen Trey, "Women in the War Economy—World War II," *Review of Radical Political Economics* 4, no. 3 (1972): 40–57. On the Depression-era scapegoating of married women, see Patrice Ruane, "From Pin Money Workers to Essential Workers: Lessons about Women's Employment and the COVID-19 Pandemic from the Great Depression and the Great Recession," *UCLA Journal of Gender and Law* 29, no. 2 (2022).

6. On the need for women's labor during WWII, see Trey, "Women in the War Economy—World War II." On the workforce participation of US mothers before and during the war, see Emily D. Cahan, *Past Caring: A History of U.S. Preschool Care and Education for the Poor, 1820–1965* (New York: National Center for Children in Poverty, 1989), https://www.researchconnections .org/sites/default/files/pdf/rc2088.pdf.

7. On the role of the Lanham Act in providing childcare during World War II, see Riley, "Caring for Rosie's Children"; Stoltzfus, *Child Care*; Eleanor Ferguson Straub, "Government Policy toward Civilian Women during World War II" (PhD diss., Emory University, 1973), https://www.proquest.com/pqdtglobal/docview/302719120/citation/7D8E27CC5AE 84C95PQ/1; Trey, "Women in the War Economy—WWII." For Lenroot's letter to Kerr, see "Letter from Katharine F. Lenroot to Florence Kerr," August 15, 1941, file 21-6-4, acc. 69-A-1959, RG 102, WNRC, cited in Straub, "Government Policy toward Civilian Women during World War II," 267–68.

8. On Congress's initial refusal to use Lanham Act funds for childcare and their eventual concession, see "Minutes of Meeting of War Services Committee of the American Public Welfare Association," August 27, 1942, 24, file "American Public Welfare Association," file 10-4-4-7, acc. 52-A-69, RG 102, WNRC, cited in Straub, "Government Policy toward Civilian Women during World War II," 268–71. On the services provided through the childcare centers, see William M. Tuttle Jr., *"Daddy's Gone to War": The Second World War in the Lives of America's Children* (Oxford: Oxford University Press, 1993); Stoltzfus, *Child Care*. For McNutt's quote, see Trey, "Women in the War Economy—World War II."

9. On the changing workforce participation of married women and women with children, see Cahan, *Past Caring*. On the limits of the Lanham Act childcare centers, see Casey Stockstill, *False Starts: The Segregated Lives of Preschoolers* (New York: NYU Press, 2023). On the situation in Mobile, see "Labor Market Developments Report Entailing the Ratio of Non-Whites and Women in the Workforce, Labor Demands, Labor Turnover, Training, Absenteeism, Overstaffing, and Related Community Problems such as DayCare, Laundries and Transportation," June 12, 1943, Office for Emergency Management, War Manpower Commission, Region VII, 1942–1945, National Archives at Atlanta, National Archives Identifier: 281508, NAIL Control Number: NRCA-211-WMC12-WMLABORRPT, https://catalog.archives.gov/id/281508.

10. On efforts to support men's reentry into the economy, see Suzanne Mettler, *Soldiers to Citizens: The G.I. Bill and the Making of the Greatest Generation* (Oxford: Oxford University Press, 2005); Sarah Turner and John Bound, "Closing the Gap or Widening the Divide: The Effects of the G.I. Bill and World War II on the Educational Outcomes of Black Americans," *Journal of Economic History* 63, no. 1 (2003): 145–77. On how men's return affected women's employment, see Goldin, *Understanding the Gender Gap*; Trey, "Women in the War Economy—World War II."

11. On women's desire to remain in the workforce after World War II, see A. G. Mezerik, "Getting Rid of the Women," *Atlantic Monthly*, June 1945. See also Stephanie Coontz, *The Way We Never Were: American Families and the Nostalgia Trap* (New York: Basic Books, 1993); Milkman, *Gender at Work*; Trey, "Women in the War Economy—World War II."

12. For the quoted passages, see Ruth Young and Catherine Filene Shouse, "The Woman Worker Speaks," *Independent Woman*, October 1945, 274–75, quoted in Trey, "Women in the War Economy—World War II." See also Coontz, *The Way We Never Were*; Milkman, *Gender at Work*; Riley, "Caring for Rosie's Children"; Straub, "Government Policy toward Civilian Women during World War II"; Trey, "Women in the War Economy—World War II."

13. On how the media and the medical establishment framed women as "crazy" and "dangerous," see Coontz, *The Way We Never Were*, 34–35. See also Susan M. Hartmann, *The Home Front and Beyond: American Women in the 1940s* (Boston: Twayne Publishing, 1983); Carol A. B. Warren, *Madwives: Schizophrenic Women in the 1950s* (New Brunswick, NJ: Rutgers University Press, 1987).

14. On postwar social welfare policy developments in Europe, see Kaspar Burger, "A Social History of Ideas Pertaining to Childcare in France and in the United States," *Journal of Social History* 45, no. 4 (2012): 1005–25; Kimberly J. Morgan, "The Politics of Mothers' Employment: France in Comparative Perspective," *World Politics* 55, no. 2 (2003): 259–89; Roosa Tikkanen et al., "International Health Care System Profiles: France," Commonwealth Fund, June 5, 2020, https://www.commonwealthfund.org/international-health-policy-center/countries /france).

15. For cross-national differences in social welfare policies, see "Maternity Leave by Country," World Population Review, 2023, https://worldpopulationreview.com/country-rankings /maternity-leave-by-country; "Countries with Universal Healthcare," World Population Review, 2023, https://worldpopulationreview.com/country-rankings/countries-with-universal -healthcare.

16. On continued gender inequalities, see Caitlyn Collins, *Making Motherhood Work: How Women Manage Careers and Caregiving* (Princeton, NJ: Princeton University Press, 2019); Sarah Damaske, *For the Family?: How Class and Gender Shape Women's Work* (Oxford: Oxford University Press, 2011); Paula England, "The Gender Revolution: Uneven and Stalled," *Gender & Society* 24, no. 2 (2010): 149–66; Paula England and Nancy Folbre, "The Cost of Caring," *ANNALS of the American Academy of Political and Social Science* 561, no. 1 (1999): 39–51; Kathleen Gerson, *The Unfinished Revolution: Coming of Age in a New Era of Gender, Work, and Family* (Oxford: Oxford University Press, 2011); Arlie Russell Hochschild, *The Second Shift: Working Families and the Revolution at Home* (New York: Penguin Books, 1989); Aliya Hamid Rao, *Crunch Time: How Married Couples Confront Unemployment* (Berkeley: University of California, 2020); William J. Scarborough, Ray Sin, and Barbara Risman, "Attitudes and the Stalled Gender Revolution: Egalitarianism, Traditionalism, and Ambivalence from 1977 through 2016," *Gender & Society* 33, no. 2 (2018): 173–200; Anne-Marie Slaughter, *Unfinished Business: Women Men Work Family* (New York: Random House, 2015). For men's and women's time spent in unpaid work, see "Time Spent in Paid and Unpaid Work, by Sex," OECD, 2023, https://stats.oecd.org/index.aspx?queryid=54757. For women's labor force participation rate as of 2023, see Alicia Wallace, "There Are More Women in the Workforce Than Ever Before," CNN, July 7, 2023, https://www.cnn.com/2023/07/07/economy/women -labor-force-participation/index.html. For men's labor force participation as of 2023, see "Labor Force Participation Rate for People Ages 25 to 54 in May 2023 Highest Since January 2007," Bureau of Labor Statistics, June 7, 2023, https://www.bls.gov/opub/ted/2023/labor -force-participation-rate-for-people-ages-25-to-54-in-may-2023-highest-since-january -2007.htm. On gender pay gaps, see Jasmine Tucker and Kayla Patrick, *Low-Wage Jobs Are Women's Jobs: The Overrepresentation of Women in Low-Wage Work* (Washington, DC: National Women's Law Center, 2017).

17. On self-help culture, see Micki McGee, *Self Help, Inc.: Makeover Culture in American Life* (Oxford: Oxford University Press, 2007). On guilt, see Collins, *Making Motherhood Work*; Caitlyn Collins, "Is Maternal Guilt a Cross-National Experience?," *Qualitative Sociology* 44, no. 1 (2021): 1–29.

INTRODUCTION

1. On the link between national-level income inequality and gender pay gaps, see Francine D. Blau and Lawrence M. Kahn, "Wage Structure and Gender Earnings Differentials: An International Comparison," *Economica* 63, no. 250 (1996): S29–62.

2. For a living wage calculator, see "Living Wage," https://livingwage.mit.edu/.

3. On the prevalence of life insurance, see LIMRA, *Facts about Life 2021* (Windsor, CT: LIMRA, September 2021), https://www.limra.com/siteassets/newsroom/fact-tank/fact-sheets /facts-of-life-2021-format-vfinal.pdf. On the nationwide shortage of affordable housing, see Ikra Rafi Clarke and Diane Yente, *Addressing America's Affordable Housing Crisis* (Washington, DC: Urban Institute, 2023), https://housingmatters.urban.org/research-summary/addressing -americas-affordable-housing-crisis. On the RAD program, see HUD, *Rental Assistance Demonstration (RAD)* (Washington, DC: US Department of Housing and Urban Development, 2023), https://www.hud.gov/RAD.

4. On the prevalence of welfare, see Gilbert Crouse et al., *Welfare Indicators and Risk Factors* (Washington, DC: US Department of Health and Human Services, 2022), https://aspe.hhs .gov/sites/default/files/documents/85da9415ece89b2989ad290755d38f7b/welfare -indicators-rtc.pdf.

5. For Indiana's welfare rules, see *TANF* (Indianapolis, IN: State of Indiana Family and Social Services Administration), https://www.in.gov/fssa/dfr/files/TANF-Brochure-English.pdf. See also "About TANF," State of Indiana Family and Social Services Administration, https:// www.in.gov/fssa/dfr/tanf-cash-assistance/about-tanf/. For more on how welfare works in the US, see "Policy Basics: Temporary Assistance for Needy Families," Center on Budget and Policy Priorities, March 1, 2022, https://www.cbpp.org/research/family-income-support /temporary-assistance-for-needy-families. For more on how families experience welfare rules, see Kathryn J. Edin and H. Luke Shaefer, *$2.00 a Day: Living on Almost Nothing in America* (Boston: Mariner Books, 2015); Kathryn Edin and Laura Lein, *Making Ends Meet: How Single Mothers Survive Welfare and Low-Wage Work* (New York: Russell Sage Foundation, 1997); Joan Maya Mazelis, *Surviving Poverty* (New York: NYU Press, 2016). On how food stamps work in Indiana, see "EBT (Hoosier Works card)," State of Indiana Family and Social Services Administration, https://www.in.gov/fssa/dfr/ebt-hoosier-works-card/. For more on food stamp exclusions, see Jennifer Randles, "Fixing a Leaky U.S. Social Safety Net: Diapers, Policy, and Low-Income Families," *RSF: The Russell Sage Foundation Journal of the Social Sciences* 8, no. 5 (2022): 166–83; Jennifer Randles, "'Willing to Do Anything for My Kids': Inventive Mothering, Diapers, and the Inequalities of Carework," *American Sociological Review* 86, no. 1 (2021): 35–59.

6. On the federal Earned Income Tax Credit program, see "Earned Income Tax Credit," United States Government, https://www.benefits.gov/benefit/939. See also "Earned Income Tax Credit (EITC) Assistant," US Internal Revenue Service, 2020, https://apps.irs.gov/app/eitc /results/. On Indiana's Earned Income Credit program, see "Indiana Earned Income Credit 2020," State of Indiana, 2020. See also *State Earned Income Tax Credits* (Washington, DC: Urban Institute, 2023), https://www.urban.org/policy-centers/cross-center-initiatives/state -and-local-finance-initiative/state-and-local-backgrounders/state-earned-income-tax -credits. On the Child Tax Credit, see *Policy Basics: The Child Tax Credit* (Washington, DC: Center on Budget and Policy Priorities, 2022), https://www.cbpp.org/research/policy-basics -the-child-tax-credit. On the sliding scale costs associated with affordable housing programs, see *Calculating Rent and Housing Assistance Payments* (Washington, DC: US Department of Housing and Urban Development, 2019), https://www.hud.gov/sites/dfiles/PIH/documents /HCV_Guidebook_Calculating_Rent_and_HAP_Payments.pdf. On the sliding scale costs associated with extended day childcare programs affiliated with Head Start, see "Head Start," Human Services, Inc., 2023, https://www.hsi-indiana.com/head-start/.

7. On the exclusion of diapers from nutrition assistance programs, see "Are Diapers or Baby Wipes Eligible for Purchase with Supplemental Nutrition Assistance Program Benefits?," AskUSDA, https://ask.usda.gov/s/article/Are-diapers-or-baby-wipes-eligible-for-purchase -with-Supplemental-Nutrition-Assistance-Program. On the lack of WIC coverage for diapers and wipes, see "How Do I Apply for WIC?," Indiana Department of Health, https://www .in.gov/health/wic/. See also Randles, "'Willing to Do Anything for My Kids'"; Randles,

"Fixing a Leaky U.S. Social Safety Net." On the legal loopholes in the Affordable Care Act, see Lisa Myers and Carroll Ann Mears, "Businesses Claim Obamacare Has Forced Them to Cut Employee Hours," NBC News, August 13, 2013, https://www.nbcnews.com/news/world/businesses-claim-obamacare-has-forced-them-cut-employee-hours-flna6c10911846; Robert Pear, "Public Sector Cuts Part-Time Shifts to Bypass Insurance Law," *New York Times*, February 20, 2014, https://www.nytimes.com/2014/02/21/us/public-sector-cuts-part-time-shifts-to-duck-insurance-law.html.

8. On the benefits cliff or the "cliff effect," see Susan Roll and Jean East, "Financially Vulnerable Families and the Child Care Cliff Effect," *Journal of Poverty* 18, no. 2 (2014): 169–87. On Indiana's income limits for rental assistance and public housing, see *2021 Adjusted Home Income Limits* (Indianapolis, IN: US Department of Housing and Urban Development, 2021), https://www.huduser.gov/portal/datasets/home-datasets/files/HOME_IncomeLmts_State_IN_2021.pdf. On Indiana's income limits for childcare subsidies, see "What are the income limits for the child care and development fund?," Indiana Family & Social Services Administration, https://faqs.in.gov/hc/en-us/articles/360042511751-What-are-the-income-limits-for-the-Child-Care-and-Development-Fund-. On Indiana's income limits for Head Start and Early Head Start, see "Indiana Head Start," Benefits.Gov, https://www.benefits.gov/benefit/1909. On Indiana's income limits for Medicaid, see "Eligibility Guide," Indiana Medicaid for Members, https://www.in.gov/medicaid/members/apply-for-medicaid/eligibility-guide/#Adults. On Indiana's income limits for TANF, see "About TANF," Indiana Family and Social Services Administration, https://www.in.gov/fssa/dfr/tanf-cash-assistance/about-tanf/. On Indiana's income limits for food stamps, see "Indiana Supplemental Nutrition Assistance Program," Benefits.Gov, https://www.benefits.gov/benefit/1070

9. On welfare time limits, see "State Policies on Lifetime Time Limits," Urban Institute, June 2002, https://www.urban.org/sites/default/files/publication/71751/900525.PDF. For Indiana's time limits, see Adam Yahya Rayes, "Indiana Senate Passes Bill with 'Modest' Increases to TANF Eligibility Limit, Payments," WFYI, January 30, 2023, https://www.wfyi.org/news/articles/indiana-senate-passes-bill-with-modest-increases-to-tanf-eligibility-limit-payments. On the soft diversion tactics used to push welfare recipients out of the program before they reach the time limit, see Mary Corcoran, Sandra K. Danziger, Ariel Kalil, and Kristin S. Seefeldt, "How Welfare Reform Is Affecting Women's Work," *Annual Review of Sociology* 26 (2000): 241–69; Kristin S. Seefeldt, "Serving No One Well: TANF Nearly Twenty Years Later," *Journal of Sociology & Social Welfare* 44, no. 2 (2017): 3–28. On asset limits on welfare eligibility in Indiana, see "About TANF," Indiana Family and Social Services Administration, https://www.in.gov/fssa/dfr/tanf-cash-assistance/about-tanf/.

10. On women's role as unpaid childcare providers for their families, see Suzanne M. Bianchi et al., "Housework: Who Did, Does or Will Do It, and How Much Does It Matter?," *Social Forces* 91, no. 1 (2012): 55–63; Caitlyn Collins, *Making Motherhood Work: How Women Manage Careers and Caregiving* (Princeton, NJ: Princeton University Press, 2019); Lyn Craig and Bridget Jenkins, "The Composition of Parents' and Grandparents' Child-Care Time: Gender and Generational Patterns in Activity, Multi-Tasking and Co-Presence," *Ageing and Society* 36, no. 4 (2016): 785–810; Lyn Craig and Killian Mullan, "How Mothers and Fathers Share Childcare: A Cross-National Time-Use Comparison," *American Sociological Review* 76, no. 6 (2011): 834–61; Dawn Marie Dow, *Mothering While Black* (Berkeley: University of California Press, 2019); Arlie Russell Hochschild, *The Second Shift: Working Families and the Revolution at Home* (New York: Penguin Books, 1989); Scott Schieman, Leah Ruppanner, and Melissa A. Milkie, "Who Helps with Homework? Parenting Inequality and Relationship Quality among Employed Mothers and Fathers," *Journal of Family and Economic Issues* 39, no. 1 (2018): 49–65. For more on the role that women play in building and maintaining kin relationships and supporting members of their family, see Marjorie L. DeVault, *Feeding the Family: The Social Organization of Caring as Gendered Work* (Chicago: University of Chicago, 1994); Naomi Gerstel and Sally K. Gallagher, "Kinkeeping and Distress: Gender, Recipients of Care, and

Work-Family Conflict," *Journal of Marriage and Family* 55, no. 3 (1993): 598–608; Mazelis, *Surviving Poverty*; Carolyn J. Rosenthal, "Kinkeeping in the Familial Division of Labor," *Journal of Marriage and Family* 47, no. 4 (1985): 965–74; Carol Stack, *All Our Kin* (New York: Harper & Row, 1974). For more on women's role in caring for elderly family members, see Sara Arber and Jay Ginn, "The Meaning of Informal Care: Gender and the Contribution of Elderly People," *Ageing & Society* 10, no. 4 (1990): 429–54; Sara Arber and Jay Ginn, "Gender Differences in Informal Caring," *Health & Social Care in the Community* 3, no. 1 (1995): 19–31; Christian Deindl and Martina Brandt, "Support Networks of Childless Older People: Informal and Formal Support in Europe," *Ageing & Society* 37, no. 8 (2017): 1543–67; Tina Schmid, Martina Brandt, and Klaus Haberkern, "Gendered Support to Older Parents: Do Welfare States Matter?," *European Journal of Ageing* 9, no. 1 (2012): 39–50. On women's role as family health managers, see Kate Cairns, Josée Johnston, and Norah MacKendrick, "Feeding the 'Organic Child': Mothering through Ethical Consumption," *Journal of Consumer Culture* 13, no. 2 (2013): 97–118; Sinikka Elliott and Sarah Bowen, "Defending Motherhood: Morality, Responsibility, and Double Binds in Feeding Children," *Journal of Marriage and Family* 80, no. 2 (2018): 499–520; Norah MacKendrick, "More Work for Mother: Chemical Body Burdens as a Maternal Responsibility," *Gender & Society* 28, no. 5 (2014): 705–28; Eliza K. Pavalko and Shari Woodbury, "Social Roles as Process: Caregiving Careers and Women's Health," *Journal of Health and Social Behavior* 41, no. 1 (2000): 91–105; Usha Ranji and Alina Salganicoff, "Balancing on Shaky Ground: Women, Work, and Family Health," Kaiser Family Foundation, October 2014, http://files.kff.org/attachment/balancing-on-shaky-ground-women-work-and-family-health-data-note; Jennifer A. Reich, "Neoliberal Mothering and Vaccine Refusal: Imagined Gated Communities and the Privilege of Choice," *Gender & Society* 28, no. 5 (2014). On women's role as family budget managers, see John P. Bartkowski, "One Step Forward, One Step Back: 'Progressive Traditionalism' and the Negotiation of Domestic Labor in Evangelical Families," *Gender Issues* 17, no. 4 (1999): 37–61; Allison Daminger, "The Cognitive Dimension of Household Labor," *American Sociological Review* 84, no. 4 (2019): 609–33; Caitlin Daniel, "Economic Constraints on Taste Formation and the True Cost of Healthy Eating," *Social Science & Medicine* 148 (2016): 34–41. On women's role in community volunteer efforts, see Rachel Karniol, Efrat Grosz, and Irit Schorr, "Caring, Gender Role Orientation, and Volunteering," *Sex Roles* 49, no. 1/2 (2003): 11–21; Lydia K. Manning, "Gender and Religious Differences Associated with Volunteering in Later Life," *Journal of Women & Aging* 22, no. 2 (2010): 125–35; Brittany Murray et al., "Civil Society Goes to School: Parent-Teacher Associations and the Equality of Educational Opportunity," *RSF: The Russell Sage Foundation Journal of the Social Sciences* 5, no. 3 (2019): 41–63; Linn Posey-Maddox, "Professionalizing the PTO: Race, Class, and Shifting Norms of Parental Engagement in a City Public School," *American Journal of Education* 119, no. 2 (2013): 235–60. On men's and women's time use, see "American Time Use Survey Summary," US Bureau of Labor Statistics, 2022, https://www.bls.gov/news.release/atus.nr0.htm. See also "Time Spent in Primary Activities for the Civilian Population," US Bureau of Labor Statistics, June 22, 2023, https://www.bls.gov/news.release/atus.t08A.htm.

11. On the gender breakdown of the US workforce, see "Labor Force Statistics from the Current Population Survey," US Bureau of Labor Statistics, 2023, https://www.bls.gov/cps/cpsaat02.htm. On gender pay gaps and the dangers of not including part-time and part-year workers in those calculations, see Lauren Hoffman and Isabela Salas-Betsch, "Including All Women Workers in Wage Gap Calculations," Center for American Progress, 2022, https://www.americanprogress.org/article/including-all-women-workers-in-wage-gap-calculations/. On the overrepresentation of women in low-wage jobs, see Jasmine Tucker and Kayla Patrick, *Low-Wage Jobs Are Women's Jobs: The Overrepresentation of Women in Low-Wage Work* (Washington, DC: National Women's Law Center, 2017). On gender pay gaps, see Wendy Chun-Hoon, "5 Fast Facts: The Gender Wage Gap," *US Department of Labor* (blog), March 14, 2023, http://blog.dol.gov/2023/03/14/5-fast-facts-the-gender-wage-gap. On variations in the

gender wage gap, see Michelle J. Budig and Melissa J. Hodges, "Differences in Disadvantage: Variation in the Motherhood Penalty across White Women's Earnings Distribution," *American Sociological Review* 75, no. 5 (2010): 705–28; Elise Gould, Jessica Schieder, and Kathleen Geier, *What Is the Gender Pay Gap and Is It Real?: The Complete Guide to How Women Are Paid Less Than Men and Why It Can't Be Explained Away* (Washington, DC: Economic Policy Institute, 2016), https://www.epi.org/publication/what-is-the-gender-pay-gap-and-is-it-real/; Ariane Hegewisch et al., *Separate and Not Equal? Gender Segregation in the Labor Market and the Gender Wage Gap* (Washington, DC: Institute for Women's Policy Research, 2010); Kathrin Leuze and Susanne Strauss, "Why Do Occupations Dominated by Women Pay Less? How 'Female-Typical' Work Tasks and Working-Time Arrangements Affect the Gender Wage Gap among Higher Education Graduates," *Work, Employment and Society* 30, no. 5 (2016): 802–20; Charlotta Magnusson, "Why Is There a Gender Wage Gap According to Occupational Prestige?: An Analysis of the Gender Wage Gap by Occupational Prestige and Family Obligations in Sweden," *Acta Sociologica* 53, no. 2 (2010): 99–117; Casey Stockstill and Grace Carson, "Are Lighter-Skinned Tanisha and Jamal Worth More Pay? White People's Gendered Colorism toward Black Job Applicants with Racialized Names," *Ethnic and Racial Studies* 45, no. 5 (2022): 896–917; Kim A. Weeden, Youngjoo Cha, and Mauricio Bucca, "Long Work Hours, Part-Time Work, and Trends in the Gender Gap in Pay, the Motherhood Wage Penalty, and the Fatherhood Wage Premium," *RSF: The Russell Sage Foundation Journal of the Social Sciences* 2, no. 4 (2016): 71–102; Wei-hsin Yu and Janet Chen-Lan Kuo, "The Motherhood Wage Penalty by Work Conditions: How Do Occupational Characteristics Hinder or Empower Mothers?," *American Sociological Review* 82, no. 4 (2017): 744–69. On the motherhood wage penalty as an explanation for larger gender pay gaps, see Joeli Brearley, *The Motherhood Penalty* (New York: Simon & Schuster, 2022).

12. On the importance of pro-union policies, see David Brady, Regina S. Baker, and Ryan Finnigan, "When Unionization Disappears: State-Level Unionization and Working Poverty in the United States," *American Sociological Review* 78, no. 5 (2013): 872–96; Henry S. Farber and Bruce Western, "Accounting for the Decline of Unions in the Private Sector, 1973–1998," *Journal of Labor Research* 22, no. 3 (2001): 459–85; David Jacobs and Lindsey Myers, "Union Strength, Neoliberalism, and Inequality: Contingent Political Analyses of U.S. Income Differences since 1950," *American Sociological Review* 79, no. 4 (2014): 752–74. For more on the importance of strong minimum wage laws, see Anne Penketh et al., "Which Are the Best Countries in the World to Live in If You Are Unemployed or Disabled?," *Guardian*, April 15, 2015, https://www.theguardian.com/politics/2015/apr/15/which-best-countries -live-unemployed-disabled-benefits. On cross-national variations in programs providing support for people who are unemployed, see "Most of World Lacks Unemployment Insurance," International Labour Organization, June 21, 2000, https://www.ilo.org/global /about-the-ilo/newsroom/news/WCMS_007901. For a list of countries that set minimum standards for paid sick leave, see Hye Jin Rho, Shawn Fremstad, and Jared Gaby-Biegel, "Contagion Nation 2020: United States Still the Only Wealthy Nation without Paid Sick Leave," CEPR, March 19, 2020, https://cepr.net/report/contagion-nation-2020-united-states -still-the-only-wealthy-nation-without-paid-sick-leave. For a list of countries that require employers to provide paid vacation time for their employees, see "People in These Countries Get the Most Paid Vacation Days," World Economic Forum, August 22, 2018, https://www .weforum.org/agenda/2018/08/average-paid-vacation-time-days-by-country/. On how shorter hours and stronger worker protections increase productivity, see Marion Collewet and Jan Sauermann, "Working Hours and Productivity," *Labour Economics* (2017): 96–106; John Pencavel, "The Productivity of Working Hours," *Economic Journal* 125, no. 589 (2015): 2052–76; Cynthia Fuchs Epstein and Arne L. Kalleberg, *Fighting for Time: Shifting Boundaries of Work and Social Life* (New York: Russell Sage Foundation, 2004); Kijong Kim and Rania Antonopoulos, "Unpaid and Paid Care: The Effects of Child Care and Elder Care on the Standard of Living," *SSRN Electronic Journal*, October 19, 2011; Robert Buchele and Jens Christiansen,

"Worker Rights Promote Productivity Growth," *Challenge* 38, no. 5 (1995): 32–37. On the importance of affordable housing programs, see Matthew Desmond, *Poverty, by America* (New York: Crown, 2023); Christine Whitehead and Kathleen Scanlon, *Social Housing in Europe II: A Review of Policies and Outcomes* (London: London School of Economics and Political Science, 2008); Ally Schweitzer, "How European-Style Public Housing Could Help Solve the Affordability Crisis," NPR, February 25, 2020, https://www.npr.org/local/305/2020/02/25/809315455/how-european-style-public-housing-could-help-solve-the-affordability-crisis. On the importance of robust cash benefit programs, see Edin and Lein, *Making Ends Meet*; Edin and Shaefer, *$2.00 a Day*; Kelley Fong, Rachel A. Wright, and Christopher Wimer, "The Cost of Free Assistance: Why Low-Income Individuals Do Not Access Food Pantries," *Journal of Sociology & Social Welfare* 43, no. 1 (2016): 71–94. On cross-national variations in retirement pensions and programs, see Rob Smith, "These Countries Have the Most Generous Pensions," World Economic Forum, 2018, https://www.weforum.org/agenda/2018/02/average-pension-country-wise/. See also *Pensions at a Glance 2021* (Paris: OECD and G20 Indicators, 2021), https://www.oecd.org/els/public-pensions/oecd-pensions-at-a-glance-19991363.htm. On effective childcare systems, see Claire Cain Miller, "How Other Nations Pay for Child Care. The U.S. Is an Outlier," *New York Times*, October 6, 2021, https://www.nytimes.com/2021/10/06/upshot/child-care-biden.html. For more on effective eldercare systems, see Max Fisher, "These Are the Best and Worst Countries to Be Elderly," *Washington Post*, October 3, 2013, https://www.washingtonpost.com/news/worldviews/wp/2013/10/03/these-are-the-best-and-worst-countries-to-be-elderly/. For a list of countries with single-payer, universal healthcare, see "Foreign Countries with Universal Health Care," NY Department of Health, https://www.health.ny.gov/regulations/hcra/univ_hlth_care.htm. For a list of countries that offer free college or university tuition, see "Countries with Free College 2023," World Population Review, https://worldpopulationreview.com/country-rankings/countries-with-free-college.

13. On the dismantling of the US social safety net, see Mitchell Barnes et al., "The Social Insurance System in the US: Policies to Protect Workers and Families," Brookings, June 23, 2021, https://www.brookings.edu/research/the-social-insurance-system-in-the-u-s-policies-to-protect-workers-and-families/. On the stagnant federal minimum wage, see "Living Wage Calculator," MIT, https://livingwage.mit.edu/. On the declining value of welfare benefits, see Gina Azito Thompson, Diana Azevedo-McCaffrey, and Da'Shon Carr, "Increases in TANF Cash Benefit Levels Are Critical to Help Families Meet Rising Costs," Center on Budget and Policy Priorities, February 3, 2023, https://www.cbpp.org/research/income-security/increases-in-tanf-cash-benefit-levels-are-critical-to-help-families-meet-0. On attacks on unions, see Jasmine Kerrissey, "Collective Labor Rights and Income Inequality," *American Sociological Review* 80, no. 3 (2015): 626–53; Tom VanHeuvelen, "The Right to Work, Power Resources, and Economic Inequality," *American Journal of Sociology* 125, no. 5 (2020): 1255–1302. On the state of US paid leave policies, see Molly Weston Williamson, "The State of Paid Family and Medical Leave in the U.S. in 2023," Center for American Progress, January 5, 2023, https://www.americanprogress.org/article/the-state-of-paid-family-and-medical-leave-in-the-u-s-in-2023/. On the prevalence of unsafe working conditions, see "A Safe Workplace Is Sound Business," OSHA, US Department of Labor, https://www.osha.gov/safety-management. On the dangers of overwork, see "Employee Overtime: Hours, Pay and Who Is Covered," OSHA, US Department of Labor, https://www.oshaeducationcenter.com/articles/employee-overtime. On inequalities in overtime pay, see Sherrod Brown, "Brown Introduces Bill to Make Millions of American Workers Eligible for Overtime Pay," United States Senate, 2023, https://www.brown.senate.gov/newsroom/press/release/sherrod-brown-introduces-bill-millions-american-workers-eligible-overtime-pay. On the shortage of affordable housing, see Andrew Aurand, Dan Emmanuel, and Daniel Threet, *The Gap: A Shortage of Affordable Homes* (Washington, DC: National Low Income Housing Coalition, 2020), https://reports.nlihc

.org/sites/default/files/gap/Gap-Report_2020.pdf. On the prevalence of substandard housing, see "General Housing Data—All Occupied Units," American Housing Survey, US Census Bureau 2023, https://www.census.gov/programs-surveys/ahs/data/interactive/ahstablecreator .html. See also Kyle G. Horst, "One in 20 Americans Live in Inadequate Housing," DS News, August 5, 2022, https://dsnews.com/news/08-05-2022/1-in-20-americans. On the prevalence of housing insecurity, see "How Much Do Americans Spend on Housing?," USA Facts, May 15, 2023, https://usafacts.org/data-projects/housing-costs. On the prevalence of food insecurity, see "Hunger and Poverty in America," Food Research and Action Center, https:// frac.org/hunger-poverty-america. On gaps in health insurance coverage, see Sam Hughes, Emily Gee, and Nicole Rapfogel, "Health Insurance Costs Are Squeezing Workers and Employers," Center for American Progress, November 29, 2022, https://www.americanprogress .org/article/health-insurance-costs-are-squeezing-workers-and-employers/. On gaps in affordable childcare, see *Experiences of U.S. Households with Children during the Delta Variant Outbreak* (NPR, Robert Wood Johnson Foundation, Harvard T. H. Chan School of Public Health, 2021), https://media.npr.org/assets/img/2021/10/19/households-children-virus-poll .pdf. See also Anya Kamenetz and Mansee Khurana, "1 in 3 Working Families Is Struggling to Find the Child Care They Desperately Need," NPR, October 19, 2021, https://www.npr.org /2021/10/19/1047019536/families-are-struggling-to-find-the-child-care-they-desperately -need. On the under-resourcing of US schools, see "Closing America's Education Funding Gaps," The Century Foundation, July 22, 2020, https://tcf.org/content/report/closing-americas -education-funding/.

14. On cross-national differences in mental health, see *How's Life? 2020: Measuring Well-Being* (Paris: OECD Publishing, 2021), https://www.oecd-ilibrary.org/economics/deaths-of-despair -have-fallen-in-some-of-the-oecd-countries-where-rates-are-highest-but-increased -elsewhere_a56e5715-en; Sophie Putka, "Why Are Americans Getting Unhappier?," *Discover Magazine*, June 19, 2021, https://www.discovermagazine.com/mind/why-are-americans -getting-unhappier; Julie Ray, "Americans' Stress, Worry and Anger Intensified in 2018," Gallup, April 25, 2019, https://news.gallup.com/poll/249098/americans-stress-worry-anger -intensified-2018.aspx. On cross-national differences in health and sickness, see Giuliano Bonoli and Frank Reber, "The Political Economy of Childcare in OECD Countries: Explaining Cross-National Variation in Spending and Coverage Rates," *European Journal of Political Research* 49, no. 1 (2010): 97–118; Thomas A. Diprete et al., "Do Cross-National Differences in the Costs of Children Generate Cross-National Differences in Fertility Rates?," *Population Research and Policy Review* 22, no. 5 (2003): 439–77; Thomas J. Kane, *The Price of Admission: Rethinking How Americans Pay for College* (Washington, DC: Brookings, 1999); Uwe E. Reinhardt, Peter S. Hussey, and Gerard F. Anderson, "U.S. Health Care Spending in an International Context," *Health Affairs* 23, no. 3 (2004): 10–25; Uwe E. Reinhardt, Peter S. Hussey, and Gerard F. Anderson, "Cross-National Comparisons of Health Systems Using OECD Data, 1999," *Health Affairs* 21, no. 3 (2002): 169–81. On cross-national variations in life expectancy, see "Life Expectancy at Birth, Total (Years)," World Bank, https://data.worldbank .org/indicator/SP.DYN.LE00.IN. On differences in productivity and work hours, see David Johnson, "These Are the Most Productive Countries in the World," *Time*, January 4, 2017, https://time.com/4621185/worker-productivity-countries/; "GDP per Hour Worked," OECD, http://data.oecd.org/lprdty/gdp-per-hour-worked.htm; "Hours Worked," OECD, http://data .oecd.org/emp/hours-worked.htm. On differences in poverty rates, see "Poverty Rate," OECD, https://data.oecd.org/inequality/poverty-rate.htm. On differences in economic growth, see "GDP Growth (Annual %)," World Bank, https://data.worldbank.org/indicator/NY.GDP .MKTP.KD.ZG?locations=FR-US-DE-SE-AU. See also Max Roser et al., "Economic Growth," Our World in Data, 2023, https://ourworldindata.org/economic-growth. On how underinvestment in the social safety net drives polarization, see Arlie Russell Hochschild, *Strangers in Their Own Land: Anger and Mourning on the American Right* (New York: The New Press,

2016); Cynthia Miller-Idriss, *Hate in the Homeland: The New Global Far Right* (Princeton, NJ: Princeton University Press, 2022).

15. On the New Deal and its promise for America, see Jacob S. Hacker, *The Great Risk Shift: The New Economic Insecurity and the Decline of the American Dream* (Oxford: Oxford University Press, 2019); Roger L. Martin and Mihnea Moldoveanu, "Capital Versus Talent: The Battle That's Reshaping Business," *Harvard Business Review*, July 2023; Heidi Shierholz et al., *Latest Data Release on Unionization Is a Wake-up Call to Lawmakers: We Must Fix Our Broken System of Labor Law* (Washington, DC: Economic Policy Institute, 2022), https://www.epi.org/publication /latest-data-release-on-unionization-is-a-wake-up-call-to-lawmakers/; Julian E. Zelizer, *The Fierce Urgency of Now: Lyndon Johnson, Congress, and the Battle for the Great Society* (New York: Penguin Books, 2015).

16. On how big businesses and billionaires tried to persuade us that we don't need a social safety net, see Naomi Oreskes and Erik M. Conway, *The Big Myth: How American Business Taught Us to Loathe Government and Love the Free Market* (New York: Bloomsbury, 2023). See also Ronald P. Formisano, *Plutocracy in America: How Increasing Inequality Destroys the Middle Class and Exploits the Poor* (Baltimore: Johns Hopkins University Press, 2015); Martin Gilens, *Affluence and Influence* (Princeton, NJ: Princeton University Press, 2014); Jacob S. Hacker and Paul Pierson, "Winner-Take-All Politics: Public Policy, Political Organization, and the Precipitous Rise of Top Incomes in the United States," *Politics & Society* 38, no. 2 (2010): 152–204; Dale L. Johnson, "Rule by Divide and Conquer," in *Social Inequality, Economic Decline, and Plutocracy: An American Crisis*, ed. Dale L. Johnson, *Critical Political Theory and Radical Practice* (Cham, Switzerland: Springer International Publishing, 2017), 91–108; Prabhir Vishnu Poruthiyil, "Big Business and Fascism: A Dangerous Collusion," *Journal of Business Ethics* 168, no. 1 (2021): 121–35.

17. On the history of neoliberal ideas in the US, see Formisano, *Plutocracy in America*; Gilens, *Affluence and Influence*; Hacker and Pierson, "Winner-Take-All Politics"; Johnson, "Rule by Divide and Conquer," in *Social Inequality, Economic Decline, and Plutocracy*; Oreskes and Conway, *The Big Myth*; Poruthiyil, "Big Business and Fascism: A Dangerous Collusion." On critiques of Hayek, see John W. Compton, *The End of Empathy: Why White Protestants Stopped Loving Their Neighbors* (Oxford: Oxford University Press, 2020); Francis Fukuyama, "Friedrich A. Hayek, Big-Government Skeptic," *New York Times*, May 6, 2011. For Friedman's quote about corporations' obligations, see Milton Friedman, "A Friedman Doctrine—The Social Responsibility of Business Is to Increase Its Profits," *New York Times*, September 13, 1970, https:// www.nytimes.com/1970/09/13/archives/a-friedman-doctrine-the-social-responsibility-of -business-is-to.html. For Friedman's quote about cutting taxes, see Richard Morrison, "Remembering Milton Friedman," *Tax Foundation* (blog), 2013, https://taxfoundation.org/remembering -milton-friedman/.

18. On the messages promoted by neoliberal economists, see Elizabeth Popp Berman, *Thinking Like an Economist: How Efficiency Replaced Equality in U.S. Public Policy* (Princeton, NJ: Princeton University Press, 2022), Hacker, *The Great Risk Shift*; Daniel Abramson Hirschman, "Inventing the Economy or: How We Learned to Stop Worrying and Love the GDP" (thesis, University of Michigan, 2016), http://deepblue.lib.umich.edu/handle/2027.42/120713. For Friedman's quote about paying people to be poor, see Greg Ip and Mark Whitehouse, "How Milton Friedman Changed Economics, Policy and Markets," *Wall Street Journal*, November 17, 2006, https://www.wsj.com/articles/SB116369744597625238.

19. On the role of neoliberal economics in contemporary US policymaking, see Berman, *Thinking Like an Economist*; Daniel Hirschman and Elizabeth Popp Berman, "Do Economists Make Policies? On the Political Effects of Economics," *Socio-Economic Review* 12, no. 4 (2014): 779–811.

20. On the great risk shift, see Hacker, *The Great Risk Shift*. See also Berman, *Thinking Like an Economist*; Hirschman, "Inventing the Economy." On declining corporate tax rates, see "Historical U.S. Federal Corporate Income Tax Rates & Brackets, 1909–2020," Tax Foundation, August 24, 2021, https://taxfoundation.org/historical-corporate-tax-rates-brackets/ See also

"United Sates Federal Corporate Tax Rate," Trading Economics, 2023, https://tradingeco nomics.com/united-states/corporate-tax-rate/. On declining personal tax rates, see "Histori-cal U.S. Federal Individual Income Tax Rates & Brackets, 1862–2021," Tax Foundation, August 24, 2021, https://taxfoundation.org/historical-income-tax-rates-brackets/. On the elimination of regulations, see Amelia Arsenault and Manuel Castells, "Switching Power: Rupert Murdoch and the Global Business of Media Politics: A Sociological Analysis," *International Sociology* 23, no. 4 (2008): 488–513; Andrew Austin, "Advancing Accumulation and Managing Its Discontents: The U.S. Antienvironmental Countermovement," *Sociological Spectrum* 22, no. 1 (2002): 71–105; James William Coleman, *The Criminal Elite: The Sociology of White Collar Crime* (New York: Macmillan, 2001); Ken-Hou Lin and Megan Tobias Neely, *Divested: Inequality in Financialized America* (Oxford: Oxford University Press, 2020); Peter Cleary Yeager, *The Limits of Law: The Public Regulation of Private Pollution* (Cambridge: Cam-bridge University Press, 1993). On the consequences of reduced regulation for tax payments, see Brooke Harrington, *Capital without Borders: Wealth Managers and the One Percent* (Cam-bridge, MA: Harvard University Press, 2017). On the consequences of reduced regulation for workers, see Art Budros, "The New Capitalism and Organizational Rationality: The Adop-tion of Downsizing Programs, 1979–1994," *Social Forces* 76, no. 1 (1997): 229–50. On anti-union legislation, see "Collective Labor Rights and Income Inequality"; VanHeuvelen, "The Right to Work, Power Resources, and Economic Inequality." On the political barriers to cutting Social Security and Medicare, see Robert H. Binstock, "From Compassionate Ageism to Intergenerational Conflict?," *The Gerontologist* 50, no. 5 (October 2010): 574–85; Jacob S. Hacker, "Privatizing Risk without Privatizing the Welfare State: The Hidden Politics of Social Policy Retrenchment in the United States," *American Political Science Review* 98, no. 2 (May 2004): 243–60. On cuts to social programs at the federal level, see Richard Kogan and Kath-leen Bryant, "Program Spending outside Social Security and Medicare Historically Low as a Percent of GDP and Projected to Fall Further," Center on Budget and Policy Priorities, March 8, 2019, https://www.cbpp.org/research/federal-budget/program-spending-outside -social-security-and-medicare-historically-low-as-a. On cuts to social welfare spending at the state level, see Michael Leachman, Kathleen Masterson, and Eric Figueroa, "A Punishing Decade for School Funding," Center on Budget and Policy Priorities, November 29, 2017, https:// www.cbpp.org/research/state-budget-and-tax/a-punishing-decade-for-school-funding.

21. On changes in economic growth over time, see Chad Stone et al., "A Guide to Statistics on Historical Trends in Income Inequality," Center on Budget and Policy Priorities, January 13, 2020, https://www.cbpp.org/research/poverty-and-inequality/a-guide-to-statistics-on-historical -trends-in-income-inequality. On the failure of trickle-down economics, see David Hope and Julian Limberg, "The Economic Consequences of Major Tax Cuts for the Rich," *Socio-Economic Review* 20, no. 2 (2022): 539–59. On wealth hoarding, see Harrington, *Capital without Borders*; Ken-Hou Lin and Donald Tomaskovic-Devey, "Financialization and U.S. Income Inequality, 1970–2008," *American Journal of Sociology* 118, no. 5 (2013): 1284–329; Donald Tomaskovic-Devey and Ken-Hou Lin, "Income Dynamics, Economic Rents, and the Financialization of the U.S. Economy," *American Sociological Review* 76, no. 4 (2011): 538–59. For the historical wealth data cited here, see Edward N. Wolff, "Household Wealth Trends in the United States, 1962 to 2019: Median Wealth Rebounds . . . but Not Enough" (working paper 28383, National Bureau of Economic Research, January 2021), https://www.nber.org /system/files/working_papers/w28383/w28383.pdf. On the growing share of wealth held by high-income families, see "Trends in the Distribution of Family Wealth, 1989 to 2019," Con-gressional Budget Office, September 2022, https://www.cbo.gov/publication/58533. See also Ajay Chaudry et al., *Poverty in the United States: 50-Year Trends and Safety Net Impacts* (Wash-ington, DC: US Department of Health and Human Services, 2016); Daniel Hirschman, "Rediscovering the 1%: Knowledge Infrastructures and the Stylized Facts of Inequality," *American Journal of Sociology* 127, no. 3 (2021): 739–86; Juliana Menasce Horowitz, Ruth Igiel-nik, and Rakesh Kochhar, "Trends in Income and Wealth Inequality," in *Most Americans Say*

There Is Too Much Economic Inequality in the U.S., but Fewer Than Half Call It a Top Priority (Washington, DC: Pew Research Center, 2020), https://www.pewresearch.org/social-trends /2020/01/09/trends-in-income-and-wealth-inequality/; Lin and Tomaskovic-Devey, "Financialization and U.S. Income Inequality, 1970–2008"; Chad Stone et al., "A Guide to Statistics on Historical Trends in Income Inequality," Center on Budget and Policy Priorities, January 13, 2020, https://www.cbpp.org/research/poverty-and-inequality/a-guide-to-statistics-on-historical -trends-in-income-inequality. For historical comparisons of wealth by income percentile, see "DFA: Distributional Financial Accounts," Board of Governors of the Federal Reserve, last updated September 22, 2023, https://www.federalreserve.gov/releases/z1/dataviz/dfa /distribute/table/.

22. For related arguments, see John R. Bowman and Alyson M. Cole, "Do Working Mothers Oppress Other Women? The Swedish 'Maid Debate' and the Welfare State Politics of Gender Equality," *Signs: Journal of Women in Culture and Society* 35, no. 1 (2009): 157–84; Altheira Caldera, "Challenging Capitalistic Exploitation: A Black Feminist/Womanist Commentary on Work and Self-Care," *Feminist Studies* 46, no. 3 (2020): 707–16; Patricia Hill Collins, *Black Feminist Thought: Knowledge, Consciousness, and the Politics of Empowerment* (New York: Routledge, 2000); Patricia Hill Collins, "Black Women and Motherhood," in *Motherhood and Space: Configurations of the Maternal through Politics, Home, and the Body*, ed. Sarah Hardy and Caroline Wiedmer (New York: Palgrave Macmillan, 2005), 149–59; Angela Y. Davis, *Women, Race, and Class* (New York: Vintage Books, 1983); Evelyn Nakano Glenn, *Forced to Care: Coercion and Caregiving in America* (Cambridge, MA: Harvard University Press, 2010); Hochschild, *The Second Shift*; Candace Howes, Carrie Leana, and Kristin Smith, "Paid Care Work," in *For Love or Money: Care Provision in the United States*, ed. Nancy Folbre (New York: Russell Sage Foundation, 2012); Zora Neale Hurston, *Their Eyes Were Watching God* (Philadelphia: J. B. Lippincott and Co., 1937); Jacqueline Jones, *Labor of Love, Labor of Sorrow: Black Women, Work and the Family, from Slavery to the Present* (New York: Basic Books, 2010); Katherine Kaufka, "The Commodification of Domestic Care: Illegitimacy of Care Work and the Exploitation of Migrant Workers," *Georgetown Immigration Law Journal* 18, no. 1 (2004): 159–78; Cameron Lynne Macdonald, *Shadow Mothers: Nannies, Au Pairs, and the Micropolitics of Mothering* (Berkeley: University of California Press, 2011); Lynet Uttal and Mary Tuominen, "Tenuous Relationships: Exploitation, Emotion, and Racial Ethnic Significance in Paid Child Care Work," *Gender & Society* 13, no. 6 (1999): 758–80; Deborah Gray White, *Too Heavy a Load: Black Women in Defense of Themselves, 1894–1994* (New York: W. W. Norton, 1999).

23. For more on the various ways that sociologists conceptualize and measure social class, see ed. Annette Lareau and Dalton Conley, *Social Class: How Does It Work?* (Washington, DC: Russell Sage Foundation, 2010).

24. On same-sex couples' division of household labor, see Mignon R. Moore, "Gendered Power Relations among Women: A Study of Household Decision Making in Black, Lesbian Stepfamilies," *American Sociological Review* 73, no. 2 (2008): 335–56; Sondra E. Solomon, Esther D. Rothblum, and Kimberly F. Balsam, "Money, Housework, Sex, and Conflict: Same-Sex Couples in Civil Unions, Those Not in Civil Unions, and Heterosexual Married Siblings," *Sex Roles* 52, no. 9 (2005): 561–75; Suzanne Taylor Sutphin, "Social Exchange Theory and the Division of Household Labor in Same-Sex Couples," *Marriage & Family Review* 46, no. 3 (2010): 191–206; Debra Umberson et al., "Instrumental- and Emotion-Focused Care Work during Physical Health Events: Comparing Gay, Lesbian, and Heterosexual Marriages," *Journals of Gerontology: Series B* 72, no. 3 (2017): 498–509; Katherine Weisshaar, "Earnings Equality and Relationship Stability for Same-Sex and Heterosexual Couples," *Social Forces* 93, no. 1 (2014): 93–123. For Indiana's demographic composition, see "QuickFacts: Indiana; United States," US Census Bureau, https://www.census.gov/quickfacts/fact/table/IN,US /PST045222. For Indiana's voting record, see "2020 Election Results: Indiana," *Politico*, 2020, https://www.politico.com/2020-election/results/indiana/. On Mike Pence, see "A Timeline of Mike Pence's Discrimination against the LGBT Community," Indiana Democratic Party,

https://www.indems.org/a-timeline-of-mike-pences-discrimination-against-the-lgbt-community/.

25. On the intersectional forces that shape women's lives, see Michaela Assouline and Sharon Gilad, "The Intersectionality of Deservingness for State Support," *Public Administration Review* 82, no. 3 (2022): 487–502; Hae Yeon Choo and Myra Marx Ferree, "Practicing Intersectionality in Sociological Research: A Critical Analysis of Inclusions, Interactions, and Institutions in the Study of Inequalities," *Sociological Theory* 28, no. 2 (2010): 129–49; Collins, *Black Feminist Thought*; Collins, "Black Women and Motherhood"; Kimberlé Crenshaw, "Mapping the Margins: Intersectionality, Identity Politics, and Violence against Women of Color," *Stanford Law Review* 43, no. 6 (1991): 1241–99; Davis, *Women, Race, and Class*; bell hooks, *Ain't I a Woman: Black Women and Feminism* (New York: Routledge, 2014).

CHAPTER 1: MAKING THEM MOTHERS-IN-WAITING

1. On adults' influences on children's gendered toy preferences, see Joe L. Bosh and Rebecca L. Woods, "Parents' Influence on Infants' Gender-Typed Toy Preferences," *Sex Roles* 79, no. 5 (2018): 358–73; Karin A. Martin, "William Wants a Doll, Can He Have One? Feminists, Child Care Advisors, and Gender Neutral Child Rearing," *Gender & Society* 19, no. 4 (2005): 456–79. On the socialization of girls into meekness and boys into strength, see Heidi M. Gansen, "Push-Ups versus Clean-Up: Preschool Teachers' Gendered Beliefs, Expectations for Behavior, and Disciplinary Practices," *Sex Roles*, July 19, (2018); Karin A. Martin, "Becoming a Gendered Body: Practices of Preschools," *American Sociological Review* 63, no. 4 (1998): 494–511; Michael A. Messner. "Barbie Girls versus Sea Monsters: Children Constructing Gender," in *Sociological Perspectives on Sport* (London: Routledge, 2015); Michael A. Messner, Margaret C. Duncan, and Kerry Jensen, "Separating the Men from the Girls: The Gendered Language of Televised Sports," *Gender & Society* 7, no. 1 (1993): 121–37; Michaela Musto, "Brilliant or Bad: The Gendered Social Construction of Exceptionalism in Early Adolescence," *American Sociological Review* 94, no. 3 (2019): 369–93. On the socialization of girls into caregiving and the ways boys are discouraged from filling these roles, see Yasemin Besen-Cassino, *The Cost of Being a Girl: Working Teens and the Origins of the Gender Wage Gap* (Philadelphia: Temple University Press, 2017); Yvonne M. Caldera and Mary A. Sciaraffa, "Parent Toddler Play with Feminine Toys: Are All Dolls the Same?," *Sex Roles* 39, no. 9 (1998): 657–68; Julia Cordero-Coma and Gøsta Esping-Andersen, "The Intergenerational Transmission of Gender Roles: Children's Contribution to Housework in Germany," *Journal of Marriage and Family* 80, no. 4 (2018): 1005–19; Ann C. Crouter, Beth A. Manke, and Susan M. McHale, "The Family Context of Gender Intensification in Early Adolescence," *Child Development* 66, no. 2 (1995): 317–29; Patricia L. East, Thomas S. Weisner, and Ashley Slonim, "Youths' Caretaking of Their Adolescent Sisters' Children: Results from Two Longitudinal Studies," *Journal of Family Issues* 30, no. 12 (2009): 1671–97; Aurora M. Sherman and Eileen L. Zurbriggen, "'Boys Can Be Anything': Effect of Barbie Play on Girls' Career Cognitions," *Sex Roles* 70, no. 5 (2014): 195–208. On adults' efforts to restrict girls' movements, see Barbara A. Morrongiello, Daniel Zdzieborski, and Jackie Normand, "Understanding Gender Differences in Children's Risk Taking and Injury: A Comparison of Mothers' and Fathers' Reactions to Sons and Daughters Misbehaving in Ways That Lead to Injury," *Journal of Applied Developmental Psychology* 31, no. 4 (2010): 322–29. On girls and women as "mothers-in-waiting," see Miranda R. Waggoner, *The Zero Trimester* (Berkeley: University of California, 2017). On the equation of womanhood and motherhood, see Sarah Thébaud and Catherine J. Taylor, "The Specter of Motherhood: Culture and the Production of Gendered Career Aspirations in Science and Engineering," *Gender & Society* 35, no. 3 (2021): 395–421.

2. For an overview of current state abortion laws, see "An Overview of Abortion Laws," Guttmacher Institute, accessed June 2022, https://www.guttmacher.org/state-policy/explore/overview-abortion-laws. For current state-level policies regarding ultrasounds as requirements

for abortion services, see "Ultrasound Requirements," Guttmacher Institute, https://www .guttmacher.org/state-policy/explore/requirements-ultrasound.

3. On nurses' salaries and the viability of nursing as a career path for upward mobility, see Sharon Brownie, Abdul Haq Wahedna, and Nigel Crisp, "Nursing as a Pathway to Women's Empowerment and Intergenerational Mobility," *Journal of Clinical Nursing* 27, no. 21–22 (2018): 4050–57; Ryan Parsons, "Moving Out to Move Up: Higher Education as a Mobility Pathway in the Rural South," *RSF: The Russell Sage Foundation Journal of the Social Sciences* 8, no. 3 (May 1, 2022): 208–29; Michael J. Petrilli, *Education for Upward Mobility* (Lanham, MD: Rowman & Littlefield, 2015).

4. For the median salary for registered nurses, see "Occupational Employment and Wage Statistics," US Bureau of Labor Statistics, April 25, 2023, https://www.bls.gov/oes/current /oes291141.htm.

5. On the messages that young girls get about sex, see Kristin Luker, *Dubious Conceptions: The Politics of Teenage Pregnancy* (Cambridge, MA: Harvard University Press, 1997); Kristin Luker, *When Sex Goes to School: Warring Views on Sex—and Sex Education—Since the Sixties* (New York: W. W. Norton, 2007). On the ineffectiveness of abstinence-only education, see John S. Santelli et al., "Abstinence-Only-Until-Marriage: An Updated Review of U.S. Policies and Programs and Their Impact," *Journal of Adolescent Health* 61, no. 3 (2017): 273–80.

6. On the frequency of unintended pregnancy worldwide, see Susheela Singh, Gilda Sedgh, and Rubina Hussain, "Unintended Pregnancy: Worldwide Levels, Trends, and Outcomes," *Studies in Family Planning* 41, no. 4 (2010): 241–50.

7. On the cost of contraception in the US, see Kate Grindlay and Daniel Grossman, "Prescription Birth Control Access among U.S. Women at Risk of Unintended Pregnancy," *Journal of Women's Health* 25, no. 3 (2016): 249–54; Sharon Cohen Landau, Molly Parker Tapias, and Belle Taylor McGhee, "Birth Control within Reach: A National Survey on Women's Attitudes toward and Interest in Pharmacy Access to Hormonal Contraception," *Contraception* 74, no. 6 (2006): 463–70; Michele Troutman, Saima Rafique, and Torie Comeaux Plowden, "Are Higher Unintended Pregnancy Rates among Minorities a Result of Disparate Access to Contraception?," *Contraception and Reproductive Medicine* 5, no. 1 (2020): 16. On the stigmatization of contraception in the US, see Krystale E. Littlejohn, *Just Get on the Pill: The Uneven Burden of Reproductive Politics* (Berkeley: University of California Press, 2021); Jessica M. Sales et al., "Relationship of STD-Related Shame and Stigma to Female Adolescents' Condom-Protected Intercourse," *Journal of Adolescent Health* 40, no. 6 (2007). On why pregnant people in the US seek abortion services, see Lawrence B. Finer et al., "Reasons U.S. Women Have Abortions: Quantitative and Qualitative Perspectives," *Perspectives on Sexual and Reproductive Health* 37, no. 3 (2005): 110–18. On teen pregnancy in the US, see Patricia L. East, Nina C. Chien, and Jennifer S. Barber, "Adolescents' Pregnancy Intentions, Wantedness, and Regret: Cross-Lagged Relations with Mental Health and Harsh Parenting," *Journal of Marriage and Family* 74, no. 1 (2012): 167–85; Lawrence B. Finer, "Unintended Pregnancy among U.S. Adolescents: Accounting for Sexual Activity," *Journal of Adolescent Health: Official Publication of the Society for Adolescent Medicine* 47, no. 3 (2010): 312–14; Lawrence B. Finer and Mia R. Zolna, "Declines in Unintended Pregnancy in the United States, 2008–2011," *New England Journal of Medicine* 374, no. 9 (2016): 843–52; Luker, *Dubious Conceptions*; Kim Ty, Dagher Rk, and Chen J, "Racial/Ethnic Differences in Unintended Pregnancy: Evidence from a National Sample of U.S. Women," *American Journal of Preventive Medicine* 50, no. 4 (2016). For cross-national differences in adolescent pregnancy outcomes, see "Adolescent Pregnancy and Its Outcomes Across Countries," Guttmacher Institute, August 2015, https://www.guttmacher.org/fact-sheet/adolescent-pregnancy-and-its-outcomes -across-countries.

8. On the Dobbs case, see *Dobbs, State Health Officer of the Mississippi Department of Health, et al. v. Jackson Women's Health Organization et al.*, 597 U.S. (2022), https://www.supremecourt.gov

/opinions/21pdf/19-1392_6j37.pdf. On *Roe v. Wade*, see *Jane ROE, et al., Appellants, v. Henry WADE*," 410 U.S. 113 (1971), https://www.law.cornell.edu/supremecourt/text/410/113. On *Planned Parenthood v. Casey*, see *Planned Parenthood of Southeastern Pennsylvania, et al. v. Robert P. Casey, et al.*, 505 U.S. 833 (1992), https://www.law.cornell.edu/supremecourt/text/505/833. On the prevalence of abortion among mothers with children before the *Dobbs* decision, see Margot Sanger-Katz, Claire Cain Miller, and Quoctrung Bui, "Who Gets Abortions in America?," *New York Times*, December 14, 2021, https://www.nytimes.com/interactive/2021 /12/14/upshot/who-gets-abortions-in-america.html. On the limited agency that US policies and culture afford to pregnant women, see: Lyz Lenz, *Belabored: A Vindication of the Rights of Pregnant Women* (New York: Hachette, 2020).

9. On the risks of the withdrawal method, see "Pull Out Method," Cleveland Clinic, last updated September 15, 2022, https://my.clevelandclinic.org/health/articles/24174-pull-out -method. On men's birth control preferences and the challenges that some women encounter in using birth control pills, see Littlejohn, *Just Get on the Pill*.

10. On the impact of anti-abortion rhetoric and policies, and their disproportionate impact on low-income women and women of color, see M. Antonia Biggs et al., "Women's Mental Health and Well-Being 5 Years after Receiving or Being Denied an Abortion: A Prospective, Longitudinal Cohort Study," *JAMA Psychiatry* 74, no. 2 (2017): 169–78; Diana Greene Foster, *The Turnaway Study: The Cost of Denying Women Access to Abortion* (New York: Simon & Schuster, 2020); Sarah Miller, Laura R. Wherry, and Diana Greene Foster, "The Economic Consequences of Being Denied an Abortion" (working paper, National Bureau of Economic Research, 2020); Corinne H. Rocca et al., "Emotions over Five Years after Denial of Abortion in the United States: Contextualizing the Effects of Abortion Denial on Women's Health and Lives," *Social Science & Medicine* 269 (2021): 113567. On how stigma and shame reduce the use of abortion services, see Kate Cockrill and Adina Nack, "'I'm Not That Type of Person': Managing the Stigma of Having an Abortion," *Deviant Behavior* 34, no. 12 (2013): 973–90; Amanda Gelman et al., "Abortion Stigma among Low-Income Women Obtaining Abortions in Western Pennsylvania: A Qualitative Assessment," *Perspectives on Sexual and Reproductive Health* 49, no. 1 (2017): 29–36; Elaine M. Hernandez and Jessica McCrory Calarco, "Health Decisions amidst Controversy: Prenatal Alcohol Consumption and the Unequal Experience of Influence and Control in Networks," *Social Science & Medicine* 286 (2021): 11431; Jessica M. Sales et al., "Relationship of STD-Related Shame and Stigma to Female Adolescents' Condom-Protected Intercourse," *Journal of Adolescent Health* 40, no. 6 (2007); Whitney Smith et al., "Social Norms and Stigma Regarding Unintended Pregnancy and Pregnancy Decisions: A Qualitative Study of Young Women in Alabama," *Perspectives on Sexual and Reproductive Health* 48, no. 2 (2016): 73–81.

11. On how tight-knit communities enforce social norms, see James S. Coleman, "Social Capital in the Creation of Human Capital," *American Journal of Sociology* 94 (1988): S95–120; Joan Maya Mazelis, "'I Got to Try to Give Back': How Reciprocity Norms in a Poor People's Organization Influence Members' Social Capital," *Journal of Poverty* 19, no. 1 (2015): 109–31; Joan Maya Mazelis, *Surviving Poverty* (New York: NYU Press, 2016); Carol Stack, *All Our Kin* (New York: Harper, 1974); Mikołaj Jan Piskorski and Andreea Gorbatâi, "Testing Coleman's Social-Norm Enforcement Mechanism: Evidence from Wikipedia," *American Journal of Sociology* 122, no. 4 (2017): 1183–222. On the changing US religious landscape, see *Modeling the Future of Religion in America* (Washington, DC: Pew Research Center, 2022), https://www.pewresearch.org/religion/2022/09/13/how-u-s-religious-composition-has -changed-in-recent-decades/. See also Roger Finke and Rodney Stark, *The Churching of America: 1776–2005* (New Brunswick, NJ: Rutgers University Press, 2005); Robin D. Perrin, Paul Kennedy, and Donald E. Miller, "Examining the Sources of Conservative Church Growth: Where Are the New Evangelical Movements Getting Their Numbers?," *Journal for the Scientific Study of Religion* 36, no. 1 (1997): 71–80; Christian Smith et al., *Young Catholic America: Emerging Adults In, Out of, and Gone from the Church* (Oxford: Oxford University Press, 2014); Mary C.

Waters, *Ethnic Options: Choosing Identities in America* (Berkeley: University of California, 1990). On religion and changing birth rates in the US, see Samuel H. Preston, "Changing Values and Falling Birth Rates," *Population and Development Review* 12 (1986): 176–95; Charles F. Westoff and Elise F. Jones, "The End of 'Catholic' Fertility," *Demography* 16 (1979): 209–17. On the rise of religious "nones," see Joseph O. Baker and Buster G. Smith, "The Nones: Social Characteristics of the Religiously Unaffiliated," *Social Forces* 87, no. 3 (2009): 1251–63. On the role of conservative Christian groups in anti-abortion politics, see Randall Balmer, *Bad Faith: Race and the Rise of the Religious Right* (Grand Rapids, MI: Eerdmans, 2021); Lyz Lenz, *God Land: A Story of Faith, Loss, and Renewal* (Bloomington: Indiana University Press, 2017); Andrew R. Lewis, *The Rights Turn in Conservative Christian Politics: How Abortion Transformed the Culture Wars* (Cambridge: Cambridge University Press, 2017); Kristin Luker, *Abortion and the Politics of Motherhood* (Berkeley: University of California Press, 1985); Patricia Miller, *Good Catholics: The Battle over Abortion in the Catholic Church* (Berkeley: University of California Press, 2014); Andrew L. Whitehead and Samuel L. Perry, *Taking America Back for God: Christian Nationalism in the United States* (Oxford: Oxford University Press, 2020); William Saletan, *Bearing Right: How Conservatives Won the Abortion War* (Berkeley: University of California, 2004); Daniel K. Williams, "The Partisan Trajectory of the American Pro-Life Movement: How a Liberal Catholic Campaign Became a Conservative Evangelical Cause," *Religions* 6, no. 2 (2015): 451–75. On Amy Coney Barrett's religious and political leanings and her role in overturning *Roe v. Wade*, see Stephanie Kirchgaessner, "Amy Coney Barrett: Spotlight Falls on Secretive Catholic Group People of Praise," *Guardian*, September 26, 2020, https://www.theguardian.com/us-news/2020/sep/26/amy-coney-barrett -supreme-court-donald-trump-people-of-praise; Bess Levin, "Amy Coney Barrett, Last Seen Helping Effectively Outlaw Abortion in Texas, Says Judges Can't Let 'Personal Biases' Affect Rulings," *Vanity Fair*, September 13, 2021, https://www.vanityfair.com/news/2021/09/amy -coney-barrett-partisan-hacks; Samantha Raphelson, "Pressed On Landmark Contraception Case, Barrett Again Declines to Answer," NPR, October 14, 2020, https://www.npr.org /sections/live-amy-coney-barrett-supreme-court-confirmation/2020/10/14/923713602 /pressed-on-landmark-contraception-case-barrett-again-declines-to-answer.

12. On the belief that adoption is a suitable substitute for abortion, see Irin Carmon, "Amy Coney Barrett's Adoption Myths," *New York Magazine*, December 3, 2021, https://nymag.com /intelligencer/2021/12/amy-coney-barrett-adoption-myths.html. On the US child welfare system and its punishment of women, see Kelley Fong, Rachel A. Wright, and Christopher Wimer, "The Cost of Free Assistance: Why Low-Income Individuals Do Not Access Food Pantries," *Journal of Sociology & Social Welfare* 43, no. 1 (2016): 71–94; Kelley Fong, "Child Welfare Involvement and Contexts of Poverty: The Role of Parental Adversities, Social Networks, and Social Services," *Children and Youth Services Review, Economic Causes and Consequences of Child Maltreatment*, 72 (2017): 5–13; Kelley Fong, "Concealment and Constraint: Child Protective Services Fears and Poor Mothers' Institutional Engagement," *Social Forces* 97, no. 4 (2019): 1785–810; Kelley Fong, "Getting Eyes in the Home: Child Protective Services Investigations and State Surveillance of Family Life," *American Sociological Review* 85, no. 4 (2020): 610–38; Jennifer A. Reich, *Fixing Families: Parents, Power, and the Child Welfare System* (London: Routledge, 2012); Dorothy Roberts, *Shattered Bonds: The Color of Child Welfare* (New York: Civitas Books, 2002); Dorothy Roberts, *Torn Apart: How the Child Welfare System Destroys Black Families—and How Abolition Can Build a Safer World* (New York: Basic Books, 2022).

13. On how companies skirt rules for worker benefits, see Lisa Myers and Carroll Ann Mears, "Businesses Claim Obamacare Has Forced Them to Cut Employee Hours," NBC News, August 13, 2013, https://www.nbcnews.com/news/world/businesses-claim-obamacare-has -forced-them-cut-employee-hours-flna6c10911846; Robert Pear, "Public Sector Cuts Part-Time Shifts to Bypass Insurance Law," *New York Times*, February 20, 2014, https://www

.nytimes.com/2014/02/21/us/public-sector-cuts-part-time-shifts-to-duck-insurance-law
.html. See also "Affordable Care Act," US Department of Labor, https://www.dol.gov/agencies
/ebsa/laws-and-regulations/laws/affordable-care-act/for-employers-and-advisers.

14. On severe postpartum mental distress, see Rachel VanderKruik et al., "The Global Prevalence
of Postpartum Psychosis: A Systematic Review," *BMC Psychiatry* 17 (2017): 272.

15. On rising rates of opioid addiction and death, see "Drug Overdose Death Rates," National
Institute on Drug Abuse, 2023, https://nida.nih.gov/research-topics/trends-statistics/over
dose-death-rates. On the role of opioid addiction and death in rising rates of child removals,
see Angélica Meinhofer and Yohanis Angleró-Díaz, "Trends in Foster Care Entry among
Children Removed from Their Homes Because of Parental Drug Use, 2000 to 2017," *JAMA
Pediatrics* 173, no. 9 (2019): 881–83; Troy Quast, Eric A. Storch, and Svetlana Yampolskaya,
"Opioid Prescription Rates and Child Removals: Evidence from Florida," *Health Affairs* 37,
no. 1 (2018): 134–39. On rates of child removal in Indiana and nationally, see "Child Welfare and Substance Use Disorder Treatment Statistics," National Center on Substance
Abuse and Child Welfare, https://ncsacw.acf.hhs.gov/research/child-welfare-and-treatment
-statistics.aspx.

16. On the placement of children following removal, see Megan L. Dolbin-MacNab and Lyn M.
O'Connell, "Grandfamilies and the Opioid Epidemic: A Systemic Perspective and Future Priorities," *Clinical Child and Family Psychology Review* 24, no. 2 (2021): 207–37. For the number
of US children being raised by people other than their parents, see "Who Takes Care of
Children When Their Parents Can't?," Urban Institute, 2003, https://webarchive.urban.org
/publications/900662.html. On how the US child welfare system prioritizes family placements, see Laura Radel et al., *Children Living Apart from Their Parent: Highlights from the National Survey of Children in Nonparental Care* (Washington, DC: US Department of Health
and Human Services, 2016); *Placement of Children with Relatives* (Washington, DC: Children's Bureau, 2018). On the number of Indiana children being raised by nonparental caregivers, see George Myers, "The Rise of 'Grandfamilies': Opioid Crisis Requires More Hoosier
Grandparents to Raise Children," *Kokomo Tribune*, September 3, 2017, https://www.kokomo
tribune.com/news/local_news/the-rise-of-grandfamilies-opioid-crisis-requires-more
-hoosier-grandparents-to-raise-children/article_0f4285e6-8f51-11e7-8421-f35a3787df2e
.html.

17. On the number of children living with only their mothers, see Paul Hermez and Chanell
Washington, "Number of Children Living Only with Their Mothers Has Doubled in Past 50
Years," US Census Bureau, 2021, https://www.census.gov/library/stories/2021/04/number
-of-children-living-only-with-their-mothers-has-doubled-in-past-50-years.html.

18. On how the burden of parental absence disproportionately falls to women, see Kristina Brant,
"When Mamaw Becomes Mom: Social Capital and Kinship Family Formation amid the
Rural Opioid Crisis," *RSF: The Russell Sage Foundation Journal of the Social Sciences* 8, no. 3
(2022): 78–98; Natallie Gentles-Gibbs and Jordan Zema, "It's Not about Them without
Them: Kinship Grandparents' Perspectives on Family Empowerment in Public Child Welfare," *Children and Youth Services Review* 108 (2020): 104650. On the toll that childcare re-
sponsibilities take on nonparental caregivers, see Margot Trotter Davis et al., "Parenting a
6-Year-Old Is Not What I Planned in Retirement: Trauma and Stress among Grandparents
Due to the Opioid Crisis," *Journal of Gerontological Social Work* 63, no. 4 (2020): 295–315;
Dolbin-MacNab and O'Connell, "Grandfamilies and the Opioid Epidemic"; Anna C. Hansen et al., "Sources of Stress and Strength: Contextualizing the Experience of Grandparents
Rearing Grandchildren in Appalachia," *Journal of Intergenerational Relationships* 20, no. 1
(2022): 39–59.

19. On grandparent care in the context of parental opioid addiction, see Brant, "When Mamaw
Becomes Mom"; Gentles-Gibbs and Zema, "It's Not about Them without Them"; Roberts,
Shattered Bonds; Roberts, *Torn Apart*; Sara Stulac et al., "Children and Families of the Opioid

Epidemic: Under the Radar," *Current Problems in Pediatric and Adolescent Health Care* 49, no. 8 (2019): 100637.

20. On how the policy response to the crack cocaine epidemic affected Black families, see Daphne Joslin and Anne Brouard, "The Prevalence of Grandmothers as Primary Caregivers in a Poor Pediatric Population," *Journal of Community Health* 20, no. 5 (1995): 383–401; Roberts, *Shattered Bonds*. On child removals and placements during the crack cocaine epidemic, as well as the consequences of those placements for parents and nonparental caregivers, see K. Haglund, "Parenting a Second Time Around: An Ethnography of African American Grandmothers Parenting Grandchildren Due to Parental Cocaine Abuse," *Journal of Family Nursing* 6, no. 2 (2000), https://elibrary.ru/item.asp?id=3919110; Meredith Minkler and Kathleen M. Roe, *Grandmothers as Caregivers: Raising Children of the Crack Cocaine Epidemic* (Newbury Park, CA: SAGE Publications, 1993).

21. On racial inequalities in pregnancy and birth-related complications, see Tressie McMillan Cottom, *Thick: And Other Essays* (New York: New Press, 2019); Latoya Hill, Samantha Artiga, and Usha Ranji, "Racial Disparities in Maternal and Infant Health: Current Status and Efforts to Address Them," Kaiser Family Foundation, November 1, 2022, https://www.kff.org/racial-equity-and-health-policy/issue-brief/racial-disparities-in-maternal-and-infant-health-current-status-and-efforts-to-address-them/; Dorothy Roberts, *Killing the Black Body: Race, Reproduction, and the Meaning of Liberty* (New York: Knopf Doubleday, 2014).

22. On mother blaming and the guilt that comes with it, see Elizabeth M. Armstrong, *Conceiving Risk, Bearing Responsibility: Fetal Alcohol Syndrome and the Diagnosis of Moral Disorder* (Baltimore: John Hopkins University Press, 2008); Caitlyn Collins, *Making Motherhood Work: How Women Manage Careers and Caregiving* (Princeton, NJ: Princeton University Press, 2019); Hernandez and Calarco, "Health Decisions amidst Controversy"; Jennifer A. Reich, *Calling the Shots: Why Parents Reject Vaccines* (New York: NYU Press, 2016); Waggoner, *The Zero Trimester*.

23. On cross-national differences in maternal morbidity and mortality, see "Maternal and Infant Morality," OECD, https://stats.oecd.org/index.aspx?queryid=30116. On the risks of pregnancy and childbirth in the US, see Rachelle Joy Chadwick and Don Foster, "Negotiating Risky Bodies: Childbirth and Constructions of Risk," *Health, Risk & Society* 16, no. 1 (2014): 68–83; Barbara Katz Rothman, "Pregnancy, Birth and Risk: An Introduction," *Health, Risk & Society* 16, no. 1 (2014): 1–6. On increasing rates of maternal and infant mortality, see Hill, Artiga, and Ranji, "Racial Disparities in Maternal and Infant Health."

24. On how racial disparities in maternal mortality differ by education, see Eugene Declercq and Laurie C. Zephyrin, *Maternal Mortality in the United States: A Primer* (New York: The Commonwealth Fund, 2020). On racism and health, see Cottom, *Thick and Other Essays*; William A. Darity, "Employment Discrimination, Segregation, and Health," *American Journal of Public Health* 93, no. 2 (2003): 226–31; Joe Feagin and Zinobia Bennefield, "Systemic Racism and U.S. Health," *Social Sciences & Medicine* 103 (2014): 7–14; Bridget J. Goosby, Jacob E. Cheadle, and Colter Mitchell, "Stress-Related Biosocial Mechanisms of Discrimination and African American Health Inequities," *Annual Review of Sociology* 44, no. 1 (2018): 319–40; Anthony Hatch, *Blood Sugar: Racial Pharmacology and Food Justice in Black America* (Minneapolis: University of Minnesota Press, 2016); Ayah Nuriddin, Graham Mooney, and Alexandre I. R. White, "Reckoning with Histories of Medical Racism and Violence in the USA," *Lancet*, October 3, 2020; Deirdre Cooper Owens and Sharla M. Fett, "Black Maternal and Infant Health: Historical Legacies of Slavery," *American Journal of Public Health* 109, no. 10 (2019): 1342–45; Whitney N. Laster Pirtle, "Racial Capitalism: A Fundamental Cause of Novel Coronavirus (COVID-19) Pandemic Inequities in the United States," *Health Education & Behavior* 47, no. 4 (2020): 504–8; Roberts, *Killing the Black Body*; David R. Williams and Michelle Sernthal, "Understanding Racial-ethnic Disparities in Health: Sociological Contributions," *Journal of Health and Social Behavior* 51, no. 1 (2010): 515–27.

25. On pregnancy-related fears, see Mary Regan and Katie McElroy, "Women's Perceptions of Childbirth Risk and Place of Birth," *Journal of Clinical Ethics* 24, no. 3 (September 2013): 239–52.
26. On postpartum sleep deprivation, see Lauren P. Hunter, Jacqueline D. Rychnovsky, and Susan M. Yount, "A Selective Review of Maternal Sleep Characteristics in the Postpartum Period," *Journal of Obstetric, Gynecologic & Neonatal Nursing* 38, no. 1 (2009): 60–68. On postpartum memory problems, see Matthew Brett and Sallie Baxendale, "Motherhood and Memory: A Review," *Psychoneuroendocrinology* 26, no. 4 (2001): 339–62; Jodi L. Pawluski, "Memory and Motherhood: Is It Better Than What We Think?," *Journal of Women's Health* 31, no. 8 (2022): 1067–68. On postpartum dental problems, see Stefanie L. Russell, Jeannette R. Ickovics, and Robert A. Yaffee, "Exploring Potential Pathways between Parity and Tooth Loss among American Women," *American Journal of Public Health* 98, no. 7 (2008): 1263–70. On postpartum depression and anxiety, see Saba Mughal, Yusra Azhar, and Waquar Siddiqui, "Postpartum Depression," *StatPearls*, October 7, 2022, http://www.ncbi.nlm.nih.gov /books/NBK519070/; Jiani Zhou et al., "Treatment of Substance Use Disorders among Women of Reproductive Age by Depression and Anxiety Disorder Status, 2008–2014," *Journal of Women's Health* (2002) 28, no. 8 (2019): 1068–76. On health disparities between mothers and non-mothers at later life, see Kei M. Nomaguchi and Melissa A. Milkie, "Costs and Rewards of Children: The Effects of Becoming a Parent on Adults' Lives," *Journal of Marriage and Family* 65, no. 2 (May 2003): 356–74; Kei Nomaguchi and Melissa A. Milkie, "Parenthood and Well-Being: A Decade in Review," *Journal of Marriage and Family* 82, no. 1 (2020): 198–223; Debra Umberson, Tetyana Pudrovska, and Corinne Reczek, "Parenthood, Childlessness, and Well-Being: A Life Course Perspective," *Journal of Marriage and Family* 72, no. 3 (2010): 612–29; Gema Zamarro and María J. Prados, "Gender Differences in Couples' Division of Childcare, Work and Mental Health during COVID-19," *Review of Economics of the Household* 19, no. 1 (2021): 11–40. On differences in the well-being of employed and nonemployed mothers, see Elizabeth Mendes, Lydia Saad, and Kyley McGeeney, "Stay-at-Home Moms Report More Depression, Sadness, Anger," Gallup, May 18, 2012, https://news.gallup .com/poll/154685/Stay-Home-Moms-Report-Depression-Sadness-Anger.aspx; Ann Meier et al., "Mothering Experiences: How Single Parenthood and Employment Structure the Emotional Valence of Parenting," *Demography* 53, no. 3 (2016): 649–74; Ronald C. Kessler and James A. McRae, "The Effect of Wives' Employment on the Mental Health of Married Men and Women," *American Sociological Review* 47, no. 2 (1982): 216–27. On differences in men's and women's experiences while caring for children, see Richard J. Petts and Daniel L. Carlson, "Managing a Household during a Pandemic: Cognitive Labor and Parents' Psychological Well-Being," *Society and Mental Health*, May 11, 2023. On the prevalence of the belief that women always want to have children and are "naturally" better suited for childcare, see Long Doan and Natasha Quadlin, "Partner Characteristics and Perceptions of Responsibility for Housework and Child Care," *Journal of Marriage and Family* 81, no. 1 (2019): 145–63; Kim Parker, Juliana Menasce Horowitz, and Anna Brown, *Americans' Complex Views on Gender Identity and Transgender Issues* (Washington, DC: Pew Research Center, 2022), https://www .pewresearch.org/social-trends/2022/06/28/americans-complex-views-on-gender-identity-and -transgender-issues/.
27. On the risk of disease and death following routine vaccinations, see Chinmay Patel and Hitesh H. Shah, "Vaccine-Associated Kidney Diseases: A Narrative Review of the Literature," *Saudi Journal of Kidney Disease Transplant* 30, no. 5 (2019): 1002–9. On vaccine misinformation, see Sahil Loomba et al., "Measuring the Impact of COVID-19 Vaccine Misinformation on Vaccination Intent in the UK and USA," *Nature Human Behavior* 5 (2021): 337–48; Reich, *Calling the Shots*; Mengcen Qian, Shin-Yi Chou, and Ernest K. Lai, "Confirmatory bias in health decisions: Evidence from the MMR-autism controversy," *Journal of Health Economics* 70 (2020). On how medical mistrust compounds fears of vaccination, particularly among Black families, see Courtney Thornton and Jennifer A. Reich, "Black

Mothers and Vaccine Refusal: Gendered Racism, Healthcare, and the State," *Gender & Society* 36, no. 4 (2022). On the role that mothers play in family health decision-making, see Hernandez and Calarco, "Health Decisions amidst Controversy"; Usha Ranji and Alina Salganicoff, "Balancing on Shaky Ground"; Waggoner, *Zero Trimester.*

28. On cross-national variations in maternal guilt and their origins in social safety net policies, see Caitlyn Collins, "Is Maternal Guilt a Cross-National Experience?," *Qualitative Sociology* 44, no. 1 (2021): 1–29; Collins, *Making Motherhood Work.*

29. On cross-national differences in infant and child mortality, see Ashish P. Thakrar et al., "Child Mortality in the US and 19 OECD Comparator Nations: A 50-Year Time-Trend Analysis," *Health Affairs* 37, no. 1 (2018). On causes of child death, see "Child Death," National Center for Health Statistics, https://www.cdc.gov/nchs/fastats/child-health.htm. On the role of guns in child mortality, see Matt McGough, Krutika Amin, Nirmita Panchal, and Cynthia Cox, "Child and Teen Firearm Mortality in the US and Peer Countries," Kaiser Family Foundation, July 18, 2023. On how we expect mothers to protect children from harm, see Norah MacKendrick, *Better Safe Than Sorry* (Berkeley: University of California Press, 2018); Margaret Nelson, *Parenting Out of Control: Anxious Parents in Uncertain Times* (New York, NY: NYU Press, 2010); Reich, "Neoliberal Mothering and Vaccine Refusal"; Ranji and Salganicoff, "Balancing on Shaky Ground"; Reich, *Calling the Shots*; Viviana Zelizer, *Pricing the Priceless Child: The Changing Social Value of Children* (Princeton, NJ: Princeton University Press, 1994); Waggoner, *Zero Trimester.*

30. On how women's vulnerability is a product of their location in intersecting hierarchies of power and marginalization, see Patricia Hill Collins, "Black Women and Motherhood," in *Motherhood and Space: Configurations of the Maternal through Politics, Home, and the Body,* ed. Sarah Hardy and Caroline Wiedmer (New York: Palgrave Macmillan, 2005), 149– 59; Dawn Marie Dow, "Negotiating 'The Welfare Queen' and 'The Strong Black Woman': African American Middle-Class Mothers' Work and Family Perspectives," *Sociological Perspectives* 58, no. 1 (2015): 36–55; Kathryn Edin and Laura Lein, *Making Ends Meet: How Single Mothers Survive Welfare and Low-Wage Work* (New York: Russell Sage Foundation, 1997); Sinikka Elliott and Sarah Bowen, "Defending Motherhood: Morality, Responsibility, and Double Binds in Feeding Children," *Journal of Marriage and Family* 80, no. 2 (2018): 499– 520; Fong, Wright and Wimer, "The Cost of Free Assistance: Why Low-Income Individuals Do Not Access Food Pantries"; Fong, "Getting Eyes in the Home"; Reich, *Fixing Families*; Roberts, *Shattered Bonds*; Roberts, *Torn Apart.*

CHAPTER 2: LEAVING WOMEN WITH NO CHOICE

1. On employment bias against mothers and mothers-in-waiting, see Stephen Benard, In Paik, and Shelley J. Correll, "Cognitive Bias and the Motherhood Penalty," *Hastings Law Journal* 59 (2008): 1359; Mary Blair-Loy, *Competing Devotions: Career and Family among Women Executives* (Cambridge, MA: Harvard University Press, 2009); Michelle J. Budig and Paula England, "The Wage Penalty for Motherhood," *American Sociological Review* 66, no. 2 (2001): 204–25; Shelley J. Correll, Stephen Benard, and In Paik, "Getting a Job: Is There a Motherhood Penalty?," *American Journal of Sociology* 112, no. 5 (2007): 1297–339; Joan R. Kahn, Javier García-Manglano, and Suzanne M. Bianchi, "The Motherhood Penalty at Midlife: Long-Term Effects of Children on Women's Careers," *Journal of Marriage and Family* 76, no. 1 (2014): 56–72; Natasha Quadlin, "The Mark of a Woman's Record: Gender and Academic Performance in Hiring," *American Sociological Review* 83, no. 2 (2018): 331–60; Sarah Thébaud and Catherine J. Taylor, "The Specter of Motherhood: Culture and the Production of Gendered Career Aspirations in Science and Engineering," *Gender & Society* 35, no. 3 (2021): 395–421. On the gender segregation of the US economy, see Olga Alonso-Villar, Coral Del Rio, and Carlos Gradin, "The Extent of Occupational Segregation in the United States: Dif-

ferences by Race, Ethnicity, and Gender," *Industrial Relations: A Journal of Economy and Society* 51, no. 2 (2012): 179–212; Erin A. Cech, "The Self-Expressive Edge of Occupational Sex Segregation," *American Journal of Sociology* 119, no. 3 (2013): 747–89; Philip N. Cohen, Matt L. Huffman, and Stefanie Knauer, "Stalled Progress?: Gender Segregation and Wage Inequality among Managers, 1980–2000," *Work and Occupations* 36, no. 4 (2009): 318–42; David A. Cotter, Joan M. Hermsen, and Reeve Vanneman, "The Effects of Occupational Gender Segregation across Race," *Sociological Quarterly* 44, no. 1 (2003): 17–36; Gordon Gauchat, Maura Kelly, and Michael Wallace, "Occupational Gender Segregation, Globalization, and Gender Earnings Inequality in U.S. Metropolitan Areas," *Gender & Society* 26, no. 5 (2012): 718–47; Claudia Goldin, *Understanding the Gender Gap: An Economic History of American Women* (Oxford: Oxford University Press, 1992); Ruth Milkman, *Gender at Work: The Dynamics of Job Segregation by Sex during World War II* (Champaign: University of Illinois, 1987); Ellen Mutari, Marilyn Power, and Deborah M. Figart, "Neither Mothers Nor Breadwinners: African-American Women's Exclusion from US Minimum Wage Policies, 1912–1938," *Feminist Economics* 8, no. 2 (2002): 37–61; Haya Stier and Meir Yaish, "Occupational Segregation and Gender Inequality in Job Quality: A Multi-Level Approach," *Work, Employment and Society* 28, no. 2 (2014): 225–46. On how families use women's low pay and "flexible" work to justify treating them as the default caregiver, see Jessica McCrory Calarco et al., "By Default: How Mothers in Different-Sex Dual-Earner Couples Account for Inequalities in Pandemic Parenting," *Socius* (2021); Sarah Damaske, *For the Family?: How Class and Gender Shape Women's Work* (Oxford: Oxford University Press, 2011); Allison Daminger, "De-gendered Processes, Gendered Outcomes: How Egalitarian Couples Make Sense of Non-egalitarian Household Practices," *American Sociological Review* 85, no. 5 (2020): 806–29; Kathleen Gerson, *Hard Choices: How Women Decide about Work, Career and Motherhood* (Berkeley: University of California Press, 1985); Evelyn Nakano Glenn, *Forced to Care: Coercion and Caregiving in America* (Cambridge, MA: Harvard University Press, 2010); Arlie Russell Hochschild, *The Second Shift: Working Families and the Revolution at Home* (New York: Penguin, 1989).

2. On how women (especially low-income women, women of color, and immigrant women) are relegated to underpaid caregiving roles, see John R. Bowman and Alyson M. Cole, "Do Working Mothers Oppress Other Women? The Swedish 'Maid Debate' and the Welfare State Politics of Gender Equality," *Signs: Journal of Women in Culture and Society* 35, no. 1 (2009): 157–84; Altheira Caldera, "Challenging Capitalistic Exploitation: A Black Feminist/ Womanist Commentary on Work and Self-Care," *Feminist Studies* 46, no. 3 (2020): 707–16; Patricia Hill Collins, *Black Feminist Thought: Knowledge, Consciousness, and the Politics of Empowerment* (New York: Routledge, 2000); Patricia Hill Collins, "Black Women and Motherhood," in *Motherhood and Space: Configurations of the Maternal through Politics, Home, and the Body*, ed. Sarah Hardy and Caroline Wiedmer (New York: Palgrave Macmillan, 2005), 149–59; Angela Y. Davis, *Women, Race, and Class* (New York: Vintage Books, 1983); Glenn, *Forced to Care*; Candace Howes, Carrie Leana, and Kristin Smith, "Paid Care Work," in *For Love or Money: Care Provision in the United States*, ed. Nancy Folbre (New York: Russell Sage Foundation, 2012); Zora Neale Hurston, *Their Eyes Were Watching God* (Philadelphia: J. B. Lippincott and Co., 1937); Jacqueline Jones, *Labor of Love, Labor of Sorrow: Black Women, Work and the Family, from Slavery to the Present* (New York: Basic Books, 2010); Katherine Kaufka, "The Commodification of Domestic Care: Illegitimacy of Care Work and the Exploitation of Migrant Workers," *Georgetown Immigration Law Journal* 18, no. 1 (2004): 159–78; Cameron Lynne Macdonald, *Shadow Mothers: Nannies, Au Pairs, and the Micropolitics of Mothering* (Berkeley: University of California Press, 2011); Lynet Uttal and Mary Tuominen, "Tenuous Relationships: Exploitation, Emotion, and Racial Ethnic Significance in Paid Child Care Work," *Gender & Society* 13, no. 6 (1999): 758–80; Deborah Gray White, *Too Heavy a Load: Black Women in Defense of Themselves, 1894–1994* (New York: W. W. Norton, 1999).

3. On stay-at-home mothers' desire for paid employment, see Kelly Musick, Ann Meier, and

Sarah Flood, "How Parents Fare: Mothers' and Fathers' Subjective Well-Being in Time with Children," *American Sociological Review* 81, no. 5 (2016): 1069–95; Ann Meier et al., "Mothering Experiences: How Single Parenthood and Employment Structure the Emotional Valence of Parenting," *Demography* 53, no. 3 (2016): 649–74; Hochschild, *The Second Shift*; Ronald C. Kessler and James A. McRae, "The Effect of Wives' Employment on the Mental Health of Married Men and Women," *American Sociological Review* 47, no. 2 (1982): 216–27; Caitlyn Collins, "Is Maternal Guilt a Cross-National Experience?," *Qualitative Sociology* 44, no. 1 (2021): 1–29. On stay-at-home mothers' use of part-time and informal paid work to make ends meet, see Michael Dunn, "Making Gigs Work: Digital Platforms, Job Quality and Worker Motivations," *New Technology, Work and Employment* 35, no. 2 (2020): 232–49; ed. Elana Levine, *Cupcakes, Pinterest, and Ladyporn: Feminized Popular Culture in the Early Twenty-First Century* (Champaign: University of Illinois Press, 2015); Sinikka Pöllänen and Laura Voutilainen, "Crafting Well-Being: Meanings and Intentions of Stay-at-Home Mothers' Craft-Based Leisure Activity," *Leisure Sciences* 40, no. 6 (2018): 617–33; Alexandrea J. Ravenelle, *Hustle and Gig: Struggling and Surviving in the Sharing Economy* (Berkeley: University of California Press, 2019); Deborah Whitehead, "Startup Culture: MLMs, Mormons, and Entrepreneurship," *Mormon Studies Review* 10 (2023): 31–41.

4. On the Affordable Care Act and the high cost of insurance available to people without employer-sponsored plans, see Ilana Graetz et al., "The U.S. Health Insurance Marketplace: Are Premiums Truly Affordable?," *Annals of Internal Medicine* 161, no. 8 (2014): 599–604; Carmen M. Gutierrez, "The Institutional Determinants of Health Insurance: Moving Away from Labor Market, Marriage, and Family Attachments under the ACA," *American Sociological Review* 83, no. 6 (2018): 1144–70; Wei Ye and Javier M. Rodriguez, "Highly Vulnerable Communities and the Affordable Care Act: Health Insurance Coverage Effects, 2010–2018," *Social Science & Medicine* 270 (2021): 113670. On variations in college completion, see Melanie Hanson, *College Dropout Rates* (Mt. Laurel, NJ: Education Data Initiative, 2022), https://educationdata.org/college-dropout-rates.

5. For more on Indiana's state-subsidized childcare programs, see "Indiana Child Care Development Fund (CCDF)," Firefly, https://fireflyin.org/programs-services/child-abuse-prevention/child-care-and-development-fund-ccdf/. See also "2016 Poverty Guidelines," ASPE, https://aspe.hhs.gov/2016-poverty-guidelines.

6. On nonstandard schedules and the challenges they create with respect to childcare, see Lyn Craig and Judith E. Brown, "Feeling Rushed: Gendered Time Quality, Work Hours, Nonstandard Work Schedules, and Spousal Crossover," *Journal of Marriage and Family* 79, no. 1 (2017): 225–42; Lyn Craig and Abigail Powell, "Non-Standard Work Schedules, Work-Family Balance and the Gendered Division of Childcare," *Work, Employment and Society* 25, no. 2 (2011): 274–91; Anita Ilta Garey, "Constructing Motherhood on the Night Shift: 'Working Mothers' as 'Stay-at-Home Moms,'" *Qualitative Sociology* 18, no. 4 (1995): 415–37; Sanna Moilanen et al., "Mothers' Non-Standard Working and Childcare-Related Challenges: A Comparison between Lone and Coupled Mothers," *International Journal of Sociology and Social Policy* 36, no. 1/2 (2016): 36–52; Brooke Richardson, Susan Prentice, and Donna Lero, "'I'm Kind of in a Dilemma': The Challenges of Non-Standard Work Schedules and Childcare," *Community, Work & Family* 26, no. 4 (2021): 428–443.

7. On the types of jobs available to low-income single mothers, see Damaske, *For the Family?*; Kathryn Edin and Laura Lein, *Making Ends Meet: How Single Mothers Survive Welfare and Low-Wage Work* (New York: Russell Sage Foundation, 1997); Sharon Hays, *Flat Broke with Children: Women in the Age of Welfare Reform* (Oxford: Oxford University Press, 2004); Allison J. Pugh, *The Tumbleweed Society: Working and Caring in an Age of Insecurity* (Oxford: Oxford University Press, 2015).

8. For more on internalized stigma around government dependency, see Joan Maya Mazelis, *Surviving Poverty* (New York: NYU Press, 2016); Katherine S. Newman, *Falling from Grace: The Experience of Downward Mobility in the American Middle Class* (New York: Free Press,

1988); Jessi Streib, *Privilege Lost: Who Leaves the Upper Middle Class and How They Fall* (Oxford: Oxford University Press, 2020).

9. For more on the administrative burden the US has attached to poverty programs, and for more on how those burdens disproportionately impact low-income women and women of color, see Pamela Herd and Donald P. Moynihan, *Administrative Burden: Policymaking by Other Means* (New York: Russell Sage Foundation, 2019); Leslie Paik, *Trapped in a Maze: How Social Control Institutions Drive Family Poverty and Inequality* (Berkeley: University of California Press, 2021).

10. On the challenges that low-income families face in affording diapers, see Jennifer Randles, "'Willing to Do Anything for My Kids': Inventive Mothering, Diapers, and the Inequalities of Carework," *American Sociological Review* 86, no. 1 (2021): 35–59; Jennifer Randles, "Fixing a Leaky U.S. Social Safety Net: Diapers, Policy, and Low-Income Families," *RSF: The Russell Sage Foundation Journal of the Social Sciences* 8, no. 5 (2022): 166–83. For comparisons of the costs, health benefits, and environmental impact of cloth and disposable diapers, see Courtney Schley, "Cloth vs. Disposable Diapers: Which Kind Should I Use?," *New York Times*, May 15, 2018.

11. On employer discrimination against mothers and mothers-in-waiting, see Natalia Ramirez Campos, "Reentering the Workforce after a Gap in Employment: Biases, Stereotypes, and Gender Roles" (thesis, Middle Tennessee State University, 2018), https://www.proquest.com/docview/2111945103/abstract/B18075FC4B244409PQ/1; Christine A. Henle et al., "Eldercare and Childcare: How Does Caregiving Responsibility Affect Job Discrimination?," *Journal of Business and Psychology* 35, no. 1 (2020); Joan R. Kahn, Javier García-Manglano, and Suzanne M. Bianchi, "The Motherhood Penalty at Midlife: Long-Term Effects of Children on Women's Careers," *Journal of Marriage and Family* 76, no. 1 (2014): 56–72; Bryan Tomlin, "Maternity Breaks: Unemployment Spells or Relevant Experience?," *Journal of Economic Behavior & Organization* 198 (2022): 673–81. On gender differences in mothers' and fathers' likelihood of being involuntarily terminated from their jobs, see Benjamin Artz, "Are Mothers More Likely Than Fathers to Lose Their Jobs?," *Journal of Family and Economic Issues* (2023).

12. On the creativity that mothers display in making ends meet, see Damaske, *For the Family*; Kathryn Edin and Maria J. Kefalas, *Promises I Can Keep: Why Poor Women Put Motherhood Before Marriage* (Berkeley: University of California Press, 2011); Edin and Lein, *Making Ends Meet*; Kathryn J. Edin and H. Luke Shaefer, *$2.00 a Day: Living on Almost Nothing in America* (Boston: Mariner Books, 2015); Mazelis, *Surviving Poverty*; Pugh, *The Tumbleweed Society*; Carol Stack, *All Our Kin* (New York: Harper, 1974); Ana Villalobos, *Motherload: Making It All Better in Insecure Times* (Berkeley: University of California Press, 2014).

13. On how childcare challenges limit American women's employment, see Caitlyn Collins, *Making Motherhood Work: How Women Manage Careers and Caregiving* (Princeton, NJ: Princeton University Press 2019); Wenjui Han and Jane Waldfogel, "Child Care Costs and Women's Employment: A Comparison of Single and Married Mothers with Pre-School-Aged Children," *Social Science Quarterly* 82, no. 3 (2001): 552–68; Sanna Moilanen et al., "Mothers' Non-Standard Working and Childcare-Related Challenges"; Richardson, Prentice, and Lero, "'I'm Kind of in a Dilemma'"; Leah Ruppanner, Stephanie Moller, and Liana Sayer, "Expensive Childcare and Short School Days = Lower Maternal Employment and More Time in Childcare? Evidence from the American Time Use Survey," *Socius* 5 (2019). On how the lack of paid family leave affects the division of household labor, see Jody Heymann et al., "Improving Health with Programmatic, Legal, and Policy Approaches to Reduce Gender Inequality and Change Restrictive Gender Norms," *Lancet* 393, no. 10190 (June 22, 2019): 2522–34; Vera Lomazzi, Sabine Israel, and Isabella Crespi, "Gender Equality in Europe and the Effect of Work-Family Balance Policies on Gender-Role Attitudes," *Social Sciences* 8, no. 1 (2019): 5.

14. On motherhood penalties, see Benard, Paik, and Correll, "Cognitive Bias and the Motherhood Penalty"; Blair-Loy, *Competing Devotions*; Budig and England, "The Wage Penalty for

Motherhood"; Correll, Benard, and Paik, "Getting a Job"; Kahn, García-Manglano, and Bianchi, "The Motherhood Penalty at Midlife"; Quadlin, "The Mark of a Woman's Record"; Thébaud and Taylor, "The Specter of Motherhood." On the daddy bonus, see Michelle J. Budig, *The Fatherhood Bonus and the Motherhood Penalty: Parenthood and the Gender Gap in Pay* (Washington, D.C.: Third Way, 2014), https://www.thirdway.org/report/the-fatherhood-bonus -and-the-motherhood-penalty-parenthood-and-the-gender-gap-in-pay.; Melissa J. Hodges and Michelle J. Budig, "Who Gets the Daddy Bonus? Organizational Hegemonic Masculinity and the Impact of Fatherhood on Earnings," *Gender & Society* 24, no. 6 (2010): 717–45.

15. On the precarity of the jobs held by lower-income American men, see David Autor, David Dorn, and Gordon Hanson, "When Work Disappears: Manufacturing Decline and the Falling Marriage Market Value of Young Men," *American Economic Review: Insights* 1, no. 2 (September 2019): 161–78; Elisabeth Jacobs and Jacob S. Hacker, "The Rising Instability of American Family Incomes, 1969–2004: Evidence from the Panel Study of Income Dynamics," Economic Policy Institute, May 28, 2008, https://www.epi.org/publication/bp213. On ideal worker norms and their gendered impact, see Youngjoo Cha, "Reinforcing Separate Spheres: The Effect of Spousal Overwork on Men's and Women's Employment in Dual-Earner Households," *American Sociological Review* 75, no. 2 (2010): 303–29; Jeffrey S. Gray, "The Fall in Men's Return to Marriage: Declining Productivity Effects or Changing Selection?," *Journal of Human Resources* 32, no. 3 (1997): 481–504; Alexandra Killewald and Margaret Gough, "Does Specialization Explain Marriage Penalties and Premiums?," *American Sociological Review* 78, no. 3 (2013): 477–502.

16. On childcare's missing middle, see Joan Williams and Heather Boushey, "The Three Faces of Work-Family Conflict: The Poor, the Professionals, and the Missing Middle," *SSRN Electronic Journal*, January 21, 2010. On the concept of the missing middle, see Theda Skocpol, *The Missing Middle: Working Families and the Future of American Social Policy* (New York: W. W. Norton, 2000).

17. On the disproportionate burden of paid and unpaid work borne by women in low-income and middle-income families, see Damaske, *For the Family*; Edin and Lein, *Making Ends Meet*; Pugh, *The Tumbleweed Society*; Villalobos, *Motherload*.

18. On the precarity of single-income families, see Damaske, *For the Family?*; Sarah Damaske, *The Tolls of Uncertainty* (Princeton, NJ: Princeton University Press, 2021); Jacob S. Hacker, *The Great Risk Shift: The New Economic Insecurity and the Decline of the American Dream* (Oxford: Oxford University Press, 2019); Arne L. Kalleberg, *Good Jobs, Bad Jobs: The Rise of Polarized and Precarious Employment Systems in the United States 1970s to 2000s* (New York: Russell Sage Foundation, 2013); Clare Lyonette, Gayle Kaufman, and Rosemary Crompton, "'We Both Need to Work': Maternal Employment, Childcare and Health Care in Britain and the USA," *Work, Employment and Society* 25, no. 1 (2011): 34–50. On the challenges of paying for healthcare in the United States, see Lucie Kalousova and Sarah A. Burgard, "Debt and Foregone Medical Care," *Journal of Health and Social Behavior* 54, no. 2 (2013): 204–20; Raymond Kluender et al., "Medical Debt in the US, 2009–2020," *JAMA* 326, no. 3 (July 20, 2021): 250–56; Ryan Nunn, Jana Parsons, and Jay Shambaugh, "A Dozen Facts about the Economics of the US Health-Care System," *Brookings* (blog), March 10, 2020, https://www.brookings .edu/research/a-dozen-facts-about-the-economics-of-the-u-s-health-care-system/; Matthew Rae et al., "The Burden of Medical Debt in the United States," Kaiser Family Foundation, March 10, 2022, https://www.kff.org/health-costs/issue-brief/the-burden-of-medical-debt -in-the-united-states/. On the absence of affordable housing: Matthew Desmond, *Evicted: Poverty and Profit in the American City* (New York, NY: Crown 2017); Desmond, *Poverty, by America*.

19. On the link between schooling and women's employment, see Elizabeth U. Cascio, "Maternal Labor Supply and the Introduction of Kindergartens into American Public Schools," *Journal of Human Resources* 44, no. 1 (2009): 140–70; Maria Donovan Fitzpatrick, "Preschoolers Enrolled and Mothers at Work? The Effects of Universal Prekindergarten," *Journal*

of Labor Economics 28, no. 1 (2010): 51–85; Ruppanner, Moller, and Sayer, "Expensive Child-care and Short School Days."

20. On how multi-level marketing companies like Mary Kay exploit the precarity of stay-at-home mothers and other women with limited economic opportunities, see Christopher Bradley and Hannah E. Oates, "The Multi-Level Marketing Pandemic," *Tennessee Law Review* 89, no. 2 (2022): 321–76; Krista Frederico, "She Works Hard for No Money: Understanding Women's Participation in Multi-Level Marketing Organizations" (PhD diss., University of Arizona, 2020), http://www.proquest.com/docview/2443599273/abstract/176B5ED29ED94A5BPQ /1; Susan L. Williams and Michelle Bemiller, *Women at Work: Tupperware, Passion Parties, and Beyond*, *Women at Work* (Boulder, CO: Lynne Rienner Publishers, 2022). On the prevalence of "side hustles" among parents of young children, see "One in Three Americans Have a Side Hustle," Zapier, January 14, 2021, https://zapier.com/blog/side-hustle-report/; see also Heidi Liu, "The Behavioral Economics of Multilevel Marketing," *Hastings Business Law Journal* 14, no. 1 (2018): 109–38; Rachelle L. Pavelko and Cory Barker, "It Really Works! Qualitative Content Analysis of Multilevel Marketing Organizations' Online Promotional Messaging and Recruitment Strategies," *Women's Studies in Communication* 45, no. 3 (2022): 399–421; Whitehead, "Startup Culture"; Julie Ann Wilson and Emily Chivers Yochim, "Mothering through Precarity," *Cultural Studies* 29, no. 5–6 (2015): 669–86.

21. On the lack of coverage for after-school and school-break care for families in the US, see Ruppanner et al., "Expensive Childcare and Short School Days = Lower Maternal Employment and More Time in Childcare?"

22. On the challenges that mothers face in combining parental responsibilities and paid work, see Caitlyn Collins, *Making Motherhood Work*; Damaske, *For the Family?*; Gerson, *Hard Choices*; Sharon Hays, *The Cultural Contradictions of Motherhood* (New Haven, CT: Yale University Press, 1998); Hochschild, *The Second Shift*; Pamela Braboy Jackson and Rashawn Ray, *How Families Matter: Simply Complicated Intersections of Race, Gender, and Work* (Lanham, MD: Lexington Books, 2018); Lesley D. Riley and Christopher "Pokey" Bowen, "The Sandwich Generation: Challenges and Coping Strategies of Multigenerational Families," *Family Journal* 13, no. 1 (2005): 52–58; Anne-Marie Slaughter, *Unfinished Business: Women Men Work Family* (New York: Random House, 2015). On the role that eldest daughters often play in caring for younger siblings and the toll that responsibility takes, see Harold D. Fishbein, "Sibling Set Configuration and Family Dysfunction," *Family Process* 20, no. 3 (1981): 311–18; Yang Hu, "Patriarchal Hierarchy? Gender, Children's Housework Time, and Family Structure in Post-Reform China," *Chinese Sociological Review* 50, no. 3 (2018): 310–38; Sarah Sload, "The Plight of the Eldest Daughter," *Atlantic*, November 14, 2023, https://www.theatlantic .com/family/archive/2023/11/first-born-children-eldest-daughter-family-dynamics/675986/.

23. On the stereotypes of Black single mothers, see Dawn Marie Dow, "Negotiating 'The Welfare Queen' and 'The Strong Black Woman': African American Middle-Class Mothers' Work and Family Perspectives," *Sociological Perspectives* 58, no. 1 (2015): 36–55; Edin and Lein, *Making Ends Meet*; Martin Gilens, *Why Americans Hate Welfare: Race, Media, and the Politics of Anti-poverty Policy* (Chicago: University of Chicago Press, 2009); Hays, *Flat Broke with Children*; Jill S. Quadagno, *The Color of Welfare: How Racism Undermined the War on Poverty* (Oxford: Oxford University Press, 1994). For news coverage of the campaign speech, see Washington Star, "'Welfare Queen' Becomes Issue in Reagan Campaign," *New York Times*, February 15, 1976, https://www.nytimes.com/1976/02/15/archives/welfare-queen-becomes-issue-in-reagan -campaign-hitting-a-nerve-now.html. For an analysis of the inaccuracies involved in Reagan's story, see Josh Levin, *The Queen: The Forgotten Life Behind an American Myth* (New York: Little, Brown and Company, 2019). On racial differences in poverty in single mother families, see "Poverty Status of Children by Family Structure," OJJDP, https://ojjdp.ojp.gov/statistical -briefing-book/population/faqs/. On Black women's paid workforce participation, see Dawn Marie Dow, "Integrated Motherhood: Beyond Hegemonic Ideologies of Motherhood," *Journal of Marriage and Family* 78, no. 1 (2016): 180–96; Dawn Marie Dow, *Mothering While Black*

(Berkeley: University of California Press, 2019); Edin and Lein, *Making Ends Meet*. On Black women's and white women's workforce participation, see Sandra M. Florian, "Motherhood and Employment among Whites, Hispanics, and Blacks: A Life Course Approach," *Journal of Marriage and the Family* 80, no. 1 (2018): 134–49. On racial differences in women's paid work hours and hourly pay, see Valerie Wilson, "African American Women Stand Out as Working Moms Play a Larger Economic Role in Families," *Economic Policy Institute* (blog), 2017, https://www.epi.org/blog/african-american-women-stand-out-as-working-moms-play-a -larger-economic-role-in-families/.

24. On the rarity of remote work jobs pre-pandemic, see Erik Brynjolfsson et al., "COVID-19 and Remote Work: An Early Look at US Data" (working paper, National Bureau of Economic Research, June 2020); Allison Dunatchik et al., "Gender, Parenting, and the Rise of Remote Work during the Pandemic: Implications for Domestic Inequality in the United States," *Gender & Society* 35, no. 2 (2021): 194–205; Thomas Lyttelton, Emma Zang, and Kelly Musick, "Gender Differences in Telecommuting and Implications for Inequality at Home and Work," *SSRN Electronic Journal*, July 17, 2020.

25. For the ranking of cities by quality of public transit, see "Indianapolis Ranks Last in Public Transportation," WRTV, September 13, 2019, https://www.wrtv.com/news/local-news/report -indianapolis-ranks-last-in-public-transportation. On the risks of Covid transmission on public transportation, see Nathan J. Edwards et al., "Reducing COVID-19 Airborne Transmission Risks on Public Transportation Buses: An Empirical Study on Aerosol Dispersion and Control," *Aerosol Science and Technology* 55, no. 12 (December 2, 2021): 1378–97. For more on how socioeconomic disparities in people's reliance on public transportation contributed to disparities in disease risk during the Covid-19 pandemic, see Karla Therese L. Sy et al., "Socioeconomic Disparities in Subway Use and COVID-19 Outcomes in New York City," *American Journal of Epidemiology* 190, no. 7 (2021): 1234–42.

26. On the poverty rate, see Emily A. Shrider and John Creamer, "Poverty in the United States: 2022," US Census Bureau, 2023 https://www.census.gov/library/publications/2023/demo /p60-280.html. On savings rates, see Lane Gillespie and Tori Rubloff, "Bankrate's 2023 annual emergency savings report," Bankrate, June 22, 2023, https://www.bankrate.com/banking /savings/emergency-savings-report/. On racial disparities in poverty, income, and food insecurity, see Kyle Ross and Justin Dorazio, "The Latest Poverty, Income, and Food Insecurity Data Reveal Continuing Racial Disparities," Center for American Progress, December 21, 2022, https:// www.americanprogress.org/article/the-latest-poverty-income-and-food-insecurity-data -reveal-continuing-racial-disparities/. On the economic precarity facing Black families and communities in the US, see Fenaba R. Addo, Jason N. Houle, and Daniel Simon, "Young, Black, and (Still) in the Red: Parental Wealth, Race, and Student Loan Debt," *Race and Social Problems* 8, no. 1 (2016): 64–7; Dalton Conley, *Being Black, Living in the Red: Race, Wealth, and Social Policy in America* (Berkeley: University of California Press, 2010); William A. Darity and A. Kirsten Mullen, *From Here to Equality: Reparations for Black Americans in the Twenty-First Century* (Chapel Hill: University of North Carolina Press, 2020); William A. Darity Jr., Fenaba R. Addo, and Imari Z. Smith, "A Subaltern Middle Class: The Case of the Missing 'Black Bourgeoisie' in America," *Contemporary Economic Policy* 39, no. 3 (2021): 494–502; Matthew Desmond, *Poverty, by America* (New York: Crown, 2023); Jason N. Houle and Fenaba R. Addo, "Racial Disparities in Student Debt and the Reproduction of the Fragile Black Middle Class," *Sociology of Race and Ethnicity* 5, no. 4 (2019): 562–77; Elizabeth Korver-Glenn, *Race Brokers: Housing Markets and Segregation in 21st Century Urban America* (Oxford: Oxford University Press, 2021); Maria Krysan and Kyle Crowder, *Cycle of Segregation: Social Processes and Residential Segregation* (New York: Russell Sage Foundation, 2017); Heather McGhee, *The Sum of Us: What Racism Costs Everyone and How We Can Prosper Together* (New York: One World, 2021). On preterm birth rates, see "Preterm Births as a Percent of All Births by Race/Ethnicity," Kaiser Family Foundation, April 25, 2023, https://www.kff.org /other/state-indicator/preterm-births-by-raceethnicity/; Tracy A. Manuck, "Racial and Ethnic

Differences in Preterm Birth: A Complex, Multifactorial Problem," *Seminars in Perinatology* 41, no. 8 (December 2017): 511–18. On the risk of heart disease, see Gorita M. Frierson et al., "Effect of Race and Socioeconomic Status on Cardiovascular Risk Factor Burden: The Cooper Center Longitudinal Study," *Ethnicity & Disease* 23, no. 1 (2013): 35–42. On inequalities in school funding, see Linda Darling-Hammond, "Unequal Opportunity: Race and Education," *Brookings* (blog), November 30, 1AD, https://www.brookings.edu/articles/unequal-opportunity -race-and-education/; Clare Lombardo, "Why White School Districts Have So Much More Money," NPR, February 26, 2019, https://www.npr.org/2019/02/26/696794821/why-white -school-districts-have-so-much-more-money. On inequalities in college outcomes, see Cristobal de Brey et al., "Status Trends in the Education of Racial and Ethnic Groups," National Center for Education Statistics, February 2019, https://nces.ed.gov/programs/raceindicators/indicator _red.asp; Tressie McMillan Cottom, *Lower Ed: The Troubling Rise of For-Profit Colleges* (New York: New Press, 2017). On inequalities in student debt, see Addo, Houle, and Simon, "Young, Black, and (Still) in the Red"; Cottom, *Lower Ed*; Houle and Addo, "Racial Dispar- ities in Student Debt and the Reproduction of the Fragile Black Middle Class"; Louise Seam- ster, "Black Debt, White Debt," *Contexts* 18, no. 1 (2019): 30–35. On environmental racism, see Laura Pulido, "Flint, Environmental Racism, and Racial Capitalism," *Capitalism Nature Socialism* 27, no. 3 (July 2, 2016): 1–16. On police violence, see Keon L. Gilbert and Rashawn Ray, "Why Police Kill Black Males with Impunity: Applying Public Health Critical Race Praxis (PHCRP) to Address the Determinants of Policing Behaviors and 'Justifiable' Homi- cides in the USA," *Journal of Urban Health* 93, no. 1 (2016): 122–40; Shannon Malone Gonzalez, "Making It Home: An Intersectional Analysis of the Police Talk," *Gender & Society* 33, no. 3 (2019): 363–86; Nicole Gonzalez Van Cleve, *Crook County: Racism and Injustice in America's Largest Criminal Court* (Redwood City, CA: Stanford University Press, 2016). On racial mi- croaggressions, see Kathryn Freeman Anderson and Jessie K. Finch, "The Role of Racial Microaggressions, Stress, and Acculturation in Understanding Latino Health Outcomes in the USA," *Race and Social Problems* 9, no. 3 (2017): 218–33; Kevin L. Nadal et al., "The Impact of Racial Microaggressions on Mental Health: Counseling Implications for Clients of Color," *Journal of Counseling & Development* 92, no. 1 (2014): 57–66; William A. Smith, Man Hung, and Jeremy D. Franklin, "Racial Battle Fatigue and the MisEducation of Black Men: Racial Microaggressions, Societal Problems, and Environmental Stress," *Journal of Negro Education* 80, no. 1 (2011): 63–82; Derald Wing Sue and Lisa Spanierman, *Microaggressions in Everyday Life* (Hoboken, NJ: Wiley, 2020). On wealth inequalities, see Conley, *Being Black, Living in the Red*; Darity and Mullen, *From Here to Equality*; Desmond, *Poverty, by America*; Desmond, *Evicted*; Houle and Addo, "Racial Disparities in Student Debt"; ed., Melvin Oliver and Thomas M. Shapiro, *Black Wealth / White Wealth: A New Perspective on Racial Inequality* (London: Routledge, 2006).

27. On how precarity increases the need for support while making it difficult for people in low- income communities to rely on each other, see Mazelis, *Surviving Poverty*; Stack, *All Our Kin*; Mario Luis Small, *Villa Victoria* (Chicago: University of Chicago Press, 2004). On the prev- alence of breadwinner mothers, see Sarah Jane Glynn, "Breadwinning Mothers Continue to Be the U.S. Norm," Center for American Progress, May 10, 2019. On why Black women are often both the primary breadwinner and the default parent, see Dow, *Mothering While Black*; Collins, "Black Women and Motherhood"; Evelyn Nakano Glenn, "From Servitude to Ser- vice Work: Historical Continuities in the Racial Division of Paid Reproductive Labor," *Signs: Journal of Women in Culture and Society* 18, no. 1 (1992): 1–43; Glenn, *Forced to Care*. On race and opportunities in school, see Thomas J. Espenshade and Alexandria W. Radford, *No Lon- ger Separate, Not Yet Equal: Race and Class in Elite College Admission and Campus Life* (Prince- ton, NJ: Princeton University Press, 2009); Amanda E. Lewis and John B. Diamond, *Despite the Best Intentions: How Racial Inequality Thrives in Good Schools* (Oxford: Oxford University Press, 2015); R. L'Heureux Lewis-McCoy, *Inequality in the Promised Land: Race, Resources, and Suburban Schooling* (Redwood City, CA: Stanford University Press, 2014); Edward W. Mor-

ris, "'Tuck in That Shirt!' Race, Class, Gender and Discipline in an Urban School," *Sociological Perspectives* 48, no. 1 (2005): 25–48; Edward W. Morris and Brea L. Perry, "The Punishment Gap: School Suspension and Racial Disparities in Achievement," *Social Problems* 63, no. 1 (2016); Victor M. Rios, *Punished: Policing the Lives of Black and Latino Boys* (New York: NYU Press, 2011); Karolyn Tyson, "Notes from the Back of the Room: Problems and Paradoxes in the Schooling of Young Black Students," *Sociology of Education* 76, no. 4 (2003): 326–43. On employment discrimination against Black men, see Zachary W. Brewster and Michael Lynn, "Black–White Earnings Gap among Restaurant Servers: A Replication, Extension, and Exploration of Consumer Racial Discrimination in Tipping," *Sociological Inquiry* 84, no. 4 (2014): 545–69; John M. Nunley et al., "Racial Discrimination in the Labor Market for Recent College Graduates: Evidence from a Field Experiment," *B. E. Journal of Economic Analysis and Policy* 15, no. 3 (2015): 1093–125; Devah Pager, Bart Bonikowski, and Bruce Western, "Discrimination in a Low-Wage Labor Market: A Field Experiment," *American Sociological Review* 74, no. 5 (2009): 777–99; Devah Pager and Lincoln Quillian, "Walking the Talk? What Employers Say Versus What They Do," *American Sociological Review* 70, no. 3 (2005): 355–80; David S. Pedulla, "How Race and Unemployment Shape Labor Market Opportunities: Additive, Amplified, or Muted Effects?," *Social Forces* 96, no. 4 (2018): 1477–506. On racial differences in the daddy bonus, see Budig, *The Fatherhood Bonus and the Motherhood Penalty*; Hodges and Budig, "Who Gets the Daddy Bonus?"

28. On how precarity affects Black families and their relationships, see Fenaba R. Addo and Sharon Sassler, "Financial Arrangements and Relationship Quality in Low-Income Couples," *Family Relations* 59, no. 4 (2010): 408–23; Edin and Kefalas, *Promises I Can Keep*; Kathryn Edin and Timothy J. Nelson, *Doing the Best I Can: Fatherhood in the Inner City* (Princeton, NJ: Princeton University Press, 2013); Laura Sanchez and Constance T. Gager, "Hard Living, Perceived Entitlement to a Great Marriage, and Marital Dissolution," *Journal of Marriage and Family* 62, no. 3 (2000): 708–22; Daniel Schneider, Kristen Harknett, and Matthew Stimpson, "What Explains the Decline in First Marriage in the United States? Evidence from the Panel Study of Income Dynamics, 1969 to 2013," *Journal of Marriage and Family* 80, no. 4 (2018): 791–811; Deadric T. Williams and Jacob E. Cheadle, "Economic Hardship, Parents' Depression, and Relationship Distress among Couples with Young Children," *Society and Mental Health* 6, no. 2 (2016): 73–89; Deadric T. Williams, Jacob E. Cheadle, and Bridget J. Goosby, "Hard Times and Heart Break: Linking Economic Hardship and Relationship Distress," *Journal of Family Issues* 36, no. 7 (2015): 924–50; Deadric T. Williams and Regina S. Baker, "Family Structure, Risks, and Racial Stratification in Poverty," *Social Problems* 68, no. 4 (2021): 964–85.

29. On how people in poverty rely on their social networks for support, see Mazelis, *Surviving Poverty*; Small, *Villa Victoria*; Stack, *All Our Kin*. On the pressures that women face to provide that support for others, see Glenn, *Forced to Care*; Hochschild, *The Second Shift*.

CHAPTER 3: LEAVING OTHERS MORALLY TRAPPED

1. On how resources facilitate the outsourcing of caregiving labor, see Michelle Brady, "Gluing, Catching and Connecting: How Informal Childcare Strengthens Single Mothers' Employment Trajectories," *Work, Employment and Society* 30, no. 5 (2016): 821–37; Ajay Chaudry, *Putting Children First: How Low-Wage Working Mothers Manage Child Care* (New York: Russell Sage Foundation, 2004); Sarah Damaske, *For the Family?: How Class and Gender Shape Women's Work* (Oxford: Oxford University Press, 2011); Esther de Ruijter and Tanja Van der Lippe, "Effects of Job Features on Domestic Outsourcing as a Strategy for Combining Paid and Domestic Work," *Work and Occupations* 34, no. 2 (2007): 205–30; Kathleen Gerson, *Hard Choices: How Women Decide about Work, Career and Motherhood* (Berkeley: University of California Press, 1985); Sanjiv Gupta, "Her Money, Her Time: Women's Earnings and Their Housework Hours," *Social Science Research* 35, no. 4 (2006): 975–99; Alexandra

Killewald, "Opting Out and Buying Out: Wives' Earnings and Housework Time," *Journal of Marriage and Family* 73, no. 2 (2011): 459–71; Alexandra Killewald and Margaret Gough, "Money Isn't Everything: Wives' Earnings and Housework Time," *Social Science Research* 39, no. 6 (2010): 987–1003; Daniel Schneider, "Gender Deviance and Household Work: The Role of Occupation," *American Journal of Sociology* 117, no. 4 (2012): 1029–72; Casey Stockstill, *False Starts: The Segregated Lives of Preschoolers* (New York, NY: NYU Press, 2023); Pamela Stone, *Opting Out?* (Berkeley: University of California Press, 2007).

2. On women's role in the exploitation of others, see John R. Bowman and Alyson M. Cole, "Do Working Mothers Oppress Other Women? The Swedish 'Maid Debate' and the Welfare State Politics of Gender Equality," *Signs: Journal of Women in Culture and Society* 35, no. 1 (2009): 157–84; Patricia Hill Collins, "Black Women and Motherhood," in *Motherhood and Space: Configurations of the Maternal through Politics, Home, and the Body*, ed. Sarah Hardy and Caroline Wiedmer (New York: Palgrave Macmillan, 2005), 149–59; Angela Y. Davis, *Women, Race, and Class* (New York: Vintage Books, 1983); Mary Louise Fellows and Sherene Razack, "The Race to Innocence: Confronting Hierarchical Relations among Women," *Journal of Gender, Race and Justice* 1, no. 2 (1998): 335–52; Evelyn Nakano Glenn, *Forced to Care: Coercion and Caregiving in America* (Cambridge, MA: Harvard University Press, 2010); Zora Neale Hurston, *Their Eyes Were Watching God* (Philadelphia: J. B. Lippincott and Co., 1937); Jacqueline Jones, *Labor of Love, Labor of Sorrow: Black Women, Work and the Family, from Slavery to the Present* (New York: Basic Books, 2010); Katherine Kaufka, "The Commodification of Domestic Care: Illegitimacy of Care Work and the Exploitation of Migrant Workers," *Georgetown Immigration Law Journal* 18, no. 1 (2004): 159–78; Cameron Lynne Macdonald, *Shadow Mothers: Nannies, Au Pairs, and the Micropolitics of Mothering* (Berkeley: University of California Press, 2011); Amanda Moras, "'This Should Be My Responsibility': Gender, Guilt, Privilege and Paid Domestic Work," *Gender Issues* 34, no. 1 (2017): 44–66; Lynet Uttal and Mary Tuominen, "Tenuous Relationships: Exploitation, Emotion, and Racial Ethnic Significance in Paid Child Care Work," *Gender & Society* 13, no. 6 (1999): 758–80; Deborah Gray White, *Too Heavy a Load: Black Women in Defense of Themselves, 1894-1994* (New York: W. W. Norton, 1999); Tegan Zimmerman, "Revisiting Irigaray's Essay 'Women on the Market,'" *Women's Studies* 45, no. 5 (2016): 425–43. On the necessity of care, see Susan Dodds, "Dependence, Care, and Vulnerability," in *Vulnerability: New Essays in Ethics and Feminist Philosophy* by Catriona Mackenzie, Wendy Rogers, and Susan Dodds (Oxford: Oxford University Press, 2013); Susan T. Fiske, *Social Beings: Core Motives in Social Psychology* (Hoboken, NJ: Wiley, 2018); Eva Feder Kittay, "The Ethics of Care, Dependence, and Disability," *Ratio Juris* 24, no. 1 (2011): 49–58; Alasdair C. MacIntyre, *Dependent Rational Animals: Why Human Beings Need the Virtues* (Chicago: Open Court Publishing, 1999).

3. On the role of birthing parents in same-sex couple families, see Mignon R. Moore, "Gendered Power Relations among Women: A Study of Household Decision Making in Black, Lesbian Stepfamilies," *American Sociological Review* 73, no. 2 (2008): 335–56.

4. On employer discrimination against mothers of young children, particularly in high-tech fields, see Stephen Benard, In Paik, and Shelley J. Correll, "Cognitive Bias and the Motherhood Penalty," *Hastings Law Journal* 59 (2008): 1359; Mary Blair-Loy, *Competing Devotions: Career and Family among Women Executives* (Cambridge, MA: Harvard University Press, 2009); Michelle J. Budig and Paula England, "The Wage Penalty for Motherhood," *American Sociological Review* 66, no. 2 (2001): 204–25; Shelley J. Correll, Stephen Benard, and In Paik, "Getting a Job: Is There a Motherhood Penalty?," *American Journal of Sociology* 112, no. 5 (2007): 1297–339; Christine A. Henle et al., "Eldercare and Childcare: How Does Caregiving Responsibility Affect Job Discrimination?," *Journal of Business and Psychology* 35, no. 1 (2020); Joan R. Kahn, Javier García-Manglano, and Suzanne M. Bianchi, "The Motherhood Penalty at Midlife: Long-Term Effects of Children on Women's Careers," *Journal of Marriage and Family* 76, no. 1 (2014): 56–72; Lindsey Trimble O'Connor and Erin A. Cech, "Not Just a Mothers' Problem: The Consequences of Perceived Workplace Flexibility Bias for All

Workers," *Sociological Perspectives* 61, no. 5 (2018): 808–29; Natasha Quadlin, "The Mark of a Woman's Record: Gender and Academic Performance in Hiring," *American Sociological Review* 83, no. 2 (April 2018): 331–60; Sarah Thébaud and Catherine J. Taylor, "The Specter of Motherhood: Culture and the Production of Gendered Career Aspirations in Science and Engineering," *Gender & Society* 35, no. 3 (2021): 395–421.

5. On the link between childcare and women's workforce participation, see Brady, "Gluing, Catching and Connecting"; Chaudry, *Putting Children First*; Josefina Posadas and Marian Vidal-Fernandez, "Grandparents' Childcare and Female Labor Force Participation," *IZA Journal of Labor Policy* 2, no. 1 (2013): 14; Leah Ruppanner, Stephanie Moller, and Liana Sayer, "Expensive Childcare and Short School Days = Lower Maternal Employment and More Time in Childcare? Evidence from the American Time Use Survey," *Socius* 5 (2019). On how outsourcing other domestic responsibilities facilitates women's employment, see Lyn Craig and Janeen Baxter, "Domestic Outsourcing, Housework Shares and Subjective Time Pressure: Gender Differences in the Correlates of Hiring Help," *Social Indicators Research* 125, no. 1 (2016): 271–88; Pia S. Schober, "Gender Equality and Outsourcing of Domestic Work, Childbearing, and Relationship Stability among British Couples," *Journal of Family Issues* 34, no. 1 (2013): 25–52.

6. On women's complicity in the exploitation of others, see Bowman and Cole, "Do Working Mothers Oppress Other Women?"; Patricia Hill Collins, *Black Feminist Thought: Knowledge, Consciousness, and the Politics of Empowerment* (New York: Routledge, 2000); Collins, "Black Women and Motherhood"; Davis, *Women, Race, and Class*; Fellows and Razack, "The Race to Innocence"; Glenn, *Forced to Care*; Jones, *Labor of Love, Labor of Sorrow*; Macdonald, *Shadow Mothers*; Candace Howes, Carrie Leana, and Kristin Smith, "Paid Care Work," in *For Love or Money: Care Provision in the United States*, ed. Nancy Folbre (New York: Russell Sage Foundation, 2012); Kaufka, "The Commodification of Domestic Care"; Moras, "'This Should Be My Responsibility'"; Uttal and Tuominen, "Tenuous Relationships"; Zimmerman, "Revisiting Irigaray's Essay 'Women on the Market'"; Deborah Gray White, *Too Heavy a Load: Black Women in Defense of Themselves, 1894–1994* (New York: W. W. Norton and Company, 1999). On the devaluation of caregiving labor, see Paula England, "Emerging Theories of Care Work"; Paula England and Nancy Folbre, "The Cost of Caring"; Nancy Folbre, *For Love or Money: Care Provision in the United States* (New York: Russell Sage Foundation, 2012). On the demographics of the US childcare workforce, see Childcare Workers (DataUSA, 2023), https://datausa.io/profile/soc/childcare-workers#demographics. See also Ajay Chaudry et al., *Cradle to Kindergarten: A New Plan to Combat Inequality* (New York: Russell Sage Foundation, 2017); Paula England, Michelle Budig, and Nancy Folbre, "Wages of Virtue: The Relative Pay of Care Work," *Social Problems* 49, no. 4 (2002): 455–73; Elise Gould, *Childcare Workers Aren't Paid Enough to Make Ends Meet* (Washington, DC: Economic Policy Institute, 2015); Howes, Leana, and Smith, "Paid Care Work"; Simon Workman, "The True Cost of High-Quality Child Care across the United States," Center for American Progress, June 28, 2021, https://www.americanprogress.org/article/true-cost-high-quality-child-care-across-united-states/. On staffing shortages in childcare, see Daphna Bassok et al., "New Evidence on Teacher Turnover in Early Childhood," *Educational Evaluation and Policy Analysis* 43, no. 1 (2021): 172–80; Russell L. Carson et al., "Emotional Exhaustion, Absenteeism, and Turnover Intentions in Childcare Teachers: Examining the Impact of Physical Activity Behaviors," *Journal of Health Psychology* 15, no. 6 (2010): 905–1; Garret D. Evans et al., "Ethnic Differences in Burnout, Coping, and Intervention Acceptability among Childcare Professionals," *Child and Youth Care Forum* 33, no. 5 (2004): 349–71. On childcare worker compensation, see "Childcare Workers," *Occupational Outlook Handbook* (Washington, DC: US Bureau of Labor Statistics, 2023), https://www.bls.gov/ooh/personal-care-and-service/childcare-workers.htm. See also *Characteristics of the US Childcare Workforce* (Washington, DC: Bipartisan Policy Center, 2021), https://bipartisanpolicy.org/download/?file=/wp-content/uploads/2021/05/C.-8-Characteristics-of-the-Child-Care-Workforce.pdf.

7. On the financial challenges faced by the childcare industry, see Elliot Haspel, *Crawling Behind: America's Child Care Crisis and How to Fix It* (Castroville, TX: Black Rose Writing, 2019).

8. On the incompatibility of care work with profit expectations, see Susan Donath, "The Other Economy: A Suggestion for a Distinctively Feminist Economics," *Feminist Economics* 6, no. 1 (2000): 115–23; Paula England, "The Failure of Human Capital Theory to Explain Occupational Sex Segregation," *Journal of Human Resources* 17, no. 3 (1982): 358–70; England et al., "Wages of Virtue"; England and Folbre, "The Cost of Caring"; Howes, Leana, and Smith, "Paid Care Work"; Ai-jen Poo, *The Age of Dignity* (New York: Tantor and Blackstone, 2021).

9. On how other countries solve the problem of childcare, see Donath, "The Other Economy." On childcare salaries in Norway, see "Child Care Worker Average Salary in Norway 2023," Salary Explorer, http://www.salaryexplorer.com/salary-survey.php?loc=162&loctype=1&job =699&jobtype=3. On childcare salaries in the US, see "Childcare Workers," US Bureau of Labor Statistics, https://www.bls.gov/ooh/personal-care-and-service/childcare-workers.htm.

10. On the exploitation of workers in low-profit industries, see Elizabeth L. Cline, *Overdressed: The Shockingly High Cost of Cheap Fashion* (New York: Portfolio, 2013); Jayne Dean, "Sex-Segregated Employment, Wage Inequality and Labor-Intensive Production: A Study of 33 U.S. Manufacturing Industries," *Review of Radical Political Economics* 23, no. 3–4 (1991): 244–68; Glenn, *Forced to Care*; Rick Helfenbein, "Apparel Jobs Are Still Available in Federal Prison—Is That What We Want?," *Forbes*, April 20, 2020, https://www.forbes.com/sites /rickhelfenbein/2020/04/20/troubled-economy-apparel-jobs-are-still-available-in-federal -prisonis-that-what-we-want/; Arne L. Kalleberg, *Good Jobs, Bad Jobs: The Rise of Polarized and Precarious Employment Systems in the United States 1970s to 2000s* (New York: Russell Sage Foundation, 2013). On how the US limits eligibility for social safety net programs, see Tricia Brooks et al., "Medicaid and CHIP Eligibility and Enrollment Policies as of January 2022: Findings from a 50-State Survey—Report," *KFF* (blog), March 16, 2022, https://www.kff .org/report-section/medicaid-and-chip-eligibility-and-enrollment-policies-as-of-january -2022-findings-from-a-50-state-survey-report/; Matthew Desmond, *Poverty, by America* (New York: Crown, 2023); Jacob S. Hacker, *The Divided Welfare State: The Battle over Public and Private Social Benefits in the United States* (Cambridge: Cambridge University Press, 2002); Jacob S. Hacker, *The Great Risk Shift: The New Economic Insecurity and the Decline of the American Dream* (Oxford: Oxford University Press, 2019); Joan Maya Mazelis, *Surviving Poverty* (New York: NYU Press, 2016). On how the US limits access to support from social safety net programs and stigmatizes their use, see Pamela Herd and Donald P. Moynihan, *Administrative Burden: Policymaking by Other Means* (New York: Russell Sage Foundation, 2019). On work requirements for poverty programs, see Kathryn Edin and Laura Lein, *Making Ends Meet: How Single Mothers Survive Welfare and Low-Wage Work* (New York: Russell Sage Foundation, 1997); Sharon Hays, *Flat Broke with Children: Women in the Age of Welfare Reform* (Oxford: Oxford University Press, 2004); Allison J. Pugh, *The Tumbleweed Society: Working and Caring in an Age of Insecurity* (Oxford: Oxford University Press, 2015). On work experience placements or "workfare," see Jana Blahak et al., *WorkFirst New Jersey's Community Work Experience Program: A Report to the New Jersey Department of Labor and Workforce Development* (New Brunswick, NJ: Rutgers University, 2018), https://bloustein.rutgers.edu/wp-content /uploads/2018/05/2018-WorkFirst-NJ.pdf; Michelle K. Derr, *Providing Unpaid Work Experience Opportunities for TANF Recipients: Examples from Erie County, New York; Montana; and Hamilton County, Ohio* (Washington, DC: US Department of Health and Human Services, 2008), https://aspe.hhs.gov/sites/default/files/migrated_legacy_files//42971/report.pdf; Harry J. Holzer, *Can Work Experience Programs Work for Welfare Recipients?* (Washington, DC: Brookings, 2002), https://www.brookings.edu/articles/can-work-experience-programs-work-for-welfare -recipients/; Sharon Parrott, et al., "Improving Welfare-to-Work Programs and Increasing Engagement," chapter II in *Implementing the TANF Changes in the Deficit Reduction Act: 'Win-win' Solutions for Families and States* (Washington, DC: Center on Budget and Policy Priori-

ties, 2007), https://www.cbpp.org/sites/default/files/archive/5-9-06tanf-sum.pdf; Irma Perez-Johnson et al., *Understanding the Costs of the DOL Welfare-to-Work Grants Program* (Washington, DC: US Department of Health and Human Services, 2002), https://aspe.hhs.gov/reports/understanding-costs-dol-welfare-work-grants-program-1. See also Krissy Clark, "The Welfare to Temp Work Pipeline" April 26, 2023, in *The Uncertain Hour*, podcast, https://www.marketplace.org/shows/the-uncertain-hour/.

11. On gender disparities in childcare responsibilities, see Allison Daminger, "The Cognitive Dimension of Household Labor," *American Sociological Review* 84, no. 4 (2019): 609–33; Liana C. Sayer, "More Work for Mothers? Trends and Gender Differences in Multitasking," in *Time Competition: Disturbed Balances and New Options in Work and Care*, ed. Tanja van der Lippe and Pascale Peters (Cheltenham: Edward Elgar, 2007), 41–56; Liana C. Sayer, "Trends in Women's and Men's Time Use, 1965–2012: Back to the Future?," in *Gender and Couple Relationships*, ed. Susan M. McHale et al. (New York: Springer, 2016), 43–77; Jill E. Yavorsky, Claire M. Kamp Dush, and Sarah J. Schoppe-Sullivan, "The Production of Inequality: The Gender Division of Labor across the Transition to Parenthood," *Journal of Marriage and Family* 77, no. 3 (2015): 662–79; Gema Zamarro and María J. Prados, "Gender Differences in Couples' Division of Childcare, Work and Mental Health during COVID-19," *Review of Economics of the Household* 19, no. 1 (2021): 11–40. On the devaluation of women's labor, see England, "Emerging Theories of Care Work"; England and Folbre, "The Cost of Caring"; Folbre, *For Love or Money*. On the necessity of childcare for employed mothers, see Charles L. Baum, "A Dynamic Analysis of the Effect of Child Care Costs on the Work Decisions of Low-Income Mothers with Infants," *Demography* 39, no. 1 (2002): 139–64; Brady, "Gluing, Catching and Connecting"; Wenjui Han and Jane Waldfogel, "Child Care Costs and Women's Employment: A Comparison of Single and Married Mothers with Pre-School-Aged Children," *Social Science Quarterly* 82, no. 3 (2001): 552–68; Jennifer Graves, "School Calendars, Child Care Availability and Maternal Employment," *Journal of Urban Economics* 78 (2013): 57–70; Hejun Gu, Fengqin Bian, and Ehsan Elahi, "Impact of Availability of Grandparents' Care on Birth in Working Women: An Empirical Analysis Based on Data of Chinese Dynamic Labour Force," *Children and Youth Services Review* 121 (2021); Julie E. Press, Jay Fagan, and Lynda Laughlin, "Taking Pressure Off Families: Child-Care Subsidies Lessen Mothers' Work-Hour Problems," *Journal of Marriage and Family* 68, no. 1 (2006): 155–71; Ruppanner, Moller, and Sayer, "Expensive Childcare and Short School Days." On employed mothers' reliance on the childcare labor of underpaid (often Black, Latina, or immigrant) women, see Bowman and Cole, "Do Working Mothers Oppress Other Women?"; Collins, *Black Feminist Thought*; Collins, "Black Women and Motherhood"; Davis, *Women, Race, and Class*; Fellows and Razack, "The Race to Innocence"; Glenn, *Forced to Care*; Jones, *Labor of Love, Labor of Sorrow*; Macdonald, *Shadow Mothers*; Howes et al. "Paid Care Work"; Kaufka, "The Commodification of Domestic Care"; Moras, "This Should Be My Responsibility"; Uttal and Tuominen, "Tenuous Relationhips"; White, *Too Heavy a Load*; Zimmerman, "Revisiting Irigaray's Essay 'Women on the Market.'" On the role of extended family in childcare, see Karin L. Brewster and Irene Padavic, "No More Kin Care? Change in Black Mothers' Reliance on Relatives for Child Care, 1977–94," *Gender & Society* 16, no. 4 (2002): 546–63; Chaudry, *Putting Children First*; Gu, Bian, and Elahi, "Impact of Availability of Grandparents' Care"; Shireen Kanji, "Grandparent Care: A Key Factor in Mothers' Labour Force Participation in the UK," *Journal of Social Policy* 47, no. 3 (2018): 523–42; Eunju Lee, Michael Clarkson-Hendrix, and Yeonggeul Lee, "Parenting Stress of Grandparents and Other Kin as Informal Kinship Caregivers: A Mixed Methods Study," *Children and Youth Services Review* 69 (2016): 29–38; Eunsil Oh, "Who Deserves to Work? How Women Develop Expectations of Child Care Support in Korea," *Gender & Society* 32, no. 4 (2018): 493–515; Posadas and Vidal-Fernandez, "Grandparents' Childcare and Female Labor Force Participation"; Lynet Uttal, "Using Kin for Child Care: Embedment in the Socioeconomic Networks of Extended Families," *Journal of Marriage and Family* 61, no. 4 (1999): 845–57. On childcare costs, see Workman, "The True Cost of High-Quality Child Care across

the United States." On how a lack of affordable childcare affects women's careers, see Heather Boushey, "The Role of the Government in Work–Family Conflict in the US," *Handbook of Research on Gender and Economic Life* (2013): 307–22; Karen Fox Folk and Andrea H. Beller, "Part-Time Work and Child Care Choices for Mothers of Preschool Children," *Journal of Marriage and Family* 55, no. 1 (1993): 146–57; Alice Fothergill, "Managing Childcare: The Experiences of Mothers and Childcare Workers," *Sociological Inquiry* 83, no. 3 (2013): 421–47; Jacob Alex Klerman and Arleen Leibowitz, "Child Care and Women's Return to Work after Childbirth," *American Economic Review* 80, no. 2 (1990): 284–88; Ruppanner, Moller, and Sayer, "Expensive Childcare and Short School Days"; Margaret L. Usdansky and Douglas A. Wolf, "When Child Care Breaks Down: Mothers' Experiences with Child Care Problems and Resulting Missed Work," *Journal of Family Issues* 29, no. 9 (2008): 1185–210; Joan Williams and Heather Boushey, "The Three Faces of Work-Family Conflict: The Poor, the Professionals, and the Missing Middle," *SSRN Electronic Journal*, January 21, 2010. On how mothers become the default parent, see Calarco et al., "By Default"; Javier García-Manglano, "Opting Out and Leaning In: The Life Course Employment Profiles of Early Baby Boom Women in the United States," *Demography* 52, no. 6 (October 21, 2015): 1961–93; Stone, *Opting Out?*

12. On how precarity reduces women's employment choices and pushes women into the motherhood trap, see Edin and Lein, *Making Ends Meet*; Kathryn Edin and Maria J. Kefalas, *Promises I Can Keep: Why Poor Women Put Motherhood Before Marriage* (Berkeley: University of California Press, 2011); Barbara Ehrenreich, *Nickel and Dimed: On (Not) Getting By in America* (New York: Metropolitan Books, 2001); Mazelis, *Surviving Poverty*; Gretchen Webber and Christine Williams, "Mothers in 'Good' and 'Bad' Part-time Jobs: Different Problems, Same Results," *Gender & Society* 22, no. 6 (2008): 752–77. On the types of low-income and caregiving jobs disproportionately held by women, see Damaske, *For the Family?*; Lonnie Golden, "Still Falling Short on Hours and Pay: Part-Time Work Becoming New Normal," *Economic Policy Institute* (blog), December 5, 2016, https://www.epi.org/publication/still-falling -short-on-hours-and-pay-part-time-work-becoming-new-normal/. On the composition of the childcare workforce, see "Childcare Workers," Data USA, https://datausa.io/profile/soc/childcare -workers#ethnicity. On the composition of the house cleaning workforce, see "Maids and Housekeeping Cleaners," Data USA, https://datausa.io/profile/soc/maids-housekeeping-cleaners #demographics. On the composition of the home health workforce, see "Home Health Aides," Data USA, https://datausa.io/profile/soc/home-health-aides#ethnicity.

13. On opportunity hoarding, see Charles Tilly, *Durable Inequality* (Berkeley: University of California Press, 1999). See also Jessica McCrory Calarco, *Negotiating Opportunities: How the Middle Class Secures Advantages in School* (New York: Oxford University Press, 2018); L'Heureux Lewis McCoy, *Inequality in the Promised Land: Race, Resources, and Suburban Schooling* (Palo Alto, CA: Stanford University Press, 2014).

14. On how precarity makes it easier to accept complicity in exploitation or marginalization, see Arlie Russell Hochschild, *Strangers in Their Own Land: Anger and Mourning on the American Right* (New York: The New Press, 2016); Jonathan J. B. Mijs, "The Paradox of Inequality: Income Inequality and Belief in Meritocracy Go Hand in Hand," *Socio-Economic Review* 19, no. 1 (2019): 7–35; Moras, "This Should Be My Responsibility"; Frederick Solt et al., "Economic Inequality and Belief in Meritocracy in the United States," *Research & Politics* 3, no. 4 (2016). On the precarity of food service and grocery workers, see Hannah Miao, "Walmart and McDonald's Are among Top Employers of Medicaid and Food Stamp Beneficiaries, Report Says," CNBC, November 19, 2020, https://www.cnbc.com/2020/11/19/walmart-and -mcdonalds-among-top-employers-of-medicaid-and-food-stamp-beneficiaries.html. On the relationship between privilege and exploitation, see Bowman and Cole, "Do Working Mothers Oppress Other Women?"; Collins, *Black Feminist Thought*; Collins, "Black Women in Motherhood"; Davis, *Women, Race, and Class*; Fellows and Razack, "The Race to Innocence"; Glenn, *Forced to Care*; Macdonald, *Shadow Mothers*; Moras, "'This Should Be My Responsibility'"; Uttal and Tuominen, "Tenuous Relationships."

15. On the types of situations where women are not the ones disproportionately responsible for housework and caregiving, see Daniel L. Carlson, Richard J. Petts, and Joanna R. Pepin, "Flexplace Work and Partnered Fathers' Time in Housework and Childcare," *Men and Masculinities* 24, no. 4 (2021): 547–70; Sara Raley, Suzanne M. Bianchi, and Wendy Wang, "When Do Fathers Care? Mothers' Economic Contribution and Fathers' Involvement in Child Care," *American Journal of Sociology* 117, no. 5 (2012): 1422–459. On the extreme level of outsourcing available to high-income families, see Lisa A. Keister, Sarah Thébaud, and Jill E. Yavorky, "Gender in the Elite," *Annual Review of Sociology* 48 (2022): 149–69; MacDonald, *Shadow Mothers*; Thorstein Veblen, *The Theory of the Leisure Class* (New York: Macmillan, 1899).

16. On the growing numbers of educationally and occupationally hypergamous couples, see Albert Esteve et al., "The End of Hypergamy: Global Trends and Implications," *Population and Development Review* 42, no. 4 (December 2016): 615–25; Robert Drago, David Black, and Mark Wooden, "Female Breadwinner Families: Their Existence, Persistence and Sources," *Journal of Sociology* 41, no. 4 (2005): 343–62; Pilar Gonalons-Pons and Christine R. Schwartz, "Trends in Economic Homogamy: Changes in Assortative Mating or the Division of Labor in Marriage?," *Demography* 54, no. 3 (2017): 985–1005; Wendy Wang, Kim Parker, and Paul Taylor, *Breadwinner Moms* (Washington, DC: Pew Research Center, 2013), https://www.pewresearch.org/social-trends/2013/05/29/breadwinner-moms/.

17. On gender differences in workplace flexibility: Constanze Leineweber, Helena Falkenberg, and Sophie C. Albrecht, "Parent's Relative Perceived Work Flexibility Compared to Their Partner Is Associated with Emotional Exhaustion," *Frontiers in Psychology* 9 (2018); Rachel Rinaldo and Ian Michael Whalen, "Amplifying Inequalities: Gendered Perceptions," *Gender, Work & Organizations* 30, no. 6 (2023): 1922–1940. On the costs and benefits of workplace flexibility: Sylvia Fuller and C. Elizabeth Hirsh, "'Family-Friendly' Jobs and Motherhood Pay Penalties: The Impact of Flexible Work Arrangements Across the Educational Spectrum," *Work and Occupations* 46, no. 1 (2019): 3–44; O'Connor and Cech, "Not Just a Mothers' Problem"; Christin L. Munsch, "Flexible Work, Flexible Penalties: The Effect of Gender, Childcare, and Type of Request on the Flexibility Bias," *Social Forces* 94, no. 4 (2016): 1567–91; Sarah Thébaud and David Pedulla, "When Do Work-Family Policies Work? Unpacking the Effects of Stigma and Financial Costs for Men and Women," *Work and Occupations* 49, no. 2 (2022): 229–63; Kim A. Weeden, "Is There a Flexiglass Ceiling? Flexible Work Arrangements and Wages in the United States," *Social Science Research* 34, no. 2 (2005): 454–82. On differences in hourly pay between full-time and part-time work: Fuller and Hirsh, "'Family-Friendly' Jobs and Motherhood Pay Penalties"; Kathrin Leuze and Susanne Strauß, "Why Do Occupations Dominated by Women Pay Less? How 'Female-Typical' Work Tasks and Working-Time Arrangements Affect the Gender Wage Gap among Higher Education Graduates," *Work, Employment and Society* 30, no. 5 (2016): 802–20; Clare Lyonette, Gayle Kaufman, and Rosemary Crompton, "'We Both Need to Work': Maternal Employment, Childcare and Health Care in Britain and the USA," *Work, Employment and Society* 25, no. 1 (2011): 34–50; Webber and Williams, "Mothers in 'Good' and 'Bad' Part-Time Jobs"; Weeden, "Is There a Flexiglass Ceiling?" On the challenges of returning to full-time work, see Damaske, *For the Family?*; Meg Lovejoy and Pamela Stone, "Opting Back In: The Influence of Time at Home on Professional Women's Career Redirection after Opting Out," *Gender, Work & Organization* 19, no. 6 (2012): 631–53; Pamela Stone and Meg Lovejoy, *Opting Back In: What Really Happens When Mothers Go Back to Work* (Berkeley: University of California Press, 2021); Stone, *Opting Out?*

18. On the lack of employment benefits for childcare workers, see Elise Gould, "The Erosion of Employer-Sponsored Health Insurance: Declines Continue for the Seventh Year Running," *International Journal of Health Services: Planning, Administration, Evaluation* 39, no. 4 (2009): 669–97; Gould, *Childcare Workers Aren't Paid Enough to Make Ends Meet.* On how families

manage when normal care arrangements fall through, see Fothergill, "Managing Childcare"; Usdansky and Wolf, "When Child Care Breaks Down."

19. On discrepancies between men's and women's accounts of the division of household labor, see Emily Christopher, "Capturing Conflicting Accounts of Domestic Labour: The Household Portrait as a Methodology," *Sociological Research Online*, September 2, 2020; Claudia Geist, "Men's and Women's Reports about Housework," in *Dividing the Domestic: Men, Women, and Household Work in Cross-National Perspective* by Judith Treas and Sonja Drobnič (Redwood City, CA: Stanford University Press, 2010); Yoshinori Kamo, "'He Said, She Said': Assessing Discrepancies in Husbands' and Wives' Reports on the Division of Household Labor," *Social Science Research* 29, no. 4 (2000): 459–76.

20. On fathers and nonbinary parents who serve as primary caregivers for their children, see Timothy Black and Sky Keyes, *It's a Setup: Fathering from the Social and Economic Margins* (Oxford: Oxford University Press, 2020); Noelle Chesley, "Stay-at-Home Fathers and Bread-winning Mothers: Gender, Couple Dynamics, and Social Change," *Gender & Society* 25, no. 5 (2011): 642–64; Marianne Cooper, "Being the 'Go-To Guy': Fatherhood, Masculinity, and the Organization of Work in Silicon Valley," *Qualitative Sociology* 23, no. 4 (December 2000): 379–405; Lyn Craig and Killian Mullan, "How Mothers and Fathers Share Childcare: A Cross-National Time-Use Comparison," *American Sociological Review* 76, no. 6 (2011): 834–61; Jennifer L. Hook and Satvika Chalasani, "Gendered Expectations? Reconsidering Single Fathers' Child-Care Time," *Journal of Marriage and Family* 70, no. 4 (2008): 978–90; Karen Z. Kramer and Amit Kramer, "At-Home Father Families in the United States: Gender Ideology, Human Capital, and Unemployment," *Journal of Marriage and Family* 78, no. 5 (2016): 1315–331; Raley et al., "When Do Fathers Care?"; Jennifer Randles, "The Means to and Meaning of 'Being There' in Responsible Fatherhood Programming with Low-Income Fathers," *Family Relations* 69, no. 1 (2020): 7–20; Aliya Hamid Rao, *Crunch Time: How Married Couples Confront Unemployment* (Berkeley: University of California Press, 2020). On the costs that men and nonbinary parents face when doing a disproportionate share of the caregiving, see Andrea Doucet, "Is the Stay-at-Home Dad (SAHD) a Feminist Concept? A Genealogical, Relational, and Feminist Critique," *Sex Roles* 75, no. 1 (2016): 4–14; Marianne G. Dunn, Aaron B. Rochlen, and Karen M. O'Brien, "Employee, Mother, and Partner: An Exploratory Investigation of Working Women with Stay-at-Home Fathers," *Journal of Career Development* 40, no. 1 (2013): 3–22; Munsch, "Flexible Work, Flexible Penalties"; Lamar Pierce, Michael S. Dahl, and Jimmi Nielsen, "In Sickness and in Wealth: Psychological and Sexual Costs of Income Comparison in Marriage," *Personality and Social Psychology Bulletin* 39, no. 3 (2013): 359–74; Kristen W. Springer, "Economic Dependence in Marriage and Husbands' Midlife Health: Testing Three Possible Mechanisms," *Gender & Society* 24, no. 3 (2010): 378–401; Joanna Syrda, "Spousal Relative Income and Male Psychological Distress," *Personality and Social Psychology Bulletin* 46, no. 6 (2020): 976–92.

21. On the prevalence of stay-at-home fathers, see Gretchen Livingston, "About 1 in 5 U.S. Moms and Dads Are Stay-at-Home Parents," Pew Research Center, September 9, 2018, https://www.pewresearch.org/fact-tank/2018/09/24/stay-at-home-moms-and-dads-account-for-about-one-in-five-u-s-parents/.

22. On couples' decisions to outsource caregiving labor, see Gupta, "Her Money, Her Time"; Killewald, "Opting Out and Buying Out"; Killewald and Gough, "Money Isn't Everything"; Schneider, "Gender Deviance and Household Work."

23. On how breadwinner moms take on more childcare and housework to compensate for their nontraditional gender roles, see Killewald and Gough, "Money Isn't Everything"; Christin L. Munsch, "Her Support, His Support: Money, Masculinity, and Marital Infidelity," *American Sociological Review* 80, no. 3 (2015): 469–95; Aundrea Snitker, "Not Mr. Mom: Navigating Discourses for Stay-at-Home Fathers," *The Journal of Men's Studies* 26, no. 2 (2018): 203–21. Springer, "Economic Dependence in Marriage and Husbands' Midlife Health."

24. On the division of labor in transgender families, see Carla A. Pfeffer, "'Women's Work'? Women Partners of Transgender Men Doing Housework and Emotion Work," *Journal of Marriage and Family* 72, no. 1 (2010): 165–83.

25. On the benefits of stay-at-home partners for mothers, see Doucet, "Is the Stay-At-Home Dad (SAHD) a Feminist Concept?"; Dunn, Rochlen, and O'Brien, "Employee, Mother, and Partner"; Arlie Russell Hochschild, *The Second Shift: Working Families and the Revolution at Home* (New York: Penguin, 1989); Melissa A. Milkie and Kathleen E. Denny, "Changes in the Cultural Model of Father Involvement: Descriptions of Benefits to Fathers, Children, and Mothers in Parents' Magazine, 1926–2006," *Journal of Family Issues* 35, no. 2 (2014): 223–53. On gender differences in pay between breadwinner mothers and breadwinner fathers, see Morgan Smith, "Women Are Now Out-Earning or Making the Same as Their Husbands in Nearly Half of Marriages," CNBC, April 20, 2023, https://www.cnbc.com/2023/04/20/more-women-are-out-earning-their-husbands-in-the-us.html. On how women do an outsized share of the domestic labor, even when they are the primary breadwinner, see Sarah Damaske, Jenifer L. Bratter, and Adrianne Frech, "Single Mother Families and Employment, Race, and Poverty in Changing Economic Times," *Social Science Research* 62 (2017): 120–33; Gupta, "Her Money, Her Time"; Killewald and Gough, "Money Isn't Everything"; Killewald, "Opting Out and Buying Out"; Schneider, "Gender Deviance and Household Work"; Margaret L. Usdansky and Wendy M. Parker, "How Money Matters: College, Motherhood, Earnings, and Wives' Housework," *Journal of Family Issues* 32, no. 11 (2011): 1449–473.

26. On women's attentiveness to their partners' emotional needs, see Aliya Hamid Rao, "Stand by Your Man: Wives' Emotion Work During Men's Unemployment," *Journal of Marriage and Family* 79, no. 3 (2017): 636–56.

27. On fathers' role in parenting during the Covid-19 pandemic, see Erik Brynjolfsson et al., "COVID-19 and Remote Work: An Early Look at US Data" (working paper, National Bureau of Economic Research, 2020); Daniel L. Carlson, Richard J. Petts, and Joanna R. Pepin, "Changes in US Parents' Domestic Labor during the Early Days of the COVID-19 Pandemic," *Sociological Inquiry* 92, no. 3 (2022): 1217–44; Allison Dunatchik et al., "Gender, Parenting, and the Rise of Remote Work during the Pandemic: Implications for Domestic Inequality in the United States," *Gender & Society* 35, no. 2 (2021): 194–205; Thomas Lyttelton, Emma Zang, and Kelly Musick, "Gender Differences in Telecommuting and Implications for Inequality at Home and Work," *SSRN Electronic Journal*, July 17, 2020).

28. On the gendered structure of our economy, see Youngjoo Cha, "Overwork and the Persistence of Gender Segregation in Occupations," *Gender & Society* 27, no. 2 (2013): 158–84; Paula England, "The Gender Revolution: Uneven and Stalled," *Gender & Society* 24, no. 2 (2010): 149–66; Ariane Hegewisch et al., *Separate and Not Equal? Gender Segregation in the Labor Market and the Gender Wage Gap* (Washington, DC: Institute for Women's Policy Research, 2010); Trond Petersen and Laurie A. Morgan, "Separate and Unequal: Occupation-Establishment Sex Segregation and the Gender Wage Gap," *American Journal of Sociology* 101, no. 2 (1995): 329–65. On gendered pressures to prioritize paid work, see Krista M. Brumley, "The Gendered Ideal Worker Narrative: Professional Women's and Men's Work Experiences in the New Economy at a Mexican Company," *Gender & Society* 28, no. 6 (2014): 799–823; Tracy L. Dumas and Jeffrey Sanchez-Burks, "The Professional, the Personal, and the Ideal Worker: Pressures and Objectives Shaping the Boundary between Life Domains," *Academy of Management Annals* 9, no. 1 (2015): 803–43; Erin L. Kelly et al., "Gendered Challenge, Gendered Response: Confronting the Ideal Worker Norm in a White-Collar Organization," *Gender & Society* 24, no. 3 (2010): 281–303; Yvonne Lott and Anja-Kristin Abendroth, "The Non-Use of Telework in an Ideal Worker Culture: Why Women Perceive More Cultural Barriers," *Community, Work & Family* 23, no. 5 (October 19, 2020): 593–611. On gender differences in socialization, see Yasemin Besen-Cassino, *The Cost of Being a Girl: Working Teens and the Origins of the Gender Wage Gap* (Philadelphia: Temple University Press, 2017); Ann C. Crouter, Beth A. Manke, and Susan M. McHale, "The Family Context of Gender Intensification in

Early Adolescence," *Child Development* 66, no. 2 (1995): 317–29; Giulia Maria Dotti Sani, "Undoing Gender in Housework? Participation in Domestic Chores by Italian Fathers and Children of Different Ages," *Sex Roles* 74, no. 9–10 (May 2016): 411–21; Patricia L. East, Thomas S. Weisner, and Ashley Slonim, "Youths' Caretaking of Their Adolescent Sisters' Children: Results from Two Longitudinal Studies," *Journal of Family Issues* 30, no. 12 (2009): 1671–697; Constance T. Gager, Teresa M. Cooney, and Kathleen Thiede Call, "The Effects of Family Characteristics and Time Use on Teenagers' Household Labor," *Journal of Marriage and Family* 61, no. 4 (1999): 982–94; Heidi M. Gansen, "Push-Ups versus Clean-Up: Preschool Teachers' Gendered Beliefs, Expectations for Behavior, and Disciplinary Practices," *Sex Roles* 80 (2018): 393–408; Tracey Idle, Eileen Wood, and Serge Desmarais, "Gender Role Socialization in Toy Play Situations: Mothers and Fathers with Their Sons and Daughters," *Sex Roles* 28, no. 11–12 (1993): 679–91; Karin A. Martin, "William Wants a Doll, Can He Have One? Feminists, Child Care Advisors, and Gender Neutral Child Rearing," *Gender & Society* 19, no. 4 (2005): 456–79; Jocelyn Wikle, "Patterns in Housework and Childcare among Girls and Boys," *Journal of Research on Women and Gender* 5, no. 1, (2014): 17–29; Jocelyn S. Wikle, Alexander C. Jensen, and Alexander M. Hoagland, "Adolescent Caretaking of Younger Siblings," *Social Science Research* 71 (2018): 72–84.

29. On the gaslighting tactics that men use against women, see Paige Sweet, *The Politics of Surviving: How Women Navigate Domestic Violence and Its Aftermath* (Berkeley: University of California Press, 2021); Angela E. Waldrop and Patricia A. Resick, "Coping among Adult Female Victims of Domestic Violence," Journal of Family Violence 19, no. 5 (2004): 291–302.

30. On the benefits of divorce for women, see Kyle J. Bourassa, David A. Sbarra, and Mark A. Whisman, "Women in Very Low Quality Marriages Gain Life Satisfaction Following Divorce," *Journal of Family Psychology* 29, no. 3 (2015): 490–99. On differences in married and unmarried women's time use, see Joanna R. Pepin, Liana C. Sayer, and Lynne M. Casper, "Marital Status and Mothers' Time Use: Childcare, Housework, Leisure, and Sleep," *Demography* 55, no. 1 (2018): 107–33.

31. On the financial risk of divorce, see Dimitri Mortelmans, "Economic Consequences of Divorce: A Review," in *Parental Life Courses after Separation and Divorce in Europe*, ed. Michaela Kreyenfeld and Heike Trappe, vol. 12 (Cham, Switzerland: Springer International Publishing, 2020).

32. On the risk faced even by those with higher incomes, see Hacker, *The Great Risk Shift*; Heather McGhee, *The Sum of Us: What Racism Costs Everyone and How We Can Prosper Together* (New York: One World, 2021).

CHAPTER 4: GOOD CHOICES WON'T SAVE US

1. On "good choices" rhetoric, see Brian Alexander, "What Is the 'Success Sequence' and Why Do So Many Conservatives Like It?," *Atlantic*, July 31, 2018, https://www.theatlantic.com/family/archive/2018/07/get-out-of-poverty-success-sequence/566414/; Matt Bruenig, "The 'Success Sequence' Is about Cultural Beefs Not Poverty," *Naked Capitalism* (blog), August 2, 2017, https://www.nakedcapitalism.com/2017/08/matt-bruenig-success-sequence-cultural-beefs-not-poverty.html; Brian Goesling, Hande Inanc, and Angela Rachidi, *Success Sequence: A Synthesis of the Literature* (Washington, DC: Office of Planning, Research, and Evaluation, 2020).

2. On the origins of neoliberal think tanks and their role in gaslighting American society, see Naomi Oreskes and Erik M. Conway, *The Big Myth: How American Business Taught Us to Loathe Government and Love the Free Market* (New York: Bloomsbury, 2023). On the success sequence and its purported link to later life poverty, see Bradford W. Wilcox and Wendy Wang, *The Power of the Success Sequence* (Washington, DC: American Enterprise Institute, 2022), https://www.aei.org/research-products/report/the-power-of-the-success-sequence/. See also Ron Haskins and Isabel V. Sawhill, *Creating an Opportunity Society* (Washington, DC: Brookings, 2009). As evidence of public attention to the success sequence, see David Leonhardt,

"Marriage, Baby Carriage and Poverty," *New York Times*, June 28, 2017, https://www.nytimes.com/2017/06/28/opinion/millenials-marriage-children-poverty.html; George F. Will, "Listen up, Millennials. There's Sequence to Success," *Washington Post*, July 5, 2017, https://www.washingtonpost.com/opinions/listen-up-millenials-theres-sequence-to-success/2017/07/05/.

3. On how success sequence research shows only correlation and not causation, see Goesling, Inanc, and Rachidi, *Success Sequence*; Richard V. Reeves, Edward Rodrigue, and Alex Gold, "Following the Success Sequence? Success Is More Likely if You're White," Brookings, August 6, 2015, https://www.brookings.edu/research/following-the-success-sequence-success-is-more-likely-if-youre-white/. On why the federal poverty line is not an effective measure of success, see Areeba Haider and Justin Schweitzer, "The Poverty Line Matters, but It Isn't Capturing Everyone It Should," Center for American Progress, March 5, 2020, https://www.americanprogress.org/article/poverty-line-matters-isnt-capturing-everyone/; Celine-Marie Pascale, "Why the Federal Poverty Line Doesn't Begin to Tell the Story of Poverty in the U.S.," *Los Angeles Times*, September 24, 2021, https://www.latimes.com/opinion/story/2021-09-24/federal-poverty-level-us-families.

4. On perceptions of marriage as the key to success, see Kathryn Edin and Maria J. Kefalas, *Promises I Can Keep: Why Poor Women Put Motherhood Before Marriage* (Berkeley: University of California Press, 2011); Amanda Gelman et al., "Abortion Stigma among Low-Income Women Obtaining Abortions in Western Pennsylvania: A Qualitative Assessment," *Perspectives on Sexual and Reproductive Health* 49, no. 1 (2017): 29–36; Whitney Smith et al., "Social Norms and Stigma Regarding Unintended Pregnancy and Pregnancy Decisions: A Qualitative Study of Young Women in Alabama," *Perspectives on Sexual and Reproductive Health* 48, no. 2 (2016): 73–81; Abigail Weitzman et al., "Desire for and to Avoid Pregnancy during the Transition to Adulthood," *Journal of Marriage and Family* 79, no. 4 (2017): 1060–75.

5. On the profitability of small businesses in the US, see "Survival of Private Sector Establishments by Opening Year," US Bureau of Labor Statistics, https://www.bls.gov/bdm/us_age_naics_00_table7.txt. On the income of small business owners in the US, see "Small-Business Options: Occupational Outlook for Self-Employed Workers," US Bureau of Labor Statistics, May 2018, https://www.bls.gov/careeroutlook/2018/article/self-employment.htm.

6. On the stipulations regarding child support and TANF in Indiana, see "TANF Benefits and Child Support," Indiana Department of Child Services, https://www.in.gov/dcs/child-support/custodial-party-information/tanf-benefits-and-child-support/. On child support pass-through programs in other states, see "Child Support Pass-Through and Disregard Policies for Public Assistance Recipients," National Conference of State Legislatures, 2023, https://www.ncsl.org/human-services/child-support-pass-through-and-disregard-policies-for-public-assistance-recipients.

7. On crisis pregnancy centers, see Amy G. Bryant and Jonas J. Swartz, "Why Crisis Pregnancy Centers Are Legal but Unethical," *AMA Journal of Ethics* 20, no. 3 (2018): 269–77; Katrina Kimport, J. Parker Dockray, and Shelly Dodson, "What Women Seek from a Pregnancy Resource Center," *Contraception* 94, no. 2 (2016): 168–72.

8. On the eligibility rules for unemployment, see "Indiana Unemployment Insurance," Benefits.gov, https://www.benefits.gov/benefit/1707.

9. On how white evangelical Christian churches view birth control, see Melissa J. Wilde and Sabrina Danielsen, "Fewer and Better Children: Race, Class, Religion, and Birth Control Reform in America," *American Journal of Sociology* 119, no. 6 (2014): 1710–60; Melissa J. Wilde, *Birth Control Battles: How Race and Class Divided American Religion* (Berkeley: University of California Press, 2019).

10. On rising rates of single motherhood and how policymakers used them as justification for welfare reform, see Kathryn Edin and Laura Lein, *Making Ends Meet: How Single Mothers Survive Welfare and Low-Wage Work* (New York: Russell Sage Foundation, 1997); Edin and Kefalas, *Promises I Can Keep*; Melanie Heath, *One Marriage Under God: The Campaign to Promote Marriage in America* (New York: NYU Press, 2012).

11. On the pro-marriage rhetoric undergirding TANF, see "TANF Funds and Healthy Marriage Activities," National Healthy Marriage Resource Center, https://www.fatherhood.gov/sites /default/files/resource_files/e000001301.pdf. On declining welfare expenditures, see "Policy Basics: Temporary Assistance for Needy Families," Center on Budget and Policy Priorities, March 1, 2022, https://www.cbpp.org/research/family-income-support/temporary-assistance -for-needy-families. On how federal matching grants incentivize states to fund marriage pro- motion campaigns, see Robert Pear and David D. Kirkpatrick, "Bush Plans $1.5 Billion Drive for Promotion of Marriage," *New York Times*, January 14, 2004, https://www.nytimes .com/2004/01/14/us/bush-plans-1.5-billion-drive-for-promotion-of-marriage.html. On current federal matching funds for marriage promotion, as of 2023, see "Healthy Marriage & Re- sponsible Fatherhood," Office of Family Assistance, last updated July 25, 2023, https://www .acf.hhs.gov/ofa/programs/healthy-marriage-responsible-fatherhood. On the beneficiaries of marriage promotion spending, see "HMRF Project Map," Office of Family Assistance, https://www.acf.hhs.gov/ofa/map/hmrf-grantee-map. On the changing percentage of TANF spending that goes toward cash welfare benefits, see Gina Azito Thompson, Diana Azevedo- McCaffrey, and Da'Shon Carr, "Increases in TANF Cash Benefit Levels Are Critical to Help Families Meet Rising Costs," Center on Budget and Policy Priorities, February 3, 2023, https://www.cbpp.org/research/income-security/increases-in-tanf-cash-benefit-levels-are -critical-to-help-families-meet-0.

12. For the quote from the DHHS website, see "Healthy Marriage," Office of Family Assistance, last updated October 23, 2020, https://www.acf.hhs.gov/ofa/programs/healthy-marriage -responsible-fatherhood/healthy-marriage.

13. On the rhetoric used to argue that unmarried parenthood causes poverty and precarity, see Eduardo Porter, "Politicians Push Marriage, but That's Not What Would Help Children," *New York Times*, March 22, 2016, https://www.nytimes.com/2016/03/23/business/for-the -sake-of-the-children-not-marriage-but-help.html. On poverty and precarity as the primary drivers of divorce and breakup, see Amelia Karraker and Kenzie Latham, "In Sickness and in Health? Physical Illness as a Risk Factor for Marital Dissolution in Later Life," *Journal of Health and Social Behavior* 56, no. 3 (2015): 420–35; Alexandra Killewald, "Money, Work, and Marital Stability: Assessing Change in the Gendered Determinants of Divorce," *Ameri- can Sociological Review* 81, no. 4 (2016): 696–719; Laura Sanchez and Constance T. Gager, "Hard Living, Perceived Entitlement to a Great Marriage, and Marital Dissolution," *Journal of Marriage and Family* 62, no. 3 (2000): 708–22x; Deadric T. Williams and Jacob E. Cheadle, "Economic Hardship, Parents' Depression, and Relationship Distress among Couples with Young Children," *Society and Mental Health* 6, no. 2 (2016): 73–89. On poverty and precarity as the primary reason why couples don't marry, see Edin and Kefalas, *Promises I Can Keep*; Daniel T. Lichter, Christie D. Batson, and J. Brian Brown, "Welfare Reform and Marriage Promotion: The Marital Expectations and Desires of Single and Cohabiting Mothers," *Social Service Review* 78, no. 1 (March 2004): 2–25. On poverty and precarity as the primary drivers of children's life chances, see Elizabeth Thomson, Thomas L. Hanson, and Sara S. McLana- han, "Family Structure and Child Well-Being: Economic Resources vs. Parental Behaviors," *Social Forces* 73, no. 1 (1994): 221–42; Elizabeth Thomson and Sara S. McLanahan, "Reflec- tions on 'Family Structure and Child Well-Being: Economic Resources vs. Parental Social- ization,'" *Social Forces* 91, no. 1 (2012): 45–53; Jane Waldfogel, Terry-Ann Craigie, and Jeanne Brooks-Gunn, "Fragile Families and Child Wellbeing," *Future of Children* 20, no. 2 (2010): 87–112.

14. On marriage advocates' misuse of data, see Beth Skilken Catlett and Julie E. Artis, "Critiqu- ing the Case for Marriage Promotion: How the Promarriage Movement Misrepresents Do- mestic Violence Research," *Violence Against Women* 10, no. 11 (2004): 1226–44; Melanie Heath, "State of Our Unions: Marriage Promotion and the Contested Power of Heterosexu- ality," *Gender & Society* 23, no. 1 (2009): 27–48; Heath, *One Marriage Under God*. For critiques of Vance's *Hillbilly Elegy*, see Betsy Rader, "I Was Born in Poverty in Appalachia. 'Hillbilly

Elegy' Doesn't Speak for Me," *Washington Post*, September 1, 2017, https://www.washingtonpost .com/opinions/i-grew-up-in-poverty-in-appalachia-jd-vances-hillbilly-elegy-doesnt-speak-for -me/2017/08/30/734abb38-891d-11e7-961d-2f373b3977ee_story.html. For the text of Vance's speech, see Bess Levin, "GOP Senate Candidate J.D. Vance: If People Love Their Kids, They'll Stay in Violent Marriages," *Vanity Fair*, July 25, 2002, https://www.vanityfair.com /news/2022/07/jd-vance-violent-marriages. See also Cameron Joseph, "JD Vance Suggests People in 'Violent' Marriages Shouldn't Get Divorced," *Vice*, July 25, 2022, https:// www.vice.com/en/article/93abve/jd-vance-suggests-people-in-violent-marriages-shouldnt -get-divorced. On the circumstances under which divorce can be beneficial for children, see Paul R. Amato, Laura Spencer Loomis, and Alan Booth, "Parental Divorce, Marital Conflict, and Offspring Well-Being during Early Adulthood," *Social Forces* 73, no. 3 (1995): 895–915; Thomas L. Hanson, "Does Parental Conflict Explain Why Divorce Is Negatively Associated with Child Welfare?," *Social Forces* 77, no. 4 (1999): 1283–316; Susan M. Jekielek, "Parental Conflict, Marital Disruption and Children's Emotional Well-Being," *Social Forces* 76, no. 3 (1998): 905–36.

15. On the ineffectiveness of marriage promotion programs, see Catlett and Artis, "Critiquing the Case for Marriage Promotion"; Wendy D. Manning et al., *Healthy Marriage Initiative Spending and U.S. Marriage & Divorce Rates, a State-Level Analysis* (Bowling Green, OH: National Center for Family & Marriage Research, 2012).

16. On how financial precarity and relationship stress increase the risk of intimate partner violence, see Catlett and Artis, "Critiquing the Case for Marriage Promotion"; Alfred DeMaris, "Till Discord Do Us Part: The Role of Physical and Verbal Conflict in Union Disruption," *Journal of Marriage and Family* 62, no. 3 (2000): 683–92; Shelley D. Golden, Krista M. Perreira, and Christine Piette Durrance, "Troubled Times, Troubled Relationships: How Economic Resources, Gender Beliefs, and Neighborhood Disadvantage Influence Intimate Partner Violence," *Journal of Interpersonal Violence* 28, no. 10 (2013): 2134–55; Daniel Schneider, Kristen Harknett, and Sara McLanahan, "Intimate Partner Violence in the Great Recession," *Demography* 53, no. 2 (April 2016): 471–505; Deadric T. Williams, Jacob E. Cheadle, and Bridget J. Goosby, "Hard Times and Heart Break: Linking Economic Hardship and Relationship Distress," *Journal of Family Issues* 36, no. 7 (2015): 924–50. On the prevalence of intimate partner abuse and violence in the United States, see M. C. Black et al., *National Intimate Partner and Sexual Violence Survey: 2010 Summary Report* (Washington, DC: National Center for Injury Prevention and Control, 2011); Catherine Elizabeth Kaukinen and Ráchael A. Powers, "The Role of Economic Factors on Women's Risk for Intimate Partner Violence: A Cross-National Comparison of Canada and the United States," *Violence Against Women* 21, no. 2 (2015): 229–48; Joseph H. Michalski, "Explaining Intimate Partner Violence: The Sociological Limitations of Victimization Studies," *Sociological Forum* 20, no. 4 (2005): 613–40. See also Jennifer L. Truman and Rachel E. Morgan, *Nonfatal Domestic Violence, 2003–2012* (Washington, DC: Bureau of Justice Statistics, 2014). On the prevalence of intimate partner abuse and violence in other countries: Lynnmarie Sardinha et al., "Global, Regional, and National Prevalence Estimates of Physical or Sexual, or Both, Intimate Partner Violence against Women in 2018," *Lancet* 399, no. 10327 (February 2022).

17. For more on how marriage encourages the kind of economic interdependence that makes it more difficult for women to leave difficult or dangerous relationships, see Demie Kurz, "Separation, Divorce, and Woman Abuse," *Violence Against Women* 2, no. 1 (1996): 63–81; Stacy J. Rogers, "Dollars, Dependency, and Divorce: Four Perspectives on the Role of Wives' Income," *Journal of Marriage and Family* 66, no. 1 (2004): 59–74; Liana C. Sayer and Suzanne M. Bianchi, "Women's Economic Independence and the Probability of Divorce: A Review and Reexamination," *Journal of Family Issues* 21, no. 7 (2000): 906–43; Heeju Sohn, "Health Insurance and Risk of Divorce: Does Having Your Own Insurance Matter?," *Journal of Marriage and Family* 77, no. 4 (2015): 982–95; Jan E. Stets and Murray A. Straus, "The Marriage License as a Hitting License: A Comparison of Assaults in Dating, Cohabiting, and Married

Couples," *Journal of Family Violence* 4, no. 2 (1989): 161–80. On the number of attempts that it takes to leave abusive relationships, see Paige Sweet, *The Politics of Surviving: How Women Navigate Domestic Violence and Its Aftermath* (Berkeley: University of California Press, 2021); Angela E. Waldrop and Patricia A. Resick, "Coping among Adult Female Victims of Domestic Violence," *Journal of Family Violence* 19, no. 5 (2004): 291–302. On women's trajectories after leaving difficult or dangerous relationships, see Andrew J. Cherlin et al., "The Influence of Physical and Sexual Abuse on Marriage and Cohabitation," *American Sociological Review* 69, no. 6 (2004): 768–89; Debra Kalmuss and Judith A. Seltzer, "Continuity of Marital Behavior in Remarriage: The Case of Spouse Abuse," *Journal of Marriage and Family* 48, no. 1 (1986): 113–20.

18. On demand for mental health services, see C. Holly A. Andrilla et al., "Geographic Variation in the Supply of Selected Behavioral Health Providers," *American Journal of Preventive Medicine* 54, no. 6, Supplement 3 (2018): S199–207; Sara B. Oswalt et al., "Trends in College Students' Mental Health Diagnoses and Utilization of Services, 2009–2015," *Journal of American College Health* 68, no. 1 (2020): 41–51.

19. On rising pandemic home prices, see Francesca Mari, "Will Real Estate Ever Be Normal Again?," *New York Times*, November 12, 2021, https://www.nytimes.com/2021/11/12/magazine /real-estate-pandemic.html. See also Ronda Kaysen, "What's Up with the Crazy Housing Market?," *New York Times*, July 8, 2022, https://www.nytimes.com/2022/07/08/realestate /housing-market.html.

20. For the public service announcement, see "1973 Ad Council Stay in School PSA," YouTube, https://www.youtube.com/watch?v=2A1ElBikFas. On the push for college for all, see Megan M. Holland, "College for All and Community College for None: Stigma in High-Achieving High Schools," *Teachers College Record* 117, no. 5 (2015): 1–52; Suneal Kolluri and William Tierney, "College for All in Capitalist America: The Post-Secondary Emphasis in the Neoliberal Age," *Tertiary Education and Management* 24, no. 3 (July 3, 2018): 242–53. For President Obama's comments, see Doug Lederman, "College for All," *Inside Higher Ed*, February 24, 2009, https://www.insidehighered.com/news/2009/02/25/college-all.

21. On the returns to higher education, see Michael Hout, "Social and Economic Returns to College Education in the United States," *Annual Review of Sociology* 38 (2012): 379–400. On the relationship between college and income/employment, see "Employment Projections," US Bureau of Labor Statistics, https://www.bls.gov/emp/chart-unemployment-earnings -education.htm. On the relationship between college, marriage, and divorce, see Kelly Raley, Megan Sweeney, and Danielle Wondra, "The Growing Racial and Ethnic Divide in U.S. Marriage Patterns," *Future of Children* 25 (2015): 89–109. On the relationship between college and health-related decision-making, see Elizabeth M. Lawrence, "Why Do College Graduates Behave More Healthfully Than Those Who Are Less Educated?," *Journal of Health and Social Behavior* 58, no. 3 (2017): 291–306. On the relationship between college and health, see Dana Goldman and James P. Smith, "The Increasing Value of Education to Health," *Social Science & Medicine* 72, no. 10 (2011): 1728–37. On the relationship between college and longevity, see Anne Case and Angus Deaton, "Rising Morbidity and Mortality in Midlife among White Non-Hispanic Americans in the 21st Century," *Proceedings of the National Academy of Sciences* 112, no. 49 (2015): 15078–83; Hedwig Lee and Kathleen Mullan Harris, "Mapping the Color Line: Racial/Ethnic and Gender Disparities in Life Expectancy across the United States," *Annals of Internal Medicine* 175, no. 8 (2022): 1185–86; Ellen R. Meara, Seth Richards, and David M. Cutler, "The Gap Gets Bigger: Changes in Mortality and Life Expectancy, by Education, 1981–2000," *Health Affairs* 27, no. 2 (2008): 350–56.

22. On the relationship between financial resources and educational attainment, see Vickie Choitz and Patrick Reimherr, *Mind the Gap: High Unmet Financial Need Threatens Persistence and Completion for Low-Income Community College Students*, Center for Law and Social Policy, Inc. (Washington, DC: Center for Law and Social Policy, 2013), https://eric.ed.gov/?id= ED544243; Rachel E. Dwyer, Laura McCloud, and Randy Hodson, "Debt and Graduation

from American Universities," *Social Forces* 90, no. 4 (2012): 1133–55; Sara Goldrick-Rab et al., "Reducing Income Inequality in Educational Attainment: Experimental Evidence on the Impact of Financial Aid on College Completion," *American Journal of Sociology* 121, no. 6 (2016): 1762–817; Jason N. Houle and Cody Warner, "Into the Red and Back to the Nest? Student Debt, College Completion, and Returning to the Parental Home among Young Adults," *Sociology of Education* 90, no. 1 (2017): 89–108; Ranita Ray, *The Making of a Teenage Service Class: Poverty and Mobility in an American City* (Berkeley: University of California Press, 2017); Tabitha G. Wilbur and Vincent J. Roscigno, "First-Generation Disadvantage and College Enrollment/Completion," *Socius* 2 (2016). On changing college costs, see Elizabeth Popp Berman, *Creating the Market University: How Academic Science Became an Economic Engine* (Princeton, NJ: Princeton University Press, 2011); Sara Goldrick-Rab, *Paying the Price: College Costs, Financial Aid, and the Betrayal of the American Dream* (Chicago: University of Chicago Press, 2016); Laura T. Hamilton and Kelly Nielsen, *Broke: The Racial Consequences of Underfunding Public Universities* (Chicago: University of Chicago Press, 2021); Thomas J. Kane, *The Price of Admission: Rethinking How Americans Pay for College* (Washington, DC: Brookings, 1999); Suzanne Mettler, *Degrees of Inequality: How the Politics of Higher Education Sabotaged the American Dream* (New York: Basic Books, 2014). On the falling value of the Pell Grant, see Sara Goldrick-Rab, "The Real College Barrier for Working-Poor Families," *Slate*, December 11, 2013, https://slate.com/human-interest/2013/12/college-affordability-pell-grants-are-inadequate.html.

23. On how rising costs force students to work more hours for pay during college, see Natasha Yurk Quadlin and Daniel Rudel, "Responsibility or Liability? Student Loan Debt and Time Use in College," *Social Forces* 94, no. 2 (2015): 589–614. On how college students' paid work hours influence their academic achievement, see Goldrick-Rab, *Paying the Price*; So-Hyun Joo, Dorothy Bagwell Durband, and John Grable, "The Academic Impact of Financial Stress on College Students," *Journal of College Student Retention: Research, Theory & Practice* 10, no. 3 (2008): 287–305; Susan Lightweis, "The Challenges, Persistence, and Success of White, Working-Class, First-Generation College Students," *College Student Journal* 48, no. 3 (2014): 461–67. On college students' ineligibility for social safety net programs, see "SNAP Work Requirements," US Department of Agriculture Food and Nutrition Service, https://www.fns.usda.gov/snap/work-requirements; *Supporting Postsecondary Completion for TANF Recipients through Work-Study Programs* (Washington, DC: US Department of Health and Human Services, 2016), https://www.acf.hhs.gov/sites/default/files/documents/ofa/work_study_issue_brief_final.pdf. On rates of college completion, see Melanie Hanson, "College Dropout Rates," Education Data Initiative, last updated October 29, 2023, https://educationdata.org/college-dropout-rates. On the incompatibility of college courses with work requirements for US government poverty programs, see Goldrick-Rab, *Paying the Price*; LaDonna Pavetti and Gina Azito Thompson, *College Support Programs Tailored to TANF Parents Can Expand Employment Opportunities, Increase Earnings, and Promote Equity* (Washington, DC: Center on Budget and Policy Priorities, 2023), https://www.cbpp.org/research/income-security/college-support-programs-tailored-to-tanf-parents-can-expand-employment. On college debt among students who do not complete their degrees, see Tara Siegel Bernard, "They Got the Debt, but Not the Degree," *New York Times*, June 1, 2022, https://www.nytimes.com/2022/06/01/your-money/student-loan-debt-degree.html. See also Melanie Hanson, "Student Loan Debt Statistics," Education Data Initiative, last updated August 20, 2023, https://educationdata.org/student-loan-debt-statistics. On the impact of student debt on later life choices, see Fenaba R. Addo, Jason N. Houle, and Daniel Simon, "Young, Black, and (Still) in the Red: Parental Wealth, Race, and Student Loan Debt," *Race and Social Problems* 8, no. 1 (2016): 64–76; Jason N. Houle and Fenaba R. Addo, "Racial Disparities in Student Debt and the Reproduction of the Fragile Black Middle Class," *Sociology of Race and Ethnicity* 5, no. 4 (2019): 562–77; Jason N. Houle and Lawrence Berger, "Is Student Loan Debt Discouraging Homeownership among Young Adults?," *Social Service Review* 89, no. 4 (2015): 589–621; Houle and Warner,

"Into the Red and Back to the Nest?"; Arielle Kuperberg and Joan Maya Mazelis, "Social Norms and Expectations about Student Loans and Family Formation," *Sociological Inquiry* 92, no. 1 (2022): 90–126; Joan Maya Mazelis and Arielle Kuperberg, "Student Loan Debt, Family Support, and Reciprocity in the Transition to Adulthood," *Emerging Adulthood*, March 12, 2022. On racial differences in the impact of student debt, see Dalton Conley, *Being Black, Living in the Red: Race, Wealth, and Social Policy in America* (Berkeley: University of California Press, 2010); Jason N. Houle, "Disparities in Debt: Parents' Socioeconomic Resources and Young Adult Student Loan Debt," *Sociology of Education* 87, no. 1 (2014): 53–69; ed. Melvin Oliver and Thomas M. Shapiro, *Black Wealth / White Wealth: A New Perspective on Racial Inequality* (London: Routledge, 2006); Louise Seamster, "Black Debt, White Debt," *Contexts* 18, no. 1 (2019): 30–35; Louise Seamster and Raphaël Charron-Chénier, "Predatory Inclusion and Education Debt: Rethinking the Racial Wealth Gap," *Social Currents* 4, no. 3 (2017): 199–207.

24. On declining college wage premiums, see Jared Ashworth and Tyler Ransom, "Has the College Wage Premium Continued to Rise? Evidence from Multiple U.S. Surveys," *Economics of Education Review* 69 (2019): 149–54. On inequalities in the college wage premium, see Paul Attewell and Dirk Witteveen, "Occupational Marginalization, Underemployment, and Earnings Inequality among College Graduates," *Research in Social Stratification and Mobility* 83 (2023): 100761; Rachel Tolbert Kimbro et al., "Race, Ethnicity, and the Education Gradient in Health," *Health Affairs* 27, no. 2 (March 2008): 361–72. On changing college enrollment over time, see Melanie Hanson, "College Enrollment & Student Demographic Statistics," Education Data Initiative, October 1, 2023, https://educationdata.org/college-enrollment -statistics. On how the increase in college enrollment led to increased competition among college graduates, see Randall Collins, *The Credential Society: An Historical Sociology of Education and Stratification* (New York: Columbia University Press, 1979); Herbert L. Smith, "Overeducation and Underemployment: An Agnostic Review," *Sociology of Education* 59, no. 2 (1986): 85–99. For more on how current generations of young people face more economic precarity than previous ones, see Houle and Addo, "Racial Disparities in Student Debt and the Reproduction of the Fragile Black Middle Class"; Houle and Berger, "Is Student Loan Debt Discouraging Homeownership among Young Adults?"; Mazelis and Kuperberg, "Student Loan Debt, Family Support, and Reciprocity in the Transition to Adulthood"; Stella Min and Miles G. Taylor, "Racial and Ethnic Variation in the Relationship Between Student Loan Debt and the Transition to First Birth," *Demography* 55, no. 1 (2018): 165–88; Robert H. Scott III and Steven Bloom, "Student Loan Debt and First-Time Home Buying in USA," *International Journal of Housing Markets and Analysis* 15, no. 1 (2021): 80–93; Jennifer M. Silva, *Coming Up Short: Working-Class Adulthood in an Age of Uncertainty* (Oxford: Oxford University Press, 2013); Jessi Streib, *Privilege Lost: Who Leaves the Upper Middle Class and How They Fall* (Oxford: Oxford University Press, 2020). On underemployment among recent college graduates, see "The Labor Market for Recent College Graduates: Underemployment," Federal Reserve Bank of New York, https://www.newyorkfed.org/research/college-labor -market/college-labor-market_underemployment_rates.html. On the incomes of recent college graduates, see "The Labor Market for Recent College Graduates: Wages," Federal Reserve Bank of New York, https://www.newyorkfed.org/research/college-labor-market/index.html# /wages.

25. On gender differences in the college wage premium, see *The Permanent Detour: Underemployment's Long-Term Effects on the Careers of College Grads* (Indianapolis, IN: Strada Institute 2018), https://www.economicmodeling.com/wp-content/uploads/2022/04/permanent_detour _underemployment_report.pdf. See also "Mean Earnings in the United States in 2021, by Highest Educational Degree Earned and Gender," Statista, https://www.statista.com/statistics /184248/mean-earnings-by-educational-attainment-and-gender/.

26. On how feminization leads to a decline in wages and occupational prestige, see Philip N. Cohen and Matt L. Huffman, "Occupational Segregation and the Devaluation of Women's

Work across U.S. Labor Markets," *Social Forces* 81, no. 3 (2003): 881–908; Asaf Levanon, Paula England, and Paul Allison, "Occupational Feminization and Pay: Assessing Causal Dynamics Using 1950–2000 U.S. Census Data," *Social Forces* 88, no. 2 (2009): 865–91; Paula England, Paul Allison, and Yuxiao Wu, "Does Bad Pay Cause Occupations to Feminize, Does Feminization Reduce Pay, and How Can We Tell with Longitudinal Data?," *Social Science Research* 36, no. 3 (2007): 1237–56. For more on how and why feminine-typed occupations are compensated at lower rates than masculine-typed occupations, see Philip N. Cohen and Matt L. Huffman, "Working for the Woman? Female Managers and the Gender Wage Gap," *American Sociological Review* 72, no. 5 (2007): 681–704; Philip N. Cohen, Matt L. Huffman, and Stefanie Knauer, "Stalled Progress? Gender Segregation and Wage Inequality among Managers, 1980–2000," *Work and Occupations* 36, no. 4 (2009): 318–42; David A. Cotter, Joan M. Hermsen, and Reeve Vanneman, "The Effects of Occupational Gender Segregation across Race," *Sociological Quarterly* 44, no. 1 (2003): 17–36; Gordon Gauchat, Maura Kelly, and Michael Wallace, "Occupational Gender Segregation, Globalization, and Gender Earnings Inequality in U.S. Metropolitan Areas," *Gender & Society* 26, no. 5 (2012): 718–47; Ariane Hegewisch et al., *Separate and Not Equal? Gender Segregation in the Labor Market and the Gender Wage Gap* (Washington, DC: Institute for Women's Policy Research, 2010); Jerry A. Jacobs and Ronnie J. Steinberg, "Compensating Differentials and the Male-Female Wage Gap: Evidence from the New York State Comparable Worth Study," *Social Forces* 69, no. 2 (1990): 439–68; Kathrin Leuze and Susanne Strauß, "Why Do Occupations Dominated by Women Pay Less? How 'Female-Typical' Work Tasks and Working-Time Arrangements Affect the Gender Wage Gap among Higher Education Graduates," *Work, Employment and Society* 30, no. 5 (2016): 802–20; Trond Petersen and Laurie A. Morgan, "Separate and Unequal: Occupation-Establishment Sex Segregation and the Gender Wage Gap," *American Journal of Sociology* 101, no. 2 (September 1995): 329–65; Barbara F. Reskin, "Bringing the Men Back In: Sex Differentiation and the Devaluation of Women's Work," *Gender & Society* 2, no. 1 (1988): 58–81; Barbara F. Reskin, "Sex Segregation in the Workplace," *Annual Review of Sociology* 19, no. 1 (1993): 241–70; Barbara F. Reskin, "Getting It Right: Sex and Race Inequality in Work Organizations," *Annual Review of Sociology* 26, no. 1 (2000): 707–709; Peter Valet, "Social Structure and the Paradox of the Contented Female Worker: How Occupational Gender Segregation Biases Justice Perceptions of Wages," *Work and Occupations* 45, no. 2 (2018): 168–93. On the glass escalator for men in women-dominated occupations, see Richard R. Verdugo and Jeffrey M. Schneider, "Gender Inequality in Female-Dominated Occupation: The Earnings of Male and Female Teachers," *Economics of Education Review* 13, no. 3 (1994): 251–64; Jill E. Yavorsky and Janette Dill, "Unemployment and Men's Entrance into Female-Dominated Jobs," *Social Science Research* 85 (2020): 102373. On the mental health care workforce in 1970, see *Detailed Occupation of the Experienced Civilian Labor Force by Sex for the United States and Regions: 1980 and 1970* (Washington, DC: US Census Bureau, 1980), https://www.census.gov/content/dam/Census/library/publications/1984/demo/pc80 -s1-15.pdf. On the mental health care workforce today, see "Labor Force Statistics from the Current Population Survey," US Bureau of Labor Statistics, https://www.bls.gov/cps/cpsaat11 .htm. On the median income for mental health counselors in 1980, see Earl F. Mellor, "Weekly Earnings in 1985: A Look at More Than 200 Occupations," US Bureau of Labor Statistics, https://www.bls.gov/opub/mlr/1986/09/rpt1full.pdf. On the median income for mental health counselors in 2023, see "Substance Abuse, Behavioral Disorder, and Mental Health Counselors," US Bureau of Labor Statistics, https://www.bls.gov/ooh/community -and-social-service/substance-abuse-behavioral-disorder-and-mental-health-counselors .htm. On the growing demand for mental health care, see Andrilla et al., "Geographic Variation in the Supply of Selected Behavioral Providers"; Oswalt et al., "Trends in College Students' Mental Health Diagnoses and Utilization of Services."

27. On women's dissatisfaction with hormonal birth control, see Krystale E. Littlejohn, *Just Get*

on the Pill: The Uneven Burden of Reproductive Politics (Berkeley: University of California Press, 2021).

28. On mastitis and its complications, see Emily Wilson, Susannah L Woodd, and Lenka Benova, "Incidence of and Risk Factors for Lactational Mastitis: A Systematic Review," *Journal of Human Lactation* 36, no. 4 (2020): 673–86.

29. For Indiana's legal rules regarding accommodations for lactating workers, see "WIC Clients," Indiana Department of Health, https://www.in.gov/health/wic/breastfeeding-information/.

30. On the housework and childcare responsibilities of breadwinner mothers, see Alexandra Killewald and Margaret Gough, "Money Isn't Everything: Wives' Earnings and Housework Time," *Social Science Research* 39, no. 6 (2010): 987–1003; Daniel Schneider, "Gender Deviance and Household Work: The Role of Occupation," *American Journal of Sociology* 117, no. 4 (2012): 1029–72.

31. On the sacrifices that women make for their husbands' jobs, see Youngjoo Cha, "Reinforcing Separate Spheres: The Effect of Spousal Overwork on Men's and Women's Employment in Dual-Earner Households," *American Sociological Review* 75, no. 2 (2010): 303–29; Caitlyn Collins, *Making Motherhood Work: How Women Manage Careers and Caregiving* (Princeton, NJ: Princeton University Press, 2019); Sarah Damaske, *For the Family?: How Class and Gender Shape Women's Work* (Oxford: Oxford University Press, 2011); Kathleen Gerson, *Hard Choices: How Women Decide about Work, Career and Motherhood* (Berkeley: University of California Press, 1985); Arlie Russell Hochschild, *The Second Shift: Working Families and the Revolution at Home* (New York: Penguin Books, 1989); Killewald and Gough, "Money Isn't Everything"; Aliya Hamid Rao, *Crunch Time: How Married Couples Confront Unemployment* (Berkeley: University of California Press, 2020); Schneider, "Gender Deviance and Household Work"; Jaclyn S. Wong, "Competing Desires: How Young Adult Couples Negotiate Moving for Career Opportunities," *Gender & Society* 31, no. 2 (2017): 171–96.

32. For the quoted *New York Times* article, see Elizabeth M. Fowler, "Computer Personnel in Demand," *New York Times*, October 15, 1980, https://timesmachine.nytimes.com/timesmachine/1980/10/15/issue.html.

33. For economists' advice for parents in the 1980s, see Estelle James et al., "College Quality and Future Earnings: Where Should You Send Your Child to College?," *American Economic Review* 79, no. 2 (1989): 251–52. For Obama's advice to parents, see "President Obama Launches 'Educate to Innovate' Campaign for Excellence in Science, Technology, Engineering & Math (Stem) Education," White House for President Barack Obama, November 23, 2009, https://obamawhitehouse.archives.gov/the-press-office/president-obama-launches-educate-innovate-campaign-excellence-science-technology-en.

34. For the median salary of software engineers, see "Computer Hardware Engineers," US Bureau of Labor Statistics, https://www.bls.gov/ooh/architecture-and-engineering/computer-hardware-engineers.htm. On how worker salaries for similar jobs vary across industries, see "High-Tech Industries: An Analysis of Employment, Wages, and Output," US Bureau of Labor Statistics, https://www.bls.gov/opub/btn/volume-7/high-tech-industries-an-analysis-of-employment-wages-and-output.htm.

35. For more on the push for STEM as a solution to social inequities and the limitations of this approach, see Kristin Cipollone, Amy E. Stich, and Lois Weis, "STEM for All: Student Identities and the Paradox of STEM Democratization," *Teachers College Record* 122, no. 2 (2020): 1–67; Margaret Eisenhart and Carrie D. Allen, "Hollowed Out: Meaning and Authoring of High School Math and Science Identities in the Context of Neoliberal Reform," *Mind, Culture, and Activity* 23, no. 3 (July 2, 2016): 188–98; Eric (Rico) Gutstein, "The Common Core State Standards Initiative: A Critical Response," *Journal of Urban Mathematics Education* 3, no. 1 (July 9, 2010): 9–18; Lois Weis et al., "In the Guise of STEM Education Reform: Opportunity Structures and Outcomes in Inclusive STEM-Focused High Schools," *American Educational Research Journal* 52, no. 6 (2015): 1024–59. On the discrimination that

women face in high-tech fields, see Erin A. Cech and Mary Blair-Loy, "Perceiving Glass Ceilings? Meritocratic versus Structural Explanations of Gender Inequality among Women in Science and Technology," *Social Problems* 57, no. 3 (2010): 371–97; Cynthia Cockburn, *Machinery of Dominance: Women, Men and Technical Know-How* (London: Pluto Press, 1987); Ethel L. Mickey, "When Gendered Logics Collide: Going Public and Restructuring in a High-Tech Organization," *Gender & Society* 33, no. 4 (2019): 509–33; Sarah Thébaud and Catherine J. Taylor, "The Specter of Motherhood: Culture and the Production of Gendered Career Aspirations in Science and Engineering," *Gender & Society* 35, no. 3 (2021): 395–421; Carroll Seron et al., "'I Am Not a Feminist, but . . . ': Hegemony of a Meritocratic Ideology and the Limits of Critique among Women in Engineering," *Work and Occupations* 45, no. 2 (2018): 131–67. On efforts to increase representation of women in STEM, see Sarah K. White, "18 organizations Advancing Women in Tech," CIO, March 1, 2023, https://www.cio.com/article/215709/16-organizations-for-women-in-tech.html.

36. On how disproportionate housework and childcare responsibilities affect women's careers, see Marianne Bertrand, Emir Kamenica, and Jessica Pan, "Gender Identity and Relative Income within Households," *Quarterly Journal of Economics* 130, no. 2 (2015): 571–614; Cha, "Reinforcing Separate Spheres"; Collins, *Making Motherhood Work*; Damaske, *For the Family?*; Dawn Marie Dow, *Mothering While Black* (Berkeley: University of California Press, 2019); Gerson, *Hard Choices*; Hochschild, *The Second Shift*; Pamela Stone, *Opting Out?* (Berkeley: University of California Press, 2007). On employers' gendered expectations for workers, see Ronald J. J. Burke and Cary L. Cooper, *Long Work Hours Culture: Causes, Consequences and Choices* (Bingley, UK: Emerald Group Publishing, 2008); Tracy L. Dumas and Jeffrey Sanchez-Burks, "The Professional, the Personal, and the Ideal Worker: Pressures and Objectives Shaping the Boundary between Life Domains," *Academy of Management Annals* 9, no. 1 (2015): 803–43; Jerry A. Jacobs and Kathleen Gerson, "Overworked Individuals or Overworked Families?: Explaining Trends in Work, Leisure, and Family Time," *Work and Occupations* 28, no. 1 (2001): 40–63; Erin L. Kelly et al., "Gendered Challenge, Gendered Response: Confronting the Ideal Worker Norm in a White-Collar Organization," *Gender & Society* 24, no. 3 (2010): 281–303; Teresa A. Sullivan, "Greedy Institutions, Overwork, and Work-Life Balance," *Sociological Inquiry* 84, no. 1 (2014): 1–15. On the penalties that workers face for allowing care responsibilities to interfere with paid work, see Sylvia Fuller and C. Elizabeth Hirsh, "'Family-Friendly' Jobs and Motherhood Pay Penalties: The Impact of Flexible Work Arrangements across the Educational Spectrum," *Work and Occupations* 46, no. 1 (2019): 3–44; Christin L. Munsch, "Flexible Work, Flexible Penalties: The Effect of Gender, Childcare, and Type of Request on the Flexibility Bias," *Social Forces* 94, no. 4 (2016): 1567–91; Richard J. Petts, Trenton D. Mize, and Gayle Kaufman, "Organizational Policies, Workplace Culture, and Perceived Job Commitment of Mothers and Fathers Who Take Parental Leave," *Social Science Research* 103 (2022): 102651; Sarah Thébaud and David S. Pedulla, "When Do Work-Family Policies Work? Unpacking the Effects of Stigma and Financial Costs for Men and Women," *Work and Occupations* 49, no. 2 (2022): 229–63. On gender differences in workers' use of flexible work and leave policies, see Jane Herr, Radha Roy, and Jacob Alex Klerman, *Gender Differences in Needing and Taking Leave* (Washington, DC: US Department of Labor, 2020), https://www.dol.gov/sites/dolgov/files/OASP/evaluation/pdf/WHD_FMLAGenderShortPaper_January2021.pdf. On men's reluctance to take paid family leave, see Jessica Grose, "Why Dads Don't Take Parental Leave," *New York Times*, February 19, 2020, https://www.nytimes.com/2020/02/19/parenting/why-dads-I-take-parental-leave.html. On the consequences of fathers' involvement (or lack thereof) in children's early lives, see Lenna Nepomnyaschy and Jane Waldfogel, "Paternity Leave and Fathers' Involvement with Their Young Children," *Community, Work & Family* 10, no. 4 (2007): 427–53; Richard J. Petts and Chris Knoester, "Paternity Leave-Taking and Father Engagement," *Journal of Marriage and Family* 80, no. 5 (2018): 1144–62; Erin M. Rehel, "When Dad Stays Home Too: Paternity Leave, Gender, and Parenting," *Gender & Society* 28, no. 1 (2014): 110–32.

37. On the judgment that mothers face in the workforce, see Tyler G. Okimoto and Madeline E. Heilman, "The 'Bad Parent' Assumption: How Gender Stereotypes Affect Reactions to Working Mothers," *Journal of Social Issues* 68, no. 4 (2012): 704–24.

38. On how women's careers shape their decisions about whether to have children, see Catherine Hill, Christianne Corbett, and Andresse St. Rose, "Why So Few? Women in Science, Technology, Engineering, and Mathematics," *American Association of University Women* (Boston: American Association of University Women, 2010). On gender differences in STEM graduates' likelihood of having jobs that use their degrees, see Mary Ann Mason and Marc Goulden, "Do Babies Matter? The Effect of Family Formation on the Lifelong Careers of Academic Men and Women," *Academe* 88, no. 6 (2002): 21–27.

39. On employers' underinvestment in women in STEM, see Cech and Blair-Loy, "Perceiving Glass Ceilings?"; Seron et al., "'I Am Not a Feminist, But . . . '"; Hadas Mandel and Assaf Rotman, "The Stalled Gender Revolution and the Rise of Top Earnings in the United States, 1980 to 2017," *Sociological Science* 9 (April 11, 2022): 136–58. See also Natasha Quadlin, "The Mark of a Woman's Record: Gender and Academic Performance in Hiring," *American Sociological Review* 83, no. 2 (April 2018): 331–60.

CHAPTER 5: THE MERITOCRACY MYTH

1. For the full text of Franklin's letter, see Benjamin Franklin, "On the Price of Corn and Management of the Poor," 1766, https://founding.com/founders-library/american-political-figures/benjamin-franklin/on-the-price-of-corn-and-management-of-the-poor/.

2. On Franklin's life and work, see Walter Isaacson, *Benjamin Franklin: An American Life* (New York: Simon & Schuster, 2004). For Franklin's writing on success and merit, see Benjamin Franklin, "The Way to Wealth," *Poor Richard's Almanac* (1758; CreateSpace Independent Publishing Platform, 2016). On the rhetoric of good choices, see Claude S. Fischer et al., *Inequality by Design: Cracking the Bell Curve Myth* (Princeton, NJ: Princeton University Press 2020); Shamus Khan and Colin Jerolmack, "Saying Meritocracy and Doing Privilege," *Sociological Quarterly* 54, no. 1 (2013): 9–19; Stephen J. McNamee and Robert K. Miller, *The Myth of Meritocracy* (Lanham, MD: Rowman & Littlefield, 2009); Jonathan J. B. Mijs, "The Unfulfillable Promise of Meritocracy: Three Lessons and Their Implications for Justice in Education," *Social Justice Research* 29, no. 1 (2016): 14–34; Jonathan J. B. Mijs, "The Paradox of Inequality: Income Inequality and Belief in Meritocracy Go Hand in Hand," *Socio-Economic Review* (2019): 1–29; Michael J. Sandel, *The Tyranny of Merit: What's Become of the Common Good?* (New York: Farrar, Straus and Giroux, 2020); Natasha Warikoo, *The Diversity Bargain* (Chicago: University of Chicago Press, 2016); Natasha Kumar Warikoo and Christina Fuhr, "Legitimating Status: Perceptions of Meritocracy and Inequality among Undergraduates at an Elite British University," *British Educational Research Journal* 40, no. 4 (2014): 699–717.

3. On the moralized and often racialized language that white low-income mothers use to distinguish themselves from low-income Black and Latino families, see Margie L. Kiter Edwards, "We're Decent People: Constructing and Managing Family Identity in Rural Working-Class Communities," *Journal of Marriage and Family* 66, no. 2 (2004): 515–29. On stereotypes of low-income mothers, and particularly Black and Latina mothers, see Dawn Marie Dow, "Negotiating 'The Welfare Queen' and 'The Strong Black Woman': African American Middle-Class Mothers' Work and Family Perspectives," *Sociological Perspectives* 58, no. 1 (2015): 36–55; Josh Levin, *The Queen: The Forgotten Life Behind an American Myth* (New York: Little, Brown and Company, 2019).

4. On the New Thought movement and its links to Franklin's writings, see Kate Bowler, *Blessed: A History of the American Prosperity Gospel* (Oxford: Oxford University Press, 2018); Jill Lepore, "What Poor Richard Cost Benjamin Franklin," *New Yorker*, January 20, 2008, https://www.newyorker.com/magazine/2008/01/28/the-creed. For Quimby's quote, see "The Phi-

losophy of P. P. Quimby," Cornerstone Books, https://cornerstone.wwwhubs.com/quimby1 .htm. For Eddy's quote, see Mary Baker Eddy, *Science and Health with Key to the Scriptures* (Boston: Christian Science Publishing, 1875).

5. On belief in the prosperity gospel and its prevalence among different religious groups, see Bowler, *Blessed*; Steve Brouwer, Paul Gifford, and Susan D. Rose, *Exporting the American Gospel: Global Christian Fundamentalism* (London: Routledge, 2013); Christopher H. Evans, "Why You Should Know about the New Thought Movement," *Conversation*, February 16, 2017, http://theconversation.com/why-you-should-know-about-the-new-thought-movement -72256; Kevin M. Kruse, *One Nation Under God: How Corporate America Invented Christian America* (New York: Basic Books, 2015); Christopher Lane, *Surge of Piety: Norman Vincent Peale and the Remaking of American Religious Life* (New Haven, CT: Yale University Press, 2016); Beryl Satter, *Each Mind a Kingdom: American Women, Sexual Purity, and the New Thought Movement, 1875–1920* (Berkeley: University of California Press, 2001); Scott Schieman and Jong Hyun Jung, "'Practical Divine Influence': Socioeconomic Status and Belief in the Prosperity Gospel," *Journal for the Scientific Study of Religion* 51, no. 4 (2012): 738–56.

6. Joel Osteen, *The Abundance Mind-Set: Success Starts Here* (Nashville: FaithWords, 2020), 5.

7. On how the prosperity gospel promotes the kind of "good choices" rhetoric we discussed in chapter 4, see Bowler, *Blessed*; Tara Isabella Burton, "The Prosperity Gospel, Explained: Why Joel Osteen Believes That Prayer Can Make You Rich," Vox, September 1, 2017, https://www .vox.com/identities/2017/9/1/15951874/prosperity-gospel-explained-why-joel-osteen -believes-prayer-can-make-you-rich-trump; Schieman and Jung, "'Practical Divine Influence.'" On the evangelical call to spread the word of God, see Mark Ruble, "Is Christian Science Evangelical?," *Christian Science Sentinel*, January 11, 1988, https://sentinel.christian science.com/shared/view/dhmj5denmc.

8. On the popularity of Peale's ideas, see Ron Elving, "Norman Vincent Peale Was a Conservative Hero Known Well Beyond His Era," NPR, July 24, 2020, https://www.npr.org/2020 /07/24/894967922/norman-vincent-peale-was-a-conservative-hero-known-well-beyond -his-era; Mitch Horowitz, "Why the 'Power of Positive Thinking' Is Still So Popular," Big Think, October 16, 2022, https://bigthink.com/thinking/power-of-positive-thinking -controversial/.

9. Norman Vincent Peale, *The Power of Positive Thinking* (New York: Touchstone, 2003).

10. Rhonda Byrne, *The Secret* (New York: Atria Books/Beyond Words, 2006).

11. On the role of self-help books in promoting the meritocracy myth, see Dana Becker and Jeanne Marecek, "Dreaming the American Dream: Individualism and Positive Psychology," *Social and Personality Psychology Compass* 2, no. 5 (2008): 1767–80; Micki McGee, *Self-Help, Inc.: Makeover Culture in American Life* (Oxford: Oxford University Press, 2007). For quotes from Peale, see Elving, "Norman Vincent Peale Was a Conservative Hero."

12. On the prevalence of overwork, see Jerry A. Jacobs and Sarah E. Winslow, "Overworked Faculty: Job Stresses and Family Demands," *ANNALS of the American Academy of Political and Social Science* 596, no. 1 (2004): 104–29; Sharon Miki, "Lawyer Working Hours: How Many Hours Do Lawyers Work & Why?," Clio, May 4, 2021, https://www.clio.com/blog/lawyer -working-hours/; Ryan Park, "Why So Many Young Doctors Work Such Awful Hours," *Atlantic*, February 21, 2017, https://www.theatlantic.com/business/archive/2017/02/doctors -long-hours-schedules/516639/; Lydia Saad, "The 40-Hour Workweek Is Actually Longer— by Seven Hours," Gallup, August 29, 2014, https://news.gallup.com/poll/175286/hour -workweek-actually-longer-seven-hours.aspx; Joanna Veazey Brooks and Charles L. Bosk, "Remaking Surgical Socialization: Work Hour Restrictions, Rites of Passage, and Occupational Identity," *Social Science & Medicine* 75, no. 9 (2012): 1625–32. On the meritocracy myth and the tenuous relationship between hard work and success, see Khan, *Privilege*; Mijs, "The Unfulfillable Promise of Meritocracy"; Sandel, *The Tyranny of Merit*. For comparisons of work hours by income, see Carmen Ang, "Do Top Earners Work More Hours? It Depends Which Country They Live In," World Economic Forum, September 27, 2022, https://www.weforum

.org/agenda/2022/09/working-hours-america-income-economy/. On the gendered dynamics of secondary employment and gig work, see "Labor Force Statistics from the Current Population Survey," US Bureau of Labor Statistics,: https://www.bls.gov/cps/cpsaat36.htm. See also Stéphane Auray, David L. Fuller, and Guillaume Vandenbroucke, "Multiple Jobholders," Federal Reserve Bank of St. Louis, 2018, https://research.stlouisfed.org/publications/economic-synopses/2018/12/21/multiple-jobholders. On the gendered rewards for overwork, see Christin L. Munsch, Lindsey T. O'Connor, and Susan R. Fisk, "Gender and the Disparate Payoffs of Overwork," *Social Psychology Quarterly* (2023).

13. On racial differences in hiring, see Devah Pager, "The Mark of a Criminal Record," *American Journal of Sociology* 108, no. 5 (2003): 937–75; Devah Pager, Bart Bonikowski, and Bruce Western, "Discrimination in a Low-Wage Labor Market: A Field Experiment," *American Sociological Review* 74, no. 5 (2009): 777–99; Lincoln Quillian, John J. Lee, and Mariana Oliver, "Evidence from Field Experiments in Hiring Shows Substantial Additional Racial Discrimination after the Callback," *Social Forces* 99, no. 2 (2020): 732–59; Christopher Uggen et al., "The Edge of Stigma: An Experimental Audit of the Effects of Low-Level Criminal Records on Employment," *Criminology* 52, no. 4 (2014): 627–54; Bruce Western, "The Impact of Incarceration on Wage Mobility and Inequality," *American Sociological Review* 67, no. 4 (2002): 526–46. On racial disparities in legal proceedings, see George S. Bridges and Sara Steen, "Racial Disparities in Official Assessments of Juvenile Offenders: Attributional Stereotypes as Mediating Mechanisms," *American Sociological Review* 63, no. 4 (1998): 554–70; Becky Pettit and Bruce Western, "Mass Imprisonment and the Life Course: Race and Class Inequality in U.S. Incarceration," *American Sociological Review* 69, no. 2 (2004): 151–69; Michael A. Strom et al., "Skin and Bones: The Contribution of Skin Tone and Facial Structure to Racial Prototypicality Ratings," *PLOS ONE* 7, no. 7 (2012); Nicole Gonzalez Van Cleve, *Crook County: Racism and Injustice in America's Largest Criminal Court* (Redwood City, CA: Stanford University Press, 2016); Loïc J. D. Wacquant, "From Slavery to Mass Incarceration: Rethinking the 'Race Question' in the US," in *Race, Law and Society, Edited by Ian Haney Lopez* (London: Routledge, 2002).

14. On Americans' belief in the myth of meritocracy, see Victor Tan Chen, "Getting Ahead by Hard Work vs. Luck or Help from Others," July 18, 2015, https://victortanchen.com/gss-getting-ahead-by-hard-work-vs-luck-or-help-from-others/. For cross-national comparisons in belief in the meritocracy myth, see Jonathan J. B. Mijs, "Visualizing Belief in Meritocracy, 1930–2010," *Socius* 4 (2018).

15. For the Pew Research Center statistics reported here, see "Typology Detailed Tables," in *Beyond Red vs. Blue: The Political Typology* (Washington, DC: Pew Research Center, 2014), https://www.pewresearch.org/politics/2014/06/26/typology-detailed-tables/. See also Michael Dimock et al., *Beyond Red vs. Blue: The Political Typology* (Washington, DC: Pew Research Center, 2014), https://www.pewresearch.org/politics/wp-content/uploads/sites/4/2014/06/6-26-14-Political-Typology-release1.pdf. For similar results from other studies, see Caroll Doherty, Jocelyn Kiley, and Nida Asheer, *In a Politically Polarized Era, Sharp Divides in Both Partisan Coalitions* (Washington, DC: Pew Research Center, 2019), https://www.pewresearch.org/politics/2019/12/17/in-a-politically-polarized-era-sharp-divides-in-both-partisan-coalitions/.

16. On the psychological benefits of belief in the meritocracy myth, see Arthur S. Alderson and Tally Katz-Gerro, "Compared to Whom? Inequality, Social Comparison, and Happiness in the United States," *Social Forces* 95, no. 1 (2016): 25–54. On how inequality amplifies the psychological benefits of belief in the meritocracy myth, see Tim Futing Liao, "Income Inequality, Social Comparison, and Happiness in the United States," *Socius* 7 (2021); Lucía Macchia, Anke C. Plagnol, and Nattavudh Powdthavee, "Buying Happiness in an Unequal World: Rank of Income More Strongly Predicts Well-Being in More Unequal Countries," *Personality and Social Psychology Bulletin* 46, no. 5 (2020): 769–80.

17. On the limits of upward mobility in the US, see Raj Chetty et al., "Is the United States Still

a Land of Opportunity? Recent Trends in Intergenerational Mobility," *American Economic Review* 104, no. 5 (May 2014): 141–47; Michael Hout, "A Summary of What We Know about Social Mobility," *ANNALS of the American Academy of Political and Social Science* 657, no. 1 (2015): 27–36; Jacob Shane and Jutta Heckhausen, "University Students' Causal Conceptions about Social Mobility: Diverging Pathways for Believers in Personal Merit and Luck," *Journal of Vocational Behavior* 82, no. 1 (2013): 10–19; Lauren A. Rivera, *Pedigree: How Elite Students Get Elite Jobs* (Princeton, NJ: Princeton University Press, 2016). On the risk of downward mobility, see Katherine S. Newman, *Falling from Grace: The Experience of Downward Mobility in the American Middle Class* (New York: Free Press, 1988); Jessi Streib, *Privilege Lost: Who Leaves the Upper Middle Class and How They Fall* (Oxford: Oxford University Press, 2020). On Americans' growing sense of hopelessness, see Anne Case and Angus Deaton, *Deaths of Despair and the Future of Capitalism* (Princeton, NJ: Princeton University Press, 2020). On how the meritocracy myth promotes a sense of agency to overcome obstacles, see Naa Oyo A. Kwate and Ilan H. Meyer, "The Myth of Meritocracy and African American Health," *American Journal of Public Health* 100, no. 10 (2010): 1831–34. On how the meritocracy myth offers hope to those who are struggling, see N. T. Feather, "Judgments of Deservingness: Studies in the Psychology of Justice and Achievement," *Personality and Social Psychology Review* 3, no. 2 (1999): 86–107; Danielle Gaucher et al., "Compensatory Rationalizations and the Resolution of Everyday Undeserved Outcomes," *Personality and Social Psychology Bulletin* 36, no. 1 (2010): 109–18; Shane and Heckhausen, "University Students' Causal Conceptions about Social Mobility."

18. On the lasting harm of belief in the meritocracy myth, see N. Krieger and S. Sidney, "Racial Discrimination and Blood Pressure: The CARDIA Study of Young Black and White Adults," *American Journal of Public Health* 86, no. 10 (1996): 1370–78; Kwate and Meyer, "The Myth of Meritocracy and African American Health."

19. On the reassurance that the meritocracy myth offers to people in more privileged positions, see Arlie Russell Hochschild, *Strangers in Their Own Land: Anger and Mourning on the American Right* (New York: The New Press, 2016); Shamus Khan, *Privilege: The Making of an Adolescent Elite* (Princeton, NJ: Princeton University Press, 2012); Rachel Sherman, *Uneasy Street: The Anxieties of Affluence* (Princeton, NJ: Princeton University Press, 2019). On rich people's attitudes toward luck and success, see Robert H. Frank, *Success and Luck: Good Fortune and the Myth of Meritocracy* (Princeton NJ: Princeton University Press, 2016). On the effects of meritocracy-based messaging, see Shannon K. McCoy and Brenda Major, "Priming Meritocracy and the Psychological Justification of Inequality," *Journal of Experimental Social Psychology* 43, no. 3 (2007): 341–51.

20. On the psychological benefits of downward social comparison, see Alderson and Katz-Gerro, "Compared to Whom?" On how inequality amplifies the psychological benefits of downward social comparison, see Liao, "Income Inequality, Social Comparison, and Happiness in the United States"; Macchia et al., "Buying Happines in an Unequal World." On how the prosperity gospel encourages its adherents to focus on their blessings, see Anthea Butler, *White Evangelical Racism: The Politics of Morality in America* (Chapel Hill: UNC Press, 2021); Eric D. Knowles and Brian S. Lowery, "Meritocracy, Self-Concerns, and Whites' Denial of Racial Inequity," *Self and Identity* 11, no. 2 (2012): 202–22.

21. On how the meritocracy myth encourages judgment of people who rely on government programs, see Heather E. Bullock, "Justifying Inequality: Social Psychological Analysis of Beliefs about Poverty and the Poor," in *The Colors of Poverty: Why Racial and Ethnic Disparities Persist*, ed. Ann Chih Lin and David R. Harris (New York: Russell Sage Foundation, 2008), 52–75; Jessica McCrory Calarco, Ilana S. Horn, and Grace A. Chen, "'You Need to Be More Responsible': The Myth of Meritocracy and Teachers' Accounts of Homework Inequalities," *Educational Researcher* 51, no. 8 (2022): 515–23; Ilana Seidel Horn, "Turnaround Students in High School Mathematics: Constructing Identities of Competence Through Mathematical Worlds," *Mathematical Thinking and Learning* 10, no. 3 (August 11, 2008): 201–39; Ilana Se-

idel Horn, "Teacher Discourse and the Construction of School Mathematics," *For the Learning of Mathematics* 32, no. 1 (2012): 25–27; Warikoo and Fuhr, "Legitimating Status." On the prevalence of the belief that people in poverty aren't doing enough to improve their lives, see "American Attitudes about Poverty and the Poor," Population Reference Bureau, May 30, 2002, https://www.prb.org/resources/american-attitudes-about-poverty-and-the-poor/. On the federal poverty line, see "Poverty Guidelines," U.S. Department of Health and Human Services, Office of the Assistant Secretary for Planning and Evaluation 2023, https://aspe.hhs.gov/topics/poverty-economic-mobility/poverty-guidelines.

22. On universal programs and their notion of deservingness, see Juliana Uhuru Bidadanure, "The Political Theory of Universal Basic Income," *Annual Review of Political Science* 22 (2019): 481–501; Helen B. Marrow, "Deserving to a Point: Unauthorized Immigrants in San Francisco's Universal Access Healthcare Model," *Social Science & Medicine* 74, no. 6 (2012): 846–54; Anne L. Schneider and Helen M. Ingram, *Deserving and Entitled: Social Constructions and Public Policy* (Albany: State University of New York Press, 2005). On how the US social safety net is structured to force beneficiaries to prove their deservingness by navigating complex bureaucratic hurdles, see Pamela Herd and Donald P. Moynihan, *Administrative Burden: Policymaking by Other Means* (New York: Russell Sage Foundation, 2019); Donald Moynihan, Pamela Herd, and Hope Harvey, "Administrative Burden: Learning, Psychological, and Compliance Costs in Citizen-State Interactions," *Journal of Public Administration Research and Theory* 25, no. 1 (2015): 43–69; Leslie Paik, *Trapped in a Maze: How Social Control Institutions Drive Family Poverty and Inequality* (Berkeley: University of California Press, 2021). On work requirements, see Kathryn Edin and Laura Lein, *Making Ends Meet: How Single Mothers Survive Welfare and Low-Wage Work* (New York: Russell Sage Foundation, 1997); Carolyn J. Heinrich and Joh Karl Scholz, *Making the Work-Based Safety Net Work Better: Forward-Looking Policies to Help Low-Income Families* (New York: Russell Sage Foundation, 2009). On the weigh-ins required for WIC recipients, see Sinikka Elliott and Sarah Bowen, "Defending Motherhood: Morality, Responsibility, and Double Binds in Feeding Children," *Journal of Marriage and Family* 80, no. 2 (2018): 499–520; Kelley Fong, Rachel A. Wright, and Christopher Wimer, "The Cost of Free Assistance: Why Low-Income Individuals Do Not Access Food Pantries," *Journal of Sociology & Social Welfare* 43, no. 1 (2016): 71–94; Kelley Fong, "Concealment and Constraint: Child Protective Services Fears and Poor Mothers' Institutional Engagement," *Social Forces* 97, no. 4 (2019): 1785–810. On the drug tests required for welfare recipients, see Darrel Thompson, *Drug Testing and Public Assistance* (Washington, DC: Center for Law and Social Policy, 2019), https://www.clasp.org/wp-content/uploads/2022/01/2019_drug-testing-and-public-_0.pdf.

23. On how the insufficiency of food stamp and WIC benefits affects families' food choices, see Kathryn Edin, Melody Boyd, and James Mabli, *SNAP Food Security In-Depth Interview Study* (Arlington, VA: US Department of Agriculture, Food and Nutrition Service, Office of Research and Analysis, 2013), https://www.mathematica.org/publications/snap-food-security-indepth-interview-study; Elliott and Bowen, "Defending Motherhood"; Elise Gifford, "Low-Income Mothers and Their Pursuit of Food in a Rural Massachusetts County: A Qualitative Study from a Feminist Point of View" (thesis, University of Massachusetts Amherst, 2011); Annie Hardison-Moody et al., "How Social, Cultural, and Economic Environments Shape Infant Feeding for Low-Income Women: A Qualitative Study in North Carolina," *Journal of the Academy of Nutrition and Dietetics* 118, no. 10 (2018): 1886.

24. On the early history of mass incarceration in the US, see Andrew H. Browning, "The Moralization of Poverty in the Panic of 1819," *Journal of the Early Republic* 40, no. 4 (2020): 715–20; Michael Meranze, "The Penitential Ideal in Late Eighteenth-Century Philadelphia," *Pennsylvania Magazine of History and Biography* 108, no. 4 (1984): 420; Robert R. Sullivan, "The Birth of the Prison: The Case of Benjamin Rush," *Eighteenth-Century Studies* 31, no. 3 (1998): 333–44. See also Michel Foucault, *Discipline and Punish: The Birth of the Prison*, trans. A Sheridan (Oxford, UK: Vintage, 1979); James B. Jacobs, *Stateville: The Penitentiary in Mass Society*

(Chicago: University of Chicago Press, 2015); Dario Melossi and Massimo Pavarini, *The Prison and the Factory: Origins of the Penitentiary System* (New York: Springer, 2018); Michael Meranze, *Laboratories of Virtue: Punishment, Revolution, and Authority in Philadelphia, 1760–1835* (Chapel Hill: University of North Carolina Press, 1996). For more on religion's role in the stigmatization of immigrants and low-income workers, see William J. Phalen, *American Evangelical Protestantism and European Immigrants, 1800–1924* (Jefferson, NC: McFarland, 2014); Melissa J. Wilde and Sabrina Danielsen, "Fewer and Better Children: Race, Class, Religion, and Birth Control Reform in America," *American Journal of Sociology* 119, no. 6 (2014): 1710–60.

25. On the Black Codes and their relationship to the modern system of mass incarceration, see Michelle Alexander, *The New Jim Crow: Mass Incarceration in the Age of Colorblindness* (New York: The New Press, 2020); Douglas A. Blackmon, *Slavery by Another Name: The Re-Enslavement of Black Americans from the Civil War to World War II* (New York: Anchor, 2008); W. E. Burghardt Du Bois, *Black Reconstruction* (San Diego: Harcourt Brace, 1935); Eric Foner, *Reconstruction: America's Unfinished Revolution, 1863–1877* (New York: Harper Perennial Modern Classics, 2014); Henry Louis Gates Jr., "How Reconstruction Still Shapes American Racism," *Time*, April 2, 2019, https://time.com/5562869/reconstruction-history/; Tera W. Hunter, *To 'Joy My Freedom: Southern Black Women's Lives and Labors after the Civil War* (Cambridge, MA: Harvard University Press, 1998); Wacquant, "From Slavery to Mass Incarceration." On the role that incarcerated people played in early US manufacturing, see Meranze, "The Penitential Ideal in Late Eighteenth-Century Philadelphia"; Meranze, *Laboratories of Virtue*.

26. On the parallels between the early and modern histories of incarceration, see Alexander, *The New Jim Crow*; Browning, "The Moralization of Poverty in the Panic of 1819"; Foucault, *Discipline and Punish*; James C. Garman, *Detention Castles of Stone and Steel: Landscape, Labor, and the Urban Penitentiary* (Knoxville: University of Tennessee Press, 2005); Evelyn Nakano Glenn, *Forced to Care: Coercion and Caregiving in America* (Cambridge, MA: Harvard University Press, 2010); Alex Lichtenstein, *Twice the Work of Free Labor: The Political Economy of Convict Labor in the New South* (New York: Verso Books, 1996); Matthew J. Mancini, *One Dies, Get Another: Convict Leasing in the American South, 1866–1928* (Columbia: University of South Carolina Press, 1996); Meranze, "The Penitential Ideal in Late Eighteenth-Century Philadelphia"; Meranze, *Laboratories of Virtue*; Vivien M. L. Miller, "Reinventing the Penitentiary: Punishment in Florida, 1868–1923," *American Nineteenth Century History* 1, no. 1 (2000): 82–106; Christopher Muller, "Freedom and Convict Leasing in the Postbellum South," *American Journal of Sociology* 124, no. 2 (2018): 367–405; ed. Mary Pattillo, Bruce Western, and David Weiman, *Imprisoning America: The Social Effects of Mass Incarceration* (New York: Russell Sage Foundation, 2006); Becky Pettit, *Invisible Men: Mass Incarceration and the Myth of Black Progress* (New York: Russell Sage Foundation, 2012); Wacquant, "From Slavery to Mass Incarceration: Rethinking the 'Race Question' in the US." On the number of people incarcerated in the US, see "Mass Incarceration: The Whole Pie 2023," Prison Policy Initiative, https://www.prisonpolicy.org/reports/pie2023.html. On the demographics of people incarcerated in prisons in the US, see "Inmate Race," Federal Bureau of Prisons, https://www.bop.gov/about/statistics/statistics_inmate_race.jsp. On the demographics of people incarcerated in US jails, see "Jail Inmates in 2021—Statistical Trends," Bureau of Justice Statistics, https://bjs.ojp.gov/library/publications/jail-inmates-2021-statistical-tables. On the relationship between income and incarceration, see Bernadette Rabuy and Daniel Kopf, *Prisons of Poverty: Uncovering the Pre-Incarceration Incomes of the Imprisoned* (Northampton, MA: Prison Policy Initiative, 2015). On the role that incarcerated people currently play in the US workforce, see Jaron Browne, "Rooted in Slavery: Prison Labor Exploitation," *Race, Poverty & the Environment* 14, no. 1 (2007): 42–44; Lan Cao, "Made in the USA: Race, Trade, and Prison Labor," *New York University Review of Law & Social Change* 43 (2019): 1; Neveen Hammad, "Shackled to Economic Appeal: How Prison Labor Facilitates Modern Slavery While Perpetuating

Poverty in Black Communities," *Virginia Journal of Social Policy & the Law* 26 (2019): 65; Robert P. Weiss, "'Repatriating' Low-Wage Work: The Political Economy of Prison Labor Reprivatization in the Postindustrial United States," *Criminology* 39, no. 2 (2001): 253–92. For the ACLU report quoted here, see *Captive Labor: Exploitation of Incarcerated Workers* (Chicago: ACLU and the University of Chicago Law School, 2022), https://www.aclu.org/wp -content/uploads/legal-documents/2022-06-15-captivelaborresearchreport.pdf.

27. On the employment-related challenges faced by formerly incarcerated people in the US, see Shawns D. Bushway, Michael A. Stoll, and David Weiman, *Barriers to Reentry?: The Labor Market for Released Prisoners in Post-Industrial America* (New York: Russell Sage Foundation, 2007); Pager, "The Mark of a Criminal Record"; Pager et al., "Discrimination in a Low-Wage Labor Market"; Uggen et al., "The Edge of Stigma"; Western, "The Impact of Incarceration on Wage Mobility and Inequality." On the likelihood of reincarceration, see Susan Lockwood et al., "The Effect of Correctional Education on Postrelease Employment and Recidivism: A 5-Year Follow-Up Study in the State of Indiana," *Crime & Delinquency* 58, no. 3 (2012): 380–96; Stephen J. Tripodi, Johnny S. Kim, and Kimberly Bender, "Is Employment Associated with Reduced Recidivism?: The Complex Relationship between Employment and Crime," *International Journal of Offender Therapy and Comparative Criminology* 54, no. 5 (2010): 706–20; Christy A. Visher, Laura Winterfield, and Mark B. Coggeshall, "Ex-Offender Employment Programs and Recidivism: A Meta-Analysis," *Journal of Experimental Criminology* 1, no. 3 (2005): 295–316.

28. On the origins of the concept of race, see Lee D. Baker, *From Savage to Negro: Anthropology and the Construction of Race, 1896–1954* (Berkeley: University of California Press, 1998); Luana Ross, *Inventing the Savage: The Social Construction of Native American Criminality* (Austin: University of Texas Press, 2010). On how racial categories were developed to justify exploitation, see Martha R. Bireda, *A Time for Change: How White Supremacy Ideology Harms All Americans* (London: Rowman & Littlefield, 2021); Edwin Black, *War against the Weak: Eugenics and America's Campaign to Create a Master Race* (New York: Dialog Press, 2012); Du Bois, *Black Reconstruction*; ed. Joe R. Feagin, *Systemic Racism: A Theory of Oppression* (London: Routledge, 2013); Joe R. Feagin, *The White Racial Frame: Centuries of Racial Framing and Counter-Framing* (London: Routledge, 2020); Barbara J. Fields and Karen E. Fields, *Racecraft: The Soul of Inequality in American Life* (New York: Verso Books, 2022); Ruth Frankenburg, *White Women, Race Matters: The Social Construction of Whiteness* (London: Routledge, 1993); Stefan Kuhl, *The Nazi Connection: Eugenics, American Racism, and German National Socialism* (Oxford: Oxford University Press, 2002); Neda Maghbouleh, *The Limits of Whiteness: Iranian Americans and the Everyday Politics of Race* (Redwood City, CA: Stanford University Press, 2017); Heather McGhee, *The Sum of Us: What Racism Costs Everyone and How We Can Prosper Together* (New York: One World, 2021); Ladelle McWhorter, "Where Do White People Come From? A Foucaultian Critique of Whiteness Studies," *Philosophy & Social Criticism* 31, no. 5–6 (2005): 533–56; Charles W. Mills, *The Racial Contract* (Ithaca, NY: Cornell University Press, 2014); Ann Morning, "Does Genomics Challenge the Social Construction of Race?," *Sociological Theory* 32, no. 3 (2014): 189–207; Ross, *Inventing the Savage*; Audrey Smedley and Brian D. Smedley, "Race as Biology Is Fiction, Racism as a Social Problem Is Real: Anthropological and Historical Perspectives on the Social Construction of Race," *American Psychologist* 60, no. 1 (2005): 16–26; Mary C. Waters, *Ethnic Options: Choosing Identities in America* (Berkeley: University of California, 1990); Ritchie Witzig, "The Medicalization of Race: Scientific Legitimization of a Flawed Social Construct," *Annals of Internal Medicine* 125, no. 8 (1996): 675–79. On how the racist denial of humanity facilitates exploitation, see Celeste Watkins-Hayes and Elise Kovalsky, "The Discourse of Deservingness: Morality and the Dilemmas of Poverty Relief in Debate and Practice," in *The Oxford Handbook of the Social Science of Poverty*, ed. David Brady and Linda Burton (Oxford: Oxford University Press, 2016). On how racist ideas make the meritocracy myth seem more plausible, see Black, *War*

against the Weak; Steven A. Farber, "U.S. Scientists' Role in the Eugenics Movement (1907–1939): A Contemporary Biologist's Perspective," *Zebrafish* 5, no. 4 (2008): 243–45; Kuhl, *The Nazi Connection*; Tukufu Zuberi, *Thicker Than Blood* (Minneapolis: University of Minnesota Press, 2001); Tukufu Zuberi and Eduardo Bonilla-Silva, *White Logic, White Methods: Racism and Methodology* (Lanham, MD: Rowman & Littlefield, 2008).

29. On Americans' perceptions of the link between race, poverty, and incarceration, see Richard Carl Fording, *Race and the Politics of Welfare Reform* (Ann Arbor: University of Michigan Press, 2010); Martin Gilens, *Why Americans Hate Welfare: Race, Media, and the Politics of Antipoverty Policy* (Chicago: University of Chicago Press, 2009); Kenneth J. Neubeck and Noel A. Cazenave, *Welfare Racism: Playing the Race Card against America's Poor* (London: Routledge, 2001); Sanford F. Schram, Joe Brian Soss, and Richard Carl Fording, *Race and the Politics of Welfare Reform* (Ann Arbor: University of Michigan Press, 2010). On the Black percentage of the US population, see "QuickFacts," US Census Bureau, https://www.census .gov/quickfacts/fact/table/US/PST045222. On the Black percentage of the incarcerated population, see John Gramlich, "Black Imprisonment Rate in the U.S. Has Fallen by a Third since 2006," Pew Research Center, May 6, 2020, https://www.pewresearch.org/short-reads /2020/05/06/share-of-black-white-hispanic-americans-in-prison-2018-vs-2006/. On the origins of racial differences in poverty and mass incarceration, see Alexander, *The New Jim Crow*; Blackmon, *Slavery by Another Name*; Du Bois, *Black Reconstruction*; Pettit and Western, "Mass Imprisonment and the Life Course"; Victor M. Rios, *Punished: Policing the Lives of Black and Latino Boys* (New York: NYU Press, 2011); Van Cleve, *Crook County*; Wacquant, "From Slavery to Mass Incarceration." On the Black percentage of welfare recipients, see *Characteristics and Financial Circumstances of TANF Recipients Fiscal Year (FY) 2020* (Washington, DC: Administration for Children and Families, 2020), https://www.acf.hhs.gov /sites/default/files/documents/ofa/fy2020_characteristics_data_final.pdf. On the Black percentage of food stamp recipients, see Heather Hartline-Grafton and Ellen Vollinger, "New USDA Report Provides Picture of Who Participates in SNAP," Food Research & Action Center, https://frac.org/blog/new-usda-report-provides-picture-of-who-participates-in-snap. On the Black percentage of Medicaid recipients, see "Distribution of the Nonelderly with Medicaid by Race/Ethnicity," KFF, https://www.kff.org/medicaid/state-indicator/medicaid -distribution-nonelderly-by-raceethnicity. On the Black percentage of free/reduced price lunch recipients, see "Number and Percentage of Public School Students," National Center for Education Statistics, https://nces.ed.gov/programs/digest/d17/tables/dt17_216.60.asp. On racialized perceptions of Covid-19 and their relationship to support for Covid mitigation policies, see Salil D. Benegal, "The Spillover of Race and Racial Attitudes into Public Opinion about Climate Change," *Environmental Politics* 27, no. 4 (July 4, 2018): 733–56; Allison Harell and Evan Lieberman, "How Information about Race-Based Health Disparities Affects Policy Preferences: Evidence from a Survey Experiment about the COVID-19 Pandemic in the United States," *Social Science & Medicine* 277 (2021): 113884.

30. On the spillover effects of racist policies, see McGhee, *The Sum of Us*. On how racial wage gaps have changed over time, see Siwei Cheng et al., "Educational Variations in Cohort Trends in the Black-White Earnings Gap among Men: Evidence from Administrative Earnings Data," *Demography* 56, no. 6 (December 2, 2019): 2253–77. On rising death rates among white people, see Anne Case and Angus Deaton, "Rising Morbidity and Mortality in Midlife among White Non-Hispanic Americans in the 21st Century," *Proceedings of the National Academy of Sciences* 112, no. 49 (December 8, 2015): 15078–8; Case and Deaton, *Deaths of Despair and the Future of Capitalism*.

31. On how the meritocracy myth promotes benevolence toward big businesses and billionaires, see McNamee and Miller, *The Myth of Meritocracy*. For the quotes about Musk, see Ryan Mac, Cade Metz, and Kate Conger, "'I Don't Really Have a Business Plan': How Elon Musk Wings It," *New York Times*, May 3, 2022, https://www.nytimes.com/2022/05/03/technology/elon -musk-twitter-plan.html. On Americans' attitudes toward billionaires, see Andrew Daniller,

"Americans' Views about Billionaires Have Grown Somewhat More Negative Since 2020," Pew Research Center, July 28, 2021, https://www.pewresearch.org/short-reads/2021/07/28 /americans-views-about-billionaires-have-grown-somewhat-more-negative-since-2020.

32. On Elon Musk's wealth, see "The World's Real Time Billionaires," *Forbes*, 2023, https:// www.forbes.com/real-time-billionaires/. For the *Wall Street Journal* article quoted here, see Christopher Mims, "Are You 'Extremely Hardcore' or Not? How Elon Musk Is Dividing Silicon Valley's Elite," *Wall Street Journal*, December 24, 2022, https://www.wsj.com/articles /elon-musk-leadership-analysis-extremely-hardcore-11671832630. On Musk's ultimatum, see Dan Milmo, "Elon Musk Gives Twitter Staff Deadline to Commit to Being 'Hardcore,'" *Guardian*, November 16, 2022, https://www.theguardian.com/technology/2022/nov/16/elon-musk -gives-twitter-staff-deadline-to-commit-to-being-hardcore.

33. On Johnson's anti-aging regime, see Ashlee Vance, "How to Be 18 Years Old Again for Only $2 Million a Year," Bloomberg, January 25, 2023, https://www.bloomberg.com/news/features /2023-01-25/anti-aging-techniques-taken-to-extreme-by-bryan-johnson. On Franklin's wealth, see Fox Butterfield, "From Ben Franklin, a Gift That's Worth Two Fights," *New York Times*, April 21, 1990, https://www.nytimes.com/1990/04/21/us/from-ben-franklin-a-gift-that-s -worth-two-fights.html.

34. For Biden's proposed billionaire tax bill, see "Billionaires Income Tax Act," US Senate Committee on Finance, https://www.finance.senate.gov/imo/media/doc/Billionaires%20 Income%20Tax.pdf. On the revenue that bill would have generated, see Tami Luhby, "Here's How Democrats Want to Tax Billionaires to Pay for Their Social Spending Plans," CNN, October 25, 2021, https://www.cnn.com/2021/10/25/politics/billionaires-tax-plan-capital -gains/index.html. On federal education spending, see "Department of Education," USA Spending, 2023, https://www.usaspending.gov/agency/department-of-education?fy=2023. On Manchin's role in killing the bill, see Jonathan Weisman, "Manchin Denounces the Democrats' Plan to Tax Billionaires as Divisive," *New York Times*, October 27, 2021, https://www .nytimes.com/2021/10/27/us/politics/manchin-billionaires-tax.html.

35. For changes in the federal income tax rate over time, see "Historical U.S. Federal Individual Income Tax Rates & Brackets, 1862–2021," Tax Foundation, August 24, 2021, https://tax foundation.org/historical-income-tax-rates-brackets/. On the number of billionaires in the 1980s, see Bob Lord, "America Only Had a Handful of Billionaires 40 Years Ago. We're Now Creating 'Centibillionaires'—and Unless We Tax Them, Trillionaires," *Fortune*, April 5, 2023, https://fortune.com/2023/04/05/america-billionaires-40-years-creating-centibillionaires -tax-them-trillionaires-bob-lord/. On the number of billionaires today, see Willy Staley, "How Many Billionaires Are There, Anyway?," *New York Times*, April 7, 2022, https://www.nytimes .com/2022/04/07/magazine/billionaires.html.

36. On how shares of the wealth have changed over time, see Juliana Menasce Horowitz, Ruth Igielnick, and Rakesh Kochhar, "Trends in U.S. Income and Wealth Inequality," in *Most Americans Say There Is Too Much Economic Inequality in the U.S., but Fewer Than Half Call It a Top Priority* (Washington, DC: Pew Research Center, 2020), https://www.pewresearch.org /social-trends/2020/01/09/trends-in-income-and-wealth-inequality/.

37. On tax loopholes, see Brooke Harrington, "Trust and Estate Planning: The Emergence of a Profession and Its Contribution to Socioeconomic Inequality," *Sociological Forum* 27, no. 4 (2012): 825–46; Brooke Harrington, *Capital without Borders: Wealth Managers and the One Percent* (Cambridge, MA: Harvard University Press, 2017); Brooke Harrington, "Turning Vice into Virtue: Institutional Work and Professional Misconduct," *Human Relations* 72, no. 9 (2019): 1464–96; Rob Reich, *Just Giving: Why Philanthropy Is Failing Democracy and How It Can Do Better* (Princeton, NJ: Princeton University Press, 2020). On the tax rates paid by extremely wealthy individuals, see Jesse Eisinger, Jeff Ernthausen, and Paul Kiel, "The Secret IRS Files: Trove of Never-Before-Seen Records Reveal How the Wealthiest Avoid Income Tax," ProPublica, June 8, 2021, https://www.propublica.org/article/the-secret-irs-files-trove -of-never-before-seen-records-reveal-how-the-wealthiest-avoid-income-tax.

38. On favorable perceptions of the rich, see Bram P. Buunk et al., "The Affective Consequences of Social Comparison: Either Direction Has Its Ups and Downs," *Journal of Personality and Social Psychology* 59, no. 6 (1990): 1238–49; Rebecca L. Collins, "For Better or Worse: The Impact of Upward Social Comparison on Self-Evaluations," *Psychological Bulletin* 119, no. 1 (1996): 51–69; Joshua J. Guyer and Thomas I. Vaughan-Johnston, "Social Comparisons (Upward and Downward)," in *Encyclopedia of Personality and Individual Differences*, ed. Virgil Zeigler-Hill and Todd K. Shackelford (Cham, Switzerland: Springer International Publishing, 2020), 5011–15.

CHAPTER 6: THE MARS/VENUS MYTH

1. For the book, see John Gray, *Men Are from Mars, Women Are from Venus: The Classic Guide to Understanding the Opposite Sex* (New York: Harper Paperbacks, 2012). On the popularity of the book, see Daisy Schofield, "What the Return of Old-School Dating Manuals Tells Us about Modern Love," *Vice*, April 7, 2023, https://i-d.vice.com/en/article/dy3yw7/dating-manual -books-relationships-tiktok-trend.

2. Gray, *Men Are from Mars, Women Are from Venus*, 7–11.

3. On the myths that help maintain the appearance of a biologically rooted gender binary, see Alice H. Eagly, *Sex Differences in Social Behavior: A Social-Role Interpretation* (London: Psychology Press, 1987); Anne Fausto-Sterling, *Myths of Gender: Biological Theories about Women and Men* (New York: Basic Books, 2008); Cordelia Fine, *Delusions of Gender: How Our Minds, Society, and Neurosexism Create Difference* (New York: W. W. Norton, 2010); Cordelia Fine, *Testosterone Rex: Myths of Sex, Science, and Society* (New York: W. W. Norton, 2017); Candace West and Don H. Zimmerman, "Doing Gender," *Gender & Society* 1, no. 2 (1987): 125–51.

4. On men's use of personality-based explanations to justify gender inequalities in the division of household labor, see Allison Daminger, "De-gendered Processes, Gendered Outcomes: How Egalitarian Couples Make Sense of Non-egalitarian Household Practices," *American Sociological Review* 85, no. 5 (2020): 806–29.

5. On how the myth establishes a gender hierarchy, see Jennifer L. Berdahl, "Harassment Based on Sex: Protecting Social Status in the Context of Gender Hierarchy," *Academy of Management Review* 32, no. 2 (2007): 641–58; Chris Brickell, "The Sociological Construction of Gender and Sexuality," *Sociological Review* 54, no. 1 (2006): 87–113; Kate Manne, *Down Girl: The Logic of Misogyny* (Oxford: Oxford University Press, 2018); Barbara J. Risman and Georgiann Davis, "From Sex Roles to Gender Structure," *Current Sociology* 61, no. 5–6 (2013).

6. On homophobia, see Dana M. Britton, "Homophobia and Homosociality: An Analysis of Boundary Maintenance," *Sociological Quarterly* 31, no. 3 (1990): 423–39; C. J. Pascoe, *Dude, You're a Fag: Masculinity and Sexuality in High School* (Berkeley: University of California Press, 2011); Stephen Valocchi, "Not Yet Queer Enough: The Lessons of Queer Theory for the Sociology of Gender and Sexuality," *Gender & Society* 19, no. 6 (2005): 750–70. On transphobia, see Kyla Bender-Baird, "Peeing under Surveillance: Bathrooms, Gender Policing, and Hate Violence," *Gender, Place & Culture* 23, no. 7 (July 2, 2016): 983–88; Charlotte Jones and Jen Slater, "The Toilet Debate: Stalling Trans Possibilities and Defending 'Women's Protected Spaces,'" *Sociological Review* 68, no. 4 (2020): 834–51; Meredith G. F. Worthen, "Hetero-Cis–Normativity and the Gendering of Transphobia," *International Journal of Transgenderism* 17, no. 1 (2016): 31–57. On sexism and misogyny, see Manne, *Down Girl*; Paige L. Sweet, "The Sociology of Gaslighting," *American Sociological Review* 84, no. 5 (2019): 851–75; Kelly Wilz, "Bernie Bros and Woman Cards: Rhetorics of Sexism, Misogyny, and Constructed Masculinity in the 2016 Election," *Women's Studies in Communication* 39, no. 4 (2016): 357–60.

7. On Darwin's efforts to prove the biological origins of Victorian-era gender relations, see Rosemary Jann, "Darwin and the Anthropologists: Sexual Selection and Its Discontents," *Victorian Studies* 37, no. 2 (1994): 287–306. On Darwin's theories of sexual selection, see

Charles Darwin, *The Descent of Man, and Selection in Relation to Sex* (London: John Murray, 1871). For critiques of the notion of a strict gender binary rooted in biological and physiological sex differences, see Claire Ainsworth, "Sex Redefined," *Nature* 518, no. 7539 (2015): 288–91; Fine, *Delusions of Gender*; Fine, *Testosterone Rex*; Matthew Gutmann, Robin G. Nelson, and Agustín Fuentes, "Epidemic Errors in Understanding Masculinity, Maleness, and Violence: An Introduction to Supplement 23," *Current Anthropology* 62, no. S23 (February 2021): S5–12; Abigail Anderson et al., "The Myth of Man the Hunter: Women's Contribution to the Hunt across Ethnographic Contexts," *PLOS ONE* 18, no. 6 (June 28, 2023); Kristen Hawkes, James O'Connell, and Nicholas Blurton Jones, "Hunter-Gatherer Studies and Human Evolution: A Very Selective Review," *American Journal of Physical Anthropology* 165, no. 4 (2018): 777–800; Jann, "Darwin and the Anthropologists"; Richard Borshay Lee and Irven DeVore, *Man the Hunter* (London: Routledge, 1968).

8. On women's role in hunter-gatherer societies, see Anderson et al., "The Myth of Man the Hunter." For media coverage of this research, see "Men Are Hunters, Women Are Gatherers. That Was the Assumption. A New Study Upends It," *Goats and Soda*, podcast, NPR, July 1, 2023, https://www.npr.org/sections/goatsandsoda/2023/07/01/1184749528/men-are-hunters-women-are-gatherers-that-was-the-assumption-a-new-study-upends-i.

9. On the role of religion in reifying the Mars/Venus myth, see Megan C. Haggard et al., "Religion's Role in the Illusion of Gender Equality: Supraliminal and Subliminal Religious Priming Increases Benevolent Sexism," *Psychology of Religion and Spirituality* 11, no. 4 (2019): 392–98; Patricia Homan and Amy Burdette, "When Religion Hurts: Structural Sexism and Health in Religious Congregations," *American Sociological Review* 86, no. 2 (2021): 234–55; Charles W. Peek, George D. Lowe, and L. Susan Williams, "Gender and God's Word: Another Look at Religious Fundamentalism and Sexism," *Social Forces* 69, no. 4 (1991): 1205–21. On the history of ideas about women's inferiority, see Kimberly A. Hamlin, *From Eve to Evolution: Darwin, Science, and Women's Rights in Gilded Age America* (Chicago: University of Chicago Press, 2015).

10. On the prevalence of misogynistic ideas in the US and internationally, see Kelly Beaver, "One in Three Men Believe Feminism Does More Harm Than Good: Global Survey," Ipsos, March 4, 2022, https://www.ipsos.com/en-us/news-polls/international-womens-day-2022-us-release.

11. On the prevalence of belief in a biologically rooted gender binary, see Travis Mitchell, *Americans' Complex Views on Gender Identity and Transgender Issues* (Washington, DC: Pew Research Center, 2022), https://www.pewresearch.org/social-trends/2022/06/28/americans-complex-views-on-gender-identity-and-transgender-issues/. See also Laura Meckler, "Most Americans Support Anti-Trans Policies Favored by GOP, Poll Shows," *Washington Post*, May 5, 2023, https://www.washingtonpost.com/education/2023/05/05/trans-poll-gop-politics-law. For an example of how the prevalence of sexist beliefs emboldens more extreme misogynists, see Kelsey Koberg, "The Woke Mob Is Everywhere: Here's Where It Came from and How One Critic Believes It Can Be Stopped," *Fox News*, July 24, 2021, https://www.foxnews.com/media/the-woke-mob-is-everywhere-heres-where-it-came-from-and-victor-davis-hansons-solution-for-stopping-it.

12. On the complexity of sex, gender, and sexuality, see Morgan Carpenter, "Intersex Variations, Human Rights, and the International Classification of Diseases," *Health and Human Rights* 20, no. 2 (December 2018): 205–14; Dillon E. King, "The Inclusion of Sex and Gender Beyond the Binary in Toxicology," *Frontiers in Toxicology* 4 (July 22, 2022): 929219.

13. On Americans' beliefs regarding the biological origins of sex and gender, see Meckler, "Most Americans Support Anti-Trans Policies Favored by GOP."

14. On the percentage of babies who are born with intersex traits, see Carpenter, "Intersex Variations, Human Rights, and the International Classification of Diseases"; King, "The Inclusion of Sex and Gender Beyond the Binary in Toxicology"; Carolina Medina and Lindsay Mahowald, "Key Issues Facing People with Intersex Traits," Center for American Progress, October 26, 2021, https://www.americanprogress.org/article/key-issues-facing-people-intersex

-traits/. On the prevalence of green eyes, see Cathy Lovering, "Eye Spy: Worldwide Eye Color Percentages," Healthline, last updated April 19, 2023, https://www.healthline.com /health/eye-health/eye-color-percentages. On variations in hormones, hormone response, and internal anatomy, see Mary K. Bloodsworth-Lugo, *In-Between Bodies: Sexual Difference, Race, and Sexuality* (Albany: State University of New York Press, 2007); Eagly, *Sex Differences in Social Behavior*; Anne Fausto-Sterling, *Sexing the Body: Gender Politics and the Construction of Sexuality* (New York: Basic Books, 2000); Deborah A. Prentice and Dale T. Miller, "Essentializing Differences Between Women and Men," *Psychological Science* 17, no. 2 (2006): 129–35; Wendy Wood and Alice H. Eagly, "Biosocial Construction of Sex Differences and Similarities in Behavior," in *Advances in Experimental Social Psychology*, ed. James M. Olson and Mark P. Zanna, vol. 46 (Cambridge, MA: Academic Press, 2012), 55–123. On how people's sex traits can vary over the life course, see Ricky Kanabar et al., "Correlates of Testosterone Change as Men Age," *Aging Male* 25, no. 1 (December 31, 2022): 29–40; Allan Mazur and Joel Michalek, "Marriage, Divorce, and Male Testosterone," *Social Forces* 77, no. 1 (1998): 315–30. On the effect of caregiving on testosterone, see John Archer, "Testosterone and Human Aggression: An Evaluation of the Challenge Hypothesis," *Neuroscience & Biobehavioral Reviews* 30, no. 3 (2006): 319–45; Anne E. Storey et al., "Hormonal Correlates of Paternal Responsiveness in New and Expectant Fathers," *Evolution and Human Behavior* 21, no. 2 (2000): 79–95; A. Voorthuis, M. J. Bakermans-Kranenburg, and M. H. van Ijzendoorn, "Testosterone Reactivity to Infant Crying and Caregiving in Women: The Role of Oral Contraceptives and Basal Cortisol," *Infant Behavior and Development* 56 (2019): 101191. On how drops in testosterone promote sensitivity in caregiving, see Alison S. Fleming et al., "Testosterone and Prolactin Are Associated with Emotional Responses to Infant Cries in New Fathers," *Hormones and Behavior* 42, no. 4 (2002): 399–413; Lee T. Gettler et al., "Longitudinal Evidence That Fatherhood Decreases Testosterone in Human Males," *Proceedings of the National Academy of Sciences* 108, no. 39 (2011): 16194–99; Gwen E. Gustafson et al., "Affective Reactivity to Cry Sounds Predicts Young Women's Reactivity and Behavior in a Simulated Caregiving Task," *Infant Behavior and Development* 56 (2019): 101193; Darby E. Saxbe et al., "Fathers' Decline in Testosterone and Synchrony with Partner Testosterone during Pregnancy Predicts Greater Postpartum Relationship Investment," *Hormones and Behavior* 90 (2017): 39–47; Darby E. Saxbe et al., "High Paternal Testosterone May Protect against Postpartum Depressive Symptoms in Fathers, but Confer Risk to Mothers and Children," *Hormones and Behavior* 95 (2017): 103–12.

15. On sexuality as a spectrum, see Bloodsworth-Lugo, *In-Between Bodies*; Fausto-Sterling, *Sexing the Body*; Judith Lorber, "Beyond the Binaries: Depolarizing the Categories of Sex, Sexuality, and Gender," *Sociological Inquiry* 66, no. 2 (1996): 143–60; Valocchi, "Not Yet Queer Enough." On declining US support for gay and lesbian relationships and changing gender identities, see Jeffrey M. Jones, "Fewer in U.S. Say Same-Sex Relations Morally Acceptable," Gallup, June 16, 2023, https://news.gallup.com/poll/507230/fewer-say-sex-relations-morally -acceptable.aspx. On variations in these views across demographic groups, see also Justin McCarthy, "U.S. Same-Sex Marriage Support Holds at 71% High," Gallup, June 5, 2023, https://news.gallup.com/poll/506636/sex-marriage-support-holds-high.aspx.

16. On gender as a social construct, see Judith Butler, *Gender Trouble: Feminism and the Subversion of Identity* (New York: Routledge, 2006); Helana Darwin, "Challenging the Cisgender/ Transgender Binary: Nonbinary People and the Transgender Label," *Gender & Society* 34, no. 3 (2020): 357–80; Lorber, "Beyond the Binaries"; West and Zimmerman, "Doing Gender." On the lack of evidence for strict gender differences in communication styles, see Erina L. MacGeorge et al., "The Myth of Gender Cultures: Similarities Outweigh Differences in Men's and Women's Provision of and Responses to Supportive Communication," *Sex Roles* 50, no. 3 (2004): 143–75. On the lack of evidence for strict gender differences in psychological traits, see Bobbi J. Carothers and Harry T. Reis, "Men and Women Are from Earth: Examining the Latent Structure of Gender," *Journal of Personality and Social Psychology* 104, no. 2 (2013): 385–407.

17. On experimental evidence of differences in how adults interact with babies on the basis of perceived gender, see Denis K. Burnham and Mary B. Harris, "Effects of Real Gender and Labeled Gender on Adults' Perceptions of Infants," *Journal of Genetic Psychology* 153, no. 2 (1992): 165–83; Tracey Idle, Eileen Wood, and Serge Desmarais, "Gender Role Socialization in Toy Play Situations: Mothers and Fathers with Their Sons and Daughters," *Sex Roles* 28, no. 11–12 (1993): 679–91; Barbara A. Morrongiello and Kerri Hogg, "Mothers' Reactions to Children Misbehaving in Ways That Can Lead to Injury: Implications for Gender Differences in Children's Risk Taking and Injuries," *Sex Roles* 50, no. 1 (2004): 103–18; Barbara A. Morrongiello, Daniel Zdzieborski, and Jackie Normand, "Understanding Gender Differences in Children's Risk Taking and Injury: A Comparison of Mothers' and Fathers' Reactions to Sons and Daughters Misbehaving in Ways That Lead to Injury," *Journal of Applied Developmental Psychology* 31, no. 4 (2010): 322–29; Eileen Wood, Serge Desmarais, and Sara Gugula, "The Impact of Parenting Experience on Gender Stereotyped Toy Play of Children," *Sex Roles* 47, no. 1 (2002): 39–49. On the effect of parents' gender stereotypes on their interactions with children, see Josh L. Boe and Rebecca J. Woods, "Parents' Influence on Infants' Gender-Typed Toy Preferences," *Sex Roles* 79, no. 5 (2018): 358–73.

18. On preschool teachers' gendered treatment of children, see Heidi M. Gansen, "Push-Ups versus Clean-Up: Preschool Teachers' Gendered Beliefs, Expectations for Behavior, and Disciplinary Practices," *Sex Roles*, July 19, 2018. On middle school teachers' gendered treatment of students, see Michela Musto, "Brilliant or Bad: The Gendered Social Construction of Exceptionalism in Early Adolescence," *American Sociological Review* 84, no. 3 (2019): 369–93.

19. For the Pew Research Center data cited here, see Kim Parker, Juliana Menasce Horowitz, and Renee Stepler, *On Gender Differences, No Consensus on Nature vs. Nurture* (Washington, DC: Pew Research Center, 2017), https://www.pewresearch.org/social-trends/2017/12/05/on -gender-differences-no-consensus-on-nature-vs-nurture/. On gender differences in socialization, see Patricia A. Adler, Steven J. Kless, and Peter Adler, "Socialization to Gender Roles: Popularity among Elementary School Boys and Girls," *Sociology of Education* 65, no. 3 (1992): 169–87; Tracy L. Dietz, "An Examination of Violence and Gender Role Portrayals in Video Games: Implications for Gender Socialization and Aggressive Behavior," *Sex Roles* 38, no. 5–6 (1998): 425–42; Heidi M. Gansen, "Reproducing (and Disrupting) Heteronormativity: Gendered Sexual Socialization in Preschool Classrooms," *Sociology of Education* 90, no. 3 (2017): 255–72; Gansen, "Push-Ups Versus Clean-Up"; Idle, Wood, and Desmarais, "Gender Role Socialization in Toy Play Situations"; Emily W. Kane, "'No Way My Boys Are Going to Be Like That!': Parents' Responses to Children's Gender Nonconformity," *Gender & Society* 20, no. 2 (2006): 149–76; Karin A. Martin, "Becoming a Gendered Body: Practices of Preschools," *American Sociological Review* 63, no. 4 (1998): 494–511; Musto, "Brilliant or Bad"; Barrie Thorne, *Gender Play* (New Brunswick, NJ: Rutgers University Press, 1999).

20. On men's willingness to abandon egalitarian gender ideals, see Calarco et al., "By Default"; Daminger, "De-Gendered Processes, Gendered Outcomes"; Aliya Hamid Rao, *Crunch Time: How Married Couples Confront Unemployment* (Berkeley: University of California Press, 2020); Jaclyn S. Wong, "Competing Desires: How Young Adult Couples Negotiate Moving for Career Opportunities," *Gender & Society* 31, no. 2 (2017): 171–96. On the disconnect between support for gender equality in the workplace and gender equality at home, see William J. Scarborough, Ray Sin, and Barbara Risman, "Attitudes and the Stalled Gender Revolution: Egalitarianism, Traditionalism, and Ambivalence from 1977 through 2016," *Gender & Society* 33, no. 2 (2018): 173–200.

21. On men's use of egalitarian attitudes as a shield, see Ellen Lamont, "The Limited Construction of an Egalitarian Masculinity: College-Educated Men's Dating and Relationship Narratives," *Men and Masculinities* 18, no. 3 (2015): 271.

22. On how learned helplessness manifests inequality, see Peter Glick et al., "Beyond Prejudice as Simple Antipathy: Hostile and Benevolent Sexism across Cultures," *Journal of Personality and Social Psychology* 79, no. 5 (2000): 763–75.

23. On Carlson's firing and the prevalence of misogynistic rhetoric across Fox News's platforms and programs, see Mary Yang, "Fired Tucker Carlson Producer: Misogyny and Bullying 'Trickles Down from the Top,'" NPR, April 28, 2023, https://www.npr.org/2023/04/28/1172 584447/tucker-carlson-firing-misogyny-abuse-fox-news-abby-grossberg. On Fox's long track record of promoting sexist and misogynistic rhetoric, see Eliana Dockterman, "The True Story behind *Bombshell* and the Fox News Sexual Harassment Scandal," *Time*, December 16, 2019, https://time.com/5748267/bombshell-true-story-fox-news/; Martin Gelin, "The Misogyny of Climate Deniers," *New Republic*, August 28, 2019, https://www.biologicaldiversity .org/news/media-archive/a2019/climate_newrepublic_8.28.19.pdf; Karla Mantilla, "Gendertrolling: Misogyny Adapts to New Media," *Feminist Studies* 39, no. 2 (2013): 563–570; Drue Allison Marr, "Three Networks, Two Candidates, One Problem: Sexist News Commentary during Hillary Clinton's Presidential and Sarah Palin's Vice-Presidential Campaigns," *Young Scholars in Writing* 16 (2019): 39–50.

24. On how new media facilitates the spread of sexism and misogyny, see Sarah Benet-Weiser and Kate M. Miltner, "#MasculinitySoFragile: Culture, Structure, and Networked Misogyny," *Feminist Media* Studies 16, no. 1 (2016): 171–174; Kirsti Cole, "'It's Like She's Eager to Be Verbally Abused': Twitter, Trolls, and (En)Gendering Disciplinary Rhetoric," *Feminist Media Studies* 15, no. 2 (2015): 356–358; Diane Felmless, Paulina Inara Rodis, and Amy Zhang, "Sexist Slurs: Reinforcing Feminine Stereotypes Online," *Sex Roles* 83 (2020): 16–28; Karla Mantilla, *Gendertrolling: How Misogyny Went Viral* (New York: Bloomsbury, 2015); Whitney Phillips, *This Is Why We Can't Have Nice Things: Mapping the Relationship between Online Trolling and Mainstream Culture* (Cambridge, MA: MIT Press, 2015).

25. On Che's attack on Biles, see Kylie Cheung, "Michael Che and the 'Edgy,' Male Comedian's Obsession with Rape Jokes," *Salon*, July 30, 2021, https://www.salon.com/2021/07/30 /michael-che-comedians-rape-jokes/. On the hateful language directed by a colleague toward Representative Alexandria Ocasio-Cortez, see Luke Broadwater and Catie Edmondson, "A.O.C. Unleashes a Viral Condemnation of Sexism in Congress," *New York Times*, July 23, 2020, https://www.nytimes.com/2020/07/23/us/alexandria-ocasio-cortez-sexism -congress.html. For the response from Ocasio-Cortez's colleagues, see also "Alexandria Ocasio-Cortez Denounces 'Sexist Slur by Congressman,'" BBC, July 23, 2020, https://www .bbc.com/news/world-us-canada-53521143. On ProPublica's investigation into the Border Patrol Facebook group, see A. C. Thompson, "Inside the Secret Border Patrol Facebook Group Where Agents Joke about Migrant Deaths and Post Sexist Memes," ProPublica, July 1, 2019, https://www.propublica.org/article/secret-border-patrol-facebook-group-agents -joke-about-migrant-deaths-post-sexist-memes. On the LAPD case, see Libor Jany, "LAPD Officer Is Suing the Department, Alleging Supervisors Ignored Sexual Harassment," *Los Angeles Times*, March 16, 2023, https://www.latimes.com/california/story/2023-03-16/an -lapd-cop-told-her-superiors-she-was-being-subjected-to-sexism-at-work-they-demoted -her-now-shes-suing.

26. On men's efforts to couch sexism and misogyny in humor, see Thomas E. Ford, "Effects of Sexist Humor on Tolerance of Sexist Events," *Personality and Social Psychology Bulletin* 26, no. 9 (2000): 1094–107; Thomas E. Ford, Erin R. Wentzel, and Joli Lorion, "Effects of Exposure to Sexist Humor on Perceptions of Normative Tolerance of Sexism," *European Journal of Social Psychology* 31, no. 6 (2001): 677–91; Thomas E. Ford et al., "More Than 'Just a Joke': The Prejudice-Releasing Function of Sexist Humor," *Personality and Social Psychology Bulletin* 34, no. 2 (2008): 159–70; Robyn K. Mallett, Thomas E. Ford, and Julie A. Woodzicka, "What Did He Mean by That? Humor Decreases Attributions of Sexism and Confrontation of Sexist Jokes," *Sex Roles* 75, no. 5 (2016): 272–84; Marinella Paciello et al., "Online Sexist Meme and Its Effects on Moral and Emotional Processes in Social Media," *Computers in Human Behavior* 116 (2021).

27. On how couching sexism and misogyny in humor discourages women from pushing back, see

Mallett, Ford, and Woodzicka, "What Did He Mean by That?"; Raúl Pérez and Viveca S. Greene, "Debating Rape Jokes vs. Rape Culture: Framing and Counter-Framing Misogynistic Comedy," *Social Semiotics* 26, no. 3 (2016): 265–82; Melanie Proulx, "Shameless Comedy: Investigating Shame as an Exposure Effect of Contemporary Sexist and Feminist Rape Jokes," *Comedy Studies* 9, no. 2 (July 3, 2018): 183–99.

28. On laughter in moments of benign incongruity, see A. Peter McGraw and Caleb Warren, "Benign Violations: Making Immoral Behavior Funny," *Psychological Science* 21, no. 8 (2010); Mary K. Rothbart, "Incongruity Problem-Solving and Laughter," in ed. Anthony J. Chapman and Hugh C. Foot, *Humor and Laughter* (London: Routledge, 1996). On the social purpose of laughter, see also Erving Goffman, *The Presentation of Self in Everyday Life* (New York: Anchor, 1959).

29. On profit pressures, see Donald Tomaskovic-Devey and Ken-Hou Lin, "Income Dynamics, Economic Rents, and the Financialization of the U.S. Economy," *American Sociological Review* 76, no. 4 (2011): 538–59; Dale L. Johnson, "The Political Economy of Financialization and Its Consequences," in *Social Inequality, Economic Decline, and Plutocracy: An American Crisis*, ed. Dale L. Johnson (Cham, Switzerland: Springer International Publishing, 2017), 23–39. On the pressure workers, especially men, face to be the "ideal worker," see Youngjoo Cha, "Reinforcing Separate Spheres: The Effect of Spousal Overwork on Men's and Women's Employment in Dual- Earner Households," *American Sociological Review* 75, no. 2 (2010): 303–29; Jeffrey S. Gray, "The Fall in Men's Return to Marriage: Declining Productivity Effects or Changing Selection?," *Journal of Human Resources* 32, no. 3 (1997): 481–504; Alexandra Killewald and Margaret Gough, "Does Specialization Explain Marriage Penalties and Premiums?," *American Sociological Review* 78, no. 3 (2013): 477–502.

30. On how husbands' paid work influences wives' time on paid work, see Cha, "Reinforcing Separate Spheres." On how men's earnings vary depending on the amount of paid work their wives perform, see Killewald and Gough, "Does Specialization Explain Marriage Penalties and Premiums?" On how the financial benefits of having a stay-at-home wife vary for men at different parts of the income spectrum, see Brian Aronson and Lisa A. Keister, "Overwork, Specialization, and Wealth," *Journal of Marriage and Family* 81, no. 5 (2019): 1053–73.

31. On how being the ideal worker is easier with a stay-at-home partner, see Cha, "Reinforcing Separate Spheres"; Jerry A. Jacobs and Kathleen Gerson, "Overworked Individuals or Overworked Families?: Explaining Trends in Work, Leisure, and Family Time," *Work and Occupations* 28, no. 1 (2001): 40–63. On why men can't simply reject these pressures, see Parker et al., *On Gender Differences*. On gender differences in the rewards for meeting ideal worker norms, see Krista M. Brumley, "The Gendered Ideal Worker Narrative: Professional Women's and Men's Work Experiences in the New Economy at a Mexican Company," *Gender & Society* 28, no. 6 (2014): 799–823; Krista M. Brumley, "'It's More Appropriate for Men': Management and Worker Perceptions of the Gendered Ideal Worker," *Sociological Spectrum* 38, no. 6 (November 2, 2018): 406–21; Tracy L. Dumas and Jeffrey Sanchez-Burks, "The Professional, the Personal, and the Ideal Worker: Pressures and Objectives Shaping the Boundary between Life Domains," *Academy of Management Annals* 9, no. 1 (2015): 803–43; Krista Lynn Minnotte and Michael C. Minnotte, "The Ideal Worker Norm and Workplace Social Support among U.S. Workers," *Sociological Focus* 54, no. 2 (2021): 120–37; Christin L. Munsch, "Flexible Work, Flexible Penalties: The Effect of Gender, Childcare, and Type of Request on the Flexibility Bias," *Social Forces* 94, no. 4 (2016): 1567–91; Christin L. Munsch, Lindsey T. O'Connor, and Susan R. Fisk, "Gender and the Disparate Payoffs of Overwork," *Social Psychology Quarterly* (2023). On how the absence of a social safety net incentivizes workers to maximize their income, see Jacob S. Hacker, *The Great Risk Shift: The New Economic Insecurity and the Decline of the American Dream* (Oxford: Oxford University Press, 2019).

32. On how religious teachings treat women as the lesser, helper sex, see Haggard et al., "Reli-

gion's Role in the Illusion of Gender Equality"; Kimberly A. Hamlin, *From Eve to Evolution: Darwin, Science, and Women's Rights in Gilded Age America* (Chicago: University of Chicago Press, 2015); Homan and Burdette, "When Religion Hurts"; Peek et al., "Gender and God's Word." On Tate's model of manhood, see Adam James, "A Problem Called Andrew Tate," *Shortform* (blog), August 24, 2022, https://medium.com/the-shortform/a-problem-called -andrew-tate-daaa422331e4; Lisa Miller, "Tate-Pilled," *Intelligencer*, March 14, 2023, https:// nymag.com/intelligencer/article/andrew-tate-jail-investigation.html; Emmeline Saunders, "Big Brother's Andrew Tate Sparks Fury by Claiming Depression Is 'Laziness,'" *Mirror*, September 8, 2017, http://www.mirror.co.uk/3am/celebrity-news/big-brothers-andrew-tate -sparks-11133888. For Tate's comments about women's place in the home and the kitchen, see TateEmpire, "Tate on Why Women Should Be in the Kitchen," YouTube, August 9, 2022, https://www.youtube.com/watch?v=kx9YwxclBRY. For the quote from Tate about women being better with children and men being better at fighting, see Yash Nair, Mateusz Miter, and Michael Dawson, "50 Most Controversial Andrew Tate Quotes," Dot Esports, August 30, 2023, https://dotesports.com/streaming/news/40-most-controversial-andrew-tate-quotes. For Tate's quote about women being "intrinsically lazy" and uninterested in conquest or profit, see Wayne the Wolf, "Why Women Are Lazy by Nature! Andrew Tate Proves It," YouTube, August 23, 2022, https://www.youtube.com/watch?v=9C-wBbdPvNs. For Tate's quote about women prioritizing their roles as wives and mothers, see Mike Jansen, "What Did Andrew Tate Say about Kylie Jenner?," Rebel Celebrity, 2023, https://rebelcelebrity.com/what-andrew-tate-say -kylie-jenner/. For Tate's quote about women being men's property, see Piers Morgan Uncensored, "Piers Morgan Challenges Andrew Tate over His View," Facebook, October 7, 2022, https://www.facebook.com/piersmorganuncensored/videos/piers-morgan-challenges-andrew -tate-over-his-view-that-women-are-the-property-of/823155822169871/.

33. On Tate's popularity and appeal, see James Brinsford, "Andrew Tate's Popularity with Women Revealed," *Newsweek*, April 9, 2023, https://www.newsweek.com/andrew-tate-popularity -women-revealed-1793001. On Tate's popularity with boys and young men, see also Miller, "Tate-Pilled"; Madeline Will, "Misogynist Influencer Andrew Tate Has Captured Boys' Attention. What Teachers Need to Know," Education Week, February 2, 2023, https://www .edweek.org/leadership/misogynist-influencer-andrew-tate-has-captured-boys-attention -what-teachers-need-to-know/2023/02.

34. On how the Mars/Venus myth inoculates men against guilt for women's undue burden, see Calarco et al., "By Default"; Daminger, "De-Gendered Processes, Gendered Outcomes"; Jenny H. van Hooff, "Rationalising Inequality: Heterosexual Couples' Explanations and Justifications for the Division of Housework along Traditionally Gendered Lines," *Journal of Gender Studies* 20, no. 1 (2011): 19–30.

35. On the history and pseudoscience of hysteria, see Joanna Kempner, *Not Tonight: Migraine and the Politics of Gender and Health* (Chicago: University of Chicago Press, 2014); Krystale E. Littlejohn, *Just Get on the Pill: The Uneven Burden of Reproductive Politics* (Berkeley: University of California Press, 2021); Sweet, "The Sociology of Gaslighting." On Hippocrates and hysteria, see also Ada McVean, "The History of Hysteria," McGill Office for Science and Society, July 31, 2017, https://www.mcgill.ca/oss/article/history-quackery/history-hysteria; Cecilia Tasca et al., "Women and Hysteria in the History of Mental Health," *Clinical Practice and Epidemiology in Mental Health* (2012): 110. On Freud and hysteria, see also Sander L. Gilman et al., *Hysteria Beyond Freud* (Berkeley: University of California Press, 1993). On how hysteria was blamed for falling birth rates among white women, see Laura Briggs, "The Race of Hysteria: 'Overcivilization' and the 'Savage' Woman in Late Nineteenth-Century Obstetrics and Gynecology," *American Quarterly* 52, no. 2 (2000): 246–73; Laura L. Lovett, *Conceiving the Future: Pronatalism, Reproduction, and the Family in the United States, 1890–1938* (Chapel Hill: University of North Carolina Press, 2007). On the inclusion of hysteria in the *Diagnostic and Statistical Manual*, see Carol S. North, "The Classification of Hysteria and Related Disorders:

Historical and Phenomenological Considerations," *Behavioral Sciences* 5, no. 4 (2015): 496–517. On modern use of the term to control women, see Alison Espach, "What It Really Means When You Call a Woman 'Hysterical,'" *Vogue*, March 10, 2017, https://www.vogue.com/article /trump-women-hysteria-and-history.

36. On how the Mars/Venus myth makes it easy for men to dismiss women as crazy or incompetent, see Littlejohn, *Just Get on the Pill*; Cynthia A. Stark, "Gaslighting, Misogyny, and Psychological Oppression," *Monist* 102, no. 2 (2019): 221–35; Sweet, "The Sociology of Gaslighting." On the prevalence of online abuse of women, see Beaver, "One in Three Men Believe Feminism Does More Harm than Good."

37. On how a stronger social safety net would improve women's safety and security by making them less dependent on men, see Holly Bell, "Cycles within Cycles: Domestic Violence, Welfare, and Low-Wage Work," *Violence Against Women* 9, no. 10 (2003): 1245–62; Demie Kurz, "Women Welfare, and Domestic Violence," *Social Justice* 25, no. 1 (1998): 105–22; Ellen K. Scott, Andrew S. London, and Nancy A. Myers, "Dangerous Dependencies: The Intersection of Welfare Reform and Domestic Violence," *Gender & Society* 16, no. 6 (2002): 878–97; Heeju Sohn, "Health Insurance and Risk of Divorce: Does Having Your Own Insurance Matter?," *Journal of Marriage and Family* 77, no. 4 (2015): 982–95. On how a stronger social safety net would leave even the privileged among us better off in an absolute sense, see Morris Altman, "A Behavioral Theory of Economic Welfare and Economic Justice: A Smithian Alternative to Pareto Optimality," *International Journal of Social Economics* 27, no. 11 (2000): 1098–131; Erling Barth, Karl O. Moene, and Fredrik Willumsen, "The Scandinavian Model—an Interpretation," *Journal of Public Economics* 117 (2014): 60–72; David Kiefer and Codrina Rada, "Profit Maximising Goes Global: The Race to the Bottom," *Cambridge Journal of Economics* 39, no. 5 (2015): 1333–350; Peter H. Lindert, *Making Social Spending Work* (Cambridge: Cambridge University Press, 2021).

38. On who benefits most from the "white-supremacist capitalist patriarchy," see bell hooks, *Feminist Theory: From Margin to Center* (Boston: South End Press, 2000).

CHAPTER 7: THE SUPERMOM MYTH

1. On Johnson's allegations, see Richard Beck, *We Believe the Children: A Moral Panic in the 1980s* (New York: Public Affairs, 2015); Mary de Young, *The Day Care Ritual Abuse Moral Panic* (Jefferson, NC: McFarland, 2004).

2. On the California case and its resolution, see Beck, *We Believe the Children*; Clyde Haberman, "The Trial That Unleashed Hysteria over Child Abuse," *New York Times*, March 10, 2014, https://www.nytimes.com/2014/03/10/us/the-trial-that-unleashed-hysteria-over-child -abuse.html; David Shaw, "Reporter's Early Exclusives Triggered a Media Frenzy," *Los Angeles Times*, January 20, 1990, https://www.latimes.com/food/la-900120mcmartin_lat-story.html; de Young, *The Day Care Ritual Abuse Moral Panic*; Kyle Zirpolo and Debbie Nathan, "I'm Sorry," *Los Angeles Times*, October 30, 2005, https://www.latimes.com/archives/la-xpm-2005 -oct-30-tm-mcmartin44-story.html. On the role the media and the legal system played in prompting this panic, see also Shaw, "Reporter's Early Exclusives Triggered a Media Frenzy."

3. For other uses of the term "Supermom Myth," see Susan Douglas and Meredith Michaels, *The Mommy Myth: The Idealization of Motherhood and How It Has Undermined All Women* (New York: Simon & Schuster, 2005); Sharon Hays, *The Cultural Contradictions of Motherhood* (New Haven, CT: Yale University Press, 1998); Becky Kopitzke, *The SuperMom Myth: Conquering the Dirty Villains of Motherhood* (Uhrichsville, OH: Barbour Publishing, 2015). On how American culture has constructed the dangers to children and the responsibility for protecting children, see Elizabeth M. Armstrong, *Conceiving Risk, Bearing Responsibility: Fetal Alcohol Syndrome and the Diagnosis of Moral Disorder* (Baltimore: Johns Hopkins University Press, 2008); Norah MacKendrick, *Better Safe Than Sorry* (Berkeley: University of California Press,

2018); Margaret Nelson, *Parenting Out of Control: Anxious Parents in Uncertain Times* (New York: NYU Press, 2010); Jennifer A. Reich, *Calling the Shots: Why Parents Reject Vaccines* (New York: NYU Press, 2016); Miranda R. Waggoner, *The Zero Trimester* (Berkeley: University of California Press, 2017). On how the media used the Supermom myth to drum up fear in the Johnson case, see Beck, *We Believe the Children*, xxiv; de Young, *The Day Care Ritual Abuse Moral Panic*, 12.

4. For more on the relationship between evangelical Christianity and homeschooling, see Kate Henley Averett, *The Homeschool Choice: Parents and the Privatization of Education* (New York: NYU Press, 2021); Mitchell L. Stevens, *Kingdom of Children: Culture and Controversy in the Homeschooling Movement* (Princeton, NJ: Princeton University Press, 2003).

5. On how evangelical Christian moms' groups recruit and support their members, see Jocelyn Elise Crowley, "Strictly for Evangelical Parenting Support? The Case of Mothers of Preschoolers (MOPS)," *Review of Religious Research* 54, no. 4 (2012): 421–44; Lyz Lenz, *God Land: A Story of Faith, Loss, and Renewal* (Bloomington: Indiana University Press, 2017).

6. On the complicated and often conflicting advice we give to women about raising children, see Armstrong, *Conceiving Risk, Bearing Responsibility*; Kate Cairns, Josée Johnston, and Norah MacKendrick, "Feeding the 'Organic Child': Mothering through Ethical Consumption," *Journal of Consumer Culture* 13, no. 2 (2013): 97–118; Caitlin Daniel, "Economic Constraints on Taste Formation and the True Cost of Healthy Eating," *Social Science & Medicine* 148, no. Supplement C (2016): 34–41; Elaine M. Hernandez and Jessica McCrory Calarco, "Health Decisions amidst Controversy: Prenatal Alcohol Consumption and the Unequal Experience of Influence and Control in Networks," *Social Science & Medicine* 286 (2021): 114319; Nelson, *Parenting Out of Control*; Norah MacKendrick, "More Work for Mother: Chemical Body Burdens as a Maternal Responsibility," *Gender & Society* 28, no. 5 (2014): 705–28; MacKendrick, *Better Safe Than Sorry*; Jennifer A. Reich, "Neoliberal Mothering and Vaccine Refusal: Imagined Gated Communities and the Privilege of Choice," *Gender & Society* 28, no. 5 (2014): 679–704; Waggoner, *The Zero Trimester*.

7. On Gothard and the origins of modern evangelical Christian parenting, see Wilfred Bockelman, *Gothard: The Man and His Ministry: An Evaluation* (Santa Barbara, CA: Mott Media, 1976); Kristin Kobes Du Mez, *Jesus and John Wayne: How White Evangelicals Corrupted a Faith and Fractured a Nation* (New York: Liveright, 2020). On the allegations against Gothard, see Sarah Pulliam Bailey, "New Charges Allege Religious Leader, Who Has Ties to the Duggars, Sexually Abused Women," *Washington Post*, January 6, 2016, https://www.washingtonpost.com/news/acts-of-faith/wp/2016/01/06/new-charges-allege-religious-leader-who-has-ties-to-the-duggars-sexually-abused-women/.

8. On the fears promoted by evangelical Christian leaders, see Andrew L. Whitehead and Samuel L. Perry, *Taking America Back for God: Christian Nationalism in the United States* (Oxford: Oxford University Press, 2020); de Young, *The Day Care Ritual Abuse Moral Panic*.

9. On Heidi St. John, see @heidistjohn, Instagram, https://www.instagram.com/heidistjohn/?hl=en. On St. John's political career, see Elizabeth Dias and Ruth Graham, "The Growing Religious Fervor in the American Right: 'This Is a Jesus Movement,'" *New York Times*, April 6, 2023, https://www.nytimes.com/2022/04/06/us/christian-right-wing-politics.html. See also Heidi St. John for Congress, http://heidistjohnforcongress.com/. For the book quotes from St. John included here, see Heidi St. John, *Prayers for the Battlefield: Staying MomStrong in the Fight for Your Family and Faith* (Carol Stream, IL: Tyndale Momentum, 2018). See also "Heidi St. John: Quotes," Goodreads, https://www.goodreads.com/author/quotes/3468282.Heidi_St_John. For the blog quotes from St. John included here, see Heidi St. John, "Homeschooling Held Hostage," *Heidi St. John: The Busy Mom* (blog), March 19, 2020, http://heidistjohn.com/blog/homeschooling-homeschool/homeschooling-held-hostage.

10. On Karis Kimmel Murray and her popularity, see "Karis Kimmel Murray," Grace Based Families, https://gracebasedfamilies.com/staff/karis-murray/. For Murray's take on disci-

pline, see Karis Kimmel Murray, *Grace Based Discipline: How to Be at Your Best When Your Kids Are at Their Worst* (Scottsdale, AZ: Family Matters Inc., 2017), 193.

11. On the effectiveness and effects of physical discipline, see Elizabeth T. Gershoff, "Spanking and Child Development: We Know Enough Now to Stop Hitting Our Children," *Child Development Perspectives* 7, no. 2 (2013): 133–37. For longitudinal studies, see Christopher J. Ferguson, "Spanking, Corporal Punishment and Negative Long-Term Outcomes: A Meta-Analytic Review of Longitudinal Studies," *Clinical Psychology Review* 33, no. 1 (2013): 196–208. On the evidence for treating spanking as an adverse childhood experience, see Tracie O. Afifi et al., "Spanking and Adult Mental Health Impairment: The Case for the Designation of Spanking as an Adverse Childhood Experience," *Child Abuse & Neglect* 71 (2017): 24–31. On evangelical Christians' disproportionate distrust in science, see Sedona Chinn et al., "Threatening Experts: Correlates of Viewing Scientists as a Social Threat," *Public Understanding of Science* (2023); Gordon Gauchat, "Politicization of Science in the Public Sphere: A Study of Public Trust in the United States, 1974 to 2010," *American Sociological Review* 77, no. 2 (2012). On evangelical Christians' disproportionate rejection of Covid-19 restrictions, see Samuel L. Perry and Andrew L. Whitehead, "Culture Wars and COVID-19 Conduct: Christian Nationalism, Religiosity, and Americans' Behavior during the Coronavirus Pandemic," *Journal for the Scientific Study of Religion* 59, no. 3 (2020): 405–16; Samuel L. Perry, Andrew L. Whitehead, and Joshua B. Grubbs, "Save the Economy, Liberty, and Yourself: Christian Nationalism and Americans' Views on Government COVID-19 Restrictions," *Sociology of Religion* 82, no. 4 (2021): 426–46.

12. On how lack of trust in authorities shifts responsibility for children's safety to mothers, see Mackendrick, "More Work for Mother"; Reich, "Neoliberal Mothering and Vaccine Refusal." For the quotes from Lia, see Amber Lia and Wendy Speake, *Triggers: Exchanging Parents' Angry Reactions for Gentle Biblical Responses* (Montclair, NJ: Same Page Press, 2016), 125.

13. For Pearl's advice, see Debi Pearl, *Created to Be His Help Meet: Discover How God Can Make Your Marriage Glorious* (Pleasantville, TN: No Greater Joy Ministries, 2004). For the Duggars' advice, see Rebecca Dube, "The Duggars' 7 Tips for Keeping Your Marriage Sexy, Even after (a Lot of) Kids," NBC News, February 13, 2014, https://www.today.com/moms/duggars -7-tips-keeping-your-marriage-sexy-even-after-lot-2D12106530.

14. On how fear of children's unhappiness and academic/professional failure motivates mothers, see Melissa A. Milkie and Catherine H. Warner, "Status Safeguarding: Mothers' Work to Secure Children's Place in the Social Hierarchy," in *Intensive Mothering: The Cultural Contradictions of Modern Motherhood*, edited by Linda Rose Ennis (Ontario: Demeter Press, 2014), 66–85. For related arguments, see Pawan Dhingra, *Hyper Education* (New York: NYU Press, 2020); Nelson, *Parenting Out of Control*; Natasha Warikoo, *Race at the Top: Asian Americans and Whites in Pursuit of the American Dream in Suburban Schools* (Chicago: University of Chicago Press, 2022).

15. For more on how the summer care gap influences US mothers' workforce participation, see Leah Ruppanner, Stephanie Moller, and Liana Sayer, "Expensive Childcare and Short School Days = Lower Maternal Employment and More Time in Childcare? Evidence from the American Time Use Survey," *Socius* 5 (2019).

16. For the nutritional content of the crackers Monica mentioned, see "Organic Cheddar Bunnies," Annie's, https://www.annies.com/products/organic-cheddar-bunnies. On how middle- and upper-middle-class parents use diet to try to give their kids an edge in life, see Stefanie Mollborn, Bethany Rigles, and Jennifer A. Pace, "'Healthier Than Just Healthy': Families Transmitting Health as Cultural Capital," *Social Problems* 68, no. 3 (2021): 574–90. See also Sarah Bowen, Joslyn Brenton, and Sinikka Elliott, *Pressure Cooker: Why Home Cooking Won't Solve Our Problems and What We Can Do About It* (Oxford: Oxford University Press, 2019); Cairns et al., "Feeding the Organic Child"; Daniel, "Economic Constraints on Taste Formation"; Priya Fielding-Singh, *How the Other Half Eats: The Untold Story of Food and Inequality in America* (New York: Hachette Books, 2021).

17. On the difference in expected earnings between Ivy League and non–Ivy League college graduates, see Cole Claybourn, "How Much Is an Ivy League Degree Worth?," *U.S. News & World Report*, January 30, 2023, https://www.usnews.com/education/best-colleges/articles /how-much-is-an-ivy-league-degree-worth. On how money buys security in the context of inequality, see Jacob S. Hacker, *The Great Risk Shift: The New Economic Insecurity and the Decline of the American Dream* (Oxford: Oxford University Press, 2019); Katherine S. Newman, *Falling from Grace: The Experience of Downward Mobility in the American Middle Class* (New York: Free Press, 1988); Jessi Streib, *Privilege Lost: Who Leaves the Upper Middle Class and How They Fall* (Oxford: Oxford University Press, 2020). On the lengths parents will go to get their kids into Ivy League schools, see Dhingra, *Hyper Education*; Warikoo, *Race at the Top*.

18. On the lengths parents will go to get their kids into Ivy League schools, see Dhingra, *Hyper Education*; Warikoo, *Race at the Top*. On the percentage of international students at Ivy League schools, see Yoni Gutenmacher, "Admission Rates across the Ivy League: A Breakdown," *Daily Pennsylvanian*, March 29, 2018, https://www.thedp.com/article/2018/03/ivy-league -decisions-class-of-2022-penn-upenn-philadelphia-yale-university-harvard.

19. On how advice for mothers encourages this type of intensive parenting, see Bowen, Brenton, and Elliott, *Pressure Cooker*; Cairns, Johnston, and MacKendrick, "Feeding the 'Organic Child'"; Dhingra, *Hyper Education*; Fielding-Singh, *How the Other Half Eats*; MacKendrick, *Better Safe Than Sorry*; Mollborn, Rigles, and Pace, "'Healthier Than Just Healthy'"; Nelson, *Parenting Out of Control*; Reich, *Calling the Shots*; Warikoo, *Race at the Top*.

20. John Medina, *Brain Rules for Baby: How to Raise a Smart and Happy Child from Zero to Five* (Edmonds, WA: Pear Press, 2010).

21. For Medina's advice on the marshmallow test, see Medina, *Brain Rules for Baby*, 115–16.

22. For more recent research on the marshmallow test, see Tyler W. Watts, Greg J. Duncan, and Haonan Quan, "Revisiting the Marshmallow Test: A Conceptual Replication Investigating Links between Early Delay of Gratification and Later Outcomes," *Psychological Science* 29, no. 7 (2018): 1159–77. For additional research debunking claims of the original marshmallow test, see Celeste Kidd, Holly Palmeri, and Richard N. Aslin, "Rational Snacking: Young Children's Decision-Making on the Marshmallow Task Is Moderated by Beliefs about Environmental Reliability," *Cognition* 126, no. 1 (2013): 109–14; Wendy S. C. Lee and Stephanie M. Carlson, "Knowing When to Be 'Rational': Flexible Economic Decision Making and Executive Function in Preschool Children," *Child Development* 86, no. 5 (2015): 1434–48; Joseph T. McGuire and Joseph W. Kable, "Rational Temporal Predictions Can Underlie Apparent Failures to Delay Gratification," *Psychological Review* 120, no. 13 (2013): 395–410; Laura E. Michaelson and Yuko Munakata, "Trust Matters: Seeing How an Adult Treats Another Person Influences Preschoolers' Willingness to Delay Gratification," *Developmental Science* 19, no. 6 (2016): 1011–19.

23. On the devaluation of women's paid work, see Michelle J. Budig and Paula England, "The Wage Penalty for Motherhood," *American Sociological Review* 66, no. 2 (2001): 204–25; Brendan Churchill, Sabino Kornrich, and Leah Ruppanner, "Children of the Revolution: The Continued Unevenness of the Gender Revolution in Housework, Childcare and Work Time across Birth Cohorts," *Social Science Research* 111 (2023): 102868; Paula England, "The Gender Revolution: Uneven and Stalled," *Gender & Society* 24, no. 2 (2010): 149–66; Wei-hsin Yu and Janet Chen-Lan Kuo, "The Motherhood Wage Penalty by Work Conditions: How Do Occupational Characteristics Hinder or Empower Mothers?," *American Sociological Review* 82, no. 4 (2017): 744–69. On the construction of mothers as the primary and natural protectors for children, see Armstrong, *Conceiving Risk, Bearing Responsibility*; Joel Best, *Threatened Children: Rhetoric and Concern about Child-Victims* (Chicago: University of Chicago Press, 1993); Stanley Cohen, *Folk Devils and Moral Panics* (London: Routledge, 1972); Erich Goode and Nachman Ben-Yehuda, "Moral Panics: Culture, Politics, and Social Construction," *An-*

nual Review of Sociology 20 (1994): 149–71; MacKendrick, *Better Safe Than Sorry*; Nelson, *Parenting Out of Control*; Reich, *Calling the Shots*; Waggoner, *The Zero Trimester*; Viviana Zelizer, *Pricing the Priceless Child: The Changing Social Value of Children* (Princeton, NJ: Princeton University Press, 1994). On the pressure that we put on mothers to protect children, see Sinikka Elliott, Rachel Powell, and Joslyn Brenton, "Being a Good Mom: Low-Income, Black Single Mothers Negotiate Intensive Mothering," *Journal of Family Issues* 36, no. 3 (2015): 351–70; Linda Rose Ennis, *Intensive Mothering: The Cultural Contradictions of Modern Motherhood* (Ontario: Demeter Press, 2014); Hays, *The Cultural Contradictions of Motherhood*; Jane Lankes, "Negotiating 'Impossible' Ideals: Latent Classes of Intensive Mothering in the United States," *Gender & Society* 36, no. 5 (2022): 677–703; Terri LeMoyne and Tom Buchanan, "Does 'Hovering' Matter? Helicopter Parenting and Its Effect on Well-Being," *Sociological Spectrum* 31, no. 4 (2011): 399–418; Milkie and Warner, "Status Safeguarding"; Amy Romagnoli and Glenda Wall, "'I Know I'm a Good Mom': Young, Low-Income Mothers' Experiences with Risk Perception, Intensive Parenting Ideology and Parenting Education Programmes," *Health, Risk & Society* 14, no. 3 (2012): 273–90.

24. On pandemic unemployment and its disproportionate impact on women, see Manuela Angelucci et al., "Remote Work and the Heterogeneous Impact of COVID-19 on Employment and Health" (working paper, National Bureau of Economic Research, 2020); Nicole Bateman and Martha Ross, *Why Has COVID-19 Been Especially Harmful for Working Women?* (Washington, DC: Brookings, 2020); Caitlyn Collins et al., "The Gendered Consequences of a Weak Infrastructure of Care: School Reopening Plans and Parents' Employment during the COVID-19 Pandemic," *Gender & Society* 35, no. 2 (2021): 180–93; Liana Christin Landivar et al., "Early Signs Indicate That COVID-19 Is Exacerbating Gender Inequality in the Labor Force," *Socius* 6 (2020); Patrice Ruane, "From Pin Money Workers to Essential Workers: Lessons about Women's Employment and the COVID-19 Pandemic from the Great Depression and the Great Recession," *UCLA Journal of Gender and Law* 29, no. 2 (2022).

25. On the gendered work of worry, see Allison Daminger, "The Cognitive Dimension of Household Labor," *American Sociological Review* 84, no. 4 (2019): 609–33; Janani Umamaheswar and Catherine Tan, "'Dad, Wash Your Hands': Gender, Care Work, and Attitudes toward Risk during the COVID-19 Pandemic," *Socius* 6 (2020).

26. On the origins of the feminist movement, see Myra Ferree and Patricia Yancey Martin, *Feminist Organizations: Harvest of the New Women's Movement* (Philadelphia: Temple University Press, 1995). For Steinem's full interview, see Sonja Steptoe, "10 Questions for Gloria Steinem," *Time*, April 5, 2004, https://content.time.com/time/subscriber/article/0,33009,993745,00.html. For Steinem's congressional testimony, see Gloria Steinem, "Testimony before the Senate Hearings on the Equal Rights Amendment, 1970," Common Lit, https://www.commonlit.org/en/texts/testimony-before-the-senate-hearings-on-the-equal-rights-amendment.

27. For related critiques of Sandberg's message, see bell hooks, "Dig Deep: Beyond Lean In," *The Feminist Wire*, October 28, 2013, https://thefeministwire.com/2013/10/17973/. On the broader corporatization and sanitization of the feminist movement, see Val Burris, "The Dialectic of Women's Oppression: Notes on the Relation between Capitalism and Patriarchy," *Berkeley Journal of Sociology* 27 (1982): 51–74; Angela Y. Davis, *Women, Race & Class* (New York: Knopf Doubleday, 1983); Angela Y. Davis, "Women and Capitalism: Dialectics of Oppression and Liberation," in *The Black Feminist Reader* (Hoboken, NJ: Wiley, 2000); Bonnie J. Dow, *Prime-Time Feminism: Television, Media Culture, and the Women's Movement Since 1970* (Philadelphia: University of Pennsylvania, 1996); Nancy Whittier, *Feminist Generations: The Persistence of the Radical Women's Movement* (Philadelphia: Temple University Press, 2010). For Sandberg's book, see Sheryl Sandberg, *Lean In: Women, Work, and the Will to Lead* (New York: Knopf, 2013). For Sandberg's TED Talk, see TED, "Why We Have Too Few Women Leaders," YouTube, December 21, 2010, https://www.youtube.com/watch?v=18uDutylDa4.

28. On the exhaustion that comes with attempting to do it all, see Caitlyn Collins, *Making Motherhood Work: How Women Manage Careers and Caregiving* (Princeton, NJ: Princeton University Press, 2019); Sarah Damaske, *For the Family?: How Class and Gender Shape Women's Work* (Oxford: Oxford University Press, 2011); Kathleen Gerson, *Hard Choices: How Women Decide about Work, Career and Motherhood* (Berkeley: University of California Press, 1985); Hays, *The Cultural Contradictions of Motherhood*; Arlie Russell Hochschild, *The Second Shift: Working Families and the Revolution at Home* (New York: Penguin Books, 1989); Aliya Hamid Rao, *Crunch Time: How Married Couples Confront Unemployment* (Berkeley: University of California Press, 2020); Pamela Stone and Meg Lovejoy, *Opting Back In: What Really Happens When Mothers Go Back to Work* (Berkeley: University of California Press, 2021).

29. For hooks's take on *Lean In*, see hooks, "Dig Deep." For Fraser's take on *Lean In*, see Nancy Fraser, "How Feminism Became Capitalism's Handmaiden—and How to Reclaim It," *Guardian*, October 14, 2013, https://www.theguardian.com/commentisfree/2013/oct/14/feminism-capitalist-handmaiden-neoliberal.

30. On the vilification and marginalization of "dangerous" women, see Silvia Federici, *Caliban and the Witch: Women, the Body, and Primitive Accumulation* (New York: Autonomedia, 2004); bell hooks, *Ain't I a Woman: Black Women and Feminism* (New York: Routledge, 2014).

31. On women opting out of high-powered careers, see Youngjoo Cha, "Reinforcing Separate Spheres: The Effect of Spousal Overwork on Men's and Women's Employment in Dual-Earner Households," *American Sociological Review* 75, no. 2 (2010): 303–29; Pamela Stone, *Opting Out?* (Berkeley: University of California Press, 2007).

32. For Collins's cross-national research on motherhood, social safety nets, and guilt, see Collins, *Making Motherhood Work*.

33. On how changes to law and policy can shape social attitudes and norms, see Roberto Galbiati et al., "How Laws Affect the Perception of Norms: Empirical Evidence from the Lockdown," *PLOS ONE* 16, no. 9 (September 24, 2021); Jody Heymann et al., "Improving Health with Programmatic, Legal, and Policy Approaches to Reduce Gender Inequality and Change Restrictive Gender Norms," *Lancet* 393, no. 10190 (June 22, 2019): 2522–34; Vera Lomazzi, Sabine Israel, and Isabella Crespi, "Gender Equality in Europe and the Effect of Work-Family Balance Policies on Gender-Role Attitudes," *Social Sciences* 8, no. 1 (2019): 5. For the study conducted in Norway, see Andreas Kotsadam and Henning Finseraas, "The State Intervenes in the Battle of the Sexes: Causal Effects of Paternity Leave," *Social Science Research* 40, no. 6 (2011): 1611–22.

34. On how men are also capable of meeting children's needs, see Timothy Black and Sky Keyes, *It's a Setup: Fathering from the Social and Economic Margins* (Oxford: Oxford University Press, 2020); Margot Trotter Davis et al., "Parenting a 6-Year Old Is Not What I Planned in Retirement: Trauma and Stress among Grandparents Due to the Opioid Crisis," *Journal of Gerontological Social Work* 63, no. 4 (May 18, 2020): 295–315; Cameron Lynne Macdonald, *Shadow Mothers: Nannies, Au Pairs, and the Micropolitics of Mothering* (Berkeley: University of California Press, 2011); Tina Miller, "Falling Back into Gender? Men's Narratives and Practices around First-Time Fatherhood," *Sociology* 45, no. 6 (2011): 1094–109; Mignon R. Moore and Michael Stambolis-Ruhstorfer, "LGBT Sexuality and Families at the Start of the Twenty-First Century," *Annual Review of Sociology* 39 (2013): 491–507; Jennifer Randles, "The Means to and Meaning of 'Being There' in Responsible Fatherhood Programming with Low-Income Fathers," *Family Relations* 69, no. 1 (2020): 7–20; Carol Stack, *All Our Kin* (New York: Harper, 1974); Casey Stockstill, *False Starts: The Segregated Lives of Preschoolers* (New York: NYU Press, 2023).

35. On how women's gender attitudes shape their willingness to seek support with caregiving, see Averett, *The Homeschool Choice*; Ruth Gaunt and Mariana Pinho, "Do Sexist Mothers Change More Diapers? Ambivalent Sexism, Maternal Gatekeeping, and the Division of Childcare," *Sex Roles* 79, no. 3 (2018): 176–89; Eunsil Oh, "Who Deserves to Work? How Women Develop Expectations of Child Care Support in Korea," *Gender & Society* 32, no. 4 (2018): 493–515;

Sarah J. Schoppe-Sullivan et al., "Who Are the Gatekeepers? Predictors of Maternal Gate-keeping," *Parenting* 15, no. 3 (July 3, 2015): 166–86.

36. On the link between gender egalitarianism and social safety nets, see Lomazzi, Israel, and Crespi, "Gender Equality in Europe and the Effect of Work-Family Balance Policies on Gender-Role Attitudes."

CHAPTER 8: WHAT A BETTER NET WOULD MEAN

1. On the origins of the phrase "Never let a good crisis go to waste," see Owen Adams, "Never Let a Crisis Go to Waste," *Healthcare Papers* 20, no. 4 (April 2022): 4–10. On Europe's post-World War II policies, see Stephanie Coontz, *The Way We Never Were: American Families and the Nostalgia Trap* (New York: Basic Books, 1993); Lynne Davis, "Minding Children or Minding Machines . . . Women's Labour and Child Care during World War II," *Labour History*, no. 53 (1987): 86–98; Anne Hélène Gauthier, *The State and the Family: A Comparative Analysis of Family Policies in Industrialized Countries* (Oxford: Oxford University Press, 1999); Sonya Michel, *Children's Interests/Mothers' Rights: The Shaping of America's Child Care Policy* (New Haven, CT: Yale University Press, 2000); Ruth Milkman, *Gender at Work: The Dynamics of Job Segregation by Sex during World War II* (Champaign: University of Illinois, 1987); Piotr Perkowski, "Wedded to Welfare? Working Mothers and the Welfare State in Communist Poland," *Slavic Review* 76, no. 2 (2017): 455–80; Linda A. White, "Explaining Differences in Child Care Policy Development in France and the USA: Norms, Frames, Programmatic Ideas," *International Political Science Review* 30, no. 4 (2009): 385–405.

2. On the murder of George Floyd and its aftermath, see "How George Floyd Died, and What Happened Next," *New York Times*, July 29, 2022, https://www.nytimes.com/article/george-floyd.html. For more on the inequalities revealed by the Covid-19 pandemic, see Whitney N. Laster Pirtle and Tashelle Wright, "Structural Gendered Racism Revealed in Pandemic Times: Intersectional Approaches to Understanding Race and Gender Health Inequities in COVID-19," *Gender & Society* (2021).

3. On Republicans' opposition to government spending, see Robert Reich, "Republicans Aren't Going to Tell Americans the Real Cause of Our $31.4tn Debt," *Guardian*, February 1, 2023, https://www.theguardian.com/commentisfree/2023/feb/01/republicans-arent-going-to-tell-americans-the-real-cause-of-our-314tn-debt. On the CARES Act, its passage, and its provisions, see Michael B. Sauter, "Coronavirus Stimulus Checks: Here's How Many People Will Get $1,200 in Every State," *USA Today*, April 28, 2020, https://www.usatoday.com/story/money/2020/04/28/how-many-people-will-get-1200-in-every-state/111604090/.

4. On the percent of American families who benefited from pandemic relief programs, see Jennifer Graham, "How Americans Spent Their Stimulus Checks," *Deseret News*, October 12, 2021, https://www.deseret.com/2021/10/12/22688623/how-americans-spent-their-stimulus-checks-american-family-survey-2021-government-aid. On the pandemic expansion of the free lunch program, see "H.R.6201—Families First Coronavirus Response Act," Congress, https://www.congress.gov/bill/116th-congress/house-bill/6201/text/eh. On the pandemic expansion of the child tax credit, see Zachary Parolin and Megan A. Curran, "Child Poverty Set to Spike in January 2022 after Expiration of Monthly Payments," *Poverty and Social Policy Brief* 6, no. 1 (2022): 6. On the eviction moratorium, the student loan payment pause, and the increase in the value of food stamps, see "H.R.133—Consolidated Appropriations Act, 2021," Congress, https://www.congress.gov/bill/116th-congress/house-bill/133/text. See also Jim Probasco, "The Consolidated Appropriations Act of 2021: What's in It, What's Not," Investopedia, August 10, 2023, https://www.investopedia.com/congress-agrees-on-second-stimulus-here-s-what-s-in-it-and-what-s-not-5093226.

5. On how pandemic relief programs influenced the child poverty and food insecurity rates, see Parolin and Curran, "Child Poverty Set to Spike in January 2022 after Expiration of Monthly Payments." On the barriers to pandemic relief, see Stephen Roll and Michal Grinstein-Weiss,

"Did CARES Act Benefits Reach Vulnerable Americans? Evidence from a National Survey," Brookings, August 25, 2020, https://www.brookings.edu/articles/did-cares-act-benefits-reach -vulnerable-americans-evidence-from-a-national-survey/. On how the CARES Act helped families stay afloat, see James Aylward et al., "How Much Did the CARES Act Help House-holds Stay Afloat?," Federal Reserve Bank of San Francisco, July 6, 2021, https://www .frbsf.org/economic-research/publications/economic-letter/2021/july/how-much-did-cares -act-help-households-stay-afloat/.

6. On how the meat and poultry processing industry was affected by Covid-19, see "Mapping Covid-19 Outbreaks in the Food System," Food and Environment Reporting Network, April 22, 2020, https://thefern.org/2020/04/mapping-covid-19-in-meat-and-food-processing -plants/; Lewis Kendall, "'Incredibly Dangerous Job': Concerns Safety Is Slipping at US Meat Plants," *Guardian*, October 1, 2020, http://www.theguardian.com/environment/2020/oct /01/incredibly-dangerous-job-concerns-safety-is-slipping-at-us-meat-plants; Michelle A. Waltenburg et al., "Update: COVID-19 among Workers in Meat and Poultry Processing Facilities," Centers for Disease Control and Prevention, July 10, 2020, https://www.cdc.gov/ mmwr/volumes/69/wr/mm6927e2.htm.

7. On Covid shortages of food and other basic necessities, see Steve Banker, "Toilet Paper Short-ages, Empty Shelves, and Panic Buying: Just How Bad Was Grocery Service in 2020?," *Forbes*, October 1, 2021, https://www.forbes.com/sites/stevebanker/2021/10/01/toilet-paper -shortages-empty-shelves-and-panic-buying-just-how-bad-was-grocery-service-in-2020/? sh=5d4896977b1a

8. On rent and utility relief programs offered during the pandemic, see "Emergency Rental Assistance Program," US Department of the Treasury, https://home.treasury.gov/policy -issues/coronavirus/assistance-for-state-local-and-tribal-governments/emergency-rental -assistance-program. On the Covid relief checks mailed to US families, see "Covid Stimulus Checks," USAGov, https://www.usa.gov/covid-stimulus-checks.

9. On the US social safety net's missing middle, see Theda Skocpol, *The Missing Middle: Working Families and the Future of American Social Policy* (New York: W. W. Norton, 2000); Joan Williams and Heather Boushey, "The Three Faces of Work-Family Conflict: The Poor, the Profession-als, and the Missing Middle," *SSRN Electronic Journal*, January 10, 2010.

10. On the pre-pandemic rules for free and reduced-price school meals, see "Poverty Guide-lines," ASPE, https://aspe.hhs.gov/topics/poverty-economic-mobility/poverty-guidelines. On pandemic-related changes to the school lunch program, see Laura Reiley, "USDA Extends Uni-versal Free Lunch through next School Year, Bringing Relief to Millions of Food-Insecure Families," *Washington Post*, April 20, 2021, https://www.washingtonpost.com/business /2021/04/20/usda-extends-universal-free-lunch/. On other countries' school meal programs, see Maria Cross and Barbara MacDonald, *Nutrition in Institutions* (Oxford, UK: Wiley-Blackwell, 2009); Emma Patterson and Liselotte Schäfer Elinder, "Improvements in School Meal Quality in Sweden after the Introduction of New Legislation—a 2-Year Follow-Up," *European Journal of Public Health* 25, no. 4 (2015): 655–60. On pandemic-related inflation in the US, see "How the Supply Chain Caused Current Inflation, and Why It Might Be Here to Stay," *PBS NewsHour*, November 10, 2021, https://www.pbs.org/newshour/economy/how -the-supply-chain-caused-current-inflation-and-why-it-might-be-here-to-stay; Ana Maria Santacreu and Jesse LaBelle, "Global Supply Chain Disruptions and Inflation during the COVID-19 Pandemic," *Federal Reserve Bank of St. Louis Review* 104, no. 2, 2022, https:// research.stlouisfed.org/publications/review/2022/02/07/global-supply-chain-disruptions -and-inflation-during-the-covid-19-pandemic. On the Covid economic impact payments, see Sauter, "Coronavirus Stimulus Checks." See also "Economic Impact Payments," US De-partment of the Treasury, https://home.treasury.gov/policy-issues/coronavirus/assistance-for -american-families-and-workers/economic-impact-payments. On the pandemic-related ex-pansion and extension of unemployment benefits, see Nick Gwyn, "Historic Unemployment Programs Provided Vital Support to Workers and the Economy during Pandemic, Offer Road-

map for Future Reform," Center on Budget and Policy Priorities, March 24, 2022, https://
www.cbpp.org/research/economy/historic-unemployment-programs-provided-vital-support
-to-workers-and-the-economy.

11. On the plans proposed by Biden and Trump during the 2020 presidential election, see Asma
Khalid and Barbara Sprunt, "Biden Counters Trump's 'America First' with 'Build Back Better' Economic Plan," NPR, July 9, 2020, https://www.npr.org/2020/07/09/889347429/biden
-counters-trumps-america-first-with-build-back-economic-plan. On the components
of Biden's Build Back Better plan, see "The Build Back Better Framework," White House,
https://www.whitehouse.gov/build-back-better/. See also "Fact Sheet: The American Jobs
Plan," White House, March 31, 2021, https://www.whitehouse.gov/briefing-room/statements
-releases/2021/03/31/fact-sheet-the-american-jobs-plan/; "Fact Sheet: The American Families Plan," The White House, April 28, 2021, https://www.whitehouse.gov/briefing-room
/statements-releases/2021/04/28/fact-sheet-the-american-families-plan/. On the student loan
debt forgiveness plan, see "Federal Student Loan Debt Relief," Federal Student Aid, https://
studentaid.gov/manage-loans/forgiveness-cancellation/debt-relief-info.

12. On Congress's ultimate rejection of Biden's Build Back Better plan, see Clare Foran, Manu
Raju, and Ted Barrett, "Manchin Delivers Grim News for Biden's Build Back Better Plan:
'It's Dead,'" CNN, February 2, 2022, https://www.cnn.com/2022/02/01/politics/manchin
-build-back-better-dead/index.html. On the end of the eviction moratorium and its conse-
quences, see *Federal Moratorium on Evictions for Nonpayment of Rent* (Washington, DC: National Housing Law Project, 2021), https://nlihc.org/sites/default/files/Overview-of-National
-Eviction-Moratorium.pdf. On the end of the pandemic relief checks, see "Stimulus Checks,"
US Government Accountability Office, June 29, 2022, https://www.gao.gov/products/gao
-22-106044. On the end of the child tax credit payments and its consequences, see Zachary
Parolin, Sophie Collyer, and Megan Curran, "Absence of Monthly Child Tax Credit Leads
to 3.7 Million More Children in Poverty in January 2022," *Poverty and Social Policy Brief*
(2022), https://ideas.repec.org/p/aji/briefs/20417.html.

13. On the end of the pause on student loan debt and its consequences, see Annie Nova, "It's
Official: Student Loan Payments Will Restart in October, Education Department Says,"
CNBC, June 20, 2023, https://www.cnbc.com/2023/06/20/its-official-student-loan-payments
-will-restart-in-october.html. On the end of pandemic rent relief and its consequences, see
Erika Bolstad, "As Pandemic Rent Relief Ends, States Struggle to Prevent Homelessness,"
Stateline, January 23, 2023, https://stateline.org/2023/01/23/as-pandemic-rent-relief-ends
-states-struggle-to-prevent-homelessness/. On the end of the pandemic expansion of the national school lunch program, see "End of Nationwide Federal Free Lunch Program Has Some
States Scrambling," NPR, October 26, 2022, https://www.npr.org/2022/10/26/1129939058
/end-of-nationwide-federal-free-lunch-program-has-some-states-scrambling. On the rollback
of the Medicaid expansion and its consequences, see Jennifer Tolbert and Meghana Ammula,
"10 Things to Know about the Unwinding of the Medicaid Continuous Enrollment Provision," *KFF* (blog), June 9, 2023, https://www.kff.org/medicaid/issue-brief/10-things-to-know
-about-the-unwinding-of-the-medicaid-continuous-enrollment-provision/. On the addition
of new work requirements for food stamps, see "Congress Created Changes to Food Assistance. Here's What They Mean," NPR, June 2, 2023, https://www.npr.org/2023/06/02
/1179633624/snap-food-assistance-work-requirements-congress-debt-ceiling. On the addition
of new work requirements for Medicaid, see Amy Goldstein, "Push to Tie Medicaid to Work
Is Making a Comeback. Georgia Is at Forefront," *Washington Post*, June 28, 2023, https://
www.washingtonpost.com/health/2023/06/28/medicaid-work-requirements/; Madeline
Guth, "Medicaid Work Requirements Are Back on the Agenda," *KFF* (blog), April 3, 2023,
https://www.kff.org/policy-watch/medicaid-work-requirements-are-back-on-agenda/. On the
Supreme Court's affirmative action decision and its aftermath, see Zach Montague, "Affirma-
tive Action: Rejection of Affirmative Action Draws Strong Reactions from Right and Left,"
New York Times, June 29, 2023, https://www.nytimes.com/live/2023/06/29/us/affirmative

-action-supreme-court. On the end of the Covid-19 emergency declaration and its consequences for workers, see Kelly Phillips Erb, "Work from Home and Other Benefits May Be
at Risk after Covid Emergency Declaration Ends," *Forbes*, May 15, 2023, https://www
.forbes.com/sites/kellyphillipserb/2023/05/15/work-from-home-and-other-benefits
-may-be-at-risk-after-covid-emergency-declaration-ends/.

14. On Congress's decision to allow the childcare subsidies to expire, see Rachel M. Cohen, "A
Program That Saved Child Care for Millions Is Expiring. What Now?," Vox, September
29, 2023, https://www.vox.com/policy/23892133/child-care-daycare-pandemic-emergency
-providers. On the likely impact of the expiration of the program, see Julie Kashen, Laura
Valle Gutierrz, Lea Woods, and Jessica Milli, "Child Care Cliff: 3.2 Million Children Likely
to Lose Spots with End of Federal Funds," Century Foundation, June 21, 2023, https://tcf.org
/content/report/child-care-cliff/.

15. On Republicans' initial demands for cuts to the social safety net, see Kevin Freking, "House
Conservatives Unveil List of Demands to Support Spending Bill and Avoid Shutdown," PBS,
August 21, 2023, https://www.pbs.org/newshour/politics/house-conservatives-unveil-list-of
-demands-to-support-spending-bill-and-avoid-shutdown. On the situation as of September
30, when the childcare funding expired, see Zach Montague, "A Shutdown Is Looming.
What Comes Next?," *New York Times*, September 30, 2023, https://www.nytimes.com
/article/government-shutdown.html. On Trump's involvement, see Sahil Kapur, "Trump
Breaks with McCarthy, Pushing Republicans to Shut Down the Government," NBC News,
September 25, 2023, https://www.nbcnews.com/politics/congress/trump-breaks-mccarthy
-republicans-government-shutdown-rcna117192. On how Congress became even more divided over the spending bill in the wake of Trump's urging, see Lisa Mascaro and Stephen
Groves, "Congress Says It Wants to Avoid a Shutdown, but the House and Senate Are Moving
Even Further Apart," AP News, September 27, 2023, https://apnews.com/article/shutdown
-mccarthy-biden-trump-republicans-e4c37673b6507deaed2902f2166ef759. On the ousting
of Republican House Speaker Kevin McCarthy, see Catie Edmondson, "Far-Right G.O.P.
Faction Throws House into Chaos as McCarthy Is Ousted," *New York Times*, October 3,
2023. https://www.nytimes.com/live/2023/10/03/us/mccarthy-gaetz-speaker-news.

16. For Venker's op-ed, see Suzanne Venker, "The Most Obvious Solution to the Looming 'Child
Care Cliff,'" Fox News, October 2, 2023, https://www.foxnews.com/opinion/most-obvious
-solution-looming-child-care-cliff.

17. For Wright's take, see Erik Olin Wright, "Class, Exploitation, and Economic Rents: Reflec-
tions on Sørensen's 'Sounder Basis,'" *American Journal of Sociology* 105, no. 6 (2000): 1559–71;
Erik Olin Wright, "Working-Class Power, Capitalist-Class Interests, and Class Compromise,"
American Journal of Sociology 105, no. 4 (2000): 957–1002. See also Erling Barth, Karl O.
Moene, and Fredrik Willumsen, "The Scandinavian Model—an Interpretation," *Journal of
Public Economics* 117 (2014): 60–72.

18. On the benefits of universal free school lunch, see Philip M. Gleason and Carol W. Suitor,
"Eating at School: How the National School Lunch Program Affects Children's Diets,"
American Journal of Agricultural Economics 85, no. 4 (2003): 1047–61; Craig Gundersen, Brent
Kreider, and John Pepper, "The Impact of the National School Lunch Program on Child
Health: A Nonparametric Bounds Analysis," *Journal of Econometrics* 166, no. 1 (2012): 79–91;
Jessie Handbury and Sarah Moshary, "School Food Policy Affects Everyone: Retail Re-
sponses to the National School Lunch Program," *SSRN Electronic Journal*, 202. See also John
Gordanier et al., "Free Lunch for All! The Effect of the Community Eligibility Provision
on Academic Outcomes," *Economics of Education Review* 77 (2020): 101999. On the nutritional value of school lunches, see Alisha R. Farris et al., "Nutritional Comparison of Packed
and School Lunches in Pre-Kindergarten and Kindergarten Children Following the Imple-
mentation of the 2012–2013 National School Lunch Program Standards," *Journal of Nutrition
Education and Behavior* 46, no. 6 (2014): 621–26. See also Alisha R. Farris et al., "A Compar-

ison of Fruits, Vegetables, Sugar-Sweetened Beverages, and Desserts in the Packed Lunches of Elementary School Children," *Childhood Obesity* 11, no. 3 (2015): 275–80; Kristie L. Hubbard et al., "What's in Children's Backpacks: Foods Brought from Home," *Journal of the Academy of Nutrition and Dietetics* 114, no. 9 (2014): 1424–31; Inyoung Hur, Teri Burgess-Champoux, and Marla Reicks, "Higher Quality Intake from School Lunch Meals Compared with Bagged Lunches," *ICAN: Infant, Child, & Adolescent Nutrition* 3, no. 2 (2011): 70–75; Craig A. Johnston et al., "School Lunches and Lunches Brought from Home: A Comparative Analysis," *Childhood Obesity* 8, no. 4 (2012): 364–68; Junxiu Liu et al., "Trends in Food Sources and Diet Quality among US Children and Adults, 2003–2018," *JAMA Network Open* 4, no. 4 (2021).

19. On total health spending as a percentage of other countries' GDPs, see "Health Expenditure in Relation to GDP," OECD, https://www.oecd-ilibrary.org/sites/ae3016b9-en/1/3/7/index .html. On how US spending on healthcare has increased as a percentage of GDP, see Sean P. Keehan et al., "National Health Expenditure Projections, 2022–31: Growth to Stabilize Once the COVID-19 Public Health Emergency Ends: National Health Expenditure Projections for 2022–31," *Health Affairs* (2023). On rising employer and worker costs for healthcare, see Gary Claxton et al., *2022 Employer Health Benefits Survey* (San Francisco: Kaiser Family Foundation, 2022), 80, https://www.kff.org/health-costs/report/2022-employer-health-benefits -survey/. On employers who try to skirt Affordable Care Act rules, see Lisa Myers and Carroll Ann Mears, "Businesses Claim Obamacare Has Forced Them to Cut Employee Hours," NBC News, August 13, 2013, https://www.nbcnews.com/news/world/businesses-claim-obamacare -has-forced-them-cut-employee-hours-flna6c10911846; Robert Pear, "Public Sector Cuts Part-Time Shifts to Bypass Insurance Law," *New York Times*, February 20, 2014, https://www.nytimes .com/2014/02/21/us/public-sector-cuts-part-time-shifts-to-duck-insurance-law.html.

20. On the health benefits associated with strong social safety nets, see Giuliano Bonoli and Frank Reber, "The Political Economy of Childcare in OECD Countries: Explaining Cross-National Variation in Spending and Coverage Rates," *European Journal of Political Research* 49, no. 1 (2010): 97–118; Thomas A. Diprete et al., "Do Cross-National Differences in the Costs of Children Generate Cross-National Differences in Fertility Rates?," *Population Research and Policy Review* 22, no. 5 (2003): 439–77; Thomas J. Kane, *The Price of Admission: Rethinking How Americans Pay for College* (Washington, DC: Brookings, 1999); Uwe E. Reinhardt, Peter S. Hussey, and Gerard F. Anderson, "U.S. Health Care Spending in an International Context," *Health Affairs* 23, no. 3 (2004): 10–25; Uwe E. Reinhardt, Peter S. Hussey, and Gerard F. Anderson, "Cross-National Comparisons of Health Systems Using OECD Data, 1999," *Health Affairs* 21, no. 3 (2002): 169–81. On the happiness associated with stronger social safety nets, see B. Radcliff, "Class Organization and Subjective Well-Being: A Cross-National Analysis," *Social Forces* 84, no. 1 (2005): 513–30; John F. Helliwell et al., World *Happiness Report 2021* (New York: Sustainable Development Solutions Network, 2021), https://happiness-report.s3.amazonaws.com/2021/WHR+21.pdf. On how employers benefit from stronger social safety nets, see Wright, "Class, Exploitation, and Economic Rents"; Wright, "Working-Class Power, Capitalist-Class Interests, and Class Compromise." See also Barth, Moene, and Willumsen, "The Scandinavian Model—an Interpretation." On the cost-effectiveness of universal programs, see Peter H. Lindert, *Making Social Spending Work* (Cambridge: Cambridge University Press, 2021).

21. On who would have paid for Build Back Better, see "President Biden Announces the Build Back Better Framework," White House, October 28, 2021, https://www.whitehouse.gov/briefing -room/statements-releases/2021/10/28/president-biden-announces-the-build-back-better -framework/

22. On how inequality increases the value of money, see Derrick Bell, *Faces at the Bottom of the Well: The Permanence of Racism* (New York: Basic Books, 1993); William Darity, "Stratification Economics: The Role of Intergroup Inequality," *Journal of Economics and Finance* 29 (2005): 144–53; W. E. B. Du Bois, *The Philadelphia Negro: A Social Study* (Philadelphia: Uni-

versity of Pennsylvania Press, 1899); David Mosse, "A Relational Approach to Durable Poverty, Inequality and Power," *Journal of Development Studies* 46, no. 7 (2010): 1156–78; David R. Roediger, "The Wages of Whiteness," in *Class: The Anthology*, ed. Stanley Aronowitz and Michael J. Roberts (Hoboken, NJ: Wiley, 2017), 41–55; Charles Tilly, *Durable Inequality* (Berkeley: University of California Press, 1999); Charles Tilly, "Relational Origins of Inequality," *Anthropological Theory* 1, no. 3 (2001): 355–72; Donald Tomaskovic-Devey, "The Relational Generation of Workplace Inequalities," *Social Currents* 1, no. 1 (2014): 51–73; Donald Tomaskovic-Devey and Dustin Avent-Holt, "Observing Organizational Inequality Regimes," in *A Gedenkschrift to Randy Hodson: Working with Dignity*, ed. Lisa A. Keister and Vincent J. Roscigno (Bingley, UK: Emerald Publishing, February 2016): 187–212. On the wealth required to be part of the 1 percent, see Dock David Treece and Michael Adams, "Are You in the Top 1%?," *Forbes*, June 8, 2023, https://www.forbes.com/advisor/investing/financial-advisor/are-you-in-the-top-1-percent/. On how families with considerable wealth leverage those resources to secure coveted spots in elite private colleges in the US (and leverage those degrees to secure coveted jobs in elite professions), see Jessica Calarco, "Cheating in College Admissions Plays out on Several Different Levels," *Inside Higher Ed*, March 21, 2019, https://www.insidehighered.com/advice/2019/03/22/cheating-college-admissions-plays-out-several-different-levels-opinion; Anthony P. Carnevale, Peter Schmidt, and Jeff Strohl, *The Merit Myth: How Our Colleges Favor the Rich and Divide America* (New York: The New Press, 2020); Sam Friedman and Daniel Laurison, *The Class Ceiling: Why It Pays to Be Privileged* (Bristol, UK: Policy Press, 2019); Daniel Golden, *The Price of Admission: How America's Ruling Class Buys Its Way into Elite Colleges—and Who Gets Left Outside the Gates* (New York: Three Rivers Press, 2007); Daniel Golden, "The Story behind Jared Kushner's Curious Acceptance into Harvard," ProPublica, November 18, 2016, https://www.propublica.org/article/the-story-behind-jared-kushners-curious-acceptance-into-harvard; Anthony Abraham Jack, *The Privileged Poor: How Elite Colleges Are Failing Disadvantaged Students* (Cambridge, MA: Harvard University Press, 2019); Lauren A. Rivera, *Pedigree: How Elite Students Get Elite Jobs* (Princeton, NJ: Princeton University Press, 2016); Mitchell L. Stevens, *Creating a Class: College Admissions and the Education of Elites* (Cambridge, MA: Harvard University Press, 2009). On how wealthy individuals and families leverage their wealth to hoard desirable real estate and drive up home values in ways that prevent other families with fewer resources from buying homes in those same neighborhoods, thus amplifying segregation and stratification, see Camille Zubrinsky Charles, "The Dynamics of Racial Residential Segregation," *Annual Review of Sociology* 29, no. 1 (2003): 167–207; Stefanie DeLuca, Philip M. E. Garboden, and Peter Rosenblatt, "Segregating Shelter: How Housing Policies Shape the Residential Locations of Low-Income Minority Families," *ANNALS of the American Academy of Political and Social Science* 647, no. 1 (2013): 268–99; Elizabeth Korver-Glenn, *Race Brokers: Housing Markets and Segregation in 21st Century Urban America* (Oxford: Oxford University Press, 2021); Lauren J. Krivo and Robert L. Kaufman, "Housing and Wealth Inequality: Racial-Ethnic Differences in Home Equity in the United States," *Demography* 41, no. 3 (2004): 585–605; Maria Krysan and Kyle Crowder, *Cycle of Segregation: Social Processes and Residential Segregation* (New York: Russell Sage Foundation, 2017); Ann Owens, "Neighborhoods and Schools as Competing and Reinforcing Contexts for Educational Attainment," *Sociology of Education* 83, no. 4 (2010): 287–311; Richard V. Reeves, *Dream Hoarders: How the American Upper Middle Class Is Leaving Everyone Else in the Dust, Why That Is a Problem, and What to Do about It* (Washington, DC: Brookings, 2018); Tilly, *Durable Inequality*.

23. On political differences in support for expanding the social safety net, see Carroll Doherty, Jocelyn Kiley, and Nida Asheer, *In a Politically Polarized Era, Sharp Divides in Both Partisan Coalitions* (Washington, DC: Pew Research Center, 2019), https://www.pewresearch.org/politics/2019/12/17/in-a-politically-polarized-era-sharp-divides-in-both-partisan-coalitions/. On gender differences in support for government spending on childcare, see

"State of Childcare in the United States," Century Foundation, June 21, 2023, https://tcf.org /content/commentary/americans-agree-child-care-should-be-more-affordable-and -available/. On the membership of the 117th Congress, see *Membership of the 117th Congress: A Profile* (Washington, DC: Congressional Research Service, 2022), https://crsreports.congress .gov/product/pdf/R/R46705.

24. On the cost of EpiPens in the US, see Dylan Scott, "It's Not Just about Abortion," Vox, June 26, 2022, https://www.vox.com/23137822/abortion-birth-control-health-care-roe -wade. On the cost of similar devices in the UK, see "EpiPen Price by Country 2023," World Population Review, https://worldpopulationreview.com/country-rankings/epipen-price-by -country. On the history of price increases for the EpiPen, see Tara Suter, "Manchin Received Large Campaign Contributions from Daughter's Company amid EpiPen Scandal," Open Secrets, September 21, 2021, https://www.opensecrets.org/news/2021/09/manchin-large -campaign-contributions-epipen-scandal/. See also "The Cost of EpiPens in the United States from November 2004 to May 2016," Statista, https://www.statista.com/statistics /629242/rising-costs-of-epipens-in-us/. On the lawsuit against Mylan, see Proskauer, "$264 Million Settlement in EpiPen Price Gouging Litigation," *Minding Your Own Business* (blog), July 29, 2022, https://www.proskauer.com/blog/264-million-settlement-in-epipen-price -gouging-litigation. On Bresch's relationship to Manchin and contributions to his campaigns, see Ryan Grim, "Heather Bresch, Joe Manchin's Daughter, Played Direct Part in EpiPen Price Inflation Scandal," *Intercept*, September 7, 2021, https://theintercept.com/2021/09/07 /joe-manchin-epipen-price-heather-bresch/; David Wright, "Manchin Defends CEO Daughter after Company Raised EpiPen Price," CNN, September 7, 2016, https://www.cnn.com/2016/09 /07/politics/manchin-defends-bresch-mylan-epipen-price/index.html.

25. On the donations Manchin took during Build Back Better negotiations, see Mike Tony, "Manchin's Campaign Contributions Surpassed $1.5 Million as His Leverage Loomed toward End of 2021," *Charleston Gazette-Mail*, February 1, 2022, https://www.wvgazettemail .com/news/energy_and_environment/manchins-campaign-contributions -surpassed-1-5-million-as-his-leverage-loomed-toward-end-of-2021/article_f30208fb -e716-52bf-be4b-a89ffacc2180.html. On Manchin's efforts to gut the Build Back Better Act, see Jeff Stein, "Manchin's $1.8 Trillion Spending Offer Appears No Longer to Be on the Table," *Washington Post*, January 8, 2021, https://www.washingtonpost.com/us-policy/2022 /01/08/manchin-white-house-talks/; Erik Wasson and Steven T. Dennis, "Manchin Balks at Biden's Corporate Tax Increase, Favors 25% Rate," Bloomberg, April 5, 2021, https://www .bloomberg.com/news/articles/2021-04-05/manchin-balks-at-biden-s-corporate-tax -increase-favors-25-rate. On donations to Sinema, see Jack Crosbie, "New Financial Disclo- sures Show Kyrsten Sinema Is Raking in Cash from Big GOP Donors," *Rolling Stone*, January 31, 2022, https://www.rollingstone.com/politics/politics-news/kyrsten-sinema-fundraising -republican-donors-1293087/; Brian Schwartz, "Kyrsten Sinema Raises over $1.5 Million in Fourth Quarter While Opposing Key Pieces of Biden Agenda," CNBC, January 31, 2022, https://www.cnbc.com/2022/01/31/kyrsten-sinema-raised-over-1point5-million-as-she -fought-key-biden-goals.html. On Manchin and Sinema's refusal to support the bill, see Robert Reich, "Where Egos Dare: Manchin and Sinema Show How Senate Spotlight Cor- rupts," *Guardian*, January 23, 2022, https://www.theguardian.com/commentisfree/2022/jan /22/where-egos-dare-manchin-sinema-senate-voting-rights-filibuster. On Manchin's deal- breaking vote against the Voting Rights Act, see Joe Manchin, "Why I'm Voting against the For the People Act," Senator Joe Manchin, June 8, 2021, https://www.manchin.senate.gov /newsroom/op-eds/why-im-voting-against-the-for-the-people-act.

26. On Republican senators' opposition, see "Build Back Better Act," Ballotpedia, https://bal lotpedia.org/Build_Back_Better_Act. On Republican representatives' opposition, see "Roll Call 385—Bill Number: H.R. 5376," Clerk of the US House of Representatives, November 19, 2021, https://clerk.house.gov/Votes/2021385. On the donors who funded Republican

opposition to the bill, see Oliver Milman, "A Closer Look at Joe Manchin's Ties to the Fossil Fuel Industry," *Mother Jones*, October 21, 2021, https://www.motherjones.com/politics /2021/10/a-closer-look-at-joe-manchins-ties-to-the-fossil-fuel-industy/; Brian Schwartz, "Rupert Murdoch-Funded Fox Corp. PAC Contributes to Democrat Joe Manchin's Campaign," CNBC, July 15, 2021, https://www.cnbc.com/2021/07/15/fox-news-owner-donates-to -joe-manchins-campaign.html; Brian Schwartz and Jacob Pramuk, "Corporate Donations to Sen. Joe Manchin's PAC Surged as He Fought President Biden's Agenda," CNBC, December 21, 2021, https://www.cnbc.com/2021/12/21/joe-manchin-pac-saw-surge-of-corporate -donations-as-he-fought-biden-agenda.html; Michela Tindera, "Billionaire Republican Donors Are Now Giving to Manchin and Sinema," *Forbes*, February 4, 2022, https://www .forbes.com/sites/michelatindera/2022/02/04/billionaire-republicans-are-now -donating-to-manchin-and-sinema/; Kenneth P. Vogel and Kate Kelly, "G.O.P. Donors Back Manchin and Sinema as They Reshape Biden's Agenda," *New York Times*, November 11, 2021, https://www.nytimes.com/2021/11/21/us/politics/manchin-sinema-republican-donors .html?partner=slack&smid=sl-share. See also Crosbie, "New Financial Disclosures Show Kyrsten Sinema Is Raking in Cash from Big GOP Donors"; Schwartz, "Rupert Murdoch–Funded Fox Corp. PAC Contributes to Democrat Joe Manchin's Campaign"; On Clarence Thomas's relationship with Harlan Crow, see Abbie VanSickle, "Justice Thomas Reports Private Trips with Harlan Crow," *New York Times*, August 31, 2023, https://www.nytimes.com/2023/08/31 /us/thomas-financial-disclosures-scotus.html.

27. On the beneficiaries of federal Covid spending, see Peter Whoriskey, Douglas MacMillian, and Jonathan O'Connell, "'Doomed to Fail': Why a $4 Trillion Bailout Couldn't Revive the American Economy," *Washington Post*, October 5, 2020, https://www.washingtonpost.com /graphics/2020/business/coronavirus-bailout-spending/. On how corporations used Covid relief money to benefit executives and shareholders, see Ken Dilanian and Laura Strickler, "Theft from the Covid Relief Plan Known as PPP Was Even Worse Than We Thought," NBC News, March 28, 2022, https://www.nbcnews.com/politics/justice-department/biggest-fraud -generation-looting-covid-relief-program-known-ppp-n1279664. On the Cheesecake Factory's manipulation of pandemic relief payments, see Alex Abad-Santos, "The Cheesecake Factory Knows What You Want," Vox, December 2024, 2022, https://www.vox.com/culture/2351 6638/cheesecake-factory-restaurant-menu. On the record profits posted by the Cheesecake Factory in 2021, see "Investor Relations," Cheesecake Factory, https://investors.thecheesecakefactory .com/news-and-events/news-releases/news-release-details/2021/The-Cheesecake-Factory -Reports-Record-Revenues-in-the-Second-Quarter-of-Fiscal-2021-and-Provides-Business -Update/default.aspx.

28. On pandemic-era stock market growth, see Robert Frank, "The Wealthiest 10% of Americans Own a Record 89% of All U.S. Stocks," CNBC, October 18, 2021, https://www.cnbc .com/2021/10/18/the-wealthiest-10percent-of-americans-own-a-record-89percent -of-all-us-stocks.html. On the struggles faced by regular people in 2021, see Jacob Orchard, "Inflation Inequality: Poorest Americans Are Hit Hardest by Soaring Prices on Necessities," *The Conversation*, January 13, 2022, http://theconversation.com/inflation-inequality-poorest -americans-are-hit-hardest-by-soaring-prices-on-necessities-174853. On the growth in wealth at the top of the spectrum in 2021, see Robert Frank, "Soaring Markets Helped the Richest 1% Gain $6.5 Trillion in Wealth Last Year, According to the Fed," CNBC, April 1, 2022, https://www.cnbc.com/2022/04/01/richest-one-percent-gained-trillions-in-wealth-2021 .html. On the prevalence and politics of billionaires and their donations, see "American Billionaires by the Numbers," *Americans for Tax Fairness* (blog), May 20, 2020, https://american sfortaxfairness.org/billionaire-politics/; Lydia DePillis, "Way More CEOs Are Republicans Than Democrats. Here's the Proof," CNN Business, May 14, 2019, https://www.cnn.com /2019/05/14/business/republican-democrat-ceos/index.html; Matt Rothschild, "GOP Accepts Four Times More in Corporate Contributions Than Dems," *Wisconsin Examiner*, August

5, 2021, https://wisconsinexaminer.com/brief/gop-accepts-four-times-more-in-corporate-contributions-than-dems/; Esther Whieldon, "Political Donations by US Public Company CEOs Largely Favor Republicans," *S&P Global Market Intelligence* (blog), April 2, 2019, https://www.spglobal.com/marketintelligence/en/news-insights/trending/0Nm-AZgRK eGzfWZhvSWTFw2.

29. On how corporate profits drove pandemic inflation, see Josh Bivens, "Corporate Profits Have Contributed Disproportionately to Inflation. How Should Policymakers Respond?" (Washington, DC: Economic Policy Institute, 2022), https://www.epi.org/blog/corporate-profits-have-contributed-disproportionately-to-inflation-how-should-policymakers-respond/. On efforts to blame pandemic inflation on greedy workers, see Talmon Joseph Smith, "Wages May Not Be Inflation's Cause, but They're the Focus of the Cure," *New York Times*, April 7, 2023, https://www.nytimes.com/2023/04/07/business/economy/wages-prices.html. On how companies used the pandemic as cover to raise prices, see Alex Bitter, "Consumers Are Wising Up to 'Greedflation' as Food Companies Keep Prices High," Business Insider, April 28, 2023, https://www.businessinsider.com/shoppers-blame-greedflation-pepsico-nestle-raise-food-prices-2023-4; Lydia DePillis and Jeanna Smialek, "Why Is Inflation So Stubborn? Cars Are Part of the Answer," *New York Times*, May 20, 2023, https://www.nytimes.com /2023/05/20/business/economy/car-prices-inflation.html; Emily Peck, "Once a Fringe Theory, 'Greedflation' Gets Its Due (Though No One Calls It That)," *Axios*, May 18, 2023, https:// www.axios.com/2023/05/18/once-a-fringe-theory-greedflation-gets-its-due. On the auto industry's efforts to raise prices, see DePillis and Smialek, "Why Is Inflation So Stubborn?"; Lauren Sforza, "Wholesale Used Car Prices Drop by Largest Amount since Pandemic Began," *Hill*, July 10, 2023, https://thehill.com/business/4088856-wholesale-used-car-prices-drop-by-largest-amount-since-pandemic-began/. On the average price of US vehicles in 2023, see "Money, Money, Money," *On the Media*, WNYC Studios, podcast, July 14, 2023, https:// www.wnycstudios.org/podcasts/otm/episodes/on-the-media-money-money-money.

30. On the challenges of getting by without a car in America, see Kathryn Freeman Anderson and Joseph Galaskiewicz, "Racial/Ethnic Residential Segregation, Socioeconomic Inequality, and Job Accessibility by Public Transportation Networks in the United Sates," *Spatial Demography* 9 (2021): 341–73; Weijing Wang, Sierra Espeland, Jesus M. Barajas, and Dana Rowangould, "Rural-Nonrural Divide in Car Access and Unmet Travel Need in the United States," *Transportation* (2023); Gerard C. Wellman, "Transportation Apartheid: The Role of Transportation Policy in Social Inequality," *Public Works Management & Policy* 19, no. 4 (2014): 334–39.

31. On the role of profit in driving pandemic inflation, see Bivens, "Corporate Profits Have Contributed Disproportionately to Inflation." On policymakers' efforts to curb pandemic inflation, see Smith, "Wages May Not Be Inflation's Cause, but They're the Focus of the Cure."

32. For more on politicians who have rejected the idea of corporate and wealthy influence on politics, see Raymond Arkie, "2020 Democrats Sticking to Their No Lobbyist Money Pledge," Open Secrets, May 7, 2019, https://www.opensecrets.org/news/2019/05/2020-democrats-stick-to-no-lobbyist/. On the number of billionaires in the US, see Willy Staley, "How Many Billionaires Are There, Anyway?," *New York Times*, April 7, 2022, https://www.nytimes.com /2022/04/07/magazine/billionaires.html.

33. On efforts to promote neoliberal ideologies in the US, see Naomi Oreskes and Erik M. Conway, *The Big Myth: How American Business Taught Us to Loathe Government and Love the Free Market* (New York: Bloomsbury, 2023). See also Natalie Allison, "Army of Millionaires Fuel Senate Primary Spending Spree," *Politico*, January 24, 2022, https://www.politico.com /news/2022/01/24/millionaires-flood-senate-cash-00000895; Martin-Brehm Christensen et al., "Survival of the Richest," Oxfam International, January 16, 2023, https://www.oxfam.org/en /research/survival-richest; Ronald P. Formisano, *Plutocracy in America: How Increasing Inequality Destroys the Middle Class and Exploits the Poor* (Baltimore: Johns Hopkins University

Press, 2015); Martin Gilens, *Affluence and Influence* (Princeton, NJ: Princeton University Press, 2014); Jacob S. Hacker and Paul Pierson, "Winner-Take-All Politics: Public Policy, Political Organization, and the Precipitous Rise of Top Incomes in the United States," *Politics & Society* 38, no. 2 (2010): 152–204; Dale L. Johnson, "Rule by Divide and Conquer," in *Social Inequality, Economic Decline, and Plutocracy: An American Crisis*, ed. Dale L. Johnson, *Critical Political Theory and Radical Practice* (Cham, Switzerland: Springer International Publishing, 2017), 91–108; Prabhir Vishnu Poruthiyil, "Big Business and Fascism: A Dangerous Collusion," *Journal of Business Ethics* 168, no. 1 (2021): 121–35.

34. On voter suppression and its consequences, see Carol Anderson, *One Person, No Vote: How Voter Suppression Is Destroying Our Democracy* (New York: Bloomsbury, 2018).

35. On the appeal of neoliberal ideologies, see Daniel C. Hallin, "Mediatisation, Neoliberalism and Populisms: The Case of Trump," *Contemporary Social Science* 14, no. 1 (2019): 14–25; David Jacobs and Lindsey Myers, "Union Strength, Neoliberalism, and Inequality: Contingent Political Analyses of U.S. Income Differences since 1950," *American Sociological Review* 79, no. 4 (2014): 752–74.

36. On big money's role in media, see David Brock, *The Republican Noise Machine: Right-Wing Media and How It Corrupts Democracy* (New York: Three Rivers Press, 2005); Kevin M. Kruse, *One Nation under God: How Corporate America Invented Christian America* (New York: Basic Books, 2015); Kate Conger and Lauren Hirsch, "Elon Musk Completes $44 Billion Deal to Own Twitter," *New York Times*, October 28, 2022, https://www.nytimes.com/2022/10/27 /technology/elon-musk-twitter-deal-complete.html; Francesca Giuliani-Hoffman, "How the Washington Post Has Changed under Jeff Bezos," CNN, August 16, 2019, https://www.cnn .com/2019/08/16/media/jeff-bezos-donald-graham/index.html. On big money's role in academia, see Kristin Kobes Du Mez, *Jesus and John Wayne: How White Evangelicals Corrupted a Faith and Fractured a Nation* (New York: Liveright, 2020); Kruse, *One Nation Under God*; Paul Sullivan, "As Politics Creep into Philanthropy, Beneficiaries Come under Fire," *New York Times*, August 16, 2019, https://www.nytimes.com/2019/08/16/your-money/politics-philanthropy -protests.html. On big money's role in funding conservative and libertarian think tanks, see Oreskes and Conway, *The Big Myth*.

37. On the prevalence of neoliberal ideologies, see Hannah Hartig, "Stark Partisan Divisions in Americans' Views of 'Socialism,' 'Capitalism,'" Pew Research Center, June 25, 2019, https://www.pewresearch.org/short-reads/2019/06/25/stark-partisan-divisions-in -americans-views-of-socialism-capitalism/. On perceptions of the consequences of business regulation, see Carroll Doherty, Jocelyn Kiley, and Bridget Johnson, *Political Values: Government Regulation, Environment, Immigration, Race, Views of Islam* (Washington, DC: Pew Research Center, 2016), https://www.pewresearch.org/politics/2016/12/08/3-political-values -government-regulation-environment-immigration-race-views-of-islam/. On tech regulation, see also Emily A. Vogels, "Support for More Regulation of Tech Companies Has Declined in U.S., Especially among Republicans," Pew Research Center, May 13, 2022, https:// www.pewresearch.org/short-reads/2022/05/13/support-for-more-regulation-of -tech-companies-has-declined-in-u-s-especially-among-republicans/. On pollution, see also Kristen Bialik, "Most Americans Favor Stricter Environmental Laws and Regulations," Pew Research Center, December 14, 2016, https://www.pewresearch.org/short-reads/2016/12 /14/most-americans-favor-stricter-environmental-laws-and-regulations/.

38. For cases of ultra-wealthy people running for office, see "Top Self-Funding Candidates," Open Secrets, https://www.opensecrets.org/elections-overview/top-self-funders. On Trump's wealth, see Dan Alexander, "Yes, Trump Is Still a Billionaire (Even Though He Paid So Little in Taxes)," *Forbes*, December 22, 2022, https://www.forbes.com/sites/danalexander/2022 /12/22/yes-trump-is-still-a-billionaire-even-though-he-paid-so-little-in-taxes/. On Trump's political party affiliations, see Peter Overby, "Every Position Donald Trump Has Taken on How He Is Funding His Campaign," NPR, July 14, 2016, https://www.npr.org/2016/07 /14/485699964/every-position-donald-trump-has-taken-on-how-he-is-funding

-his-campaign. On Bloomberg's political party affiliations, see Shane Goldmacher, "Michael Bloomberg Spent More than $900 Million on His Failed Presidential Run," *New York Times*, March 20, 2020, https://www.nytimes.com/2020/03/20/us/politics/bloomberg-campaign -900-million.html. On how wealthy elites bankroll politicians, see Lee Drutman, *The Business of America Is Lobbying: How Corporations Became Politicized and Politics Became More Corporate* (Oxford: Oxford University Press, 2015); Kruse, *One Nation Under God*; Kevin Phillips, *Bad Money: Reckless Finance, Failed Politics, and the Global Crisis of American Capitalism* (New York: Penguin, 2008). Oreskes and Conway, *The Big Myth*.

39. On the voting behavior of billionaires and corporate executives, see DePillis, "Way More CEOs Are Republicans Than Democrats." On the personal donations of billionaires and corporate executives, see *American Billionaires by the Numbers* (Washington, DC: Americans for Tax Fairness, 2020), https://americansfortaxfairness.org/billionaire-politics/. On how big donors hedge their bets by making donations on both sides of races, see Whieldon, "Political Donations by US Public Company CEOs Largely Favor Republicans." On the role of out-of-state donations in Wisconsin politics, see Rothschild, "GOP Accepts Four Times More in Corporate Contributions Than Dems."

40. On the DeVos family's political donations, see Zack Stanton, "How Betsy DeVos Used God and Amway to Take Over Michigan Politics," *Politico*, January 15, 2017, https://www.politico .com/magazine/story/2017/01/betsy-dick-devos-family-amway-michigan-politics-religion -214631/. See also Craig Mauger, "DeVos Family Has Made at Least $82 Million in Political Contributions since 1999, According to Campaign Finance Disclosures," Michigan Campaign Finance Network, 2020, https://mcfn.org/node/6178/devos-family-has-made-at-least-82 -million-in-political-contributions-since-1999-according-to-campaign-finance-disclosures. On Betsy DeVos and her role in politics, see Kevin Bogardus, "Organizational Donors," Center for Public Integrity, May 26, 2005, http://publicintegrity.org/politics/organizational -donors/; Jane Mayer, "Betsy DeVos, Trump's Big-Donor Education Secretary," *New Yorker*, November 23, 2016, https://www.newyorker.com/news/news-desk/betsy-devos-trumps -big-donor-education-secretary; Valerie Strauss, "She's a Billionaire Who Said Schools Need Guns to Fight Bears. Here's What You May Not Know about Betsy DeVos," *Washington Post*, February 17, 2017, https://www.washingtonpost.com/news/answer-sheet/wp/2017/02/07 /shes-a-billionaire-who-said-schools-need-guns-to-fight-bears-heres-what-you-may-not -know-about-betsy-devos/.

41. On how big money donations are increasingly being used to elect far-right candidates, see Poruthiyil, "Big Business and Fascism." On Thiel's backing of Vance, see Jessie Balmert, "Super PAC Supporting Potential Senate Candidate J. D. Vance Gets $10 Million Donation from PayPal Cofounder," *Enquirer*, March 15, 2021, https://www.cincinnati.com/story/news/politics /elections/2021/03/15/super-pac-supporting-possible-ohio-senate-candidate-j-d-vance-gets-10 -m-donation-peter-thiel/4700540001/; Theodore Schleifer, "Peter Thiel Is Making the Biggest Political Bet of His Life," Vox, March 15, 2021, https://www.vox.com/recode/22332045/peter -thiel-jd-vance-ohio-senate-donation.

42. On Vance's anti-immigration attitudes, see Steve Peoples, "Republican Senate Candidates Promote 'Replacement' Theory," PBS, May 17, 2022, https://www.pbs.org/newshour/politics /republican-senate-candidates-promote-replacement-theory. On Vance's attitudes regarding marriage and divorce, see Kylie Cheung, "Conservatives Are Coming for No-Fault Divorce," *Jezebel*, August 3, 2022, https://jezebel.com/conservatives-are-coming-for-no-fault-divorce -1849366745; Cameron Joseph, "JD Vance Suggests People in 'Violent' Marriages Shouldn't Get Divorced," *Vice*, July 25, 2022, https://www.vice.com/en/article/93abve/jd-vance-suggests -people-in-violent-marriages-shouldnt-get-divorced; Bess Levin, "GOP Senate Candidate J. D. Vance: If People Love Their Kids, They'll Stay in Violent Marriages," *Vanity Fair*, July 25, 2022, https://www.vanityfair.com/news/2022/07/jd-vance-violent-marriages. On Vance's neoliberalism, see Amanda Marcotte, "Republicans Don't Care about Kids—Just Imaginary Children," *Salon*, May 25, 2022, https://www.salon.com/2022/05/25/dont-care-about-kids—

just-imaginary-children/; Abby Vesoulis, "Forced Parenthood and Failing Safety Nets: This Is Life in Post-*Roe* America," *Mother Jones*, August 29, 2022, https://www.motherjones.com /politics/2022/08/abortion-bans-states-social-safety-net-dobbs/. On Vance's opposition to vaccines, see Bevan Hurley, "GOP Senate Hopeful JD Vance Calls for 'Mass Civil Disobedience' over Biden Vaccines Mandate," *Independent*, September 10, 2021, https://www.independent .co.uk/news/world/americas/us-politics/biden-vaccine-mandate-gop-b1918191.html. On the relationship between neoliberalism and social conservatism, see Melinda Cooper, *Family Values: Between Neoliberalism and the New Social Conservatism* (Cambridge, MA: MIT Press, 2017).

43. For Vance's take on the social safety net, see Travis Waldron and Arthur Delaney, "J. D. Vance Ditches Past Support for Social Security Cuts," *HuffPost*, July 13, 2022, https://www.huffpost .com/entry/jd-vance-ohio-senate-blake-masters-social-security_n_62cede26e4b0eef119c132fb.

44. On the exploitation of Black women and particularly low-income Black single mothers, see Altheira Caldera, "Challenging Capitalistic Exploitation: A Black Feminist/Womanist Commentary on Work and Self-Care," *Feminist Studies* 46, no. 3 (2020): 707–16; Patricia Hill Collins, *Black Feminist Thought: Knowledge, Consciousness, and the Politics of Empowerment* (New York: Routledge, 2000); Patricia Hill Collins, "Black Women and Motherhood," in *Motherhood and Space: Configurations of the Maternal through Politics, Home, and the Body*, ed. Sarah Hardy and Caroline Wiedmer (New York: Palgrave Macmillan, 2005), 149–59; Angela Y. Davis, *Women, Race, and Class* (New York: Vintage Books, 1983); bell hooks, *Ain' I a Woman: Black Women and Feminism* (New York: Routledge, 2014); Zora Neale Hurston, *Their Eyes Were Watching God* (Philadelphia: J. B. Lippincott and Co., 1937); Jacqueline Jones, *Labor of Love, Labor of Sorrow: Black Women, Work and the Family, from Slavery to the Present* (New York: Basic Books, 2010); Deborah Gray White, *Too Heavy a Load: Black Women in Defense of Themselves, 1894–1994* (New York: W. W. Norton, 1999). On the vilification of low-income single mothers and especially low-income Black single mothers, see Dawn Marie Dow, *Mothering While Black* (Berkeley: University of California Press, 2019); Dawn Marie Dow, "Negotiating 'The Welfare Queen' and 'The Strong Black Woman': African American Middle-Class Mothers' Work and Family Perspectives," *Sociological Perspectives* 58, no. 1 (2015): 36–55; Kathryn Edin and Laura Lein, *Making Ends Meet: How Single Mothers Survive Welfare and Low-Wage Work* (New York: Russell Sage Foundation, 1997); Celeste Watkins-Hayes and Elise Kovalsky, "The Discourse of Deservingness: Morality and the Dilemmas of Poverty Relief in Debate and Practice," in *The Oxford Handbook of the Social Science of Poverty*, ed. David Brady and Linda Burton (Oxford: Oxford University Press, 2016). On the blaming of children for their parent's "bad choices," see Jessica McCrory Calarco, "Avoiding Us Versus Them: How Schools' Dependence on Privileged 'Helicopter' Parents Influences Enforcement of Rules," *American Sociological Review* 85, no. 2 (2020): 223–46; Jessica McCrory Calarco, Ilana S. Horn, and Grace A. Chen, "'You Need to Be More Responsible': The Myth of Meritocracy and Teachers' Accounts of Homework Inequalities," *Educational Researcher* 51, no. 8 (2022): 515–23.

45. On racial inequalities in family poverty, see Areeba Haider, "The Basic Facts about Children in Poverty," Center for American Progress, January 12, 2021, https://www.americanprogress .org/issues/poverty/reports/2021/01/12/494506/basic-facts-children-poverty/. On Vance's anti-immigrant attitudes, see Peoples, "Republican Senate Candidates Promote 'Replacement' Theory." On the link between neoliberalism, fascism, and eugenics, see Cooper, *Family Values*; Gabrielle Goodrow, "Bipower, Disability and Capitalism: Neoliberal Eugenics and the Future of ART Regulation," *Duke Journal of Gender Law & Policy* 26 (2019, 2018): 137; Paul Nachtwey and Eva Walther, "Survival of the Fittest in the Pandemic Age: Introducing Disease-Related Social Darwinism," *PLOS ONE* 18, no. 3 (2023); Eva Sharma and Isha Malhotra, "'Wombs-for-Hire': Biopolitics and Neoliberal Eugenics of Indian Commercial Surrogacy Industry in Amulya Malladi's *A House for Happy Mothers*," *Media Watch* 12, no. 1 (2021): 67–78.

CONCLUSION: LEVERAGING OUR LINKED FATES

1. On the Icelandic Women's Day Off, see Kirstie Brewer, "The Day Iceland's Women Went on Strike," BBC News, October 23, 2015, https://www.bbc.com/news/magazine-34602822.
2. On how Icelandic politics and culture changed in the wake of the Women's Day Off, see Edward Schneider, "Icelandic Women on the Brink of Power," *Scandinavian Studies* 64, no. 3 (1992): 417–38; Inga Minelgaite Snaebjornsson, "'President Vigdís': The End and the Beginning of Women's Agenda in Iceland," in *Women Leaders in Chaotic Environments: Examinations of Leadership Using Complexity Theory*, ed. Şefika Şule Erçetin (Cham, Switzerland: Springer International Publishing, 2016), 35–47. On the improvement of life for girls and women in Iceland, see Þorgerour H. Þorvaldsdóttir, "The Gender-Equal North: Icelandic Images of Femininity and Masculinity," in *Iceland and Images of the North*, ed. Sumarlidi Isleifsson and Daniel Chartier (Québec: Presses de l'Université du Québec, 2011). On the Human Development Index ratings in 1980, see "Augmented Human Development Index," Our World in Data, https://ourworldindata.org/grapher/human-development-index-escosura. On the Human Development Index ratings in 2015, see "Iceland: Human Development," Global Economy, https://www.theglobaleconomy.com/Iceland/human_development/. On the Human Development Index ratings in 2023, see "Human Development In-Sights," UNDP, https://hdr.undp.org/data-center/country-insights#/ranks.
3. On lingering gender inequalities in Iceland, see Katrin Olafsdottir, "Iceland Is the Best, but Still Not Equal," *Søkelys På Arbeidslivet* 35, no. 1–2 (May 8, 2018): 111–26. On the rankings of best countries for women, see Morgan Smith, "The 20 Best Countries for Women—the U.S. Isn't One of Them," CNBC, June 23, 2023, https://www.cnbc.com/2023/06/23/the-20-best-countries-for-womenthe-us-isnt-one-of-them-wef-report.html.
4. On the gap between the number of women who would prefer an egalitarian male partner and the number of men who would meet these ideals, see Long Doan and Natasha Quadlin, "Partner Characteristics and Perceptions of Responsibility for Housework and Child Care," *Journal of Marriage and Family* 81, no. 1 (2019): 145–63; Trenton D. Mize, Gayle Kaufman, and Richard J. Petts, "Visualizing Shifts in Gendered Parenting Attitudes during COVID-19," *Socius* 7 (2021); Joanna R. Pepin and David A. Cotter, "Separating Spheres? Diverging Trends in Youth's Gender Attitudes about Work and Family," *Journal of Marriage and Family* 80, no. 1 (2018): 7–24.
5. On the fundamental interdependence of human beings, see Jane Addams, "Charity and Social Justice," *North American Review* 192, no. 656 (1910): 68–81; Jane Addams, *20 Years at Hull-House* (New York: Macmillan, 1910); Maurice Hamington, "Jane Addams and a Politics of Embodied Care," *Journal of Speculative Philosophy* 15, no. 2 (2001): 105–21; Donna Ladkin, "Caring beyond Kinship: Applying Jane Addams Social Ethic to the Organizational Domain," *Paradox and Power in Caring Leadership* (March 2, 2020): 210–21; Carol Stack, *All Our Kin* (New York: Harper, 1974). On how that interdependence relates to care, see Robert N. Bellah et al., *Habits of the Heart: Individualism and Commitment in American Life* (Berkeley: University of California Press, 2007); ed. William A. Donohue, *The New Freedom: Individualism and Collectivism in the Social Lives of Americans* (London: Routledge, 2021); Claude S. Fischer, "Paradoxes of American Individualism," *Sociological Forum* 23, no. 2 (2008): 363–72; David John Frank, John W. Meyer, and David Miyahara, "The Individualist Polity and the Prevalence of Professionalized Psychology: A Cross-National Study," *American Sociological Review* 60, no. 3 (1995): 360–67; Geert Hofstede, *Culture's Consequences: Comparing Values, Behaviors, Institutions, and Organizations Across Nations* (Thousand Oaks, CA: SAGE Publications, 2001); Ken I. Kim, Hun-Joon Park, and Nori Suzuki, "Reward Allocations in the United States, Japan, and Korea: A Comparison of Individualistic and Collectivistic Cultures," *Academy of Management Journal* 33, no. 1 (1990): 188–98. For definitions and discussions of care, see Paula England, "Emerging Theories of Care Work," *Annual Review of Sociology* 31 (2005): 381–99; Paula England, Michelle Budig, and Nancy Folbre, "Wages of

Virtue: The Relative Pay of Care Work," *Social Problems* 49, no. 4 (2002): 455–73; Paula England and Nancy Folbre, "The Cost of Caring," *ANNALS of the American Academy of Political and Social Science* 561, no. 1 (1999): 39–51; Nancy Folbre, *The Invisible Heart: Economics and Family Values* (New York: The New Press, 2002); Candace Howes, Carrie Leana, and Kristin Smith, "Paid Care Work," in *For Love or Money: Care Provision in the United States*, ed. Nancy Folbre (New York: Russell Sage Foundation, 2012); Allison J. Pugh, *The Tumbleweed Society: Working and Caring in an Age of Insecurity* (Oxford: Oxford University Press, 2015).

6. Karen V. Hansen and Anita Ilta Garey, *Families in the U.S.: Kinship and Domestic Politics* (Philadelphia: Temple University Press, 1998); Karen V. Hansen, *Not-So-Nuclear Families: Class, Gender, and Networks of Care* (New Brunswick, NJ: Rutgers University Press, 2004); Joan Maya Mazelis, *Surviving Poverty* (New York: NYU Press, 2016); Mario Luis Small, *Unanticipated Gains: Origins of Network Inequality in Everyday Life* (Oxford: Oxford University Press, 2009); Stack, *All Our Kin*.

7. On inequalities in networks of care, see Evelyn Nakano Glenn, *Forced to Care: Coercion and Caregiving in America* (Cambridge, MA: Harvard University Press, 2010); Arlie Russell Hochschild, *The Second Shift: Working Families and the Revolution at Home* (New York: Penguin Books, 1989); Lynet Uttal and Mary Tuominen, "Tenuous Relationships: Exploitation, Emotion, and Racial Ethnic Significance in Paid Child Care Work," *Gender & Society* 13, no. 6 (1999): 758–80. On networks with insufficient resources to support their members' needs, see Mazelis, *Surviving Poverty*; Small, *Unanticipated Gains*; Stack, *All Our Kin*.

8. On how biased notions of "deservingness" limit the equitability and efficacy of US social policy, see Celeste Watkins-Hayes and Elise Kovalsky, "The Discourse of Deservingness: Morality and the Dilemmas of Poverty Relief in Debate and Practice," in *The Oxford Handbook of the Social Science of Poverty*, ed. David Brady and Linda Burton (Oxford: Oxford University Press, 2016), 193–220. On how current US social policy pits caregivers against care recipients, see Donna Baines, Sara Charlesworth, and Tamara Daly, "Underpaid, Unpaid, Unseen, Unheard and Unhappy? Care Work in the Context of Constraint," *Journal of Industrial Relations* 58, no. 4 (2016): 449–54; Glenn, *Forced to Care*; Cameron Lynne Macdonald, *Shadow Mothers: Nannies, Au Pairs, and the Micropolitics of Mothering* (Berkeley: University of California Press, 2011); Julia Orupabo, "Enacting Efficient Care within a Context of Rationalisation," *Sociological Review* 70, no. 1 (2022): 57–73; Ai-jen Poo, *The Age of Dignity* (New York: Tantor and Blackstone, 2021); Uttal and Tuominen, "Tenuous Relationships." On how the rigidity and complexity of US social policy creates burdens and barriers for families, see Pamela Herd and Donald P. Moynihan, *Administrative Burden: Policymaking by Other Means* (New York: Russell Sage Foundation, 2019); Donald Moynihan, Pamela Herd, and Hope Harvey, "Administrative Burden: Learning, Psychological, and Compliance Costs in Citizen-State Interactions," *Journal of Public Administration Research and Theory* 25, no. 1 (2015): 43–69; Leslie Paik, *Trapped in a Maze: How Social Control Institutions Drive Family Poverty and Inequality* (Berkeley: University of California Press, 2021).

9. On how the US's short school days and long summers negatively impact families, see Leah Ruppanner, Stephanie Moller, and Liana Sayer, "Expensive Childcare and Short School Days = Lower Maternal Employment and More Time in Childcare? Evidence from the American Time Use Survey," *Socius* 5 (2019). On the consequences of overwork for gender inequalities in caregiving within families, see Youngjoo Cha, "Reinforcing Separate Spheres: The Effect of Spousal Overwork on Men's and Women's Employment in Dual-Earner Households," *American Sociological Review* 75, no. 2 (2010): 303–29; Youngjoo Cha, "Overwork and the Persistence of Gender Segregation in Occupations," *Gender & Society* 27, no. 2 (2013): 158–84; Youngjoo Cha and Kim A. Weeden, "Overwork and the Slow Convergence in the Gender Gap in Wages," *American Sociological Review* 79, no. 3 (2014): 457–84; Juliet B. Schor, *The Overworked American: The Unexpected Decline of Leisure* (New York: Basic Books, 1993). For more on how overwork among paid care workers contributes to burnout and thus to the care crisis, see Russell L. Carson et al., "Emotional Exhaustion, Absenteeism, and Turnover In-

tentions in Childcare Teachers: Examining the Impact of Physical Activity Behaviors," *Journal of Health Psychology* 15, no. 6 (2010): 905–14; James T. Decker, Tammy Lynn Bailey, and Nikki Westergaard, "Burnout among Childcare Workers," *Residential Treatment for Children & Youth* 19, no. 4 (2002): 61–77; Joan Hildebrand and Carol Seefeldt, "Teacher Burnout and Environmental Quality in Child Care Centers," *Child Care Quarterly* 15, no. 2 (1986): 90–97; Hansung Kim and Sun Young Lee, "Supervisory Communication, Burnout, and Turnover Intention among Social Workers in Health Care Settings," *Social Work in Health Care* 48, no. 4 (2009): 364–85; Frank Perrone, Daniel Player, and Peter Youngs, "Administrative Climate, Early Career Teacher Burnout, and Turnover," *Journal of School Leadership* 29, no. 3 (2019): 191–209.

10. On the challenges that care industries face in meeting profit expectations, see Eileen Boris and Jennifer Klein, *Caring for America: Home Health Workers in the Shadow of the Welfare State* (Oxford: Oxford University Press, 2015); England and Folbre, "The Cost of Caring"; Elliot Haspel, *Crawling Behind: America's Child Care Crisis and How to Fix It* (Castroville, TX: Black Rose Writing, 2019); Howes, Leana, and Smith, "Paid Care Work." On low-profit industries in the US, see Mary Ellen Biery, "The 15 Least Profitable Industries in the U.S.," *Forbes*, October 6, 2016, https://www.forbes.com/sites/sageworks/2016/10/03/the-15-least -profitable-industries-in-the-u-s/. See also "Least Profitable Industries in the United States as of January 2022," Statista, https://www.statista.com/statistics/468436/least-profitable -industries-usa/.

11. On paid workers' representation in the US population, see David H. Montgomery, "Who's Not Working in the U.S.? Learn the Basics," Federal Reserve Bank of Minneapolis, accessed July 21, 2023, https://www.minneapolisfed.org/article/2022/whos-not-working -in-the-us-learn-the-basics. On cash benefits as the best way to ensure dignity for people in poverty, see Kathryn Edin and Laura Lein, *Making Ends Meet: How Single Mothers Survive Welfare and Low-Wage Work* (New York: Russell Sage Foundation, 1997); Jennifer Sykes et al., "Dignity and Dreams: What the Earned Income Tax Credit (EITC) Means to Low-Income Families," *American Sociological Review* 80, no. 2 (2015): 243–67; Marianne S. Ulriksen, Sophie Plagerson, and Tessa Hochfield, "Social Protection and Justice: Poverty, Redistribution and Dignity," in *Distributive Justice Debates in Political and Social Thought: Perspectives on Finding a Fair Share*, ed. Camilla Boisen and Matthew C. Murray (London: Routledge, 2015).

12. On people's intrinsic motivation to work and create, see Carmen Fischer, Charlotte P. Malycha, and Ernestine Schafmann, "The Influence of Intrinsic Motivation and Synergistic Extrinsic Motivators on Creativity and Innovation," *Frontiers in Psychology* 10 (2019), https://www .frontiersin.org/articles/10.3389/fpsyg.2019.00137; Ayelet Fishbach and Kaitlin Woolley, "The Structure of Intrinsic Motivation," *Annual Review of Organizational Psychology and Organizational Behavior* 9 (2022): 339-63; Luke Zaphir, "No, People Aren't Unemployed Because They're Lazy. We Should Stop Teaching Children Myths about Work," *Conversation*, March 3, 2021, http://theconversation.com/no-people-arent-unemployed-because-theyre-lazy -we-should-stop-teaching-children-myths-about-work-153643. On workers' desire for dignity and sustainable wages, see Randy Hodson, *Dignity at Work* (Cambridge: Cambridge University Press, 2001); Arne L. Kalleberg, *Good Jobs, Bad Jobs: The Rise of Polarized and Precarious Employment Systems in the United States 1970s to 2000s* (New York: Russell Sage Foundation, 2013); Knut Laaser and Sharon Bolton, "Absolute Autonomy, Respectful Recognition and Derived Dignity: Towards a Typology of Meaningful Work," *International Journal of Management Reviews* 24, no. 3 (2022): 373–93; Jens Jørund Tyssedal, "Work Is Meaningful if There Are Good Reasons to Do It: A Revisionary Conceptual Analysis of 'Meaningful Work,'" *Journal of Business Ethics* 185, no. 3 (2023): 533–44. On quiet quitting, see Cal Newport, "The Year in Quiet Quitting," *New Yorker*, December 29, 2022, https://www.newyorker.com/culture/2022 -in-review/the-year-in-quiet-quitting. On work-to-rule tactics, see André D. Robert and Jeffrey Tyssens, "Introduction: Mapping Teachers' Strikes: A 'Professionalist' Approach," *Paedagog-*

ica Historica 44, no. 5 (2008): 501–16; Mini Thekkechangarapatt, "Quiet Quitting in the Education Sector: Enumeration of Three Cases," *EPRA International Journal of Multidisciplinary Research (IJMR)* 9, no. 5 (2023): 83–88. On teachers' unions' use of work-to-rule tactics, see Dan McGowan, "Providence Teachers OK New Contract, Ending Work-to-Rule" (WPRI, November 16, 2018), https://www.wpri.com/news/providence-teachers-ok-new-contract-ending -work-to-rule/; Lucia Winton, "Teachers Rule, Contracts Drool: Rising up for Teachers in Providence and Beyond," *Brown Political Review*, November 28, 2018, https://brownpoliticalreview .org/2018/11/teachers-rule-contracts-drool-rising-teachers-providence-beyond/. On accusations of laziness against teachers, see Heather Berg, "An Honest Day's Wage for a Dishonest Day's Work: (Re)Productivism and Refusal," *Women's Studies Quarterly* 42, no. 1/2 (2014): 161–77; "Chicago Story Exposes the Rank Selfishness of US Teachers Unions," *New York Post*, December 10, 2020, https://nypost.com/2020/12/10/chicago-story-exposes-the-rank-selfishness -of-us-teachers-unions/. On work stoppages and slowdowns, see Robin D. G. Kelley, "'We Are Not What We Seem': Rethinking Black Working-Class Opposition in the Jim Crow South," *Journal of American History* 80, no. 1 (1993): 75–112; Jason R. Young, *Rituals of Resistance: African Atlantic Religion in Kongo and the Lowcountry South in the Era of Slavery* (Baton Rouge: Louisiana State University Press, 2007).

13. On how a universal healthcare system would reduce total US spending on health care over the long run, see Christopher Cai et al., "Projected Costs of Single-Payer Healthcare Financing in the United States: A Systematic Review of Economic Analyses," *PLOS MEDICINE* 17, no. 1 (2020); Alison P. Galvani and Meagan C. Fitzpatrick, "Cost-Effectiveness of Transitional US Plans for Universal Health Care," *Lancet* 395, no. 10238 (May 30, 2020): 1692–93. On the cost of universal childcare and early childhood education, see Daniela Viana Acosta, Maddison Erbabian, Youran Wu, and Efraim Berkovich, *Total Cost of Universal Pre-K, Including New Facilities* (Philadelphia: University of Pennsylvania, 2022), https://budgetmodel .wharton.upenn.edu/issues/2022/6/2/total-cost-of-universal-pre-k. For Elizabeth Warren's proposal, see "Universal Child Care," Elizabeth Warren for Senate, https://elizabethwarren .com/plans/universal-child-care. On how current childcare spending could be reallocated to support a broader national program, see Grover J. "Russ" Whitehurst, *Why the Federal Government Should Subsidize Childcare and How to Pay for It* (Washington, DC: Brookings, 2017), https://www.brookings.edu/research/why-the-federal-government-should-subsidize -childcare-and-how-to-pay-for-it/.

14. On the cost-effectiveness of universal programs, see Erling Barth, Karl O. Moene, and Fredrik Willumsen, "The Scandinavian Model—an Interpretation," *Journal of Public Economics* 117 (2014): 60–72; Erik Olin Wright, *Class Counts* (Cambridge: Cambridge University Press, 2000); Erik Olin Wright, "Working-Class Power, Capitalist-Class Interests, and Class Compromise," *American Journal of Sociology* 105, no. 4 (2000): 957–1002. On the stability benefits of universal programs, see Morris Altman, "Labor Rights and Labor Power and Welfare Maximization in a Market Economy—Revising the Conventional Wisdom," *International Journal of Social Economics* 27, no. 12 (2000): 1252–69; Morris Altman, "A Behavioral Theory of Economic Welfare and Economic Justice: A Smithian Alternative to Pareto Optimality," *International Journal of Social Economics* 27, no. 11 (2000): 1098–131; Robert Buchele and Jens Christiansen, "Worker Rights Promote Productivity Growth," *Challenge* 38, no. 5 (1995): 32–37; Peter H. Lindert, *Making Social Spending Work* (Cambridge: Cambridge University Press, 2021). On how a stronger social safety net would rebalance the system of power in the US, see David Brock, *The Republican Noise Machine: Right-Wing Media and How It Corrupts Democracy* (New York: Three Rivers Press, 2005); Jacob S. Hacker and Paul Pierson, "Winner-Take-All Politics: Public Policy, Political Organization, and the Precipitous Rise of Top Incomes in the United States," *Politics & Society* 38, no. 2 (2010): 152–204; Nicole Hemmer, *Messengers of the Right: Conservative Media and the Transformation of American Politics* (Philadelphia: University of Pennsylvania Press, 2016); C. Wright Mills, *The Power Elite* (Oxford: Oxford University Press, 2000); Francie Ostrower, *Why the Wealthy Give: The Culture of Elite*

Philanthropy (Princeton, NJ: Princeton University Press, 1997); Sarah Reckhow, *Follow the Money: How Foundation Dollars Change Public School Politics* (Oxford: Oxford University Press, 2012); Megan Tompkins-Stange, *Policy Patrons: Philanthropy, Education Reform, and the Politics of Influence* (Cambridge, MA: Harvard Education Press, 2016).

15. On how unions help their members to resist exploitation, see Marc Dixon, Vincent J. Roscigno, and Randy Hodson, "Unions, Solidarity, and Striking," *Social Forces* 83, no. 1 (2004): 3–33; Randy Hodson, "Individual Voice on the Shop Floor: The Role of Unions," *Social Forces* 75, no. 4 (1997): 1183–212; Andrew W. Martin and Marc Dixon, "Changing to Win? Threat, Resistance, and the Role of Unions in Strikes, 1984–2002," *American Journal of Sociology* 116, no. 1 (July 2010): 93–129; Robert A. Penney, "Interpretation, Meaning, and Worker Solidarity," *Social Problems* 53, no. 2 (2006): 139–60; Ian Robinson, "Neoliberal Restructuring and U.S. Unions: Toward Social Movement Unionism?," *Critical Sociology* 26, no. 1–2 (2000): 109–38. On the changing role of unions in the US over time, see Henry S. Farber and Bruce Western, "Accounting for the Decline of Unions in the Private Sector, 1973–1998," *Journal of Labor Research* 22, no. 3 (September 2001): 459–85; Chad Alan Goldberg, *Citizens and Paupers: Relief, Rights, and Race, from the Freedmen's Bureau to Workfare* (Chicago: University of Chicago Press, 2007); Michael Goldfield, *The Decline of Organized Labor in the United States* (Chicago: University of Chicago Press, 1989); Ruth Milkman, "Two Worlds of Unionism: Women and the New Labor Movement," in *The Sex of Class: Women Transforming American Labor*, ed. Dorothy Sue Cobble (Ithaca, NY: Cornell University Press, 2007); Michael Wallerstein and Bruce Western, "Unions in Decline? What Has Changed and Why," *Annual Review of Political Science* 3 (2000): 355–77. On anti-union rhetoric and policies, see David T. Ellwood and Glenn Fine, "The Impact of Right-to-Work Laws on Union Organizing," *Journal of Political Economy* 95, no. 2 (1987): 250–73; Julius G. Getman and F. Ray Marshall, "The Continuing Assault on the Right to Strike," *Texas Law Review* 79, no. 3 (2001): 703–36; John V. Kane and Benjamin J. Newman, "Organized Labor as the New Undeserving Rich?: Mass Media, Class-Based Anti-Union Rhetoric and Public Support for Unions in the United States," *British Journal of Political Science* 49, no. 3 (July 2019): 997–1026; James Gray Pope, "How American Workers Lost the Right to Strike, and Other Tales," *Michigan Law Review* 103, no. 3 (2004): 518–53; Tom VanHeuvelen, "The Right to Work, Power Resources, and Economic Inequality," *American Journal of Sociology* 125, no. 5 (2020): 1255–302; Tom VanHeuvelen, "The Right to Work and American Inequality," *American Sociological Review* 88, no. 5 (2023): 810–43.

16. On union wins and Republican legislators' efforts to pass new anti-union laws, see Sam Becker, "Anti-Union Bills Bubble Up in Congress, Despite Growing Voter Support for Organized Labor," *Fast Company*, August 2, 2022, https://www.fastcompany.com/90775158/anti-union-bills-bubble-up-in-congress-despite-growing-voter-support-for-organized-labor. For current rates of union membership and pay differences between union and non-union member, see "Union Members—2022," US Bureau of Labor Statistics, 2022, https://www.bls.gov/news.release/pdf/union2.pdf. On differences in the racial attitudes of union and non-union members, see Paul Frymer and Jacob M. Grumbach, "Labor Unions and White Racial Politics," *American Journal of Political Science* 65, no. 1 (2021): 225–40. On the fact that Black workers are represented by unions at higher rates than white workers, see "Union Members—2022," US Bureau of Labor Statistics, January 19, 2023, https://www.bls.gov/news.release/pdf/union2.pdf. See also Kate Bronfenbrenner and Dorian T. Warren, "Race, Gender, and the Rebirth of Trade Unionism," *New Labor Forum* 16, no. 3/4 (2007): 142–48; John Schmitt and Kris Warner, "The Changing Face of U.S. Labor, 1983–2008," *WorkingUSA* 13, no. 2 (2010): 263–79.

17. For more on the tensions between labor unions and unpaid caregiving, see Michèle Barrett and Mary McIntosh, "The 'Family Wage': Some Problems for Socialists and Feminists," *Capital & Class* 4, no. 2 (1980): 51–72; Allan C. Carlson, "Gender, Children, and Social Labor: Transcending the 'Family Wage' Dilemma," *Journal of Social Issues* 52, no. 3 (1996): 137–61; Nancy Fraser, "After the Family Wage: Gender Equity and the Welfare State," *Political Theory*

22, no. 4 (1994): 591–618; Maurine Weiner Greenwald, "Working-Class Feminism and the Family Wage Ideal: The Seattle Debate on Married Women's Right to Work, 1914–1920," *Journal of American History* 76, no. 1 (1989): 118–49; Hansen and Garey, *Families in the U.S.*; Martha May, "The Historical Problem of the Family Wage: The Ford Motor Company and the Five Dollar Day," *Feminist Studies* 8, no. 2 (1982): 399–424; Roberta Spalter-Roth, Heidi Hartmann, and Linda M. Andrews, "Mothers, Children, and Low-Wage Work: The Ability to Earn a Family Wage," in *Sociology and the Public Agenda*, by William J. Wilson (New York: SAGE Publishing, 1993).

18. On the rhetoric used to attack union members for being "selfish," see Jonathan Roth, "Union Reform and Teacher Turnover: Evidence from Wisconsin's Act 10," (working paper, Program on Education Policy and Governance, 2017). See also Sylvia A. Allegretto and Lawrence Mishel, *The Teacher Pay Gap Is Wider than Ever: Teachers' Pay Continues to Fall Further behind Pay of Comparable Workers* (Washington, DC: Economic Policy Institute, 2016); Eric Brunner, Joshua Hyman, and Andrew Ju, "School Finance Reforms, Teachers' Unions, and the Allocation of School Resources," *Review of Economics and Statistics* 102, no. 3 (2020): 473–89; Douglas N Harris and Matthew F Larsen, *The Effects of the New Orleans Post-Katrina Market-Based School Reforms on Student Achievement, High School Graduation, and College Outcomes* (New Orleans, LA: Education Research Alliance, 2018); Michael F. Lovenheim, "The Effect of Teachers' Unions on Education Production: Evidence from Union Election Certifications in Three Midwestern States," *Journal of Labor Economics* 27, no. 4 (October 2009): 525–87. On the benefits of strong teachers' unions for student achievement, see E. Jason Baron, "The Effect of Teachers' Unions on Student Achievement in the Short Run: Evidence from Wisconsin's Act 10," *Economics of Education Review* 67 (2018): 40–57.

19. On linked fate, see Michael C. Dawson, *Behind the Mule: Race and Class in African-American Politics* (Princeton, NJ: Princeton University Press, 1995); Evelyn M. Simien, "Race, Gender, and Linked Fate," *Journal of Black Studies* 35, no. 5 (2005): 529.

20. On how illness and caregiving responsibilities put jobs at risk in the US economy, see *Sick Kids, Struggling Parents* (Ann Arbor, MI: Mott Children's Hospital, 2012), https://mottpoll .org/reports-surveys/sick-kids-struggling-parents. See also Abha Bhattarai, "RSV, Covid and Flu Are Keeping Kids out of School—and Parents out of Work," *Washington Post*, November 17, 2022, https://www.washingtonpost.com/business/2022/11/15/work-absences-childcare/.

21. On how the engineers and profiteers use their resources to defend their powerful position, see Hacker and Pierson, "Winner-Take-All Politics"; Hemmer, *Messengers of the Right*; Mills, *The Power Elite*; Benjamin I. Page, Jason Seawright, and Matthew J. Lacombe, *Billionaires and Stealth Politics* (Chicago: University of Chicago Press, 2018); Reckhow, *Follow the Money*; Tompkins-Stange, *Policy Patrons*. On the power of participatory democracy for fighting capitalistic oppression, see Nancy Fraser, "How feminism became capitalism's handmaiden—and how to reclaim it," *Guardian*, October 14, 2013, https://www.theguardian.com/commentisfree /2013/oct/14/feminism-capitalist-handmaiden-neoliberal; Erik Olin Wright, *Envisioning Real Utopias* (New York: Verso Books, 2010).

22. On the warnings that feminists sounded, see Silvia Federici, *Caliban and the Witch: Women, the Body and Primitive Accumulation* (New York: Autonomedia, 2004); bell hooks, *Ain't I A Woman? Black Women and Feminism* (Boston: South End Press, 1981), bell hooks, *Feminism is for Everybody: Passionate Politics* (Boston: South End Press, 2000).

23. On how Covid-19 affected gender-linked fate, see Christopher Stout, Kelsy Kretschmer, and Leah Ruppanner, "The Link between Familial Care, the Covid Pandemic and Gender Linked Fate," *Journal of Women, Politics & Policy* 43, no. 4 (October 2, 2022): 514–24. For Federici's quote, see Silvia Federici, *Wages Against Housework* (London: Power of Women Collective / Falling Wall Press, 1975), https://thecommoner.org/wp-content/uploads/2019 /10/04-federici.pdf. On the Wages for Housework and Welfare Rights movements, see Silvia Federici, *Revolution at Point Zero: Housework, Reproduction, and Feminist Struggle* (Binghamton, NY: PM Press, 2020); Glenn C. Loury, "The Return of the 'Undeserving Poor,'" *Atlantic*,

February 2001, https://www.theatlantic.com/magazine/archive/2001/02/the-return-of-the-undeserving-poor/302102/; Kevin Sapere, "Covid-19 Has Made Housework More Visible, but It Still Isn't Valued," *Washington Post*, April 8, 2021, https://www.washingtonpost.com/outlook/2021/04/08/covid-19-has-made-housework-more-visible-it-still-isnt-valued/; Louise Toupin, *Wages for Housework: A History of an International Feminist Movement, 1972–77* (Vancouver: University of British Columbia Press, 2018).

24. For hooks's warning, see bell hooks, *Talking Back: Thinking Feminist, Thinking Black* (Boston: South End Press, 1989), p. 36–37.

APPENDIX

1. On the value of qualitative research, see Mario Luis Small and Jessica McCrory Calarco, *Qualitative Literacy: A Guide to Evaluating Ethnographic and Interview Research* (Berkeley: University of California Press, 2022).